When The Game Stands Tall

WHEN THE GAME

STANDS TALL

THE STORY OF THE DE LA SALLE
SPARTANS AND FOOTBALL'S LONGEST
WINNING STREAK

Neil Hayes

Foreword by Tony La Russa

Frog, Ltd.
Berkeley, California

Published by Frog, Ltd.

Frog, Ltd. books are distributed by
North Atlantic Books
P.O. Box 12327
Berkeley, California 94712

Cover and interior photos by Bob Larson/Contra Costa Times
Cover and book design by Maxine Ressler

Printed in Canada

North Atlantic Books' publications are available through most bookstores. For further information, call 800-337-2665 or visit our website at www.northatlanticbooks.com.

Substantial discounts on bulk quantities are available to corporations, professional associations, and other organizations. For details and discount information, contact our special sales department.

Library of Congress Cataloging-in-Publication Data

Hayes, Neil, 1967-
  When the game stands tall : the story of the De La Salle Spartans and football's longest winning streak / by Neil Hayes.
    p. cm.
  ISBN 1-58394-086-3 (hardcover)
  1. De La Salle High School (Concord, Calif.)--Football. 2. Football--California--Concord--History. I. Title.
  GV958.D4H39 2003
  796.332'09794'63--dc22   2003017347

      3   4   5   6   7   8   9   TRANS   08   07   06   05   04   03

To Charlee, Nicholas, and Riley

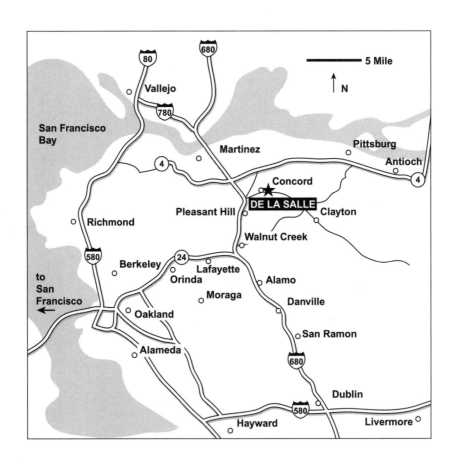

TABLE OF CONTENTS

FOREWORD
By Tony La Russa

During spring training in Arizona several years ago, George Will told the Oakland A's that Americans were fascinated by excellence, not only as a product but as a process.

How do you achieve it? And once you do, how do you sustain it?

Excellence exists in all facets of life but it's the examples in business and sports that receive the most attention. We look at Howard Schultz and Starbucks, Bill Gates at Microsoft, Bill Russell of the Celtics, Michael Jordan of the Bulls, Tiger Woods and Lance Armstrong, to name a few. We see their seemingly magical results and we can't help but wonder what their edge is and what makes them so special.

There's another ongoing example of excellence that has earned a place alongside the ones I just mentioned. It's not as well known as Michael Jordan or Bill Gates, but it's just as phenomenal.

Since 1992, De La Salle High School, competing at the highest levels in the ultra-competitive state of California, has won 138 consecutive football games. Perhaps the best way to define De La Salle's excellence is to consider this: Since 1998 they have played seven games against some of the most respected high school programs in the nation. In those seven games they never once trailed.

Can you imagine going undefeated for eleven seasons while purposely seeking out the toughest competition?

As De La Salle approached the national record for consecutive wins, the program and its coach drew more and more attention. De La Salle broke Hudson (Michigan) High School's record of 72 consecutive wins in 1997, but the pressure still hasn't gone away. Wins over Mater Dei, Long Beach Poly, and St. Louis of Honolulu are recent examples of their excellence being challenged and redefined.

As each victory extends the record winning streak, the school's football program has become a lightning rod for the controversy that inevitably attaches itself to success today. Too often there is a search for the quick, easy answer or handy label when excellence and success are analyzed. It's routine to question the success by searching for improprieties, but in De La Salle's case it only obscures the reality and distorts perceptions. If our interest in excellence is legitimate, then what we need—and what De La Salle deserves—is as complete an understanding as possible of their unique formula for success.

By pure coincidence I live in the same county in Northern California where De La Salle is located. Because of that I can personally attest to some aspects of what makes the program unique and special, the reality versus the perception.

I have had the opportunity to come into contact with various members of the De La Salle program. I have heard them speak and I have read what they have written, in particular head coach Bob Ladouceur.

What I have learned is so much more important than what I first perceived. Initially, I thought the lessons about De La Salle were only about winning in a team sport, which were valuable enough.

But now I understand that the core of the program's success extends well beyond sports. It is a remarkable blueprint that has applications not only in business but also with your family and friends.

During my forty years in baseball I have been fortunate to meet some of the coaching greats who have come to define excellence. With no disrespect to these fine managers and coaches, Bob Ladouceur is one of the finest coaches I have ever met. As I have gotten to know him on a personal basis, I also believe he is one of the finest people I have ever met.

The more I come into contact with people associated with the De La Salle program, the more I want to learn about the De La Salle story, which is why I was excited when I heard that Bob Ladouceur granted Neil Hayes the access to enlighten us all.

This book tells an important story of just how special the De La Salle program has been over the years and how The Streak has been built by average young men who come together each season and are transformed by Ladouceur and his coaches into truly remarkable teams.

Please understand that referring to these players as average young men is not meant disrespectfully, but rather the opposite. It is meant to underscore just how truly amazing they are for the very fact that they are normal and not supermen. They have accomplished great things. Their success is hard-earned, and we can all learn from their efforts.

The core of this book is about those who wear the De La Salle uniform and the unprecedented commitment they have been willing to make to hard work, teamwork beyond individual pursuit, and winning the right way whatever the obstacles.

It's a story we should want to read. It's a story we need to read.

June 2003

INTRODUCTION

his offensive linemen were confused at halftime. They sat on narrow wooden benches in the locker room, dirt and grass from their cleats scattered across the cement floor. The opposition's defensive linemen were shifting and shooting gaps, making it difficult for his linemen to execute their assignments. This wasn't something they had anticipated or practiced against, and it made them tentative and less precise.

Now they wanted to know what to do, how to adjust. They looked to their coach standing before them through wide eyes, begging for his wisdom, his guidance. They sat there in expectant silence, waiting for words that would never come.

"Why do I always have to be the problem solver?" Bob Ladouceur told them. "Group problem-solving is a skill you will use your whole life. You guys figure it out."

With that, the most successful high school football coach in history turned his back and walked away, leaving his players to discover the solution themselves. This scene has occurred frequently during Ladouceur's tenure at De La Salle High School, and it's just one of the many reasons why this coach and this program are so unique.

I have spent the past seventeen years covering football—high school football, college football, and professional football. It wasn't De La Salle's 125-game winning streak that compelled me to write the story of this man, this school, and the nation's most successful high school football program. It was moments like this that convinced me that this story had to be told.

1

This book was Bob Ladouceur's idea, which I'm sure he came to regret during the six months I followed him around with a clipboard. We were standing in the school parking lot in March of 2000 when he asked me to help him publish an essay in the Sunday "Perspective" section of my employer's newspaper, the *Contra Costa Times.* "I don't think people understand what we do here," he said.

De La Salle's is the most publicized high school football program in the country. *Sports Illustrated, The New York Times,* the *Los Angeles Times,* ABC's *World News Tonight,* and countless other media outlets have featured the man and The Streak. In many ways, however, the Spartans' success remains shrouded in mystery.

"The game by itself doesn't stand tall," Ladouceur told me later that summer. "Without intangibles, in a certain sense, it's barbarism. The violence isn't what attracts me to it. It's getting kids to play together and get along with each other. The game should be a teaching tool. It doesn't stand tall on its own."

His words resonated with me. Everybody wants to know why his teams dominate like no team in history has dominated. "Spend a year with us" is his pat answer.

I called his bluff.

I learned that this is not a typical football coach nor is this a typical football team. Thus it follows that this is not a typical football book. This is a coming-of-age story that will take you places you may not expect to go, but such a historical journey is necessary because De La Salle's success is about much more than football. It's about educators who have put personal ambition aside to shepherd young men through what are often troubled times. It's about the spirit of a school where teachers build extraordinary relationships with their students.

There is no specific training technique or motivational ploy that explains why Ladouceur's teams have not lost a game in more than a decade, but many threads intertwine with a philosophy as unique as the head coach himself: He has won more consecutive football games than any other coach in history by not emphasizing winning. Winning is a byproduct of a larger vision. It begins with a question:

How much do we owe each other?

It is each coach's and player's individual answer that makes this the most successful program in history. De La Salle separates itself from the competition because everyone from the head coach to the least accomplished player on the roster is willing to make the sacrifices necessary to be their absolute best.

This may be the hardest-working football team in the country. Many programs begin offseason conditioning work in June. De La Salle starts in January. For all but three weeks of the year players are trained using sophisticated speed and strength techniques that allow them to achieve an unparalleled level of fitness. They don't do this because their legendary coach is standing over them blowing a whistle. Sacrifices are made because a feeling of brotherhood is cultivated during emotional team meetings when players talk about the game and about how much they mean to each other.

Ladouceur and his longtime assistant Terry Eidson, the two people most responsible for De La Salle's unprecedented success, both teach religious studies, a fact that cannot be ignored. You don't have to be Catholic or even religious to appreciate how they guide boys down the path of becoming thoughtful young men.

As you will see, much is made of the "advantages" De La Salle has because it's a private school. The program's success has always been met with suspicion. Critics complain about competitive inequity and allege that players are recruited.

But De La Salle's biggest so-called "advantage" isn't the athleticism of its players but the mentality they bring to school. These are kids who want something more and have made a commitment from the first day they step on campus. Other elite teams may have a core group of ten to fifteen players that are dedicated to the sport and each other. Every player who achieves varsity status at De La Salle has done so.

Some claim there's no way the Spartans would be 125–0 if they were a public-school program, that the inevitable crests and troughs in the talent pool would lead to The Streak's demise. Others believe that De La Salle would not have such a gaudy record if they competed in talent-laden Southern California, even though the Spartans defeated Southern California superpower Mater Dei in four straight games.

The critics may even be right, but quibbling over numbers dilutes the essential point. Ladouceur may not be able to win 125 straight games at a public school. If De La Salle regularly competed against more competitive Southern California teams they probably wouldn't be 125–0.

They'd be 122–3.

This is a story with no ending. The Streak has become a meteor streaking through the night sky, burning brighter and traveling faster with each passing year. As the 2002 season dawned, however, it was in as much jeopardy as it had ever been, the program inching ever closer to testing Bob Ladouceur's philosophy of emphasizing life lessons instead of wins and losses.

Some claim his true genius may not be revealed until his team loses.

01 ▶

DE LA SALLE
A Monument to Understatement

| | | | | | | | |

de La Salle High School sits on the corner of Treat Boulevard and Winton Drive in Concord, California. The campus is a modest cluster of Spanish-style buildings, Disneyland-clean and Catholic-functional, surrounded by strip malls filled with supermarkets, nail salons, and delicatessens. It is neighbored by neat ranch-style homes framed by orange trees, rose bushes, and carefully trimmed hedges.

Nothing about the school or its surroundings suggests singular achievement. White block letters identify the school on a low brick wall on the northwestern edge of the campus. There is no billboard proclaiming this the home of football's longest winning streak. Nowhere in this sprawling community of 126,000 located twenty-nine miles east of San Francisco is a sign heralding the school's sixteen undefeated seasons, eleven state championships, and four national titles.

Visitors wander into the main office, wondering if this is the De La Salle, the school that owns the longest winning streak in the documented history of football.

At the dawn of the 2002 season, The Streak stands at a national record 125 consecutive games. Year after year, season after season, it takes on new, almost bizarre dimension, gaining size and strength, overpowering reason, overwhelming perspective. It has become a force that defies description, even by its architects.

The Oklahoma Sooners coached by Bud Wilkinson own the longest streak in college football history. They won 47 consecutive games between

5

1953 and '57. John Wooden's UCLA basketball team won 88 straight across four seasons from 1970 to '74. Hudson High School in Michigan set the previous high school football record with 72 consecutive wins from 1968 to '75. Should De La Salle continue to win, it would double Hudson's record by winning its sixth game of the 2003 season.

There is no statewide playoff system for football in California. The state is divided into ten geographical sections. De La Salle's eleven state championships are mythical since there is no statewide playoff system, but no one can dispute the school's dominance over the past quarter-century.

The De La Salle football program first came to prominence in the mid-1980s when it reeled off 44 consecutive wins. The Spartans followed that streak with one of 34, which ended with a 35–27 setback to Pittsburg High School in the 1991 North Coast Section 3A championship game. De La Salle hasn't lost since.

Since 1984, the Spartans are 204–4.

They have sought out the toughest competition in Northern California and, in recent years, the top teams from Southern California as well. In one of the most talent-rich states, that means they have defeated some of the best teams in the nation.

But it's not simply that they win. It's how they win. Since The Streak began, the Spartans have outscored opponents by an average of 40–9. Their games are typically over and their starters benched by the middle of the third quarter.

It's one of the most amazing streaks in sports and perhaps the least celebrated. The school that is home to America's most successful football team is not a football school. Trophy cases sit in an out-of-the-way foyer between the gymnasium and the cafeteria, containing only a sample of the awards bestowed upon the team over the years. The rest of the hardware can be found in the coaches' office, stuffed on shelves, behind battered file cabinets, and—because the program has generated more brass and marble mementos than it can practically house—in trash cans.

The stadium sits on the east end of campus like the afterthought it was. The school was not designed to accommodate large team sports. Passersby on busy Treat Boulevard find their view of the football field obstructed by a thick row of oleanders, which only adds to the mysteriousness of the place and the program.

Understatement has become part of the tradition. A proposal to build a history room to house the football team's memorabilia was shelved when many former players complained. What makes this program so unique is what you carry in your heart, they argued, not what you hang on the wall.

There's only one place on campus where an attempt has been made to document the team's unprecedented success, and that's in the weight room where the Spartans' league, section, and state titles are stenciled on the wall. The chart hasn't been updated since 1998. Maybe it just seemed pointless after a while.

The lack of fervor reflects the spirit of the school, the humility of a coach who has won more league championships than he has suffered defeats, and the fine line administrators walk between embracing the football program and trying to deflect attention from it.

Parents of prospective students are handed a packet that includes an eight-page brochure. In it they learn that the private, all-boys Catholic school was founded in 1965 and is run by the Christian Brothers. They will read that the school's motto is "Enter to learn, leave to serve," and that students are taught in the Lasallian tradition. They can read the school's mission statement and discover that 98 percent of De La Salle graduates go on to two-year or four-year colleges, and that one year's tuition will run their parents $8,200 plus $200 for books.

The brochure lists graduation requirements and student activities. Two paragraphs on the penultimate page inform parents that "the purpose of the athletic program at De La Salle is to help promote perseverance in the pursuit of personal and team goals, and to develop in its participants a recognition of personal achievement."

At the bottom of the page is a snapshot of a football game—linemen coiled in their stances, the quarterback crouched over center. Nowhere else is the football team, its legendary coach, or its unprecedented success so much as hinted at.

Football has given this school a national identity and as many enemies as fans. De La Salle is the only all-boys Catholic high school in Contra Costa County, which has a population of almost 1 million. The fact that the private school can draw students from a wide geographical area has long fueled accusations of recruiting from frustrated opponents.

The school and its storied football team are respected and reviled. People come from all over the country to visit the school that never loses. They almost always leave disappointed. They imagine a glorious stadium such as those that rise from the Texas prairie. They expect to see an ancient stone bowl like they might find in a steel-mining town in Western Pennsylvania. At the very least they expect to find a monument, a display, something they can commit to film or memory.

Disappointment turns to surprise when, as happens at some point during practice nearly every day, someone drives down Treat Boulevard, hangs out the window, and screams profanities at history's most successful team.

~

Bob Ladouceur walks as if he's carrying a heavy burden. In his forty-eighth year, his face is tanned and deeply lined, his eyes mysterious in the shadow of a dense brow. He still has an athlete's build after hours of solitude on the stationary bike, but there's a noticeable stoop to his shoulders and deliberateness to his stride as he trudges across the practice field, a solitary figure even in a crowd.

It is the first official day of practice and he's already looking forward to the day when the helmets are stored away in the equipment room. The first day of the season is full of hope and possibilities for many coaches, but the dawn of Ladouceur's twenty-fourth season at De La Salle brings him as much dread as joy.

He never aspired to this. He took a beating as an undersized youth football player and was forced to quit. He made himself into a star running back in high school. His college career began promisingly but was marred by injuries and left him feeling maimed by the machine of college football.

He turned his back on the game three times vowing never to return. He never considered coaching, even though his aptitude was obvious to everyone. He was young and idealistic and he wanted something more. He wanted to make a real impact on kids' lives. He wanted to look into their eyes and see that he had made a difference. How was coaching football going to give him that?

But here he was twenty-four years later, wearing a sweatshirt and shorts, a whistle around his neck, on the first day of practice, the winningest coach in America, wishing he were somewhere else. He enjoys coaching but doesn't always find it enjoyable. Pushing kids to accomplish what they don't consider achievable is a long, painful process, as much for the coach as the player.

"I'm relieved when it's all over," he says. "It's not that I don't enjoy it. But right now I'm looking at it and thinking, 'Damn, it's a long haul.'"

He is not who you expect him to be. Maybe that's why he's misunderstood and why his name is chronically mispronounced (the correct pronunciation is "LAD-a-sir"). Maybe that's why some consider him aloof and arrogant while others describe him as unassuming, intensely introspective, meticulous, and pathologically honest.

He doesn't fit the preconceived image of what America's most successful high school coach should be. He's an introvert in a profession filled with extroverts. He likes football but he doesn't need it. The game doesn't define him. He has no interest in coaching at the college or professional level, because in high school he feels he has the ability to help shape lives, and he can't think of a more noble vocation. His dream job is the lowest rung on the ladder. He talks about someday coaching the freshman team.

He's a philosopher and a tactician. He's old school and new age. Nobody works his teams harder, stresses fundamentals more, but he will tell you that the key component to his success is the most basic of human emotions—love.

His teams win in part because he doesn't emphasize victories.

He has the timeless characteristics that people respect, and something else that's more difficult to identify. There's a wisdom lurking behind those deep-set brown eyes that makes you think he has the answer to the questions you've been aching to resolve. People are drawn to him like a touchstone, but he finds himself searching for the answers he is somehow able to pass along to others.

He has become a mythic figure at this school for reasons you might not expect. He moves about campus like a ghost, appearing and disappearing as if into underground passageways, yet his presence is undeniable. Students part respectfully when he plods past with his head down, thinking, oblivious. He is the only faculty member capable of silencing eight hundred boys at an all-school assembly. First a muffled hush and then a reverential silence fills the ears.

He's the only person unaware of this phenomenon, just as he is unaware of the near-icon status he has achieved throughout the San Francisco Bay Area sports community.

"To this day he doesn't know who he is," his assistant coach, Terry Eidson, says. "That's the funny part. That's what makes him who he is, though."

Ladouceur lives in a world of contradictions. His players execute with the precision of a military drill team, but he can't find his car keys. He's the least controversial person you'll ever meet, yet his detractors and supporters parry weekly in the Letters to the Editor section of the local newspaper.

He has built his entire life around doing the right thing, yet he is openly accused of cheating.

He has turned down job offers from such prestigious coaches as Bill Walsh to remain on this campus, but he considers his a conflicted soul.

The countless accolades and awards have brought little satisfaction.

"I'm a very restless and unsettled person," he says. "I have a hard time finding peace in my life. I don't know why it's that way."

Perhaps part of the reason he is conflicted is that his unmatched professional success comes at a personal cost. He has made his family—wife Beverly, daughter Jennifer (20), and sons Danny (15) and Michael (11)—a bigger priority now than he did during his early years with De La Salle. Still, he agonizes over the time he spends away from one family while trying to create another.

"After ten years of doing it here, I'm thirty-five, thirty-six, and I've got two kids and my girl Jennifer is eight or nine years old, and my wife sits me down and says, 'I feel real cheated,'" Ladouceur recalls. "'That school got the best of you, and we got seconds.' I'll tell you something, I felt like shit. She was right. That was another life-changing moment for me. I discovered it can be done differently. That's live and learn."

Another aspect of his job that wears on him is having to answer to his success. Coaches are always asking him how he does it. No question frustrates him more. They want to know the secret to winning 125 straight games, but there is no secret. There's nothing that can be manufactured, packaged, and distributed. It's a thousand different threads wrapped around a fundamental truth.

De La Salle doesn't win because of anything Bob Ladouceur does. They win because of who he is.

"Kids respect true humility and that you stand for something more than winning," he notes. "They'll fight for you and your program if you stand for more than that. It boils down to what you believe in as a person, and I'm talking about how life should be lived and how people should be treated. Kids see all that. It's a whole package of things that have nothing to do with standing in front of a team with a piece of chalk. You can know who to block and what play to call, but it has no meaning unless the kids know who you are. Our kids aren't fighting for wins. They're fighting for a belief in what we stand for."

He has broken the game down to its DNA and discovered the secret to success. It's simple but it's not easy.

It's pulling tires across bleached grass on scorching summer afternoons. It's getting up at 5 A.M. to get to school on time to lift weights during the season. It's a coaching staff that is obsessed with the minutiae of the game. Ladouceur knows the game, make no mistake, but his genius, if he has a genius, is his ability to connect with adolescent minds. He's an absolute master of human relationships.

He has created a culture, a community, based on timeless values where teenagers hold themselves and each other accountable.

"Winning a lot of high school football games is doable," said former longtime assistant Blair Thomas. "It's no big deal. What's difficult is getting people to understand there's more to life than football. That's what he does."

Coach Ladouceur has found a way to turn selfish teens into selfless teammates by making them step back and examine their relationships.

"De La Salle would not be De La Salle without Bob Ladouceur," said former Spartans running back Patrick Walsh, now the head coach at Serra High in San Mateo. "He is not an interchangeable part. There's something in Coach Lad that knows what it takes to pull the best out of each kid. That's his gift."

He has thought about quitting. He has never seriously considered accepting one of the numerous offers he has had to move up to the college ranks. "I don't know if I like football that much," he says. In other ways he is a hostage of The Streak. It's difficult to walk away from something like that, if for no other reason than pity for the poor man who inherits the albatross.

So, he soldiers on, even if there's often someplace he'd rather be, something he'd rather do. But when all eleven of his players are playing as one, and not for themselves but for the person next to them, and when they're firing off the ball and playing with passion and every ounce of effort they can summon, it can become a symphony of male adolescence. That's when Ladouceur feels truly inspired.

That's what amazes him about The Streak. It has been accomplished by teenagers and indicates what they are capable of doing.

"I felt I was called to do this," Ladouceur says. "This is what I should be doing. As crazy as that may seem to some people—maybe they can't even understand what the heck it means—but I'm not alone. A lot of teachers at this school feel they have been called. This isn't just a job. This is a life mission."

His is the most publicized high school football team in the country. But Ladouceur has never read or seen anything that he felt encapsulates his program or begins to define it.

"If someone truly wants to understand, they have to be on the other side of the oleanders," said former De La Salle principal Brother Michael Meister. "They have to go and see. They have to look and feel."

THE MOST VULNERABLE TEAM SINCE THE STREAK BEGAN

august and September are the hottest months in San Francisco's East Bay, where hillsides are bleached brown and grass fires are a constant threat. But today a marine layer hovers over the region and a damp wind blows through the ear holes of players' new helmets, making the first day of practice feel more like the last.

"Brrr," Bob Ladouceur says, shivering. "It feels like November."

People describe De La Salle's head football coach as mysterious, probably because his face is impossible to read. His mouth is perpetually frozen between a smile and a frown. Deep crow's feet frame his eyes, which appear to retract while his brow extends when he gives somebody "The Look."

Everyone who has played football for De La Salle knows "The Look." Ladouceur rarely raises his voice. His message is instantly conveyed when his jaw muscles tighten and his lips, which are thin to begin with, disappear altogether.

It's the eyes that everybody remembers most. Those "criminal eyes," as assistant coach Terry Eidson calls them. Players swear he can peer directly into their souls and illuminate all that is hidden there. It's an urban myth, but it works for him.

"Fear slowly gives way to respect during your four years here," said former player and assistant coach Justin Alumbaugh.

Eidson pushes balls into a machine that fires hissing spirals to receivers. As the school's athletic director and the football team's defensive coordinator and special teams coach, he is both Ladouceur's superior and subordinate. It might be an awkward arrangement if these two old friends had bigger egos or if they hadn't realized long ago that their personalities interlock like puzzle pieces.

Eidson looks more like the theology teacher he is by day than the football coach he becomes in the afternoon. His beard is slowly turning gray, and his wire-rimmed glasses lend him a scholarly appearance. While Ladouceur often appears weary, Eidson has boundless energy and is always alert.

Eidson is the dreamer in the program. He's the front man, media contact, and promoter. His father owned stakes in several racehorses. He grew up along the backstretch at Golden Gate Fields and Bay Meadows. He remains a handicapper in life, always convinced he's right, always ready to double his bet.

Eidson's voice leaves his mouth in a raspy whisper that is easily carried away by the wind or drowned out by the sound of metal cleats on a cement floor. He screams to be heard on the practice field, or above the screaming guitars of the heavy-metal music he favors, or above the squeals of his two young daughters.

He lives in a perpetual state of exasperation. He stands on the sideline, chewing on his lanyard, until a defensive player fails to properly execute an assignment or lines up in the wrong spot. Then he starts convulsing as if a puppeteer were jerking his strings from above. Players have grown so used to these outbursts that often they wink at each other while Eidson stomps around.

"He honestly thinks our kids are loud because of me," says his wife, Aggie, shaking her head in disbelief. "I find that so comical."

Calling Eidson Ladouceur's assistant isn't accurate. Partner is more like it. As the defensive coordinator and special teams coach Eidson controls two-thirds of the game—the most critical two parts, in his opinion.

In his role as athletic director, he is in charge of scheduling for all sports, including football. As a result, De La Salle has played in front of as many as 30,000 fans in some of the most anticipated high school football games in history. The 2002 schedule may be the most difficult yet. The Spartans will open against defending Central Coast Section champion Archbishop Mitty of San Jose before traveling to Honolulu to meet 14-time state champion St. Louis in a game that promoters are hopeful will draw as many as 40,000 fans to Aloha Stadium.

Three weeks later comes a rematch with Southern California super-power Long Beach Poly, a program that has sent more players to the NFL (39) than any other high school in the nation and poses the greatest threat to The Streak.

The opponents don't worry Ladouceur as much as the timing. Instead of playing the toughest opponents at the end of the season, like most teams, his Spartans will play two of the top programs in the nation in the first five weeks. This lends a sense of urgency to the first day of practice.

The 48 varsity players scattered across the cramped practice field come from 23 different public high school districts throughout Contra Costa County.

This group already has impressed the coaching staff with its work ethic during summer workouts presided over by head trainer and strength coach Mike Blasquez. Ex-players claim that De La Salle's off-season regimen is more demanding than anything they have encountered while playing in college or the NFL.

The California Interscholastic Federation mandates that players participate in "conditioning week" before they are allowed to don pads and commence hitting. It's a joke at De La Salle, where Ladouceur has created a culture that embraces work. A senior on the 2001 team kept track of the hours he and his teammates spent working out. The final number was 995 hours, and that was before practice started.

"If I didn't show up, they would run that program and work just as hard or harder knowing I wasn't there because they believe wholeheartedly in what we do," trainer Blasquez said. "They know what they're doing is the absolute right way to do it. They believe they need to work as hard as they do."

The 2002 team is markedly different than its immediate predecessors. The 1999 team had unlimited potential but didn't believe it had anything left to learn. That team, that season, was a bear. When it finally was over, another undefeated season in the books, the coaching staff did something it rarely does. They all met at a local bar and raised their glasses, not in celebration or satisfaction, but in relief. Thank God that's over.

Last season's roster (2001) was full of seniors who embraced leadership roles and made the coaches' jobs easy. There are no leaders on the 2002 team, at least not yet, but leaders always emerge.

This team has talent. De La Salle always has talent, regardless of whether the athletes are recruited to the campus, drawn like a moth to a flame, or created through the sweat and science of the strength and speed programs.

Running back Maurice Drew was compared to Barry Sanders after his breakout four-touchdown performance against Long Beach Poly in 2001.

Drew is 5'7", 190 pounds, and can bench-press 330 pounds, squat 515, and run the 40-yard dash in 4.4 seconds. He's a human ricochet with a football under his arm, bounding around the field at wild angles, would-be tacklers never sure where his next step will take him.

He is a typical De La Salle student who spends as much as an hour on traffic-clogged freeways each morning. He attended public elementary school in Antioch. One day his mother fed his key chain through his belt loop so he wouldn't lose it. When school officials informed her that it was a gang sign, Andrea Drew immediately enrolled her son in the nearest Catholic grammar school.

He was a youth football legend. After watching De La Salle dismantle his hometown team, young Maurice knew which high school he would attend. What he didn't know was that his mother had already arrived at the same decision.

It required sacrifice. His parents were divorced and his mother traveled on business. He moved in with his grandparents in Pinole, thirty miles away, so his retired grandfather could drive him back and forth to school every day.

"I knew it was a disciplined environment that would allow him to grow up and be a mature adult," Andrea said. "I didn't know he would develop this kind of friendship with the football players. They do everything together."

∽

Attention to detail is one of the things that separates De La Salle from the competition. Ladouceur gives players vigilant feedback. Not even the slightest misstep or hesitation goes unnoticed. He has been known to spend forty-five minutes during a spring practice teaching the importance of his offensive linemen's splits. Every player's technique, whether he is an offensive lineman or a wide receiver, is constantly being refined.

"He brings tremendous focus to every practice," former junior varsity coach Pat Hayes said of Ladouceur. "I don't know how he does it, because sometimes he absolutely hates it. But these guys will not get cheated out of one minute. They are being taught every moment of every day until the end of the season. He will not let them down."

Other coaches often say they want to copy De La Salle's practice plan.

"No, you don't," Eidson quickly replies. That's because there is no practice plan, or at least no set daily schedule that is distributed to the coaching staff, as is commonplace in most programs. They wing it, mostly. The staff has been together for so long that each coach knows his role. There are no huge egos here.

Joe Aliotti is a former star high school and college quarterback from nearby Pittsburg (California) who devised the game plan that defeated De La Salle in 1991. He might be a successful head coach himself if he hadn't left a political morass at Pittsburg High to become De La Salle's dean of students in 1998.

He is in charge of discipline and patrols the campus like a beat cop. His job at the school is so consuming that he often is unable to get to practice on time. He refers to his role as "quality control," which includes quarterbacking the scout team in a shirt, tie, and loafers.

"Get your head up!" Aliotti yells at young quarterback Britt Cecil encouragingly. "You're going to make mistakes."

Mark Panella is a mortgage broker. He was Ladouceur's starting quarterback in 1984. Except for four years spent as an assistant at St. Mary's College in the early 1990s, he has mentored De La Salle quarterbacks ever since.

If Ladouceur is the stern father figure, Panella is the empathetic older brother who invites quarterbacks to his house for a home-cooked meal and a film session on Wednesday nights. He stands deep in the backfield during practices with his hat pulled low and snuff packed into his bottom lip, seeing the field through his quarterback's eyes.

Justin Alumbaugh coaches the linebackers and helps Ladouceur with the offensive linemen. He played offense and defense on the 1997 De La Salle team that broke Hudson, Michigan's, national record of 72 straight wins. Players love Alumbaugh. He only recently graduated from UCLA but is already being groomed as Ladouceur's eventual replacement, prompting other coaches to call him "The Chosen One."

Mike Blasquez's physique is the best advertisement for his training techniques. He is a former body builder who originally came to the school as an athletic trainer. He later assumed strength-and-conditioning duties and has lifted the football program to new heights by combining Ladouceur's philosophy with his science.

Because his off-season workouts are so comprehensive, Blasquez spends more time with the players throughout the year than anyone else on the staff.

"He has put us at a level where we could compete with elite teams," Ladouceur said. "Without him, forget it. We just couldn't have done it."

Nate Geldermann and his twin brother Jason were the twin terrors of their grammar school, bullying other students and creating havoc in the hallways. That destructive energy was channeled into football when they came to De La Salle. They became two of the fiercest, most dominating players in school history.

Nate coaches the defensive line the same way he played. Sometimes Ladouceur has to tell him to tone it down, just as he did when Geldermann was a player.

The staff is fueled by pessimism and obsessed with preparation. Strengths are overlooked, weaknesses magnified. Despite the presence of Drew, they consider this one of their weaker teams. Inexperience at quarterback and a lack of returning starters on the lines could have Streak-ending implications.

The quarterback situation is the result of a dilemma that Ladouceur faced at the beginning of the 2001 season. It was Matt Gutierrez's team— no dilemma there. He was a three-year starter and the best pure passer the program had ever produced. Senior Brian Callahan, son of then-Oakland Raiders offensive coordinator and current head coach Bill Callahan, was one of the hardest-working and most respected players on the team. Everybody knew that junior Britt Cecil was the future, but Ladouceur couldn't deny Callahan the backup job during 2001.

Thus, Cecil entered his senior season having not started a game since his sophomore year, and having never thrown a pass at the varsity level. He had the tools to be an effective runner and passer, but you could see the doubt swimming in his powder-blue eyes.

Panella tapped his index finger against his temple in explanation.

It's all in Cecil's head.

"I don't want to pay attention to how he's doing," Panella said. "I want to see how he's doing it. He's got to trust himself and believe he's doing the right thing. If he believes he's doing the right thing, it will become apparent to the rest of the team. He has a lot of self-doubt. That will be his biggest obstacle."

The speed, precision, and execution of the offensive line has always been the signature of the program. It's five players in complete synchronicity, firing off the ball as one, like a wave crashing on a beach. No team gets off the ball quicker or holds blocks longer. This advantage allows De La Salle's linemen to successfully compete against larger opponents. The only way to neutralize the Spartans' get-off is to beat them across the line of scrimmage. No opponent ever has.

Three starters return on the offensive line. It's the other two spots that worry Ladouceur most. "Who are my right tackle candidates?" he asked during a preseason meeting. The question was answered with blank stares.

"We're so in trouble on the line," Geldermann said, summing up the mood.

Three television camera crews, including ESPN, film the first day of full-contact practice, when Ladouceur hopes linemen will start catching his eye. Players are so used to the media attention they ignore the cameras.

One player stands out because of his potential. Chris Biller is a 5'10", 205-pound ball of explosive power, a permanent grin masking a mean streak. He dominated at the JV level last season but has never played in a varsity game.

Biller feels a tingling sensation down his arms after blocking Eric Sandie on the first day in pads. Twenty-four hours later, he is unable to raise his arms to snap his chinstrap and is sent to a specialist for tests.

An MRI reveals no fractures or herniated discs but detects spinal stenosis, a non-football-related narrowing of the spinal canal. Dr. John Wilhelmy makes the diagnosis. He has served as a team doctor for various high school football programs in the East Bay since the early 1970s. He consults two cervical spine specialists who conclude that it is unsafe for anyone with Biller's condition to play contact sports.

The bad news follows the practice-field death of a local junior-college player. On the surface, there is no connection between the incidents. The junior-college player went into cardiac arrest during a routine drill; Biller's problem is skeletal. Still, Ladouceur's cautious instincts are heightened. He won't even consider allowing Biller back on the field unless the doctors and his parents are convinced there will be no long-term risks.

Biller is devastated. He did not come to De La Salle for the college preparatory classes. He was a ball boy when his older brother was a Spartans offensive lineman, and he wants nothing more than the same for himself.

"I don't blame them if they say they don't want me to play," he said. "I might come to the same decision if I was in their shoes. But in my mind I've played before. I want use of my body, but every sixteen-year-old kid thinks the same thing: It won't happen to me. My spine won't break. I'm just praying they say the canals are pretty small, it's dangerous but it's your decision. Then I'd play. I'd play in a second. My mom has a lot of trust in me. I'm a pretty mature kid. I think she'd go along with it. At least I hope she would."

He stands on the sideline during practices, watching disconsolately as the collisions continue, day after day, with no linemen rising above the rest. Even the three returning starters, Erik Sandie, John Chan, and Cole Smith, struggle to get off the ball and to strike with the speed and ferocity Ladouceur demands.

"I feel like burning this tape it's so bad," Ladouceur says after pointing out the same incorrect first step again and again.

"If they want to play like shit, I don't care," Eidson says, shrugging.

"We're freakin' dogshit," a disgusted Geldermann tells his defensive linemen. "If you want to get your ass kicked that's your problem. It's not like I'm getting my ass kicked."

After two weeks in pads it's obvious that Ladouceur doesn't know anything more about his team than he did before Day 1. Cecil is still performing like a junior varsity quarterback, at least to Ladouceur's exacting eye. The offensive line lacks the aggression and intensity that always has been a trademark of his teams.

This team is shaping up to be the most vulnerable since The Streak began, and it must navigate the most difficult schedule in school history. De La Salle has finished undefeated for ten straight years, but there's a strong feeling among Ladouceur and his staff that this could be the year The Streak ends.

That doesn't stop *USA Today* from publishing its preseason Super 25 Football rankings. De La Salle, winner of three of the past four *USA Today* national championships, is ranked No. 1. Long Beach Poly is fourth, and St. Louis of Honolulu is twenty-first. Below an action photo of Maurice Drew running away from a Poly defender in his four-touchdown performance last season is the headline:

"125 and counting."

~

Eidson insisted on coaching the special teams units when he was elevated to the varsity staff in 1982. He wanted a team he could call his own, and De La Salle's special teams were ordinary.

Ladouceur was all too willing to give Eidson that responsibility.

"Before Terry came there was nothing special about our special teams," Ladouceur said. "It was an afterthought for me. I felt I had so many other things to worry about, it was always last on the list."

Eidson wanted to make his special teams a cornerstone of the program, and the kickoff coverage team the cornerstone of the special teams. He succeeded in creating a game-breaking unit for the team and an alter ego for himself—Cobra.

"The whole environment around Cobra is a little cultish, and I don't want to use that word loosely," former player Patrick Walsh says. "This cult is centered on good special teams play and creates special memories for kids. What is the value in that? That's what coaching is about, creating positive memories for kids."

Eidson has succeeded on that front. One former player wrote a song for the kickoff team to the tune of the popular movie theme "Ghost-busters." He changed the words to Wedge Busters, and soon the nickname was shortened to Busters. To this day, if the kickoff team allows even a mediocre return, Eidson receives complaints from former Busters, who fear that the coach has grown soft.

It is more than a point of pride. The efficiency of these elite units is one of the primary reasons why De La Salle is so dominant. Players must fill out an application before they are considered, as if they were applying for a job or admission into college.

"Walt Michaels, former coach of the New York Jets, summed up what kind of man plays on special teams," concludes the application's introductory paragraph. "A man with no fear belongs in two places—a mental institution and on special teams." The paragraph ends with a question: "Are you that man?"

The seven questions range from serious to silly and reflect the nature of the process and the man who drafted it. Players are required to state which special teams unit they are applying for and why Eidson should consider them for such an important assignment.

"Do you like girls?" That's question No. 5 and Eidson's personal favorite. Players aren't sure how to respond. If they write "no," then they may not be selected for the manly assignment. If they answer "yes," the coach might consider this a distraction. Most admit they like girls, but only after the football season has concluded.

"What would you do if you saw your mother running with the football?" That's the last question. It comes from an article on special teams that Eidson read years ago. If the response is "push her out of bounds," the player is best suited to offense. If it's "tackle her," then he is a candidate for defense. If the answer is "knock her head off," it's a sure sign of a committed special teams player.

Most players state matter-of-factly that they would cream their mother in such a situation. Former star running back and linebacker D.J. Williams took it a step farther. He included a videotape with his application that began with his mother dressed in a football uniform and ended with her son, then a 6'1", 220-pound manchild who would become one of the most intensely recruited high school athletes in history, leveling her after she caught the ball.

The extra effort gave D.J.'s mother recurring back pain but did not land her son a spot on the kickoff team. As a two-way star at running back and linebacker, he was just too valuable.

But that's how far players will go to please the Cobra.

Eidson's Cobra persona evolved over time. He and his special teams units would watch a movie together every year. The movie always involved a good guy who did something borderline psychotic. Cobra would bring the movie's posters to practice, and his players would kneel and bow reverentially in front of them.

One year they watched Sylvester Stallone's *Cobra*. Not long afterward a player showed up with a toy-store version of Cobra sunglasses and a gun. Eidson put on the glasses and walked onto the field. The first chant of "Cobra! Cobra!" was heard. A tradition was born.

Eidson has accessorized through the years. Cobra now wears a black leather jacket with silver studs, black pants, and black zip-up boots when he makes his weekly appearance. The cobra tattoo on his right biceps is the result of his wife's dare.

He'll often read an article from a tabloid to inspire his troops. "Man shot three times drives self home" is a time-tested favorite, as is the tabloid story about the 113-year-old granny who warded off a burglar by grabbing his crotch and jabbing him with a screwdriver.

Each year Eidson designs a new version of the "Cobra Corps" T-shirt. A hooded snake, poised to strike, adorns the front. An image from the most recent movie night is on the back. Before the 2002 season the team watched *Black Hawk Down*. Thus, the 2002 shirts feature a Black Hawk helicopter above a line from the movie: It's about the man next to you.

Only players who make a big special teams play will earn a T-shirt.

"Kids will do anything to get one of those shirts," senior tackle John Chan said. "You still see guys wearing them six or seven years later."

The coveted payouts go both ways. Players have honored Cobra in their own unique manner before the practice when the special teams units are announced. In 2000 players smashed watermelons on the field, then rolled around in the sticky mess. In 2001 they wore diapers and sucked on pacifiers while playing leapfrog.

This year's tribute begins with a banner. Chan grins when it is raised. "Cobra Wears Panties" is written in big, block letters.

What happens next is the kind of unbridled display that makes outsiders scratch their heads, while it forges insiders into a team. Erik Sandie places a Slip and Slide along the home sideline and attaches it to a hose. Erich Faustman produces an assortment of extra large women's underwear and thongs purchased at a discount store.

"It was a team effort," Chan explains.

Dressing in women's clothes has always been the ultimate in hilarity at an all-boys school. Players wear women's underwear and nothing else as they race across the grass and slide headfirst on the long, plastic runway, sending water spraying in all directions.

"This is classic," Chan says proudly. "We definitely stepped it up this year."

Afterward, the players who will comprise the special teams units are announced amidst much pomp and circumstance. Senior De'Montae Fitzgerald, who clashed with Eidson throughout his junior season, is named captain of the special teams, and he is thus entitled to wear the spiked leather jacket during noncontact practices.

The ultimate in "Cobra Theater," as Mark Panella likes to call it, occurred in 1990. But its roots were in the 1989 game against Pinole Valley, when De La Salle shocked its league rival with a 28–22 come-from-behind win at Owen Owens Field.

The Spartans already had lost two games that season—18–16 to St. Francis and 14–13 to El Cerrito—and Pinole Valley had the offensive weapons to knock De La Salle out of the playoff chase.

That game will always be remembered for the Toomer brothers. Pinole took a 16–14 lead on the final play of the third quarter. Amani Toomer, who would go on to star at Michigan and for the NFL's New York Giants, fielded the ensuing kickoff on his own 15-yard line, avoided several tacklers, and bolted up the right sideline.

Toomer is the fastest player in De La Salle history. In fact, there was only one player on the field who had a chance to catch him. That was his brother Don, who played cornerback for Pinole. But Don, a senior, couldn't catch his younger brother, a sophomore, and De La Salle took a momentary lead. The teams exchanged scores again before Pinole took the field for one final possession.

They drove to the Spartans' 13-yard line in the final minutes. Pinole backup quarterback Chris Singleton, who would go on to play baseball for the Chicago White Sox, Baltimore Orioles, and Oakland A's, played the entire second half after an injury to Pinole starter Ryan Deadrich.

Rob Kroha deflected Singleton's third-down pass. Mike Shea and Matt Clizbe defended his fourth-down attempt to seal the victory, thereby securing a Spartans win and setting the stage for Cobra's finest hour months later.

De La Salle played Pinole Valley for the league championship the following season. Two nights before the rematch, Eidson dug a shallow grave in the east end zone. He punched air vents in the plywood sheet he placed over the crude hole and carefully replaced the sod.

Cobra came out in his usual attire the next afternoon. The team gathered around him in the east end zone as he pointed to the spot where Pinole's last-gasp pass had fallen incomplete the year before.

That's where Pinole fantasies of a league title had been buried, he told wide-eyed players. A ghost now roamed the end zone, and one never knew when the Ghost of Pinole would rise up and attempt to reclaim the dreams of championship it had lost on this field the year before.

Eidson had a friend who had been a star running back at Pinole. The friend agreed to wear his old high school jersey and hide in the "grave" until the signal was given. When Cobra said "rise," the ghost leapt out of the grave as players shrieked.

That's when things went awry. It was a simple plan. The ghost would pretend to attack Cobra. Cobra would fight him off before retrieving a chainsaw hidden behind the bleachers. He would then chase the ghost off the field with the chainsaw, exorcising him forever.

They didn't anticipate startled players chasing the ghost themselves. Eidson's friend wasn't in the same physical condition as the last time he wore that jersey. By the time Eidson reached the chainsaw his friend was on the verge of collapse.

Cobra chased him from the field, disengaged chainsaw roaring, with the Ghost of Pinole on his final gasp. The Ghost sat in his truck for ninety minutes waiting for his fluttering heart to calm. A trainer was sent to check his vital signs periodically.

"Don't you think this Cobra shit has gone far enough?" Aggie Eidson asked her husband later that night.

"WHAT?" Terry asked, innocently. "IT'S SOMEHOW MY FAULT?"

∼

Eidson steers the white van out of the parking lot and toward the highway, his favorite heavy-metal CD reverberating through overmatched factory speakers. Archbishop Mitty scouting reports litter the floor. Defensive backs coach Terrell Ward, the only African American member of the staff, sits in the back seat, reading the sports page.

"That's the difference between me and Lad," Eidson says, shouting above the ear-bleeding wall of sound. "I like chaos. I like music that goes in four different directions. He likes things all laid out and mellow. He thinks Fleetwood Mac's Greatest Hits is the greatest album ever made."

The Spartans have just finished their annual scrimmage with James Logan High School. No one bothered to keep score, but had this been an actual game, the nation's longest winning streak would've been in jeopardy.

"We have a lot of work ahead but we'll get there if you're willing," Ladouceur told players afterward, when they gathered around him in the late afternoon sun. "We can't make you great players. We can offer you the opportunity to become great players. You're ninety percent of the equation. We're ten percent."

The bus takes the players back to De La Salle's campus, some fifty miles to the north. The day drags on for the coaches. Eidson and Ward drive to Foothill Community College in San Jose to scout Archbishop Mitty's season-opening game against Gunderson. The Spartans will host Archbishop Mitty in their own season opener in seven days. Ladouceur and Aliotti follow in another car, and Panella, Geldermann, and Alumbaugh ride in yet another.

"A lot of teams would wait a couple more years before testing us, but they want to see where they stand," Eidson says of Mitty, which was the Central Coast Section's runner-up in 2001. "If the game stays close it can be a huge confidence builder for their program. If they get torn apart it's like, 'Well, I guess we're not that good.' That's why I give them credit for playing us."

At Foothill College, a Mitty fan notices Ward's green De La Salle cap and asks, surprised: "You're not here to scout, are you? You don't need to do that."

He's right, of course. Archbishop Mitty is ranked twenty-third in the state in one preseason poll, but few believe it poses a serious threat to De La Salle.

Ladouceur already has broken down film of three of Mitty's games from last season and methodically assembled a detailed scouting report, but he wants to see if the Mitty coaches have added any new wrinkles. He prefers to scout teams personally so he can gauge speed and size and secondary coverages.

There are seven De La Salle coaches on hand, as well as Pat Hayes, who arrives separately. He labors up the steps, the aluminum bleachers bending under his weight. Hayes carries more than 300 pounds on his 5'10" frame. His long white hair makes him look more like a member of the Grateful Dead than a high school football coach.

He was a teacher and junior varsity assistant coach at De La Salle for thirteen years. His current role is difficult to define. He holds no official title, but he scouts, clips articles about upcoming opponents in local newspapers, and mainly hangs out, the target of almost constant good-humored ridicule from Ladouceur's younger assistants.

Ladouceur has a binder on his lap filled with identical pages divided into quadrants, each one containing an X to represent the center and circles for the guards and tackles on either side. Panella barks out down, distance, and whether the play will begin from the middle of the field or the right or left hash mark, information that Ladouceur dutifully notes in the left-hand corner of each quadrant before every play. He begins diagramming as soon as the play starts to unfold.

One longtime former assistant claims that Ladouceur has the gift of spatial intelligence. He can see order among chaos, like a math prodigy who looks at an equation and sees a solution when others see a jumble of letters and numbers.

He diagrams eleven individual assignments down to the smallest detail, such as whether the defensive tackles are lining up on the inside or outside shoulders of the offensive tackles, or if they are playing straight up. He can see the left guard pulling and the tight end releasing and running a shallow crossing route.

His assistants fill in blanks, such as calling out the routes run by out-side receivers. Aliotti jots down Mitty's personnel groupings and the defensive fronts Gunderson employs. Eidson watches the offense and special teams.

"Second-and-6, right hash," Panella calls out.

"Straight dive," Aliotti predicts.

"Halfback in the flat," Panella counters before the right tackle jumps offside and the official whistles the play dead.

"Call me crazy, but the back was going deep behind the quarterback. It could've been a double pass," Hayes ventures.

"You're crazy," Ladouceur says, never taking his eyes off the field.

This night is equal parts scouting expedition and boys' night out. The insults and one-liners fly, as is the case whenever this group is together.

Hayes' narcolepsy is a source of great amusement. He can fall asleep in any setting, and his colleagues often wager on how long it will take for him to nod off.

"Are you still up?" Panella teases.

"The night's still young," Hayes answers, bright-eyed and confident. Then a look of enlightenment crosses his face. "Oh, shit. You guys have got a pool going, huh? I've got to start getting a cut of that shit."

When Gunderson forces Mitty to punt, Aliotti notices the punter lin-ing up shallower than normal.

"I don't see a lot of speed on that punt team," says Eidson, whose spe-cial teams units terrorize opponents weekly. "Here's a suggestion: DON'T PUNT TO US!"

Gunderson attempts a shotgun snap from its own end zone and the ball sails past the goal post for a safety.

"We can go now," Geldermann says. "We've seen enough."

Mitty has a talented running back and a big, strong tight end, but otherwise doesn't appear overly threatening, especially against a disor-ganized Gunderson team that has only twenty-eight players on its var-sity roster.

"This is just bad football," Ladouceur says, referring more to Gun-derson than to Mitty.

Mitty leads by 30 when Hayes' eyes flutter closed and his chin drops to his chest. "You couldn't even make it through the first half," Panella says with mock disgust.

Hayes jerks awake with a snort.

"There's no love on this staff," he mutters sleepily.

Midway through the third quarter the tight end lines up in the backfield and catches a screen pass for a sizable gain.

"That's their best play," Eidson says. "I wouldn't have run it."

Ladouceur has seen enough. Geldermann, Alumbaugh, and Panella have already left. The coach who owns the longest winning streak in history climbs down from the bleachers at the end of a 14-hour day and walks through the main gate, disappearing into the darkness of the parking lot, unnoticed.

The dashboard lights give Eidson's bearded face a haunting glow during the seventy-five-minute drive back to Concord. He tries to explain the sense of obligation the coaching staff feels toward the game, but most of all toward the players.

"My wife doesn't get upset with me when I'm never home during the season because she knows how hard these kids work," he says. "It's when I get home late after a basketball game that she gets upset."

So, Eidson is asked, what did he learn on this scouting expedition that he didn't already know?

"It taught me that we'll be 1–0 heading to Hawaii," he says.

1971

FOOTBALL COMES TO DE LA SALLE

| | | | | | | | |

before there were oleanders, there were walnut trees. There were no roads leading to the construction site. Brother Jerome Gallegos remembers bumpy rides through the surrounding walnut orchards just to reach the location of the new Christian Brothers high school opening in Concord.

"You couldn't even call it the boonies," he said. "There was nothing there, literally nothing."

The San Francisco province of the Christian Brothers commissioned a study in the early 1960s which concluded that Concord would experience a population boom. In fact it already had, growing from a sleepy burg of 6,953 in 1950 to a suburban community of 36,000 by 1960. With no other Catholic high schools in Contra Costa County and none slated to open in the next ten years, the Brothers completed plans to found one of three new high schools on the West Coast.

Contra Costa County was beginning its transformation from an agricultural community to a suburban enclave. Even though the population was steadily rising, this was a risky venture for the Christian Brothers, which up to that point had typically built schools in major urban centers.

There wasn't much of a student population to draw from. There were numerous quality public schools in the immediate area, including Ygnacio Valley High School, which bordered the new school's 18-acre property. As a result, some Brothers began to quietly refer to the new school as the "De La Salle experiment."

"At the ground-breaking ceremony the Diablo Valley College President talked about the experiment of the Brothers leaving the cities and coming to the suburbs," said Pete Kelly, who graduated from De La Salle in 1971 and later taught at the school for twenty years. "That was a big question. Did they belong? Would it work?"

De La Salle was built at the same time as an all-girls private school across the street, run by the Sisters of St. Joseph of Carondelet. Both schools were designed in the European monastery style, with outdoor courtyards and arcades.

Plans for De La Salle included a 12,000-volume library, administration and counseling offices, a 500-seat theater, music rooms, a cafeteria, an auditorium, and a gym with a capacity of 1,200. The chapel and in-house residence for the Christian Brothers completed the original construction project at a cost of $4.5 million.

Carondelet was completed in time for the incoming class of 1965. Construction at De La Salle lagged behind schedule, however, forcing the four Brothers, one lay teacher, and the 115-member inaugural class to take up temporary residence less than a mile away at Most Precious Blood Catholic grammar school.

The first entrance test was called a "placement test" because administrators didn't want to scare potential students away. It was scheduled for a Saturday. The test forms had not arrived at the school by Tuesday, prompting Brother Norman Cook, the founding principal, to call the company from which he had ordered them.

He was told that the tests would arrive via air mail at San Francisco International Airport on Thursday. "So I put on my blacks," Brother Norman remembers. "I had to get results and I was hoping to impress them."

His request for his package at the airmail counter created a bustle of activity, which he found curious, even if he was wearing his black robe and collar. His package had indeed arrived, he was told, and had been promptly packed in ice.

In ice?

"Here, Brother, is your most precious blood," the airport employee said as he proudly placed a box covered with ice crystals on the counter.

The package had Most Precious Blood written prominently on the

31

side. Employees had seen the address and mistaken the contents for plasma.

"We had two days to thaw it out and then we were OK," Brother Norman said.

The grammar school serving as the temporary facility had no cafeteria, forcing students to bring bag lunches from home or buy their lunch from one of six vending machines, which students referred to as the "dietary supplement center." There were no tables. Students sat on benches and ate outside the school.

The girls from Carondelet were invited to the first school dance. Money was tight, so Brother Norman was delighted to find a nearby Elks Hall with a jukebox in the corner, which meant he wouldn't have to hire a band or disc jockey.

He and several parents and faculty members were decorating the hall the night of the dance when they discovered that the jukebox only contained one record.

"We locked the doors and they danced to Bing Crosby's 'White Christmas' all night," Brother Norman chuckled. "I don't know how they ever recovered."

De La Salle was officially dedicated in September 1967, but it took several years before students and faculty were welcomed in the community. Some outsiders viewed the Brothers in their black robes and rabats with suspicion. Students from neighboring schools looked down on the new private-school students, calling the institution "Gay La Salle," "Homo High" or, even more irritating to some, "De La Who?"

It was not uncommon to see graffiti on various walls of the school on Monday mornings. "Fags" was a popular epithet. It later became school policy to have a maintenance crew erase any offensive words before the students arrived for class.

"Our kids used to get razzed by kids from other schools," Brother Jerome said. "A lot of them would not wear De La Salle jackets. They preferred being anonymous."

Athletics at the school consisted of basketball, baseball, golf, tennis, and cross-country. Soccer was added later. De La Salle competed in the now-defunct Catholic Athletic League and enjoyed limited success in the early days.

High school football was king in Contra Costa County at the time. Neighboring public schools such as Ygnacio Valley and Concord fielded high-caliber teams. Eventually the Brothers were forced to consider starting a football program. They were losing prospective students who wanted to play. The faculty was divided.

"The school was in its infancy and trying to establish an identity for itself," said Steve Quirico, who taught physical education and coached soccer and freshman baseball in 1970. "Athletics were something they wanted to get started but it really wasn't a priority. It wasn't getting a big push from the administrative side."

Administrators were busy trying to keep the doors open. The school was struggling financially, and the provincial council considered closing it. Because De La Salle was still young there were no wealthy alumni to tap, which forced the Brothers to come up with creative new ways to raise money.

It was at a dinner-dance fundraiser in the school cafeteria in 1970 that Brother Norman noticed a hulking, intense-looking man with a blond mop of hair stalking him. He appeared too young to have high school-aged children.

"Who is this guy?" Brother Norman thought. "Mafia? A private eye?"

The man finally introduced himself as Ed Hall. He was a San Francisco police officer interested in launching a football program at De La Salle.

"I thought there's no chance, none," Brother Norman said. "I told him I didn't see how we could possibly do it, but he wouldn't take no for an answer."

Hall said he would bring fellow officers from San Francisco as his unpaid assistants, and they would raise all the necessary funds themselves.

Brother Norman said he would do his best to represent Hall's cause.

Hall was determined to make it work. He regularly dropped by the school unannounced. Brother Norman's secretary would tell him that the principal was unavailable. Hall would wait in the reception area until Brother Norman finally appeared in the doorway.

"Our initial interviews were based on my persistence and his reluctance to meet with me," Hall said.

There had been increasing parental pressure to start a football program, eventually prompting Brother Norman to write a letter to the

District Council requesting permission to establish a football program at De La Salle. Because of the school's substantial operating deficit, he stressed that the program would be financed outside the existing school budget.

"We believe the athletic program which includes football as an inter-scholastic sport will greatly benefit De La Salle's recruitment of fresh-man students...," Brother Norman wrote in the letter dated November, 14, 1970. "I have visited eighth grade and CCD classes throughout Con-tra Costa County over the past five years, and the biggest obstacle I have had to contend with in getting 'thirteen-year-olds' interested in com-ing to DLS is the absence of a football program...."

The letter continued: "We believe that an inter-scholastic football program at De La Salle will enhance the other sports programs at the school.... The resultant publicity of a FEW WINS NOW AND THEN in the area of the major sports provides a *ready* springboard for selling our academic and extra-curricular program to a more disposed and receptive public."

"I was bullshitting like mad when I wrote that," Brother Norman said more than thirty years later. "I was saying anything I could to get the program going."

Brother Norman's letter helped convince the council to agree to allow De La Salle to establish a junior varsity football team for the 1971 sea-son. The idea, however, was not embraced by everyone at the school. Some considered football a necessary evil.

"The whole cost issue was a concern to some Brothers," said Al Claiborne, the athletic director at the time and the only lay teacher on staff when the school opened. "I also remember some dialogue about the safety issue of the sport."

It would be impossible to start a football program without some-one like Ed Hall. This would be a daunting task for anyone, especially someone with two young children at home and a full-time job as a San Francisco police officer.

There was no field, no equipment, and no budget. There weren't even any goal posts. The school was in such dire fiscal straits that it was being considered for closure. But Ed Hall was a man of intense singular focus.

He was thirty years old and had been an assistant at another Christian Brothers School, Sacred Heart High in his native San Francisco. Hall played football in high school and in the army and wanted a program to call his own.

"Ed Hall was very courageous," said Quirico, who was an assistant coach in the early years. "I'm sure he felt he was well equipped, but it still took a lot of guts to start that program. I can't imagine doing it myself, but he tackled it with ferocity and courage. He was trying to teach coaches his system and trying to teach kids who had never played tackle football."

The school was attracting more merit scholars than potential football stars at the time. Many students arrived at the insistence of their parents. Athletes didn't gravitate to the school. Hall remembers walking through the campus and noticing that there was no hard-core jock group similar to what is commonly found at public schools.

De La Salle in the 1970s was an academic school and a party school. It didn't fit the profile of a budding football dynasty, but the kids were tougher than they looked, and Hall was convinced that De La Salle was a sleeping giant.

"It was the 1970s," Brother Jerome recalls. "Kids were all over the place in terms of interest. It was socially chaotic. It was very difficult to get kids to dedicate themselves to something real structured like football. A lot of them didn't."

Hall threw himself into his work. His team lacked size, speed, and experience. He quickly determined that to be successful they would have to rely on the deception of the triple option. He immersed himself in learning the new offense. He organized golf tournaments and crab feeds to raise money for the fledgling program.

Chuck Lafferty, the athletic director in 1972, said of the program, "We knew we had to have someone to sell it, not only to the kids but to the community. Ed could do that. He was wonderful speaking to groups and fundraising."

Football debuted at the school in 1971, on the junior varsity level only. Players carried Ed Hall off the field after the school's first victory, a 28−0 shutout of Bishop O'Dowd. The Spartans finished their inaugural JV season with a 6−2 record, including a win over the varsity team from the California School for the Deaf. "It was like taking kids off polo horses and putting football helmets on them," Quirico said. "We had kids who didn't know how to wear shoulder pads. It was crazy."

Hall cut the victory cake after De La Salle upset perennial Catholic Athletic League power Salesian during its first varsity season the following year. A troubling trend was developing, however. The Spartans averaged 7.5 points per game that season and were shut out in three straight games late in the year.

Hall was a defensive-minded coach who put all his best players on that unit. His teams played hard, hit hard, and were rarely blown out, but his offense continued to flounder during a 3–5–1 season in 1973.

"I remember when Oakland Tech came to De La Salle in 1973," Hall said. "I kept telling our kicker not to kick the ball to No. 24. He kicked it right to him and Rickey Henderson ran it back for a touchdown. We played St. Elizabeth the following week. They had a big stud fullback, the biggest, meanest-looking guy we played against. Have you ever seen [former Oakland A's pitcher] Dave Stewart's beady eyes looking out from under a baseball cap? Well, you should've seen them from inside a football helmet."

The first "winning season" came in 1974, at least according to the yearbook, which insisted that the team's record could easily have been 7–2. The yearbook staff was using the term "winning" loosely, since the Spartans were the picture of mediocrity at 4–4–1. They did finish the CAL season with a 3–2–1 record, however, and three players were named to the all-conference team. The following season included a 6–6 tie with Moreau, which had quickly become De La Salle's chief rival, but the season ended with the Spartans posting a 2–5–2 overall record and a 2–2–2 league mark.

The Spartans were forced to play home games in the heat on Saturday afternoons because their stadium had no lights. This added to their second-class status in local football circles. Only a smattering of parents and students attended home games.

Hall remembers calling a timeout late in one game so he could talk strategy with his quarterback. His team was playing courageously and was still in the game. As he walked back to the sideline his eyes wandered. That's when he noticed four Brothers playing tennis on nearby courts, which summed up the support of the administration.

"Sometimes we were lucky to get parents and families in the stands," Brother Jerome said. "It was a very slim turnout. The support for the team was negligible. I used to feel terrible for those kids. They had very little backing."

Hall spent so much time at the school that his colleagues wondered when he slept. He raised money for aluminum bleachers that he and his assistants attempted to assemble themselves to save money. When they were finished and gazed at their handiwork from afar, they noticed that the entire structure leaned drunkenly to the right. Eventually, professional installers had to be hired.

Owen Owens sent eight of his children to either De La Salle or Carondelet. He was an avid car collector and prominent local newspaper publisher forced to retire from the business he loved after being diagnosed with leukemia at age forty.

He took great interest in philanthropy after his forced retirement and took pride in the school his children attended. He donated $5,000 for new helmets and contributed to the scoreboard and other improvements for the field that still bears his name, even though none of his four sons played football.

"I remember running the jackhammer across the asphalt so we could run conduit to the main building," Hall says. "My ears rang for a week."

Hall believed the best way to raise the visibility of his program was to schedule public schools. It wasn't a popular decision because De La Salle was still struggling for wins while playing a relatively easy non-league schedule.

But the decision seemed to pay off when De La Salle shocked Northgate 19–7 for its first victory over a Diablo Valley Athletic League school.

"For a night, anyway, I was the talk of the town," Hall said.

The school was growing but the football program was shrinking. There were only 25 players on the varsity team in 1975 and the junior varsity team, which had only 17 members in 1976, was forced to forfeit a game late in the season for lack of players.

"A lot of guys didn't want to come out because they were intimidated by Hall," noted Phil Donahue, a linebacker and tight end who graduated in 1978.

Hall had earned the nickname "Bear" because of his perceived similarity with legendary Alabama coach Paul "Bear" Bryant. While other teams had two-a-days during the summer, Hall had three-a-days and players were not allowed to leave campus between practices. When three of his players skipped practice to play golf, he tracked them down on the links and hauled them back to the practice field. When some of his players chose to attend a party rather than scout an upcoming opponent, he had his own party waiting for them on Monday. They ran for what seemed like hours.

He wore a scowl on his face and was so single-minded that he was considered a curiosity around campus. Players will never forget Hall shouting instructions to them from the back of a moving ambulance while escorting an injured player to the hospital.

"I look back on him as that old-time football guy, leather-faced and very intense," said Keith Schuler, who played for Hall his sophomore and junior years. "He probably did as much as he could with the talent he had."

The varsity finished 1–4 in league play in 1977 and 2–3 the following season. In eight years, the only championship De La Salle had won was a freshman CAL title in 1976. By that time, the losing had begun to wear on Ed Hall.

"I remember Ed running on the track and it seemed like he had the weight of the world on his shoulders," Kelly said. "He wanted to bring these kids victories and he couldn't. He was frustrated, but he was most frustrated for the kids."

Hall's resignation stunned the administration, but many of his players saw it coming. He hadn't been as intense in 1978. By the end of the season the man whose boundless energy established the program looked old and tired.

Players on his first team would never forget the first thing Hall told them.

"He was a very forward-thinking person," said Pat Mullen, who was the first quarterback at De La Salle. "He knew we were going to be good someday. He'd say, 'When De La Salle is a powerhouse you can say you were on the first team.'"

He also told them he would no longer be the coach when the sleeping giant finally awoke.

04 ►

ARCHBISHOP MITTY
A Deflating Debut

| | | | | | | | | |

the first team dinner of the 2002 season is in a Walnut Creek home that feels more like a small estate. Players eat on the patio as a waterfall trickles into a swimming pool. They gaze down at the private tennis court and batting cage below.

Parents have spent the afternoon preparing fifteen pounds of pasta, twenty loaves of garlic bread, and 180 pieces of grilled chicken. Players finish their third and fourth helpings and disappear into the house to play video games, shoot pool, or watch the Thursday night college football game on ESPN.

The team dinners began in 1982. Bob Ladouceur was searching for a remedy to the slow starts that had plagued his first three seasons as head coach. He wanted his players mentally and emotionally ready to play the night before the game. He remembered his high school coach inviting players to his home on Thursday nights for homemade ice cream and to review the game plan one last time. He started the same custom at De La Salle.

The 1982 team dominated early in games and finished undefeated for the first time in school history. Eventually, desserts turned into full-blown meals organized by the parent group. The meeting evolved along with the menu. What began as review sessions turned into intimate team-building exercises that helped make a unit that was greater than the sum of its parts. Players today look so forward to the team dinners that the locker room empties quickly after Thursday's practice. Some don't even bother to shower before piling into their cars.

For Ladouceur, Thursday nights can be pleasurable but are often a chore. This night is both. Although important work lies ahead, he's in no hurry to start the meeting as he sips bottled water in the fading light.

This is not a good team, at least by De La Salle standards, and it isn't getting any better. Practices have lacked the trademark intensity. Nobody is hitting. Quarterback Britt Cecil continues to struggle. Ladouceur had to stop his offensive linemen during a drill earlier in the week and shame them into getting off the ball and sustaining blocks, and shaming is something he loathes to do.

In more than twenty practices thus far, Ladouceur estimates he has seen maybe a half dozen offensive plays that have satisfied him. The effort he has witnessed might be good enough to beat Archbishop Mitty, against whom the Spartans will open their season tomorrow, but it could prove inadequate against St. Louis.

"It's like this team doesn't think it can lose," assistant coach Mark Panella grumbled after practice earlier in the week. "What were they, six or seven years old the last time we lost a game? They think all they have to do is put on a jersey and they'll win."

Terry Eidson was decidedly more upbeat after a chapel service earlier Thursday. Players opened up and spoke from the heart, which is almost as important as what takes place on the practice field. It was the first positive sign he had seen from this team, and it could not have come at a more opportune time.

"I feel we have a chance now," he said. "They're getting it. It's more than just a game. That's what you want to see. I think we'll get the effort."

Then he added: "Now we'll let Lad work his magic tonight."

Ladouceur removes the napkin from his lap, pushes his chair back, and contemplates the dessert tray as assistant Joe Aliotti unwraps his third ice cream bar. It's time for a wake-up call that many of Coach Lad's assistants are convinced is long overdue.

"Let's get this thing started," he says finally, rising from his chair.

Coaches separate players into position groups to make final adjustments and set goals for the following night's game. The offensive line, for example, may make 100 percent pass protection and 200 yards rushing its goal. The defensive line's goal may be to hold opposing backs to less than 75 total yards and register three sacks.

This also is a time when position coaches can talk to their units individually before Ladouceur addresses the team as a whole. Ladouceur always considers his offensive line a microcosm of his team. He tells them where they stand.

"I'm trying to warn you," he tells them. "I'm not even thinking about dominating another line right now. I just hope you guys don't embarrass yourselves."

Players gather in the garage when the position meetings break up. Ladouceur stands in the front of the room, deep in thought, his sunglasses hanging from the collar of his gray golf shirt as the sound of metal folding chairs squeaking against the polished cement floor fills the room. When everybody has settled in it gets so silent that the muffled conversations of parents can be heard through the locked door.

"First of all, when you enter somebody's home you behave like gentlemen," he begins, referring to his players' mad scramble to the dessert tray after dinner, a display that forced him to throw down his napkin and quell the riot. "You don't bum-rush the dessert counter. You clean up after yourself. You say, 'please' and 'thank you' to the parents. You're in someone else's home. I don't give a shit how you act in your own home. But when you're in somebody else's home you're a guest, an invited guest, and you behave like one. You treat the property and the people in it with respect.

"That bum-rush to the dessert tray was embarrassing and unbecoming of you as gentlemen. Like you weren't going to get a dessert, and even if you didn't, what were you going to do, throw a tantrum? Are you going to go hungry? Come on."

Maybe it's his soft-spoken manner that makes Ladouceur such a powerful public speaker. He is unflinchingly honest and direct. Even coaches sit spellbound as he paces back and forth in front of a water heater, his voice rising and falling for emphasis. He has prepared no notes. He speaks from the heart, thinking things through as he speaks, creating dramatic pauses that last an eternity.

"I'm the dean of coaches. I've been coaching longer than almost anybody else in the Bay Area. I'm not saying I'm the best coach. I'm just saying I've seen a lot. I've seen a lot of teams. I think that's my strength as a coach. I'm not a genius. I'm not brilliant as a coach. But my strength is being able to tell you guys if you're playing up to your abilities. That I do know.

"One thing to understand throughout this year is what I tell you will be my perception of the truth. I'm not going to bullshit you, I'm not going to lie to you or make up shit to try to fire you up—none of that stuff. I'm going to give you exact feedback of what I see and what I hear.

"Here's how the meeting is going to go. I'm not going to give you any pregame talk tomorrow. I don't give speeches. Don't anticipate some guy firing you up, whether it's a teammate or a coach. I don't want to do it and I don't want them to have to do it [pointing to his assistant coaches]. Do it yourself. If you sit there and say, 'I need somebody to fire me up,' that's horseshit. It doesn't happen that way. It all comes from within your own heart...."

The dim overhead light casts Ladouceur's features in shadow, creating the illusion that there are bottomless black pools where his eyes should be. Players sit like statues in their metal chairs, staring straight ahead, engrossed.

"I'm just going to talk to you tonight, because tonight, you're going to have to decide what you want to be as a team. I've had at least three or four people come up to me since the middle of last summer and ask, 'What kind of team do you have this year? What's the team like this year?' I'm honest with them. I tell them I don't know....

"Here's what I see from you. Every team needs leaders to cut the path and followers who make it wider. Every great team has to have followers, guys who will go, 'I believe in this guy, I'm going to do what he says; I'm going to follow his lead. I'm going to be right beside him, whatever he wants.' It's OK to be a follower depending upon what you're following. I'm a follower. I'm a leader and a follower and I'll gladly FOLLOW ANYTHING I BELIEVE IN OR ANY PERSON I BELIEVE IN. I will follow.

"Last year, I think we had a very good group of leaders and you acknowledged and recognized that in them and were good followers.

Those sons of bitches that left took every challenge head on, welcomed it, wanted it, couldn't wait for it. They practiced like it, too. They kicked the shit out of you in practice every week to get themselves ready for the game. When the game came they were fearless and they played like it. It looks like you guys are looking around going, 'Where are those leaders?'

"The effort you put in during the offseason was commendable but it has not translated onto the field. To be honest with you, I think a lot of you are afraid of contact and mixing it up. I'm sorry, but this game requires that of its leaders. I can talk a great game, lift a corner of the weight room, run through the agility stations, but if I don't hit and I'm not physical on that field, my leadership qualifications drop dramatically. If I'm not a tough son of a bitch on that field, my leadership credibility is diminished.

"You've got to decide what you want to be. Because I get the feeling from you as a team that you want to jump up on the throne and let us place the championship ring on your finger. You're at De La Salle and you deserve that. You guys think you DESERVE that? DO YOU THINK THOSE OTHER TEAMS DIDN'T EARN THAT AND FIGHT FOR IT AND BLEED FOR IT ON THE PRACTICE FIELD? Damn right they did. But it seems like you guys want to hop up on the throne without going through all that. WELL, YOU'RE FOOLING YOURSELF....

"I talked to the offensive line and hopefully it will be the alarm that wakes them up because next week and down the road they're going run up against lines that will tear them a new asshole unless they wake up. And then I don't know where you're going to be. I don't know what you're going to think about that.

"I had a discussion with Coach Eidson. He's concerned, rightfully, about you guys. I said, 'Hey Terry. They're either going to do it or they're not. Have we spent less time with them or prepped them less than any squad we've ever had? No. They're going to have to do it themselves.' One thing he said I agreed with. He said, 'Yeah, but I hate posers. They think they're going to do it and believe they deserve it but they won't go out there and do it.' Hey, that may be who you are.

"That's my answer to all the people that ask me what kind of team

I have. I don't know. I tell them we're ragged, not very aggressive, but we do have our moments out there. We have moments of brilliance, but for the most part we're inconsistent, mistake-prone, ragged, and not very physical. I'm not blowing smoke their way. I tell them flat out. If they continue on this path they definitely won't beat St. Louis and Poly. Now I'm being honest with you. If you do not have a jump in intensity and leadership, if you don't have a dramatic jump, I'm telling you now, and I don't mean to be pessimistic, but I just want you to understand this: There are consequences to your play. You will not beat St. Louis and you will not beat Poly with the intensity you're bringing. That's all the way across the board.

"That's where we are, and as much as you don't want to hear that, that's my assessment. Right now we're in over our heads. Do I feel that you guys can pull this off and earn the right to sit on the throne? Yeah, I do. I'm not hoping you play well tomorrow. YOU HAVE TO. You have to play well tomorrow. If we had all these big games coming up at the end of the year, I'd say, 'We've got time.' You don't have time. The time is right now. You have to play well starting tomorrow night. Now is a decision time for you as a team, as a group of seniors, as a group of returners.

"It's not going to be easy. Even if you make that decision, even if you step your game up and you guys are playing at your ability level, it's STILL NOT GOING TO BE EASY. YOU ARE STILL GOING TO FIGHT YOUR ASS OFF FOR VICTORIES IN THOSE GAMES.

"OK, I spoke long enough. But, hey, this has been building. I've been patient with you. I've been patient. I've been saying let's wait, it's only been three days, it's only been four days, it's only been a week; we've only been in pads for seven days.... Time's up. Either step up or prepare for the consequences."

There are several moments of awkward silence as his words sink in. The spell is finally broken when players are told to begin reviewing their offensive and defensive checklists, or specific things to be aware of during the game, such as when a team is prone to running a certain play out of a particular formation.

When the checklists are completed, it's the players' turn to speak.

"I don't want any saber-rattling," Ladouceur warns. "That's not what this is about. Talk about yourself, the guy playing next to you, your friend, or your group. That's fine. This is about you, mostly, and our team, if you want to speak to our team. But make sure you include your-self in it."

Ladouceur believes that his teams win because they care—not about winning, but about each other. Most people spend their lives suppress-ing the power of raw emotion, choking it back whenever it bubbles to the surface. Ladouceur taps into the individual emotional tributaries of his players and channels them into an unstoppable force.

The process begins during the offseason program when players spend countless hours together and become heavily invested in the season before it even begins. It continues during these weekly meetings, when players stand and deliver heartfelt testimonials. You can't play for Ladouceur unless you're willing to stand in front of your teammates and bare your soul. You can't play unless you're willing to cry.

Maurice Drew felt Ladouceur's wrath during a noontime film ses-sion when he was caught horsing around. It was a sign of the immatu-rity plaguing the team. Drew is the first player to stand.

"I'll start out," he says, examining his sneakers. "I'd like to apologize to the team for what I did today at lunch. I'm sorry. It won't happen again."

This is kicker Tony Binswanger's first full season on varsity. The sen-ior stands up in the back of the room and tells his teammates how much they mean to him even if the nature of his position can make it diffi-cult to feel as if he's an integral part of the team. "What we have here we'll never have in college," he says.

"The last three years I've been in love with this program," senior Erik Sandie says. "It's my life. This team is what I am. I love you guys like brothers."

Chris Mulvanny transferred to De La Salle following his sophomore year and struggled to fit in. The 190-pound defensive end clashed with his new coaches and teammates and spent the majority of the season on the bench.

He has been Geldermann's whipping boy during the first four weeks of practice. He's athletic but undisciplined, leaving his passing lane when

WHEN THE GAME STANDS TALL

he sees a direct line to the quarterback and failing to stay home to guard against reverses.

"Nobody works harder than us," he says. "Not St. Louis, not Long Beach Poly. I don't think anybody, anywhere, gets up at five in the morning to lift weights."

The testimonials continue as player after player speaks about the need to come together as a team and start performing like they know they can. The notable exception is Britt Cecil. The inexperienced quarterback remains silent, with his head down, even as Panella and his offensive teammates throw anticipatory glances his way.

They wonder when the offensive team leader will start acting like one.

"I want to hear from our quarterback," Panella finally says, the disgust apparent in his voice.

Cecil rises reluctantly to his feet, his eyes never leaving the floor.

"I hadn't really planned on saying anything because I'm unproven," he says softly, forcing those in the back to strain to hear. "Until I prove myself and prove that I can play, I don't feel like I should be talking to you guys about it."

It's almost ten o'clock when the meeting ends. Players stack chairs neatly in the corner of the garage, thank the hosts, and file silently through the door.

$\sim$

Owen Owens Field embodies the name of the team that calls it home. It's Spartan to the core. But when the sun goes down and the lights come up, and it's all decked out for a Friday night high school football game, it glows.

The stadium seats 3,500, but 6,000 can squeeze in if people stand six-deep in the end zones. The bleachers on the home sideline are actually located inside the all-purpose track and extend to within a few feet of the playing surface. A well-struck extra point can land in the condominium complex next door.

The peculiar orientation of the field makes the setting sun a factor during junior varsity games. The field is oddly crowned, peaking nearer the home sideline, which means that De La Salle players stand in a quagmire whenever it rains. The light poles aren't light poles at all. They actually are underground pipelines donated by a local oil company and erected after the waterproof adhesive was painstakingly removed. The cream-colored press box is trimmed in green. A Spartans logo is painted on one side.

The Spartans haven't lost a game on that field since 1989, but only a few old-timers know who Owen Owens was and why this unremarkable stadium bears his name.

Volunteers have already spent a day pulling weeds, repainting the goal posts, and picking up trash. They are parents of current students and alumni and call themselves "White Coats" because of the thin white jackets that identify them as they supervise various sporting events. The first White Coats show up more than four hours before the game to set up yard markers and pad the stairs that lead from the bleachers to the field. They place tarpaulins on both sidelines for players to stand on and cordon off the field with long strings of green and white flags.

"There's a charisma here," says White Coat president Tom Bruce, who patrols the field with a walkie-talkie on game nights. "There's not much to it but we keep it very clean. It makes a statement to me. It fits the demeanor and work ethic of the team. It's a very basic field and I don't think Bob would want it any other way."

When their work is done and the field is readied, and the cheerleaders are cheering and the band is blaring and the stands are packed with mothers and fathers and sisters and brothers, this humble little field has an undeniable charm.

De La Salle players stretch in silence on the practice field behind the stadium as the sun makes a spectacular descent and the golden foothills of nearby Mt. Diablo slowly fade into the darkness. Ladouceur gathers his team around him as the band marches to Notre Dame's "Victory March" and smiling cheerleaders on loan from the all-girls Catholic school across the street are tossed high into the air.

"If you're not sure on your blocking assignments, your rule is to pick out the closest guy and attack," he says. "Don't clip on special teams. Give us a chance. You guys are going to make some mistakes today, but we have to turn out on the positive side of the ledger when it's all said and done. The thing we're looking for tonight is aggression. This is it. We talked about it last night. You guys have to take that next step. You have to start rocking out there. If you do that, this evening will turn out just fine. It's a game of aggression and emotion. You have to play that way throughout the game."

This game has created an anticipatory buzz on Archbishop Mitty's San Jose campus. De La Salle has won ten consecutive North Coast Section championships and is ranked No. 1 in the state and No. 1 in the nation.

Archbishop Mitty is coming off the greatest season in school history. The school's only loss of 2001 came in the Central Coast Section championship game. It was only the second loss that the seniors suffered during their four-year high school careers.

A 46–8 demolition of Gunderson in the Monarchs' season opener lent credence to their No. 23 state ranking. An afternoon pep rally sent school spirit soaring. Fans chartered a bus to Concord hoping their team would accomplish what no other team in a decade had done—defeat De La Salle.

The hills to the east are cloaked in black against a vibrant orange sky when De La Salle players, dressed in bright green jerseys, silver pants, and silver helmets, join hands and walk onto the field in two parallel lines. There is no open display of emotion, just a quiet confidence that can be unnerving to an opponent.

Archbishop Mitty wins the toss and elects to receive. On the first play from scrimmage, running back Robert Perry runs for 13 yards. On the next play, quarterback Danny Dressman fakes a handoff up the middle and scampers for 49 yards.

Three plays into the game, the Monarchs have a first down at the 27-yard line against a program that hasn't lost a season opener since Ladouceur took over in 1979. Mitty fans are on their feet. De La Salle fans sit in silence, waiting.

Blitzing safety Matt Kavanaugh dumps Dressman for a seven-yard loss. Two running plays gain 11 yards to the De La Salle 23-yard line. De La Salle takes over on downs after Dressman falls on a fumbled snap on fourth down.

De La Salle's veer-option offense operates with such relentless precision that it's often compared to a machine. Ladouceur's teams have been shut out twice, both in his initial season, and have scored in 268 straight games, an ongoing state record.

Maurice Drew squats in his stance in the backfield, his weight on his haunches like a frog on a lily pad, his hand barely brushing the ground. The laws of physics would seem to prohibit anyone from exploding out of such an awkward stance, but Drew does, pushing the pile for 5 yards on De La Salle's first play.

Two plays later, he bursts off left tackle, spins away from a defender in the secondary, and scores from 51 yards out for the game's first touchdown.

It's the kind of stunning, game-turning play for which this team is known. De La Salle running backs average more than 10 yards per carry because of dominant line play and an infectious desire by everyone to make a "touchdown alley" block, or a downfield block that springs a running back or a receiver for a score.

The score is still 7–0 when Spartan safety Jackie Bates intercepts a Dressman pass late in the first quarter. Gino Ottoboni's ensuing 18-yard run gives the Spartans a 14-point lead, prompting the band to celebrate with another rendition of "Victory March."

Drew fields a punt after Mitty's next series and quickly dips behind his wall of blockers along the right sideline. A shuffle-step confounds one potential tackler and suddenly three green jerseys are escorting Drew down the field.

A quick cut inside leaves the kicker grasping at air at the 20. Drew continues zig-zagging toward the end zone until he crosses the goal line to complete a 55-yard punt return, just as Eidson had predicted while scouting Mitty a week earlier.

The 21-point lead snuffs any remaining drama. This looks like a typical rout.

Binswanger's 33-yard field goal makes it 24–0 at halftime. Drew's heroics overshadow some uncharacteristic sloppiness, however. There are three dropped passes, including two by senior receiver and special teams captain De'Montae Fitzgerald.

Fitzgerald is distraught at halftime. "I'm letting everyone down," he moans as Drew and receiver Cameron Colvin console him on the way to the locker room. Aliotti sees Fitzgerald sitting all alone, his head in his hands, while Edison and Ladouceur make halftime adjustments at opposite ends of the locker room.

"It's all right," he tells the emotional senior. "It's the first half of the first game. We've got a long way to go. Take it easy. You're going to be all right. Just make sure you catch the ball before you try to run with it."

The Spartans offense is lifeless in the second half. The defense, however, is turning in a surprisingly stout performance. The defensive line that was so worrisome when fall practice began is keeping Perry from ripping off any large gains.

The score remains 24–0 when Drew catches a screen pass in the right flat on the second play of the fourth quarter. A defender tackles him in the backfield and Drew lands awkwardly on his left ankle. He rolls over and leaps to his feet before trying to hop back to the huddle. Then he turns and hobbles toward the sideline.

There is fear in Drew's eyes. His intuition told him something was terribly wrong on impact. When he is unable to put any weight on his left leg he gets scared.

"I think I broke it," Drew says, grimacing, as trainer Mike Blasquez and team doctor John Wilhelmy take off his shoe and carefully examine his ankle behind the bench.

Drew was expected to carry the team, and he had through the first three quarters, racking up 131 yards on 11 carries and returning a punt 55 yards for a touchdown. The game continues on the field, but fans focus on the drama unfolding on the sideline. Drew's availability for next week's St. Louis of Hawaii game is in doubt. Considering how inconsistently the team has played in the second half, that isn't good news.

A season-ending injury isn't what scares Drew most. All he can think about is the upcoming trip to Honolulu. He has been looking forward to it for more than a year.

"I can't get hurt before Hawaii," he says to himself as he sits on a gurney, his injured ankle packed with ice and resting atop his helmet. His mother kneels by the railing separating the bleachers from the field and comforts her only son.

"It's just a cramp," All-State cornerback Damon Jenkins tells a teammate on the sideline. "Reese is too buff to get injured."

Ladouceur is updated on Drew's status by Blasquez in the waning moments of the fourth quarter. He nods and walks away, stone-faced.

There is little joy when the clock expires and long-time public-address announcer Lou Ascatigno announces that the Spartans have just captured their 126th consecutive victory. The team struggled offensively in the third quarter with Drew. It appeared lost in the fourth quarter without him.

The final score is 24–0. The Spartans didn't score a point in the second half.

"We looked pretty ragged compared to how we have looked in the past," Ladouceur tells reporters as parents and students mix with players on the field afterwards. "We didn't prep for our first game. We need to prep better."

Everyone asks about Drew. Blasquez sends him to the emergency room for X-rays. He hopes it is just a sprain. Everybody agrees that is the best-case scenario. Nobody even wants to consider any other possibility.

"That was our lowest offensive output since 1987," Eidson tells players as they sit with their elbows on their knees between rows of green mesh lockers. "You know what? You can wish it, you can talk about it and try to bond, but the bottom line is: You played that second half exactly the way you practiced the last three weeks—lethargic, walking around, dazed. We tried to warn you but it's too late. You can't put it together in one night. We had a good effort in the first half from the special teams and the defense, but the offense didn't drive it all night. We had a good individual effort from Maurice, but as an offense that was miserable. That's the truth.

"You've got to earn stuff. Nobody has gone out there and said, 'I'm going to get better today.' Nobody has practiced like that yet. You're playing a team ranked in the top twenty in the nation eight days from now. Blow it off. Keep practicing like that and we'll see what happens against St. Louis. This week we're going to play more speed and bigger guys and you're not going to scare anybody off, boys, you're not going to scare anybody off. Let me tell you something: You put yourselves in this position."

"I can't add to that at all," Ladouceur says when Eidson is through. "That was one of the most ragged performances I've seen from an offensive team from our school. That goes back a long way. I'd have to say into the early 1980s. You didn't do the things we coached you to do. We dropped balls. We didn't make plays. Maurice made plays. The rest of you didn't make plays. I know you guys were blocking the wrong people out there. You just looked bad. You played just like you practiced.

You're going to play just how you practice. You're not some comic book hero who's going to put on a cape on game day and go out there and star. It doesn't work that way. You watch too much TV if you believe that. I don't know if you guys are tough enough mentally and physically. I just don't know if you're tough enough.

"If Drew is with the team next week or not, I really don't care. I really don't. I want to see what you're made of—what a great test. We'll see you at films tomorrow. This was not good. You better have a change of heart by next week if you want to be in the game. Right now, even if you bring it next week with everything you've got I'd call it a toss-up. So you better do a little more soul-searching. Last night was not enough. When you sit and watch films tomorrow you better have your eyes glued to your position, whether you're playing or not. If there's continued ragged play I'm going to make changes. I'm not going to continue to beat a dead horse if somebody just can't do it or won't do it. All right, team prayer, and then go home."

The assistant coaches congregate behind a locked door and up a short flight of stairs from the main locker room, in the four cramped rooms that make up the coaches' offices. There they pick over what's left of the pregame meal Aliotti had purchased from a local deli and discuss their team's performance in hushed tones.

Pat Hayes sits on the tired green sofa, Justin Alumbaugh and Nate Geldermann in chairs. They all are stunned by what they witnessed and try to remember the last time the offense performed so poorly. If they play like this against St. Louis, The Streak could come to a screeching halt on the floor of Aloha Stadium.

"Bad week to stop sniffing glue," Hayes says, trying to lighten the mood.

Ladouceur, Eidson, and Aliotti have yet to make their way up the stairs when former De La Salle lineman Dalton Brown appears in the doorway. Brown's senior season at nearby St. Mary's College was interrupted when he was diagnosed with leukemia. The disease is now in remission, and he is a frequent visitor to his old school.

Brown passes out cold beers he has smuggled in under his sweatshirt.

He opens his can, the white foam oozing out of the hole in the top, and holds it high over his head in a mock toast: "Here's to 126 and 1," he says.

1970s

A COACHING LEGEND IS FORGED

t om Ladouceur got lost on his way to the airport. A salesman, he had been transferred from Detroit to the San Francisco Bay Area and was searching for a new home for his family when he took a wrong turn and found himself on a gravel road.

The rolling hills of the East Bay in 1962, three years before De La Salle High School opened for business, must have seemed as desolate as the moon's surface to a man who grew up in the crowded row houses of Detroit. Eventually the elder Ladouceur saw lighted stone gates up ahead and a sign that read "San Ramon Country Club Park."

Tom was an avid golfer who even played in the snow back home in Michigan. There were only three unsold homes left in the first phase of the new development. It was late in the afternoon and the sales office was about to close.

Tom wanted the house, but he knew he needed to talk to his wife first. Ever the charmer, he slipped the man five dollars for a promise to hold the house. That was in April. In May, Tom and Mary moved their four children into the $19,000 gray ranch-style home on Broadmoor Drive in San Ramon. Bob, the second-youngest, was in second grade.

Tom and Mary's children had been the focus of the extended family back in Detroit. With the kids gone, there was nothing to keep the rest of the family in Michigan. Tom's mother and sister bought a house on a cul-de-sac that bordered Tom and Mary's property. Mary's sister and father moved into an apartment in Walnut Creek.

San Ramon is located twenty-five miles east of Oakland, but in those years it was often referred to as "San Remote." The village had a town hall, general merchandise store, elementary school, and Methodist Church. The agricultural community wasn't even listed on the 1960 census. The 1970 census recognized 4,084 inhabitants.

"When we moved out there we were shocked," Bob said. "We felt we were really out in the country, the boondocks. The crickets were deafening. Pheasants would fly right by our house. Orchards, farms, and ranches were all that was there."

Once they adjusted they found their new surroundings idyllic in many ways. There were no fences then and endless open spaces. Parents didn't worry when their children disappeared after breakfast and didn't return until dark. Kids walked into the nearby hills at night to camp beneath the stars. Fathers organized quail hunting parties on Saturday mornings.

There was new construction all around them. Everywhere the Ladouceur children looked there were surveyors' flags, bulldozers, construction workers, and piles of dirt and lumber.

Bob and Tom Jr. acclimated quickly and were soon hunting field mice and being chased off the nine-hole golf course by the sprinklers every evening.

"We played in the newly constructed houses," Tom Jr. said. "When the frames went up they made really cool forts. We had unlimited lumber to build with."

Patricia was the oldest of the Ladouceur children by four years. Tom Jr. was fifteen months older than Bob, and Suzie two years younger. They were always playing sports, even the girls. If they weren't at home, they were at their grandmother's house.

Slowly, life fell into a comfortable routine. The Ladouceur house soon became a popular destination for neighborhood kids, who joined in the games and stayed for dinner. There always was at least one dog, if not three, adding to the chaos.

Like many women of her generation, Mary Ladouceur lived for her family. She made breakfast and packed lunches before leaving for her job as a school secretary. She was a quiet, simple woman who prayed to an army of Catholic saints and spent her Friday nights reciting the rosary across the street at Aunt Pat's.

Tom Sr. was interested in what his children did athletically, but he never joined in their games or took them to sporting events. He was always around but never engaged. But he was fun-loving and easily the most popular dad on the block, especially when his children got older. From the outside it appeared to be a model family where children were raised with traditional Catholic values. Internally there was constant friction. Tom Sr. drank, often heavily. Mary hated that. It was a divisive force.

"It helps me when I'm talking to kids about drug and alcohol abuse," Bob said. "I'm real up front with them. I tell them, look, you don't want to go down that road. It tears up a family and the fabric of relationships dramatically. I never had an interest—ever—in going down that road."

Tom Sr. pushed his sons into athletics. Bob and Tom Jr. played on one of four Little League teams in nearby Dublin. Tom Jr. was a good natural athlete but lost interest in sports at a crucial time. The more his father pushed, the more he resisted. When knee problems kept Tom Jr. from participating in high school athletics, Tom Sr. focused on his youngest son's athletic career.

"I felt that to get his approval and attention I had to play athletics," Bob said. "I liked doing it, but I knew that was a way to get him to notice me. He was very interested in our athletic careers, mine in particular."

Football didn't seem like a good fit for Bob, despite his love for the game. All he had ever wanted for Christmas was a ball or a jersey or a helmet. He remembers feeling as if he understood the game even at a young age. Everything slowed down when he stepped on the field. He couldn't wait to play.

The problem was, he was so skinny that his oldest sister called him "Chicken Wing." His mom and grandfather called him "Bones."

He weighed 110 pounds during his first year of youth football; the weight limit was 145. He took a terrible beating and became discouraged. It was a game he felt he was born to play. But it was too painful to play.

Meanwhile, the San Ramon Valley, like the rest of Contra Costa County, was booming. Ranchers and laborers were in the process of being displaced by more than 25,000 new residents. The new 680 freeway was extended to Dublin in 1966, making the entire valley more convenient for commuters. "City close, country quiet" was the slogan of one developer.

The student population at San Ramon High School illustrated the valley's transformation from an agricultural community to a modern suburb. The demographics of Bob's freshman class reflected the eclectic community. It wasn't ethnically diverse. In fact, it was overwhelmingly white. But it was diverse in other ways.

"There were kids who would occasionally ride a horse to school," said long-time family friend Blair Thomas, who grew up with the Ladouceurs and has also worked with the De La Salle football program. "There were other kids who would occasionally drive dad's Ferrari to school. It was a really odd mix of kids from different types of backgrounds and economic situations."

With his final Pop Warner season still fresh in his mind, Bob opted to skip football during his freshman and sophomore years in high school. He lifted weights instead. He draped towels over the bench his grandfather had fashioned for him. Soon he was working out in his garage lifting sand-filled weights five days per week with the conviction that his players would later display.

The weight training was a turning point in his life. He started to gain weight and feel more confident about himself at about the same time he noticed a pretty pom-pom girl with long brown hair and freckles in his biology class.

Beverly Lutgendorf would be his first and last serious girlfriend.

"There was a certain mystery to Bob," she said. "I knew that he was sensitive, too. He was different from the other guys. He didn't mess around with girls. He didn't drink. We just fell gaga. From the very start we knew we would get married someday."

Beverly's father was a captain in the Merchant Marines who was at sea for nine months at a time. Her mother suffered from periodic bouts of depression. The new couple took refuge in each other. Beverly spent more time at the Ladouceurs', where the liveliness of an extended family was a refreshing contrast to the tense silence of her home. Bob spent time with her to escape the quiet dysfunction on Broadmoor Drive.

"My mom pretty much raised us," Tom Jr. said. "My dad loved to have a great time. Everybody loved him, but he drank too much and had limited time with us."

Football remained in the back of Bob's mind. His body had changed dramatically since he began lifting weights. He was stronger, thicker, heavier. He started lifting in the backyard on crisp fall nights when many of his friends were playing for San Ramon. He kept telling himself he would join them on the playing field some day.

"He didn't feel adequate," Beverly said. "He didn't feel strong enough or big enough. Then he started weight-lifting at an age where you can really see results. He felt like he could do something. He wanted to do something."

He was working out in the San Ramon High weight room at the end of his sophomore year when coach Fred Houston noticed that Bob was stronger than most of his football players. He remembered Bob from youth football and encouraged him to come out for the team, which only made Bob more determined to make up for the years he missed.

"The weights put me in position," Bob said. "I was scared going in. I remember thinking, 'God, I hope this isn't like eighth grade.' But I got into it and I was so much faster and bigger and stronger. I thought, 'Wow, this is great.' The game was easier."

Houston was a blood-and-guts coach who would've looked as natural in starched fatigues as he did in khaki slacks and black coaching shoes on the sideline. His practices were so exhausting that many potential players were either scared away or quit. Those who remained were dedicated and believed in what they were doing, which would later become a trademark of Ladouceur's programs.

"He was tough to play for," Bob said. "Not everybody could go through his regime. We'd have two and a half weeks of two-a-days. God, it was just brutal. But he taught me a lot. He taught me it's a game of technique, repetition, and getting it right in practice before you run them in a game. Discipline. He taught me that the game is played aggressively; it's hard, tough. He taught me a lot of the fundamentals."

Houston would build a 91–50 record in sixteen years as San Ramon's head coach. He was considering leaving the profession when he became intrigued with the triple-option offense popularized by legendary University of Texas coach Darryl Royal.

Royal's triple-option spread through college football like a wildfire in the late 1960s, and by the early 1970s it was trickling down to the high-school level. The offense relied on quick, intelligent linemen capable of executing intricate schemes. It required a quick-thinking quarterback who could distribute the ball in the running game as well as the passing game, and two halfbacks with enough speed to get outside.

Houston decided to install the offense at San Ramon and immersed himself in training film, not yet realizing he would soon have a power runner with deceptive speed who would make an ideal halfback in his new triple-option scheme.

"Bob was one of the fastest guys out there," Blair Thomas recalls. "He had moves, ability, and certainly didn't mind hitting people. He immediately became the halfback in that option set-up. Even though he hadn't played in two years he was accepted as a natural and one of the starters. As time progressed it was obvious he would be a go-to guy."

The Wolves went three straight games without scoring during Ladouceur's junior season, and he and the other juniors felt that some of the seniors had quit on the team. Other seniors partied excessively, and the juniors wondered if that held the team back during a 5–2–1 season.

They resolved to solve these chemistry problems before fall practice began the following season. This was a tight group that cared about football a great deal. They wanted to succeed for themselves, but most of all they wanted to succeed for each other. They spent long hours working out over the summer to put themselves in position to have the type of season they were convinced they had been denied the year before.

"It was something we loved," Thomas said. "We loved the game. Internally, it was big for us. It was pretty much all we did. We played other sports, but what we really wanted to succeed at was football."

While Ed Hall was coaching his first team at De La Salle in 1971, San Ramon's triple-option offense led the Diablo Valley Athletic League. Ladouceur, a senior, gained 620 yards, averaging 10.2 yards per carry, and was named to the all-conference team. He was San Ramon's Most Valuable Player. He scored three touchdowns and had two more called back during a 61–14 thrashing of Piedmont. If it weren't for the penalties, he would've had 250 yards rushing in one game.

He also excelled on defense, earning second-team all-league honors as a junior. With so few available bodies, almost all Houston's players had to play both ways.

"He was dedicated but very quiet," Houston remembers about the young Ladouceur. "He thought about things. Bob was the captain, and he'd come up and tell me I should use a certain player in the game because he was better injured than the other guys were healthy. He was always right."

The two dominant conferences in Contra Costa County at the time were the Diablo Valley Athletic League and the Foothill Athletic League. On Thanksgiving Day, 1971, the DVAL champion Ygnacio Valley Warriors met the FAL champion San Ramon Wolves in what was billed as the Turkey Bowl. The man who would go on to dominate the playoffs like no other coach in history participated in the first official football playoff game held in Contra Costa County.

The game was staged at a local junior college before a sellout crowd. San Ramon led 7–6 at halftime but fell apart in the second half when Ygnacio Valley began stringing out the option. The Warriors connected on a couple of long passes and benefited from four San Ramon fumbles to win 32–19.

Bob finished his prep career with 85 yards on eleven carries and eight tackles. Nobody was more disappointed after the loss than Bob's dad.

Tom Sr. had spent three years in the Army Corps of Engineers in World War II, building pontoon bridges to allow Allied tanks to cross the Rhine River. Like many World War II-era veterans, he never discussed his war experiences, although he did say he had promised himself he would never spend another night outdoors if he made it home alive. He remained true to his word. The Ladouceurs never went camping.

"My dad must have held ten different jobs," Bob said. "If he didn't like a job he'd just quit. He never liked being told what to do, never liked any of his bosses, but he was a real talented salesman. If he had pushed it he could've sold a lot of stuff. He could've been a sales manager. He could've done a lot. He could've made a lot of money but he hardly made any money. He lived by his own leave."

Tom Sr. idolized his youngest son. He never missed a game and always was waiting at home to dissect Bob's performance, almost as if his own self-worth was directly linked to his son's performance.

"He could be very critical of other people in the family when he was drinking, but rarely Bob," Blair Thomas noted. "But if Bob made a mistake in a football game that's when it came out. If Bob fumbled or got tackled for a loss he could be ruthless."

Coaches from USC and Nebraska, among others, came to San Ramon to watch film of Ladouceur. He was only 6', 180 pounds, but he could bench-press 300 pounds and run a 4.6 40-yard dash. But recruiters weren't sure if Ladouceur's success was a product of his own ability or San Ramon's triple-option offense.

He took a recruiting visit to the University of Utah. When the school officially offered him a scholarship, Tom Sr. encouraged him to accept it. Bob did.

It was an era when young people were challenging traditional values. Sex and drugs became fashionable even in overlooked corners of the East Bay, but Ladouceur wasn't compelled to experiment in high school. In his family, you either drank or you didn't. There was no in-between. It didn't matter what friends were doing. Bob and Tom Jr. didn't want to be like their dad.

College was an eye-opening experience for someone who grew up sheltered in the San Ramon Valley. Bob was away from home for the first time. He missed Bev. He wanted to make friends and feel accepted. Everybody was drinking and smoking marijuana, and he wanted to fit in with his new teammates. He now discusses his brief flirtation with drugs and alcohol with students in his senior synthesis class. His students are then required to write a paper explaining in depth the emotional and psychological triggers that make them want to drink or not drink.

"It was an assumption that if you were from California, you were hip, you were a surfer and a smoker," he said. "I knew that wasn't me, that it wasn't my lifestyle. It wasn't what I wanted. I kind of got intimidated into experimenting with that stuff."

Ladouceur was relegated to the scout team during his freshman season at Utah, where he played against the varsity's first and second teams during two-a-day practices. Scout-team players are typically underclassmen not yet ready to contribute, or upperclassmen who never will get the chance, but they are required to practice against first-teamers every day.

It's punishing duty, especially for someone fresh out of high school playing against bigger, stronger, faster, and more mature athletes.

By the time the other freshmen arrived three weeks later, Ladouceur had taken a beating. He started at running back on the freshman team for the first two games and had a 100-yard rushing game. By Thanksgiving all he could think about was home.

Many other freshmen were permitted to go home for the holiday because the freshman season had ended. Bob's request was denied. He was told he might have a chance to play in the varsity games, which he knew was a lie. The truth was, they couldn't let all the freshmen leave because they still needed bodies for the scout team.

It wasn't fair. He had showed up three weeks before the other freshmen and done his duty. Now it was their turn. He and a dozen other players went home for Thanksgiving anyway.

For a week upon their return they were required to complete a grueling hour-long regime of sprints and stair climbing that began at 6 A.M. When Bob left campus for the summer after his freshman year, he knew he would never go back.

"The football program was run like a business," he said. "If this was college football, I didn't want any part of it. I was never playing again. I was done with it. I let my hair grow down to my shoulders."

Once again, it was Houston who spotted him in the weight room at San Ramon and revived his career. Bob spent the summer coaching youth baseball and umpiring men's softball for the local park and recreation department. He had enrolled in San Jose State as a student, but had no desire to play football.

Houston and first-year San Jose State coach Darryl Rogers had been teammates at Fresno State and remained friends. Houston called Rogers and informed him that Bob was enrolled for the fall semester. Tom Sr. also had secretly hand-delivered to Rogers newspaper articles detailing Bob's performances on the freshman team at Utah.

Rogers called Bob and encouraged him to play.

"We knew exactly who he was and we were excited he was interested in coming," said Rogers, now the athletic director at Southern Connecticut State.

Because of NCAA rules, Ladouceur would have to sit out for one year before he was eligible to play in games. He wasn't crazy about the idea of spending another year getting beat up on the practice team. He already paid his dues at Utah. He told Houston as much, and his old coach struck a deal with his former college teammate.

Bob would serve as an assistant coach under Houston at San Ramon that fall. He would join the San Jose State football team in time for the offseason conditioning program and would begin competing for a starting position during spring ball.

"I thought that was a good deal," Ladouceur said. "Fred said, 'OK, but you've got to cut your hair.'"

Ladouceur came off the bench to rush for 92 yards in the San Jose State alumni game and was offered a scholarship by the end of spring practice. When two-a-days started in the fall, he was a third-string running back and was expected to see playing time because of his pass-catching abilities.

That plan changed as Rogers prepared his team for the 1974 season opener against Santa Clara. Injuries to his teammates forced Ladouceur into the starting lineup as a redshirt sophomore. It was an exciting time. San Jose State was coming off its first winning season since 1961. Bev, Tom Sr., and all Bob's friends and family members watched from the stands as he scored a touchdown to give San Jose State an early lead.

Friend Blair Thomas, who had transferred to San Jose State after one year at Houston, was a backup quarterback who was charting plays on the sideline when Bob collected a pitch on a sweep late in the second quarter. Bob was trying to turn upfield when an opposing linebacker hit him square in the left shoulder with the crown of his helmet.

"He landed less than five feet from me," Thomas said. "He kind of popped up on one knee. I was looking at him and you could see that he was hurting. I could tell he wasn't right. He was holding his shoulder. We were real concerned for him."

A photographer captured the image moments after impact, and the photograph later appeared in the "Opponents" section of the 1975 San Jose State program. Ladouceur is recoiling from the hit, biting down hard on his mouthpiece, his shoulder already separated, his face twisted in pain. He underwent season-ending surgery the following day.

"I'll never forget when he got hit," Bev said. "Everyone in the stands inhaled. When I opened the program and saw the picture the next year, I couldn't believe it."

It was a long time before Ladouceur could raise his arm above his shoulder. Two stainless steel pins held the joint together. Thomas noticed a blood stain on Bob's T-shirt when they were home for the weekend during the offseason.

"We get his shirt off and one of the pins is sticking through the skin," Thomas recalls. "We went back to San Jose and damned if the trainer doesn't grab a pair of pliers and yank it out. I saw it. The pin was three inches long. You could see Bob's eyes watering up. You knew it hurt. I'll never forget that. I thought, 'Man, that's one tough hombre.' I was gritting my teeth and it wasn't even me."

Ladouceur was climbing back up the depth chart during spring football the following year when he shredded his left knee in the spring scrimmage. "I was in over my head," Ladouceur says. "I probably would've been better as a role player coming in for a couple downs now and then. In hindsight, I probably would've been better off as a Division II-type player."

Ladouceur underwent his second major surgery in a one-year span and missed the first four games of the 1975 season. He was riding on the team bus after a tough 27–24 loss to California when he mentioned to Rogers that he wanted to help out in some way even though he hadn't fully recovered.

"Bobby was going to be a real good player," Rogers says. "He didn't start by default. He earned it. An injury took him out and it came at the most inopportune time. He was going to play. He wasn't a Division II player. He could've been a very good Division I player. Injuries were the only thing that held him back."

The 1975 San Jose State team was one of the most star-studded rosters in school history. Future NFL standouts Steve DeBerg, Wilson Faumuina, Rick Kane, Kim Bokamper, Carl Ekern, and Louis Wright all played on a team that was 8–1 heading into the regular-season finale against a mediocre Hawaii team at Aloha Stadium.

San Jose State players enjoyed the sun and the sand all week, then got ambushed 30–20, robbing them of a chance to play in the Tangerine Bowl. Ladouceur would relate the memory to his De La Salle players before they took the same field 27 years later.

Rogers left for Michigan State after the 1975 season and would later coach the Detroit Lions. Lynn Stiles, a former assistant to UCLA head coach Dick Vermeil, was hired to replace Rogers at San Jose State.

Ladouceur had been switched to defensive back but was playing mostly on special teams during the 1976 season. A blurb under his picture in the program that year summed up his career: "A quick player who needs only to avoid injury to realize potential."

By the time San Jose State wrapped up a 7–4 season in 1976, Bob was looking forward to life after football. He felt as if the business of big-time college football had chewed him up and spit him out. He would carry the scars from shoulder and knee injuries for the rest of his life. It was time to move on.

"I got soured on football again," he remembers. "I didn't want to do it anymore."

06 ►

A FRIDAY NIGHT IN PARADISE

t he streets outside the hotel offer every imaginable temptation to a seventeen-year-old boy. It's a Friday night in paradise, a street festival in full party mode. Music from three different bands— one pulsating siren song—wafts up to the eleventh-floor keep of the De La Salle football team.

The young men watch from a balcony as the stages are erected, the tents raised, and the beer trucks unloaded. The aqua waves and white sand of nearby Waikiki Beach might as well be a hundred miles away; the players have been forbidden to swim there.

There is no sheltering them from all of Hawaii's temptations, how-ever. They have elbowed each other and snickered as they passed pros-titutes in strapless tops and short skirts, many of them not much older than the players themselves. They have even been propositioned by whispering drug dealers near the International Market.

These young men are caretakers of the nation's longest winning streak, 126 games, and they feel the enormous weight of that responsibility. Their season-opening win over Archbishop Mitty was one of the worst performances by a De La Salle team in more than a decade. Now they are twenty-four hours away from putting The Streak on the line against the 17th-ranked team in the country, on a field 2,500 miles and three time zones from home.

Organizers of the First Hawaiian Bank Football Classic are hopeful that as many as 50,000 fans to fill Aloha Stadium for a much-anticipated doubleheader—public high schools Kahuku vs. Long Beach Poly in the first game, private school powers St. Louis vs. De La Salle in the second. The De La Salle game will be televised live in Hawaii and California. De La Salle's most vulnerable team in a decade will be lining up against a St. Louis team that has been waiting years for this opportunity.

St. Louis High School began dominating under legendary coach Cal Lee in 1983. It won 17 league titles in 19 years, and 14 Hawaii state championships before being upset by Kahuku in the state championship game in 1999 and 2000. The St. Louis Crusaders had a 55-game winning streak of their own in the late 1980s and own a 17–1–1 record against out-of-state opponents as they prepare for De La Salle. They have already defeated one California team with an impressive winning streak. In 1991, the Crusaders ended Bakersfield's 39-game streak with a resounding 36–14 victory.

Lee retired with a 241–32–5 record following the 2001 season, turning the program over to longtime defensive coordinator Delbert Tengan. Heading into the 2002 season, the Crusaders were expected to dominate Hawaii football once again.

They had seven players on the preseason All-State team, including quarterback Bobby George, receiver Jason Rivers, and 6'3", 310-pound preseason all-American defensive end Tolifili Liufau. They are huge along the offensive and defensive lines, outweighing De La Salle by an average of 48 pounds per man. St. Louis has 83 players on its roster. No one plays both ways. De La Salle has 48 players; 10 will see action on offense and defense. The Crusaders hope to use their size and numbers advantage to wear the Spartans down.

High school football games drew as many as 25,000 fans to the stadium in downtown Honolulu before the University of Hawaii rose to prominence in the mid-1970s. But the emergence of Kahuku after years of St. Louis domination has sparked a revival that promoters of the doubleheader hope to exploit.

The caliber of play in Hawaii is a perennial source of island pride. St. Louis gave Hawaiian high school football credibility by being included in the *USA Today* Super 25 rankings at various times throughout the years, but there was always an underlying feeling that the program was overlooked nationally. This is a chance to prove that the best Hawaiian teams can compete with the best programs from the mainland.

"What I see in this game is a St. Louis team in the same position we were in before our first game against Mater Dei," De La Salle coach Bob Ladouceur said. "They're looking for validation and respect, and that makes them real dangerous. They're not just playing for themselves; they're playing for all the St. Louis players who always wanted to play in a game like this. That's a powerful thing."

The hype began building the minute the game was announced in February. Corporations lined up to sponsor the event. Radio, television, and newspaper ads promoted ticket sales. Schedules were adjusted so none of the other 46 high school football teams on Oahu would play games that night, ensuring that coaches and players can attend the doubleheader. Teams on the neighboring island of Maui cleared their schedules as well.

The Hawaiian High School Athletic Association website was bombarded by hits from as far away as Virginia and Indiana. Some 250 fans from American Samoa made the five-hour-plus flight to Honolulu for the games. The doubleheader is front-page news in USA Today's sports section. Local politicians fear the event will keep voters away from the Democratic primary.

The week leading up to the event seems like the run-up to a college bowl game. Cheerleaders meet the De La Salle and Long Beach Poly team planes at the airport and present players and coaches with leis. Luxury motor coaches shuttle teams to and from practices in air-conditioned comfort.

In the final twenty-four hours before kickoff, emotions reach a crescendo. De La Salle players watched their predecessors play games of national significance in recent years. Ready or not, it is now their turn. They wouldn't trade what they are about to share for all the temptations that await them on the street below.

As they gather in the eleventh-floor meeting room, the primary focus isn't on defending The Streak or even prolonging it, though such sentiment always lurks near the surface. The football family crams into a corner of the room as strength and conditioning coach Mike Blasquez starts to speak over the party raging below. They need to hear what he has to say. They know they have to come together to get through this.

"You're going into the most physically demanding moment of your life. It's going to be harder than any summer workout or any training you've done to date. Tomorrow is going to be double or triple that. You've trained for it. Physically, you're ready for that. You're trained to recover. You'll rest for twenty seconds and you'll be able to do it again. . . . You offensive linemen are going against guys fifty, sixty, seventy pounds heavier than you. I'm telling you right now, if you go out and try to wrestle those guys you will get tired and you will get beat. I've seen it every year I've been part of this program. Smaller guys have been able to battle bigger guys because of their speed and willingness to hit. That's how you overcome guys who are bigger and stronger than you. You pound them, smack them. You use your explosiveness and you blow those guys up. That's how you're going to do it. . . ."

~

It was Keith Amemiya's idea to bring De La Salle to Hawaii. The executive director of the HHSAA worked for two years to make this game a reality.

There were skeptics who scoffed at the idea. It would cost $150,000 to fly De La Salle and Long Beach Poly to Honolulu and feed, house, and shuttle the two teams to and from practice, but Amemiya knew he had the one commodity that guaranteed success.

He had De La Salle and its record winning streak.

"De La Salle is far and away the most desirable team for a Hawaiian team to play," Amemiya said while watching De La Salle practice at Aloha Stadium on Wednesday before the game.

A radio station called De La Salle athletic director (and assistant coach) Terry Eidson in the fall of 2000 to propose a season-ending game between St. Louis and De La Salle. The idea seemed preposterous to Eidson. The proposed date was just six weeks away. Both teams would require special permission from their respective state and local athletic associations, a process that might require both teams to forfeit any post-season participation. In De La Salle's case, it might even require the school to compensate the North Coast Section for lost revenue. Besides, who would pay for the airfare and accommodations?

Former coach Cal Lee, with the help of various Honolulu media organizations, kept the pressure on. It was reported that the HHSAA had agreed to allow St. Louis to bow out of the state championship game in order to play De La Salle. Lee even offered to travel to California to play De La Salle on its home field to make the game a reality.

At least one of the reports was wishful thinking. St. Louis had not received permission to play an unscheduled season-ending game, and Amemiya faxed a letter to Eidson to that effect. But the dream was out of the bottle. News of the potential matchup spread throughout the islands. The perception was that De La Salle was ducking mighty St. Louis.

"It seems like all they want to do is add to their winning streak," one of the radio station's hosts told the *Honolulu Star Bulletin.* Eidson was furious.

Amemiya called a few months later to reiterate the HHSAA's position and to inquire about the possibility of De La Salle playing St. Louis sometime in the future. Eidson said he would seriously consider playing the Hawaiian state champion—whether it be St. Louis or Kahuku—if certain conditions were met.

He wanted his team's expenses paid, for one. His second concern was scheduling. The football season typically begins earlier in Hawaii, and Eidson didn't want to be playing his season opener against a team that already had played three or four games. As the second condition, the Hawaiian opponent could play no more than two games before the proposed date, which would still give it a one-game advantage. Third and finally, the Hawaiian team could not use fifth-year seniors.

The Interscholastic League of Honolulu, which included St. Louis, allowed student-athletes who needed five years to complete a four-year education to be eligible for athletics in their fifth and final year. The practice had been outlawed in the Honolulu public school league and also in HHSAA bylaws. The private school league eventually changed the rule, but players who were already enrolled were protected under a grandfather clause.

Amemiya didn't think the fifth-year senior rule was an issue. He began the process of making the game a reality. But as the game approached, he discovered that preseason all-American defensive lineman Tolifili Liufau had completed ninth grade at a public school before transferring to St. Louis and repeating his freshman year.

He had not played or even practiced with the football team during the repeated year, and had only recently turned eighteen. Still, Liufau was the best player in the state. He could bench-press 225 pounds 38 times and had standing scholarship offers from USC, Oregon, Washington, Wisconsin, Tennessee, and Brigham Young.

Eidson and Amemiya had spoken countless times on the phone, and a mutual respect had developed. Eidson knew the St. Louis community would ridicule Amemiya if Liufau were ruled ineligible. Amemiya felt a responsibility to live up to Eidson's conditions, which he considered more than fair.

"I brought it to Terry's attention and we talked about it," Amemiya said. "We agreed we were both in a no-win situation. If [Liufau] doesn't play, St. Louis will complain, and if he does play, De La Salle will complain. In the end, we felt that him playing would be less of a distraction than if he didn't. One player wouldn't make the difference, and we didn't want anything to take away from the doubleheader."

Eidson wanted to allow Liufau to play so St. Louis would have no excuses if it lost. First he had to convince Ladouceur. Fortunately, he had experience in this area.

Eidson loves challenges. He thrives on competition. He wanted to play national powerhouses far from home. Ladouceur, meanwhile, focused on individual challenges more than the final score and was content dominating teams from Northern California. When Eidson pushed to upgrade the schedule, Ladouceur relented and was later thankful for the upgrade.

"Bob can be very little-old-ladyish," said longtime friend Blair Thomas, who filled Eidson's role as Ladouceur's chief assistant for eleven years. "Sometimes you have to convince him the other road must be taken. Sometimes you have to talk Bob into doing what's best for Bob. Terry is that guy."

It was always that way. When Eidson first proposed scheduling Southern California powerhouse Mater Dei of Santa Ana, Ladouceur resisted. It had been even more difficult for Eidson to convince him to play powerful Long Beach Poly.

Even the Hawaii trip took some finesse, although the enthusiasm of the assistant coaches made it easier for Eidson to convince Ladouceur.

"I didn't think it would be a tough sell, but it started out that way," Eidson said. "All these games are a tough sell with him. It's like dealing with your parents. The first answer is always no, and then you start working on them."

Eidson called a staff meeting—a rarity at De La Salle—to discuss the fifth-year senior issue after a preseason practice. He hadn't told anybody of his desire to let Liufau play. He told them Amemiya had inquired about the possibility of Liufau participating in the game, and as the athletic director it was his responsibility to pass the inquiry on to the staff.

"They can't start changing the rules now," Ladouceur said. "That's like us saying at the last minute that we want to play the game in California instead."

Everyone in the cramped, cluttered upstairs office nodded in agreement—everybody except Eidson, playing the role of moderator.

"But we don't want them to have any excuses if they lose," Eidson said.

"What excuse?" assistant coach Justin Alumbaugh said, throwing his hands in the air. "We've got a contract that says no fifth-year seniors. How is that an excuse?"

There were more nodding heads. Soon, everybody was talking at once and expressing the same sentiment. A deal is a deal. You can't change the rules now.

"Just so you know, I did a little research," Eidson said. "Liufau repeated the ninth grade but he didn't play football. He just turned eighteen so it's not like he's twenty-two years old. What's the difference between him and one of our defensive linemen?"

"About eighty pounds," Ladouceur shot back, prompting smiles all around.

Ever the administrator, assistant coach Joe Aliotti sympathized with Eidson, who would be cast as a villain if Liufau did not play. He suggested they throw the decision back at Amemiya. Why should it come from them? They had wanted a third party involved for this precise reason. The HHSAA negotiated a contract that said no fifth-year seniors. Why was it now De La Salle's responsibility to change the conditions a month before the game?

That's how they left it. Eidson would tell Amemiya it was the HHSAA's call. He would say they were disappointed the issue had come up at such a late date, but if the agreement were to be changed it should be by a neutral third party.

Ladouceur was in the locker room undressing for a workout when Eidson barged into the room.

"I JUST WANT YOU TO KNOW SOMETHING," he yelled at Ladouceur, who just stood there, frozen, with one leg in the air as he changed out of his shorts. "IF WE TELL THEM HE CAN'T PLAY, IT WILL DETRACT FROM THE GAME. THE HEADLINE WILL BE, 'WE DIDN'T WANT THEIR BEST KID TO PLAY.' IF YOU WANT TO LESSEN THE IMPACT OF THE GAME, THEN TELL HIM HE CAN'T PLAY AND THAT'S EXACTLY WHAT WILL HAPPEN. I DON'T WANT ANY EXCUSES."

"Then let him play," Ladouceur said, suddenly indifferent.

Eidson marched out of the room, barely able to conceal a smile, before Ladouceur could change his mind, much less his pants.

Now that Liufau will play, who will block him?

The party down on the street has grown even louder. A crowd of shrieking girls clusters around one of the three stages and screams in the fleeting silence between songs. Lights from boats twinkle on the water in the distance as Ladouceur addresses the team.

"My job as your coach is to find out what your ceiling is. I have a good idea, but exactly where it is, I don't know that right now. Neither do you ... I'm not saying you guys have to hit your ceiling tomorrow. It's the second week of the season. You're not going to reach it, but you have to make a significant gain tomorrow night ... You have to take ownership of this game. Taking ownership means getting together as a group and saying, 'Look, on this play, we're going to do this.' You can't come to us all the time because YOU'RE playing the game. Right next to each other. It doesn't matter what I know. It matters what the kid playing next to you knows. That's taking ownership. That's taking responsibility. That's what we need from YOU. That's what it's got to be or nothing good will happen tomorrow. If it comes from you everything good will happen. It's not talk. It's do."

~

There was no one in the emergency room when Maurice Drew arrived after the Mitty game. The X-rays were negative. At worst his injury was a damaged ligament; at best a mild sprain.

A high-tech machine that combines cold and compression (Blasquez always finds a way to get the latest state-of-the-art equipment for free) coupled with powerful anti-inflammatory drugs helped keep the swelling down overnight. But Drew still couldn't put any weight on his ankle when he arrived at school the following morning.

The question of Drew's availability resulted in a week of speculation. It has been a long time since De La Salle has been so dependent on one player. Now he might not be able to play one of the biggest games in school history.

Blasquez put Drew on a regimen of motion and strengthening exercises combined with soft-tissue massage. Drew didn't practice Monday. He jogged Tuesday. The team flew to Honolulu on Wednesday and had a practice scheduled for that afternoon. Curious onlookers watched as Blasquez put Drew through his paces on the sideline.

Drew could run straight ahead at about 75 percent of his usual speed, but cutting and planting on the ankle was still painful. He felt better by Thursday but was still tentative, forcing the coaching staff to make a difficult decision.

Blasquez and team physician Dr. John Wilhelmy know there is little chance of Drew's ankle suffering further damage by playing. It is a matter of pain management. The possibility of a pain-killing injection isn't considered.

"He feels a weakness in there, and an injection is not going to help that," Blasquez says. "When you use those methods to get kids ready to play it's a question of ethics. There are only a few injuries where you can mask the pain and not cause additional damage, but I won't do that and neither will the team doctor."

Blasquez wants Drew to test the ankle to see whether or not he thinks he can play. He wants Drew to run ten plays in full pads with the first-team offense during Thursday's practice. Drew needs to know what he can do and what he can expect.

"I know high school athletes," Blasquez said. "They're tentative. They're scared of the pain and they make mistakes. Maurice needs to go out there and mix it up and realize that there might be pain but he's not going to hurt himself."

The assistant coaches disagree. Why not give Drew's ankle two extra days to heal and see how it feels during pregame warmups? Why take a chance of re-injuring the ankle in practice two days before the game when it might improve significantly by kickoff?

Ladouceur defers to Blasquez, and Drew takes the practice field for a series that will determine whether the player who bailed his teammates out again and again against Mitty will be available for the first big game of the season.

The first three plays go off without incident. Drew isn't as explosive as before the injury, but he still has a burst. He takes a handoff on the fourth play and makes a spin move before being tackled. He screams in agony as he hits the ground, the sickening cry echoing across the silent practice field. Everybody freezes except for Blasquez, who rushes to Drew's side. His teammates' faces drain of color and their eyes grow wide as Blasquez kneels over Drew and eventually helps him to his feet.

"He's out of the game," Ladouceur thinks to himself.

Drew felt the same pain he experienced against Mitty. He panicked. He's walking without a limp a few minutes later. He's more scared than hurt. He has experienced the pain and now he knows what to expect.

"Look, I'm not going to clear you for this game," Blasquez told him. "I've done everything I can to help you. There's no magic potion. You will feel pretty much the way you feel today on Saturday. What I need to know is, do you feel confident enough to play full speed and without hesitation? If you do, I'll clear you. But if you look me in the eye and are unsure, I won't. I don't want an answer until Friday."

Drew ultimately convinces Blasquez to clear him. But no one knows how much he will be able to contribute as Ladouceur continues his pregame talk.

"You've got to come into games like tomorrow night's like a razor. I saw many too many guys who thought something bad was going to happen when they took [Drew] off the field. I saw it in your faces when he was on the grass screaming yesterday. I've approached this whole week thinking if he plays, great, if he doesn't, good for you [pointing to the team]. Now it's YOUR chance. Even if he does play it's still your chance. You know what happened last week. We're not going to win with last week's effort; I don't give a shit how good he is. That's what makes this game so great. It's getting all the guys doing their jobs at one time. That's hard to do. Not just doing it but doing it with passion and aggression. I can tell every time a De La Salle team takes ownership of a game. You see it on the field and you say, 'Wow. We're blowing these guys out,' or, "We're fighting like banshees out there.' It's obvious. You didn't take ownership last week....

"Offensively, we're starting to understand some things. You need to play offense with aggression and passion. Defensively, [Eidson] has prepped you for this game for a year. Ever since we've been allowed to have a football out there he's prepped you for this game. THIS GAME. I'm looking forward to this game tomorrow, I really am. Isn't this what you wanted? If this is what you wanted, this is what it takes. If it's not what you wanted you can go down to the street right now and have fun. But from what I heard from everyone in the off-season—'Yeah, let's play that team. Get Poly on the schedule. Let's play these guys.' All right. If that's what you want. If you want Long Beach, St. Louis, OK, this is what it takes. My opinion is you can do it. You can beat these guys solidly. That's my opinion. But you've got to take responsibility."

They take their football seriously in Hawaii, and nowhere is it taken more seriously than on the hilltop campus of St. Louis High School.

It has become increasingly obvious that school officials will spare no expense to gain an advantage against an opponent they've been itching to play. They've ordered new uniforms for the De La Salle game. An assistant athletic director traveled to the Bay Area to film De La Salle's preseason scrimmage against James Logan. Former Crusaders coach Cal Lee came to Concord personally to scout De La Salle's season opener against Archbishop Mitty.

A quiet confidence has spread throughout the St. Louis community. The Spartans don't look unbeatable at all. Instead, they appear ripe for an upset.

First-year coach Delbert Tengan relied on vanilla game plans and played his best players sparingly in the first two games—both blowout victories. After the second game he found an envelope in his mailbox containing a videotape of the De La Salle-Mitty game. There was no note or return address, but it bore a San Jose postmark.

Adding to the intrigue is the cameraman spotted filming De La Salle's practice at the University of Hawaii from atop a circular dormitory overlooking the field. Security guards shoo the intruder away, and HHSAA officials promise to investigate.

"Delbert claims [the cameraman] had no affiliation with the school," said Blane Gaison, a former NFL player who is serving as De La Salle's liaison during the trip. "We've heard that before. It has happened, especially before crucial games, in the past. They won't do it all the time, but if a big game is coming up they'll send someone around."

Tengan denies any wrongdoing: "We don't do that over here. There are certain ethics in football. We'll film scrimmages and preseason games but not practices. I don't know who that was up there. It could've been a Long Beach Poly alumnus."

Ladouceur has been on edge all week, as he is during most big-game weeks. The Spartans are representing Northern California football, and Ladouceur takes that responsibility seriously. He doesn't worry about losing but he doesn't want to lose to an out-of-state team.

"Word trickled in from Hawaii about how they could beat us and how we've ducked them and they've done well against California teams," Ladouceur later said of the tenor going into the trip. "I'm thinking, 'Man, I'd hate to go over there and not win that game.' The Hawaiian people were wonderful, and all the peripheral people were wonderful and supportive, but I never felt that from their [former] coach, Cal Lee, or their players. It was more like, 'You guys are afraid of us. You guys won't play us.' I don't like that."

He remembers coming to Honolulu as a college player with a San Jose State team that needed a win to secure a bowl bid and perhaps even a national ranking. That team treated the trip as a vacation and was upset by an inferior University of Hawaii team. The memory of that painful defeat has made Ladouceur uneasy since the moment the St. Louis game was first announced.

Leisure activities have been scheduled. The highlight of the trip comes when Eidson is summoned to the stage to dance with smiling Polynesians during a beachfront luau. The players laugh and point and chant "Cobra! Cobra! Cobra!" as Eidson wiggles his hips and waves his hands. Much to his embarrassment, footage shot by a local television crew is later broadcast on the local news in the Bay Area.

They are taken on a tour of the USS *Missouri* with Long Beach Poly players, and you can sense the testosterone in the air. Poly players look at the much smaller Spartan players with expressions that say: We got beat by these guys?

Several coaches and players talk with an elderly woman visiting Pearl Harbor for the first time. She tells them she had been engaged to a sailor on the doomed USS *Arizona* when the Japanese attacked in 1941. She received a letter from her fiancé on December 9. He expressed his love for her and promised to send a grass skirt as a souvenir. By the time she read the letter he had been dead for two days.

Eidson asks if any of the players are interested in visiting a Shriners hospital he saw on the way from the hotel to the practice field. Every player raises his hand to volunteer. Eidson arranges the visit.

For the most part, however, this is a business trip. There is much to accomplish in a short time. Another week of uninspired practice will result in certain defeat. The players need to focus despite the distractions. They respond with what Ladouceur would later call one of the most intense weeks of practice in De La Salle history.

Wherever De La Salle players go that week, they are met with puzzled expressions and double-takes, which only adds to their anxiety. Locals have heard so much about high school football's most dominant team, but the players they see in the hotel lobby don't look the part. This is mighty De La Salle? They are by far the smallest of the four teams participating in the doubleheader. One man who sees players pass through the lobby of the team hotel, carrying shoulder pads and helmets to the bus before practice, wonders if they are members of the junior varsity.

"They look more like a cross-country team," notes Gaison, the Spartans' liaison. "They don't have the athletes that Long Beach Poly has, but they have a little magic from somewhere."

The St. Louis Crusaders' size advantage is weighing heavily on the minds of De La Salle players as they address their teammates the night before the game. The St. Louis offensive line averages 280 pounds compared to 231 for De La Salle. The Crusaders' defensive line averages 264 pounds compared to 218 for the Spartans.

"I know I'll be going up against guys who are bigger and stronger than me," one offensive lineman begins.

"Whoa," Ladouceur interrupts. "Do you really think they're stronger?"

Senior lineman John Chan admits that he didn't play like a captain against Mitty but promises to change that against St. Louis.

There is no one on the team more respected than junior Cameron Colvin. He has been through an excruciatingly difficult family life and lost so much, but he remains appreciative of what he has. All eyes are upon him when he stands up and promises to make a name for himself the following night. "It's my coming-out party," he says.

"I'll go until I'm dead on the field and they have to carry me off on a stretcher," senior lineman Erik Sandie declares. "I will not give up. I will not let you down."

"Spent," Ladouceur says, temporarily breaking the tension. "The word is 'spent.' It's still just a game."

"There was no reason for me to scream like that on Thursday," Drew says, embarrassed. "Don't worry about my ankle. I'm going to come back and play like I did last Friday. I'm going to play better. I'm going to give it everything I've got."

"When I got here I had a message from my dad, who said this is a once-in-a-lifetime opportunity to play in a game like this," says soft-spoken linebacker Parker Hanks, choking back emotion. "Here we are in paradise playing football and we're all together. In twenty years we're going to have vivid memories of this game. We're going to remember the roar of the crowd and the expressions on our faces. I've gotten to know you guys even better this week, and it makes me want to play even harder. I'm going to make mistakes but I promise you I won't come off that field and I will not quit."

"Parker brings up a good point," Ladouceur interjects. "You're going to make mistakes, but that just means you have to put together more good plays. That's why this is such a great team sport. I'm going to do my best to call the best game for you. But I'm going to call some plays that won't be good plays. We make mistakes too, but we count on you guys to pick us up. But I guarantee you one thing: You'll do more right than wrong, and we as coaches will put you in situations to be successful."

Several other players speak about St. Louis' size advantage, and finally Eidson can't contain himself any longer. There is trepidation, even doubt, in their voices. This is a fragile team, and the players are psyching themselves out.

"We're not playing the Miami Hurricanes tomorrow. They're big. They're strong. SHIT! HAVE YOU WATCHED FILM? I'VE SEEN MIDGETS BLOCK THOSE GUYS. I'VE SEEN LITTLE GUYS RUN IN AND SACK THE QUARTERBACK ... YOU'RE ACTING LIKE YOU'RE THE LITTLE SISTERS OF THE POOR. GET YOUR KEYS, UNLOCK YOUR BRAIN, CRAWL OUT OF YOUR HEAD, PUT YOUR PADS ON AND GO HIT SOMEONE. QUIT THINKING SO MUCH. . . . GET OUT OF YOUR HEADS AND PLAY. . . !'"

Eidson is getting more excited by the moment. The raspy voice is so strained, the gesticulations so wild that at times he almost appears to levitate.

"These guys are good, but YOU ARE TOO. You will make mistakes. It's what you do after you make a mistake that's important. If you make a mistake you have to make someone pay. That's football. That's the best part of this game. If you make a mistake you've got a thousand chances to make it up, to hit, to strike. It's a simple game. It really is. These guys have some weight on them but give me a break. . . .

"I can't stand these guys. I couldn't stand them for the past eight years when I heard them say [in a mocking voice], 'We keep trying to get a game with De La Salle but they keep avoiding us.' That's a bunch of HORSESHIT. . . . I get one call from St. Louis, they never call me back, and they tell everybody we don't want to play them.

"Well, we're here to play them now, and I'll tell you what: IF YOU THINK YOU'RE PSYCHED UP YOU'RE NOT AS PSYCHED UP AS ME. I'LL TELL YOU THAT RIGHT NOW. I'VE BEEN WAITING EIGHT YEARS TO DRILL THESE GUYS. AND NOW YOU'VE GOT THE CHANCE. The chance everybody else wanted for you. It's like Coach said, 'What an opportunity.' . . . This is a game of a lifetime for you guys. All the grads say, 'Why couldn't you get this for us?' I say, 'You got Mater Dei, you got Poly. THEY get St. Louis.' It's your turn. Make something of it, for God's sake."

Blasquez passes out cups of water to emphasize the need for players to drink as much as possible to avoid cramps in the tropical climate. Hotel employees finish cleaning up the conference room, which doubles as the dining hall. The meeting is about to break up when Ladouceur stands up for the last time.

"It's like I said earlier. You wanted to play St. Louis, you've got St. Louis and all the responsibility that goes with playing a team like that, and that means you're not on the street. Get off your feet. From now until game time you're at complete rest. I don't want to see anyone on the streets tonight. Go to the room. There's no bed check. You're on your own. There's nothing to see out there anyway. We've all seen the streetwalkers out there and I see you looking at them. That's not a nice way of life. Being men, we like to look at them and check out their costumes and stuff, and when it's all said and done, we like to think those women like that stuff. They don't. They have a miserable life and you know it. They're not out there banging guys because they like it. They come from miserable backgrounds—every single one of them. They're either hooked on drugs, been molested as kids, been raped by a stepfather; whatever it is, their backgrounds are misery, and every man who pays for them contributes to it. So, it's really sad, a sad scene. You're not missing anything."

~

Bob Ladouceur and Frank Allocco run alongside Waikiki Beach, the ground flying beneath their feet, the wind rushing past, reveling in the unspoken bond shared by kindred spirits.

They have a bond that in some ways runs deeper than those between Ladouceur and any of his other assistants, and they have had it since before the first game against Mater Dei in 1998. Allocco, then in his second year as the school's basketball coach, accompanied the football team to Anaheim and worked out with Ladouceur several hours before that game, just as he is doing now.

They talked afterward, and the long, serious conversation took many unpredictable turns. They realized they had much more in common than age. They shared Catholic backgrounds, the same core values, and similar coaching philosophies. They would even recite the same favorite lines to their same favorite movies.

They continue this pregame routine in the hours leading up to the First Hawaiian Bank Football Classic. They are both in good shape. Ladouceur fiercely protects the time he spends on the stationary bike every day. Allocco is a former Notre Dame quarterback who can still beat most of his players in a game of one-on-one.

Now they run hard along the beach, leaving the other assistants behind. They stride through the park and push themselves before stopping and sucking the tropical air into their thirsty lungs. Drops of sweat fall onto the sidewalk.

"Do you ever get tired of it?" Ladouceur asks when he has regained his breath.

"Yes, sometimes I do," Allocco says.

Kickoff is only a few hours away, but Ladouceur isn't thinking about what he might call on third-and-7 or how Maurice Drew's ankle will hold up on the artificial surface. He has been thinking about this all week, ever since several assistants cornered him in the upstairs office a few days after the Mitty game.

They told him he needed to be tougher with this team. He had remained patient, but this group wasn't responding. They needed what former players referred to as the Old Lad. The problem is, the New Lad doesn't like the Old Lad. He doesn't like to yell at kids or shame them into performing. He hasn't had to do that in recent years because his teams have had such strong senior leaders. But this team doesn't just need to be coached—it needs to be led, and he is the only one who can do it.

"Do you ever feel conflicted?"

"What do you mean?" Allocco answers, trying to draw him out.

"I'm very conflicted," Ladouceur confides. "People don't understand how conflicted I feel when I'm trying to get kids to be aggressive that maybe aren't aggressive by nature. It's hard for me because I know I'm pushing them to do something that in their hearts they really don't want to do, and I wonder sometimes if by pushing them like that we're damaging them. If they're passive boys, why not let them be passive boys? I know what we have to do to win games against nationally ranked teams, but should we be trying to change their personalities? In some ways it's positive and in some ways negative. That's what I deal with every day. I haven't made peace with how far to push them and when it becomes a negative."

Allocco's teams have been nearly as successful as Ladouceur's since he arrived at the school in 1997. He coached Northgate High in neighboring Walnut Creek to a state championship before coming to De La Salle and becoming the only coach in California history to win state titles at two different schools. He shares a conversation he had with a player during a summer league game.

"I called him over and said, 'I'm worried about your future,'" Allocco tells Ladouceur. "'I see a boy who is a great student who could be valedictorian of his class. I see a boy who could be a successful musician.' I mentioned all the things he was good at but told him he wasn't great at anything because he wasn't passionate about anything. I told him, 'I'm concerned that you won't tap your potential as a man because you're so good at everything that you cruise. You coast. Until I see you create a passion in your life, I don't see you making it.'

"The kid got real upset and teared up. I really felt bad about it. But on the other hand, I think it needed to be said. It was what the kid needed to hear, but I still felt bad saying it and wondered if I should've said it afterward. Coaching is like that. It's like being a parent. You don't always know if you're doing the right thing. Only time will tell. But in your heart you do what you think is right and you move forward and hopefully the best occurs. In most cases, it does."

It's a dilemma Ladouceur will wrestle with throughout the year.

07

1978

DE LA SALLE HIRES A RELIGION TEACHER

b ob Ladouceur graduated from San Jose State University in 1976 with a degree in criminal justice. He wanted to help troubled kids, maybe become a probation officer. He spent eighteen months counseling troubled, mostly delinquent kids at juvenile hall, but he spent more time managing files than teens. He kept seeing the same faces being recycled through the system.

He watched them make glitter posters when he knew they needed to be force-fed reading, writing, and arithmetic. This was more of a detention center than a rehabilitation facility. There wasn't enough time to give these kids the kind of help they needed. When the courts decided what to do with them, they were shuffled through the system, bound to return. He became increasingly disillusioned.

"It was like putting band-aids on amputations," he recalls.

He had recently married his high school sweetheart and considered a career in law enforcement. He thought about taking the test to become a fire fighter. He didn't know what he wanted to do with his life, but he knew it wasn't this.

"He came home and his attitude became more and more cynical about kids," his wife Beverly said. "I would stick up for the kids. I would say, 'Kids aren't bad, Bob. The ones you work with have a lot of baggage, but they're not all like that.' Bob is not an optimist anyway. He had a pretty sour attitude."

He was working crazy shifts at juvenile hall, mostly at night. He decided to fill the days while his wife taught by taking classes that interested him. Theology interested him. After four semesters at St. Mary's College in nearby Moraga, he was close to fulfilling the requirements for a religious studies degree. He would later return to St. Mary's to get a master's degree in Physical Education and Administration.

"I was searching for something—a peace in my life, validation, something to ease my uneasiness," Ladouceur remembers.

His shift at juvenile hall ended early on Fridays. An old friend was coaching the junior varsity football team at Monte Vista High School in nearby Danville in 1977. He asked Ladouceur if he would be his eyes in the sky on game days.

Ladouceur had worked with Rob Stockberger in the local parks and recreation department. Rob was closer in age to Bob's older brother Tom, and he had spent plenty of time at the Ladouceur house. He and Bob grew closer as they grew older. They were very much alike and later roomed together at San Jose State.

Ladouceur wasn't even sure what offense Stockberger was running, but when he sat in the press box and put on the headphones, the world suddenly made sense.

"We had an uncanny ability to anticipate what each other was thinking," Ladouceur said. "I'd say, 'Rob, do you have a screen pass?' and he would have already sent it in. It was exciting to think that he was out coaching the game and doing very well and I thought, 'Hey, I could do this.' I could call the damn game."

He didn't realize he wanted to be a coach until he walked into the locker room at halftime and saw how players responded to Stockberger. If Ladouceur had dropped dead on the floor, the kids at juvenile hall would've stepped over him on the way to the snack machine. These kids were attentive. They *wanted* guidance. It was a look he'd been looking for but had never seen.

Bob and Tom were both assistant coaches at Monte Vista the following year. Tom helped out with the freshman team. Bob coached the varsity defensive backs and to this day considers it his most fulfilling coaching job.

"Coach Lad was a big brother to us," said Mike Shepanek, a defensive back at Monte Vista in 1978. "You looked at him and he was a total stud. He was the fastest guy on the team. He'd run sprints with us and it wasn't even close. He would get down and show us technique all the time and would run the drills before we did."

Shepanek had never played football before his senior year. He was a basketball player but decided to try out for the football team because his friends were playing. It wasn't easy, even though he was a good athlete. He was way behind fundamentally.

"He was raw, didn't know how to hit, but he was athletic," Ladouceur remembers. "I felt I could make him a football player. I could teach him the game. His improvement from the start of the season to the end was so dramatic it boosted my ego tremendously. I knew I could coach. That was the kid who convinced me of it."

The young coach and raw player had a profound impact on each other. Shepanek was a key contributor to the team and enjoyed his experience so much he didn't even go out for basketball because he didn't think it was possible to end his high school athletic career on a more satisfying note. What Ladouceur learned would serve him well in the future.

"Bob's background was such that from the time he was a player he had the skill set to take a guy like Mike Shepanek and turn him into a football player," said Stockberger, who would go on to lead the Monte Vista varsity to four section championships before retiring from the sideline and becoming an administrator. "That was probably the key factor his first couple years at De La Salle because he probably took kids who had not had a lot of football experience and made them into football players quickly, kind of like he did with Mike Shepanek."

Ladouceur had found his calling after the 1978 season. He thought he could be an effective coach, but, more important, he knew he could reach kids and make an impact in their lives. He just didn't know where to begin. If this was what he was going to do, his four years spent pursuing a criminal justice degree were wasted.

He wasn't qualified to teach anything, not even PE. He didn't even have a teaching credential when he read the article in the *Catholic Voice* a small newspaper serving the Oakland diocese. He wasn't looking for it, but there was the headline on page 11 of the Sept. 23, 1978, edition: "Hall resigning post as De La Salle coach."

The *Voice*'s sports pages were filled with fawning articles about Catholic Athletic League teams and their coaches. The Spartans had never had a winning season, but they made replacing Ed Hall seem a virtually impossible task.

Catholic Athletic League "football circles were stunned to learn of the resignation of Ed Hall, the head football coach at De La Salle, effective at the end of the season," the article began. "Hall is one of the most respected coaches in the league...." It ended: "He will certainly be a tough act to follow at De La Salle."

Ladouceur didn't know De La Salle existed until he went to scout one of Monte Vista's opponents in the fall of 1978. He and Stockberger had to stop and ask for directions. "We sat in those crappy stands in the heat of the day and watched California High beat the tar out of De La Salle," he said. "I remember watching the De La Salle kids and thinking, 'Man, these guys are horrible.'"

The article intrigued him, however. Tom and Mary couldn't afford to send their kids to Catholic school after the family left the Detroit area, but Bob had friends who had gone to Catholic grammar and high schools, and he envied the sense of community and belonging that seemed to be part of their educational experience.

When he discovered that the school was also looking to hire a religion teacher, a light went on in his head. The theology classes he had taken qualified him to teach religion. Ladouceur didn't even need a credential to teach at a private school.

"I was confident I could do the job, but I didn't have enough confidence to think they would pick me," he says. "I thought they thought I was probably too young to do this, or that I didn't have the experience, which I didn't."

After Hall resigned, De La Salle Principal Brother Michael Meister reevaluated the program and decided he wanted a teacher first and a coach second. He didn't want anyone who would berate kids or attempt to live out a personal fantasy through them. He wanted something different, a coach who believed in the Lasallian philosophy of putting the student first. He wanted a coach with a genuine respect for young people.

Athletic director Chuck Lafferty headed the search committee, which consisted of an administrative representative, a faculty representative, and a member of the parents association. Sal Siino, the long-time coach at Antioch High School, was a friend of Lafferty's and was brought in to help gauge each candidate's knowledge of the game.

The search-and-screening committee, as it was known, decided in a meeting that it would give great consideration to applicants with the twin competencies of teaching and coaching. This didn't seem to bode well for Ladouceur, who had precious little experience in both areas.

The application included ten questions of philosophical and theological nature that took Ladouceur ten typewritten pages to answer. He also included letters of recommendation from, among others, his theology professors at St. Mary's College.

"I wasn't even trying to appeal to the football side of it," he said. "I was trying to come in as a teacher. I wanted them to believe I could be a religious studies teacher. I had a feeling they weren't looking for a football coach. You could tell by the program. As it turned out, they didn't know anything about football."

Lafferty was in charge of sifting through the applications.

"When the resumes came in, I started putting the folders together," he said. "Ladouceur didn't pay any attention—of course this is not unusual—to how many letters of recommendation he had to have. Here was a twenty-three-year-old, and he submitted a file three inches thick with people just raving about the guy—football coaches from high school and college, church people, professors. He had it all.

"But the killer was it didn't matter whether I liked him or not. I knew Brother Michael was not opposed to doing the unexpected, and there was one thing in Ladouceur's file that gave him an edge—the religion courses. I'm wondering what the hell a religion teacher knows about football, but I interviewed him. Nice man. I interviewed the other candidates. Nice men. I had the faculty guys interview them all separately and everybody came back with glowing reviews about Ladouceur. He blew them away."

Ladouceur continued working at juvenile hall for the next month while awaiting word from De La Salle. He desperately wanted the job, even if people he respected thought of the fledgling program as a hopeless cause, a dead end.

"De La Salle was such a non-entity we never gave them a second thought," Tom Jr. said. "They had no lights and played on Saturdays in 106-degree heat. I thought it was a death sentence, him going there."

"I told him not to take that job," Fred Houston, his high school coach at San Ramon, recalls. "Bob told me he liked the setup because of the religious part. I'd never given that any consideration. I told him I still wasn't sure I'd do that."

He finally was called back for a second interview. After ten minutes with Ladouceur, Brother Michael was convinced he'd found his football coach.

"We went through the process three or four times, and I wasn't satisfied with the candidates," Brother Michael said. "We were clear with what we wanted and didn't want to settle for anything less. The last person we interviewed was Bob. He was the right person. It clicked right away. Bob was the one."

Others weren't so sure, for understandable reasons. As a football coach, Ladouceur had only one year of experience as a paid varsity assistant. As a teacher, he had never completed a class plan, graded a paper, or taught a class.

"We preferred someone who could teach as well as coach," Brother Michael was quoted in a *Contra Costa Times* article announcing Ladouceur's hiring. "Religious studies is a very different area for a coach to be involved in, but it rounds out our staff. This really crashes stereotypes of football personnel."

The article included a photo of the baby-faced Ladouceur wearing a plaid shirt, tie, and sports jacket. He didn't look much older than many of his players.

Hiring Ladouceur wasn't a popular decision. Several coaches with higher profiles had applied for the job, and controversy swirled around the announcement. Even Hall was less than thrilled with the decision. He had written a letter to Brother Michael recommending that assistant coach Bill Mott be named his successor.

"The shit hit the fan afterwards," Brother Michael said. "The phone calls I got—'Have you lost your mind?' 'Are you crazy?' 'You don't have a clue about football.' Nobody thought I had made a good choice because Bob was unknown."

Ladouceur found antiquated suspension helmets, hand-me-down

pants, and frayed jerseys in a pile so huge he was unable to open the door to the equipment closet on his first official day as coach. Not only was there no weight room, there wasn't a free weight on campus. This was an immediate concern to Ladouceur, who made himself into a football player by lifting weights. An old Universal machine sat in one corner of the locker room. Its cables were frayed and it was in dire need of reconditioning.

Now not only was the principal having second thoughts. So was the new coach.

Ladouceur called a team meeting for everyone interested in playing football during the 1979 season. The first thing he noticed when he walked into the classroom was the fact that there were more chairs than players. Then he looked at the players themselves. They wore colorful bandanas and had scraggly beards and long hair. One wore a T-shirt with a picture of a marijuana leaf on the front.

Ladouceur wrote 5–4 on the chalkboard. That would be the goal for the coming season, which seemed lofty for a program that had only won four games in the previous two seasons combined. The next thing he wrote caught everybody's attention: Beat Moreau.

"He had really done his homework," said his best returning defensive player, linebacker Keith Schuler. "Everybody at that school hated Moreau. We had never beaten them, and the year before they scored a 96-yard touchdown in the fourth quarter to beat us. He made that a goal, and we all looked at each other and thought, 'Exactly.'"

The season wouldn't start in August. He expected players to attend offseason workouts and weight-training sessions. For the most part, they did.

Players bought in, perhaps because he didn't ask them to do anything he wasn't willing to do himself. He worked out with them and soon began to feel their confidence in themselves start to blossom. He didn't bark orders at them. He treated them like adults.

"He set the example and everybody caught on pretty quickly," Keith Schuler said. "Guys were more motivated than I had seen them on my previous three years with the varsity. A lot of individualism was done away with quickly."

Ladouceur enlisted his friend and former teammate Blair Thomas to be his offensive coordinator. Thomas spent one year running Bill Yeoman's split-back veer offense at Houston. He and Ladouceur chose that as their base offense because it relies on quickness and precision more than size and athleticism, and they believed it gave average high school players the best chance to succeed.

Ladouceur and Thomas both played football on two different college teams, but they didn't pattern their program after Utah, Houston, or San Jose State. Their fondest football experiences had occurred at San Ramon High School, and they wanted to recreate the attitude, work ethic, and feeling of brotherhood they experienced Bob's senior year. At De La Salle, Ladouceur didn't set out to build a dynasty. He just wanted to create the type of experience that he sought but never found in college.

"Our issue wasn't whether we'd win or score a certain number of touchdowns," Thomas explained. "We wanted to train kids to play at a level of excellence that satisfied us, and we were people who didn't play for the adulation. We wanted to take the spirit of the game and infuse it in the kids. He wanted them to play with pure joy and abandonment. Winning was secondary to that. It was a by-product of playing at that level. As starry-eyed as that sounds, that is what he really believes."

08 ►

ST. LOUIS
Cameron Colvin's Coming-Out Party

| | | | | | | | | |

he couldn't see his teammates from his seat in the front pew of the First Baptist Church in Pittsburg (California), but he knew they were there: the coaches, the graduating seniors, even the principal. Mourners stole curious glances at Bob Ladouceur when he entered wearing a black leather jacket and a somber expression. The majority of the white faces in the predominantly black congregation wore Spartan letter jackets and sat on folding chairs in the aisles, collar buttons straining against thick necks. When there was no room left for them there, they were seated in the choir box.

Cameron Colvin buried his mother on Valentine's Day, 2002. Five of Veronica Colvin's eight pallbearers were De La Salle football players.

Many of Cameron's closest teammates showed up unannounced at his house on Limewood Place that morning carrying their Sunday clothes on hangers. They dressed together and escorted him to the immaculate white church in the shadow of oil refinery towers where his mother had been a trustee.

Few players have benefited from the feeling of brotherhood and community that Ladouceur creates more than Cameron. He found comfort in his teammates' presence, just as he found comfort in the family snapshot he kept in his room. The camera had captured a typical family gathering on a Sunday afternoon. He could still smell the charcoal smoldering in the barbecue. That was the way it used to be, the way he thought it would always be.

Grandma, wearing the red-and-white checkered apron, stands on the far left. Dad's in back, smiling. The father-son resemblance is profound: the same wide eyes framed by high cheekbones. Uncle George, everybody's favorite, is on the right, next to great-grandma, who always acted more like one of the kids. Cameron's two cousins were there and, of course, his sister Saimone, who looks so like her mother. Then there's little Cameron, in a white shirt and black tie, smiling, his mother's hand resting comfortingly on his shoulder.

Cameron looks at the photo and wonders what his life would've been like if not for the long, dark procession of tragedies and scandals that filled local newspapers for nearly a decade and shook this close-knit blue-collar community to its core. He wonders how his life would be different if his father hadn't died, if his mother hadn't been accused of murdering him, and if his uncle hadn't confessed to one of the most notorious crimes in Contra Costa County history.

One by one, those pictured who were closest to him disappeared from his life, until only he and Saimone were left.

His father was the first to go, and it came without warning on an August night in 1992. John Cameron Colvin was thirty-nine, a painter and carpenter. He admired civil rights leader Malcolm X. John Colvin's Muslim name was Sudan Shahied Fard. He liked the Oakland A's and Rickey Henderson. He was a quiet man who cooked for his family.

The coroner found twenty times the legal dose of morphine in John Colvin's system and ruled his death an accident caused by acute morphine intoxication. John's family suspected foul play. One year later, the local police department began a murder investigation.

Cam and Saimone were prepared for their mother's possible arrest. Still, it came as a shock when Cameron saw his mother sitting between two officers in the back seat of an unmarked police car. Soon the police were searching the house.

The prosecution painted John as the victim of a murderous plot. They claimed that Veronica had brought a bottle of pharmaceutical morphine home from her mother's house following her death from cancer in 1992. Prosecutors accused Veronica of lacing her husband's cough medicine with the morphine in order to collect on two life insurance policies John Colvin had taken out in the two years before his death.

They claimed Veronica had called to inquire about one of the policies a month before her husband died.

The prosecution planned to seek the death penalty.

The defense painted John Colvin as a closet drug user who accidentally overdosed on liquid morphine.

Veronica's arrest left Cam and Saimone dazed and disoriented. "They wouldn't let us have contact visits at first," Cam said. "We had to talk to her behind the glass. It was real awkward. It was like something you see on TV or in the movies. You'd never think you'd be in that situation."

Their great-grandma moved in and took care of Cam and Saimone in her granddaughter's absence. Veronica called often and mailed letters, drawings, and connect-the-dots pictures home to her children daily.

The trial lasted four weeks. Saimone went almost every day. She remembers her mother's lawyers taking her out to lunch after testifying on her thirteenth birthday. Cameron was in the courtroom for closing arguments.

"The jury was staring at me," he said. "Everybody was staring at the kids. It was uncomfortable. It was real tough to hear what was being said."

It ended in a mistrial. Nine jurors voted to acquit. Three believed she was guilty. The charges against Veronica Nell Colvin were dismissed on Cameron's eleventh birthday, almost five years after his father's death.

The trial attracted headlines because Veronica was the sister of George Elzie, whose own arrest and subsequent trial shocked the community.

George Elzie was a former Pittsburg High School class president and baseball star who received a scholarship to Oregon State. He returned to his hometown after college and joined the police department, where he was given several high-profile assignments and was considered a rising star.

He and his sister Veronica were extremely close, and he doted on her two kids, Cameron and Saimone. He stopped by to see them almost every day, and he let them each pick out four presents at the toy store every Christmas. It was Uncle George who told his niece and nephew that their father had passed away.

"He's the one who got me started on sports," Cam says. "When my father first died I was sitting around the house doing nothing. One day Uncle George came and said, 'We're going to sign you up for baseball.' I didn't know if I wanted to do it, but ever since he signed me up I loved it. I've loved sports ever since."

A passerby discovered twenty-eight-year-old Cynthia Kempf's body in a field south of the rural town of Brentwood on the morning of March 14, 1988. She was wearing a black hood secured with duct tape and had nine bullet holes in her back. Her death remained a mystery for six months until police linked the case to a Pittsburg police officer suspected of a string of armed robberies that had confounded authorities.

It wasn't until six years later that the community was shocked to discover that George Elzie had been one of four men who kidnapped Kempf for the purpose of gaining entrance to the Safeway store where she worked as a manager. When their attempts to divert police from the store's parking lot failed, they panicked. All four men had fired shots. They would share in the culpability.

Because he testified against the gang's ringleader, George Elzie was allowed to plead guilty to a lesser charge, kidnapping for robbery. After a trial that for a time ran concurrently with Veronica Colvin's murder trial, George was sentenced to twelve years in prison in a case that rocked Pittsburg to its foundation.

"I looked up to him a lot," Cameron said. "It was kind of hard to understand at first. My mother would tell me all the stuff that was going on in the newspaper. There were all these articles about her and my uncle. It was real tough."

It had been his mother's idea for him to attend De La Salle. He was warm to the notion, having idolized D.J. Williams, another Pittsburg youth football legend who went to the Christian Brothers school. Cameron was wavering when his junior high basketball coach Jay Lightner, who by then had become a family friend, convinced him to try De La Salle for a year. He even offered to pay Cameron's tuition so Veronica wouldn't be burdened financially. If Cameron didn't feel at home at De La Salle, Lightner promised to personally enroll him in Pittsburg High for his sophomore year.

A month into his freshman year Cam called Lightner and told him he would not be transferring. He wanted to graduate from De La Salle.

"You don't have to worry about anything," he said of his new school. "All you have to focus on is your football and your school. You don't have to worry about people back-stabbing you. Everybody is there for the same reason. Everybody wants to be the best. The place just gets in your heart."

~

Oddly enough, Veronica's death was the easiest for Cameron to accept.

"I kind of understood her death," he said. "I was happy for it. She didn't have to struggle anymore. She didn't have to worry about paying bills or my tuition. She had a lot of bills to pay. My sister was graduating. She had to pay for the senior ball and all that stuff. She had a lot on her plate. She got a rest from all that. I'm glad she got a rest. She had a tough life."

Cam had overslept on his mother's last morning at home and was rushing to get ready for school. He couldn't find his lunch money, even though Veronica had put it on the table by the front door, just like she did every weeknight.

The carpool driver hadn't arrived. Cameron was starting to panic. He went into his mother's room to see if she could take him to school. She was in the bathroom, her eyes rolling in her head and her skin tinged green.

Saimone was half awake. She had heard a strange thump come from the master bathroom. It was Veronica's head hitting the wall.

Saimone took care of them both. She studied sports medicine at Pittsburg High and had long played the role of Veronica's caregiver and administrative assistant. She sorted her mother's many medications, helped her dress when she awoke disoriented, assisted with a myriad of other chores, and always, always looked out for Cameron.

By the time Saimone reached the bathroom, Veronica was slowly sliding down the wall, eyes rolling, tears streaming down her cheeks.

Saimone dragged her mother to the bed and was holding the phone when she heard a honking horn on the street. Cameron's ride had arrived. She knew her mother wouldn't want Cam to see her like this. She pushed him out the door.

"He said he thought everything would be fine, but he knew [otherwise]," Saimone said. "He wanted to stay but he did what we told him to do."

Saimone's worst fears were confirmed when she met her mother at the hospital. Veronica's right eye was dropping and drool was pooling in the corner of her mouth. She had suffered another stroke.

Veronica slipped into a coma the following night and was placed on life support. She had suffered a second aneurysm, and the doctors couldn't operate this time. They wanted to know how long the family wanted to leave her on life support. Saimone thought it over while giving her mother a sponge bath in the hospital.

"I kept thinking, 'I shouldn't be the one to make this decision,'" Saimone remembers. "I'm too young to make this decision."

Her mother wouldn't have wanted this. So Saimone set a deadline. If Veronica didn't wake from her coma in three days, they would take her off the respirator and hope and pray she would survive. The deadline had come and gone when Cam visited his mother in the hospital. He watched as her eyes followed him across the room from beneath her closed eyelids. He told her he loved her. Saimone promised to take care of Cam.

"We knew she could hear us because she was crying," Saimone said.

That was on a Thursday night. Cam worked out with his teammates on Friday afternoon, shocking everybody. Nobody knew what to say. They knew his mother was in the hospital.

He kept telling himself she would pull through, as she had during her previous hospitalizations. Ladouceur and Aliotti told him they were there for him. Take as much time as you need, they said, again and again. Forget about offseason workouts. Get away if you need to. Come back when you're ready.

What they didn't understand was that his relationships with his teammates were all he had left. That's why he practiced on that Friday afternoon and why he stunned everybody by showing up to a voluntary workout early Saturday morning. It had been less than twelve hours since the respirator was unplugged and Veronica Colvin drifted away, leaving her children to wonder what would happen next.

"She went peacefully," Saimone told her brother.

"The whole week I was saying she's going to come out of the coma, she's going to be all right, she's going to pull through," Cam said. "But when Saimone told me that it just crushed me. It shattered me."

The football team was the only thing he had left that made sense in his life. He wasn't going to lose that, too.

"That's getting away for me, just being with the team," he said. "When I was with the team and coaches I didn't even think about it. I'm focused on what I want to do. Nothing else matters. That's my family now. I have a relationship with everybody on that team. I have forty-seven brothers."

Blasquez hugged Cameron when he saw him that Saturday morning. Then he walked Cam into the locker room and told the team to gather round for a prayer, a prayer for Veronica, whom they all knew and respected, but most of all a prayer for Cameron Colvin.

Cameron remained stoic throughout his mother's funeral service. He was just like his father, he was told; John Colvin never showed his emotions, either. Cameron didn't know what to do next. He didn't want to return to his family's Limewood Place home—too many memories. He didn't want to abandon his sister, either, and she was determined to remain in the house and build a life her mother would be proud of.

He had grown close to Jay Lightner, his former basketball coach. Jay was director of a mentoring program in nearby Antioch and had three foster children and his own young son at home. He too had lost his father, and he related to the boy. Cameron moved in with Jay and focused his emotions on football and school. Going to De La Salle had been his mother's idea. He would dedicate his junior season to her.

"When you talk about us being a family, make sure you mean it because I do," Colvin would tell his teammates in an early-season chapel service. "You guys are about the only family I have left."

Maurice Drew takes a handoff on the second play from scrimmage and bolts into the secondary behind blocks from Erik Sandie and Cole Smith. A gasp rises from the crowd at Aloha Stadium as he bursts into the open field. He blows past two defensive backs charging up to stop the run.

Drew was the first De La Salle player to emerge from the locker room before the game. He had begun testing his injured ankle midway through the fourth quarter of Long Beach Poly's 42–16 demolition of two-time defending state champion Kahuku. The first game had been sobering for De La Salle coaches, who knew the Spartans would host powerful Long Beach Poly in three short weeks, and also for the 30,050 fans that had come to watch two local powerhouses defend the honor of Hawaiian football.

With the outcome of the first game long determined, the anticipation mounted for the main event. Every eye was on Drew as he stretched and ran. "Without Drew in the lineup, The Streak is in serious jeopardy," television analyst John Veneri said as the cameras focused on Drew during pregame warm-ups. Now every eye is on him again as No. 21 heads for the end zone.

A St. Louis defender dives at his feet from behind and manages to trip him up. Drew staggers for 20 yards before falling at the St. Louis 9-yard line to complete a 51-yard play. He feels the same sharp pain in his ankle that he felt during Thursday's practice. This time he doesn't scream. He knows the pain will subside. He's OK.

Jackie Bates, who will be expected to replace Drew next season, runs the next two plays while Drew rests, but the junior has trouble keeping his feet. An incomplete pass on third down sets up a chip-shot field goal attempt for Tony Binswanger, who had wowed the crowd by kicking a 50-yard field goal in warm-ups.

Binswanger was playing varsity soccer as a sophomore when his best friend, football player Matt Kavanaugh, led him unknowingly into the coaching office and introduced him as the junior varsity's new kicker. Binswanger was stunned. Louisa Binswanger discouraged her son from playing football because she didn't want him to get hurt. Tony had never kicked a football in his life.

Kavanaugh led him to the practice field after school for a tryout. Binswanger's first extra-point attempt was true. After field goals from 30 and 35 yards sailed through the uprights, the junior varsity coach told him he had just joined the football team.

He put five of his first six kickoffs in the back of the end zone in the junior varsity season opener. He was called up to the varsity midway through his junior season and put 38 of 58 kickoffs in the end zone for touchbacks.

Now Tony Binswanger is lining up for his second field goal attempt of the season as Ladouceur watches from the sideline, his fingers on his chin. It's a chip-shot considering his leg strength, but his low, hooking attempt never has a chance. Drew's electrifying run has been wasted. The kick is wide left, and St. Louis takes over.

The Crusaders have been a run-and-shoot team since Cal Lee was hired in 1983, which means they throw the ball all over the field. This is a passing offense that only runs the ball often enough to keep the defense honest.

However, Coach Delbert Tengan made a bold decision when he discovered that De La Salle's defensive line averaged 218 pounds per man. The strategy is apparent from the moment St. Louis breaks the huddle. Instead of the offensive linemen lining up a yard or more apart in a typical run-and-shoot alignment, they stand shoe to shoe. The intent is obvious. They plan to run the ball right at the Spartans' undersized defense.

The first play is a handoff to the slot receiver running around right end. The undersized defensive linemen hold their ground and occupy their man, allowing linebacker Cole Smith and defensive backs Matt Kavanaugh and Chris Wilhelmy to tackle the ball carrier for a 2-yard loss. A fireplug fullback pounds up the middle on the next play but gains only a yard. Quarterback Bobby George throws deep for game-breaking receiver Jason Rivers on third down, but Jackie Bates and Damon Jenkins have Rivers double-covered and the pass falls harmlessly to the artificial turf. The Crusaders are forced to punt.

That puts the ball back in Spartans quarterback Britt Cecil's hands. Before the game, the De La Salle players wrote inspirational messages on the T-shirts they would wear beneath their shoulder pads. Linebacker Parker Hanks opted for "The only pain that matters is the pain you inflict." Cecil, the mild-mannered senior who has yet to morph into the take-charge guy Ladouceur wants to see, chose something more introspective and cerebral: "Persistence and determination alone are omnipotent." It's a quote from Calvin Coolidge.

Britt is going to need Coolidge's wisdom of the ages if Drew is too hobbled to make a difference. Instead, the quarterback is going to have to make a difference. Now, on De La Salle's second possession, he does—with a little help. On third and long, Cecil drops back and throws deep down the middle for Cameron Colvin.

Fans had chanted his name during pregame warm-ups. "We want three touchdowns, Cameron!" someone shouted from the seats high above the end zone. Colvin searched the crowd with a perplexed look on his face. The De La Salle cheering section was on the other side of the field. These were strangers calling his name.

"Who was that?" De'Montae Fitzgerald asked.

"I have no idea," Cameron said, still searching the crowd.

Now two St. Louis defenders run stride for stride with De La Salle's 6', 180-pound receiver. It seems an ill-advised pass until Colvin, who is slowing down to catch the underthrown ball, uses his body to shield one defender and leaps up and catches the ball over the other for a 46-yard gain.

A late hit on Colvin by a frustrated defensive back gives De La Salle a first down on the St. Louis 7-yard line. Gino Ottoboni picks up six yards on the next play. Cecil then scores on a quarterback sneak to give the Spartans a 7–0 lead. De La Salle offensive linemen crouch at the line of scrimmage when Cecil barks "down" and drop into their stances when they hear "set." A second later, when Cecil shouts "hut," they fire off the ball—a snarling, bloody-knuckled chorus line—and three separate movements become one fluid motion.

This unit isn't as quick or as synchronized as Ladouceur would like, but they are still quicker off the ball than anything the Crusaders had ever encountered.

"St. Louis is good, but De La Salle is a machine," says one of the many Hawaiian observers on the sideline.

The De La Salle offense is executing with a crisp efficiency that was absent the week before. These seem like different De La Salle players than the ones who piled into elevators after the previous night's team meeting. You could see the change as they filed through the buffet line for breakfast. They were united and self-assured. You could see their newfound resolve. The body language of all forty-eight players changed overnight.

"I thought that team grew substantially overnight," Allocco said before the game. "You could sense a big difference in their confidence this morning. They were coming together. They were accepting responsibility. That was the difference."

Crusaders' coach Tengan sticks with his running game on the second series and gains two yards before George throws another incompletion on third down. Drew snatches the ensuing punt out of the air and shoots up the sideline before being tripped up. He comes limping off the field. Bates, who can't seem to pick up his feet, gains seven yards on the next play. Cecil throws a six-yard completion to De'Montae Fitzgerald while an assistant trainer re-wraps Drew's ankle on the bench. Later, on yet another third and long, Cecil deftly sidesteps a defender and flings the ball toward Colvin.

St. Louis defensive back Joe Medeiros will make a clean interception, or at least it appears that way until Colvin leaps up and knocks the ball out of Medeiros' hands, making an acrobatic catch of the deflection and falling in a heap at the 1. The 35-yard gain leads to a touchdown that makes the score 14–0 as the first quarter expires.

This is indeed Cameron Colvin's coming-out party, just as he predicted the night before.

Ladouceur had Colvin and Fitzgerald switch positions earlier in the week. Colvin's size coupled with his leaping ability allows him to make plays downfield on the deep patterns that had been Fitzgerald's domain. Fitzgerald wasn't thrilled with the idea of becoming a possession receiver. He felt he was being punished for his dropped passes against Mitty. He knew he could get open deep, but they had only played one game. He didn't feel as if he had been given an opportunity.

"Look, some things he does better than you, and some things you do better than him," Ladouceur told Fitzgerald. "You'll get your chances."

The Spartans have 94 yards rushing and 87 passing at the end of the first quarter. St. Louis, with the most potent passing attack De La Salle has ever faced, has yet to complete a pass and has gained just two yards on the ground. The St. Louis strategy of running the ball down De La Salle's throat is backfiring. Tengan's team is facing the very situation he hoped to avoid. Now, like so many of De La Salle's opponents before them, the Crusaders find themselves behind early in the game.

In the second quarter, George hits receiver Shane Butcher for nine yards on first down, and a cheer rises from a confused crowd that doesn't understand why the Crusaders aren't opening it up. Their running back picks up five yards off right tackle, and St. Louis has its first first down of the game. It is third-and-2 on the De La Salle 45 when Mike Pittore drops the running back for a two-yard loss, forcing yet another punt.

Drew gains nine yards on the first play of De La Salle's ensuing possession, and Cecil quickly picks up the first down on a keeper. After a delay-of-game penalty, Cecil pitches the ball to Bates, who fires a pass to Fitzgerald for a 32-yard gain that would've been a 75-yard touchdown had the ball not been underthrown.

"I guarantee you I'm going to run that halfback pass tomorrow night," Ladouceur warned players in the team meeting the night before. "If those safeties are flying up and the corners are hanging out I'm going to run it and it's going to go for a score. That's a touchdown, a home run play. You guys run that right and it will be six."

Three plays later, Drew bursts off right tackle and limps untouched into the end zone. The silence in the stadium is deafening as De La Salle players celebrate their third score and a 21–0 lead.

"That offense puts you in a predicament," Tengan said later. "If you load up in the box they'll throw it over you. They attack you all over the field."

Former ESPN SportsCenter anchor Larry Beil is the play-by-play announcer for Fox Sports today. The broadcast will draw a larger local share of the television audience than the three stations reporting Democratic primary results combined. Beil tells the home viewing audience what has become obvious in the hush that envelops the stadium after Drew's touchdown.

"It's absolutely imperative that St. Louis do something positive with the football here," he says as another Binswanger kickoff sails out of the end zone.

St. Louis fans rise to their feet when George throws deep to Butcher, who is being escorted down the field by Bates and Willie Glasper. The senior receiver makes a leaping catch despite double coverage and gains 47 yards to the De La Salle 13. Three plays later George rolls to his right and tucks the ball under his arm as if he is going to run for the pylon.

When defensive backs Chris Wilhelmy and Bates abandon their receiver in the end zone to come up and meet him, he flips a soft pass over their heads and into Rivers' waiting arms for a touchdown.

Cole Smith, the senior captain, is sitting on the bench, sobbing. He has suffered a concussion—when and how he has no idea. He can't remember anything past the first two series. He is benched when Blasquez notices him stumbling off the field. He keeps trying to convince the coaches he can play.

Players unaware of his condition see him on the bench and urge him to get back on the field, prompting more sobs. In his mind, he has let his teammates down.

Bates admits at halftime that his shoes are two sizes two big, which explains why it appears like he is running on ice. De La Salle has a contract with Nike that allows players to purchase shoes at discounted prices. Bates had been sent size 13 turf shoes instead of 11. He went to Nike Town the day before looking for another pair, but none were in stock. He didn't think it would be a big deal but it is. "The turf is tackling me more than St. Louis is," he admits.

Drew is definitely not himself. They never would've caught him on the second play of the game if he had been 100 percent. He felt the pain in his foot again while returning a punt in the first quarter and is limping all the time now. He still has eight carries for 88 yards. Cecil has completed six of eight passes for 148 yards.

De La Salle dominated the first half, but St. Louis proved it could score in a hurry. With Drew hobbled, there is reason for optimism in the St. Louis locker room.

St. Louis picks up one first down before being forced to punt yet again on its first drive of the second half. Damon Jenkins returns the punt 48 yards to set up Binswanger's 42-yard field goal, which clears the uprights with 10 yards to spare. It's 24–7 De La Salle.

Predictably, Binswanger's kickoff sails into the end zone. In high school football, any kickoff that lands in the end zone is an automatic touchback. So far, thanks to Binswanger, St. Louis has begun every drive at its own 20-yard line.

"I haven't seen many kickers like that," Cal Lee said later. "Putting them in the end zone all the time is a big, big deal. That guy is a weapon."

Eidson picked up a tendency while watching film of the St. Louis offense over the summer. The Crusaders almost always run out of the shotgun formation and almost always throw to the side of the field where the running back is lined up. Eidson has his entire secondary rotate toward that side of the field on the snap of the ball.

This is proving to be an effective defensive strategy, even as Rivers makes a leaping, twisting catch over Jenkins for a 29-yard gain. George throws to slot back B.J. Batts in the left flat later in the drive and Jenkins, a three-year starter at cornerback, delivers a crushing blow to his midsection. Batts fumbles, but St. Louis somehow recovers. Batts bounces back with a spinning, leaping touchdown run to cut the lead to 10 with less than two minutes left in the third period.

"We've got a football game, everybody," Beil says in the broadcast booth.

De La Salle's special teams continue to dominate. Jenkins returns the kickoff 37 yards. Instead of sending Binswanger on the field for another field goal attempt, Ladouceur goes for it on fourth-and-2 at the St. Louis 14. Drew limps off right tackle for six yards, setting up Gino Ottoboni's 1-yard touchdown run. When Willie Glasper intercepts George's next pass, victory No. 127 is all but assured.

Butcher gets behind the secondary for a 65-yard touchdown in the waning moments that prompts more sideline hysterics from Eidson. Even Lee, the winningest coach in Hawaiian history, is forced to admit that the 31–21 final score is deceiving.

"It hurts when you lose," he says. "A lot of people think 31–21 is a good game, but if you were there you knew they had it under control."

Defensive lineman Tolifili Liufau, the fifth-year senior Eidson had convinced Ladouceur to allow to play, finishes with seven tackles, including two for loss. For St. Louis there are no excuses, which is just the way Eidson wanted it.

Tengan and the St. Louis players and coaches leave before talking with reporters. Ladouceur patiently answers questions at midfield as players celebrate with the approximately six hundred De La Salle parents and fans who made the trip. "We're not counting wins," Ladouceur says. "We're counting on them improving every week and that's how we have always approached it. We try to find a ceiling for these kids. Some of them reach it and a lot of them don't. We just work day to day and keep plugging away. Wins are the outcomes. We really don't harp on wins."

Veronica Colvin spoke often before her death about how much she was looking forward to the trip to Hawaii to watch her son play. Cameron has been thinking about her all week and even taped a picture of himself and his mother to his locker before the game. He is overcome by fatigue, emotion, and the knowledge that she is not here to share his breakout performance. He sits by himself on the bench, sobbing.

Promoter Keith Amemiya spends the night trying to conceal his nervous energy. His worst-case scenario was to have both local teams blown out, and although the St. Louis–De La Salle game was not as lopsided as the Long Beach Poly–Kahuku outcome, it has been decisive.

He insists that the doubleheader has been a success despite the final scores. Most people leave more impressed with De La Salle's performance than disappointed in St. Louis', although some grumble about Tengan's conservative game plan.

"In all my years I had never seen a program like that," says Don Botelho, who has coached football in Hawaii for forty-two years. "Their execution is outstanding. They're not very big, and they're not all great athletes, but they're all good football players. It was the best-coached football team I've ever seen."

Ladouceur can't remember ever having a team that improved so much in one week, but the shadow of Poly is already looming. They have made a significant step, players agree, but they will have to take many more steps to have any chance of beating Long Beach.

"We stepped up defensively," senior lineman Erik Sandie notes. "But we have a lot to work on before Poly."

Pizza is waiting back at the hotel. That's when several players approach Eidson. The foaming surf has tempted them all week. They haven't been allowed in the water because coaches feared that prolonged exposure to the sun would drain them before the game. How can they spend five days overlooking Waikiki without testing the water? Cameron accompanies his teammates to the beach but is too drained to swim. He returns to his hotel room alone, and when he crawls into bed and closes his eyes he can see his mother and father in the stands in Aloha Stadium next to Uncle George and Saimone. He can see their proud shining faces and imagine what it would feel like to have hugged them in his moment of triumph the way he had seen his teammates embrace their parents. He can see it all so clearly it's almost as if it really happened, which only makes him feel more empty inside.

That's how Cameron Colvin's night ends. For everybody else, it ends with a joyous midnight swim in the warm salt water, Diamondhead shining in the moonlight.

LADOUCEUR'S FIRST TEAM OF SPARTANS

One of the first things Ladouceur did after he was hired at De La Salle was order new jerseys with the school name printed proudly across the chest. The jerseys had previously been generic. He saw that as another illustration of how the school didn't embrace the football program and the football program didn't embrace the school.

Football was offered so admissions people could tell parents and prospective students that yes, there was a football program. It wasn't anything the school took pride in. Athletes avoided wearing their varsity jackets for fear of public ridicule. Students from neighboring schools screamed profanities at the players as they drove past the De La Salle campus. That was the first thing Ladouceur wanted to change. He wanted to earn the community's respect. He wanted the name-calling to stop. He wanted his players to be proud of where they went to school and the team they played for.

"Football was something outside the school," Ladouceur says of that era. "It was Ed Hall's thing. I loved the school and wanted to bring them both together. I wanted the school to be proud of the football team. The game doesn't sustain itself. Something else has to be attached to it to make it great."

His first team had more characters than any team he has coached since, and many of them remain his friends today. Then they had little grasp of the type of discipline Ladouceur would require.

It was a group that liked to have a good time on and off the field. Ladouceur was furious after he suspended two players caught smoking marijuana before the first game. He expressed his displeasure by shattering a clipboard in the locker room.

"We had some jocks, some stoners, and some bookish types," former linebacker Chris Crespi recalls. "It was an interesting team."

Players realized something else as they began preparing for the 1979 season. The offense was no longer an afterthought, as it had been under Hall. In fact, it was just the opposite. Hall believed that defense won games. Ladouceur believed that a ball-control offense that kept the defense off the field was the key to success. He believed in attacking offensively and continuing to attack until the outcome was decided.

That excited players learning the new veer offense. His philosophy toward preseason practice also was a welcome change.

The weight benches and equipment had been upgraded. The new coach accompanied his players on long runs and pushed them in weightlifting sessions. Players were in better shape than they had been and became more confident.

Instead of two weeks of three-a-day practices, as they had endured under Hall, Ladouceur scheduled one week of two-a-days.

"I always thought two-a-days were counter-productive," he says. "They turn into a survival test instead of a teaching opportunity. So much of the game is learning how to hit and move people. It's physical pad work, and you can only do so much of that."

Ladouceur set out to teach players the game once practices began. He didn't believe his players had the necessary passion and dedication. The losing mentality was difficult to shake. They weren't tough enough. They didn't know how to win. They didn't even know how to prepare.

He was attempting to install a new offense and a new attitude. He had a young hands-on staff that wasn't afraid to get in a stance or deliver a blow to a blocking dummy or even suit up and scrimmage against players in the early years. Having coaches suit up was good for morale. It also was practical because there weren't enough athletes on the thirty-three-man roster to simulate the opposing team's offense.

"It was what we looked forward to more than anything," Keith Schuler said, who was a linebacker on Ladouceur's first team. "If you were pissed off at Bob, you had a chance to get in a pop or two. Guys were flying all over the place trying to hit him."

Ladouceur grimaces at the memory.

"I'm lucky nobody got hurt," he said. "I've had coaches propose that lately. I tell them there's no way they're touching the kids."

Blair Thomas' knowledge of the veer from the year he spent under Bill Yeoman at Houston made him a natural offensive coordinator. De La Salle graduate Don De Rosa had played college ball at St. Mary's and was hired to coach the defense.

"I remember calling kids gutless," Ladouceur says. "You chickened out of that hit. You gave up on that run, that drill. So much of it was negative feedback. I don't make those comments today because our kids give so much. Coming in, there was not only a tremendous lack of pride but also a lack of understanding about what it took."

The Spartans scored five touchdowns for their first-year coach in a preseason scrimmage against Redwood, which was an accomplishment considering they had been shut out four times the previous season, finishing with negative yardage in two of those games.

The new veer offense that produced an offensive explosion in the scrimmage appeared anything but potent the following week, when quarterback Kevin Heaney fumbled the first two snaps from center in the regular-season opener against Sacred Heart of San Francisco.

Ladouceur had told numerous reporters that he would open up the offense, and here his team couldn't even execute a simple snap.

Heaney had taken a terrible beating as the starting quarterback during his junior year but impressed Ladouceur with his toughness. Asking him to master the veer was asking a lot, but Thomas was an exacting taskmaster who proved to be as good a coach as he was a quarterback.

"He was a perfectionist," said Heaney, who is now a defense attorney in Sausalito, California. "I remember he would have me out there for an hour after every practice, and that was during hell week."

Heaney finally settled down and the offense began to move. De La Salle trailed Sacred Heart 7–6 in the third quarter before scoring three quick touchdowns on a sweep, an interception return, and a perfectly executed option reverse that went for a 47-yard score.

The 26–13 win and 326 total yards was quite an accomplishment for a team that had scored only 65 points in nine games the year before. When they followed that by defeating Benicia 14–0 on a day when temperatures spiked into triple digits, the Spartans had won as many games in two weeks as they had during the entire 1978 season. With lowly California High and Half Moon Bay left on the nonleague schedule, the Spartans had a chance to enter conference play undefeated.

"I remember sitting in the locker room not knowing what to do when we were 2–0," linebacker Keith Schuler said. "We expected to win. Before we wanted to win but we didn't expect it. The mentality was changing."

California High is in San Ramon, which made the Spartans' third game of the season a homecoming for Ladouceur. He was going back to play against a team from the same league as Monte Vista, where he had worked his first coaching job the year before, and San Ramon, where he had starred for Fred Houston. The rookie coach wanted to win this game badly; it was a reasonable expectation considering the competition. The Spartans were five-point favorites in one local newspaper. No one could remember the last time De La Salle had been a five-point favorite against any team.

Cal High opened its doors in 1973 and had one of the few football programs in the area that was less distinguished than De La Salle's. The Grizzlies had yet to win their first league game and had lost nine straight dating back to the 1978 season. In fact, they hadn't won since their 20–6 romp over De La Salle the year before.

It seemed like an omen when Schuler broke his finger on the third play of the game. The veer was failing miserably. The game was scoreless with 2:34 to play. De La Salle had the ball on its own 34 when Heaney lost a fumble after being hit behind the line. It was De La Salle's eighth turnover of the game. The Grizzlies won on a last-second field goal.

As California players celebrated the rare victory, Ladouceur's team walked toward the bus, visibly shaken by the defeat.

"That was a huge ego game for me," Ladouceur said. "I didn't realize it at the time, but looking back I'm embarrassed by it. I was taking a team that was all mine back to the EBAL, the league I had come from, and we were so horrid. It was a humbling experience. I blamed the kids. I told them they were shit and garbage. I have a lot of regrets as a young coach, and that was definitely one of them."

Ladouceur had to find a way to get the offense back on track and reduce penalties. De La Salle bounced back and routed hapless Half Moon Bay 35–0, accumulating 401 total yards. The Spartans were 3–1 heading into conference play but still were not considered a threat to established teams such as St. Mary's and powerhouse Salesian.

∼

Regardless of the ups and downs on the football field, Ladouceur was reassured by the fact that he had joined a close-knit school community as dedicated to helping kids as he was. De La Salle has always been innovative, with a liberal view of education. There has never been a dress code, for example. It was one of the first schools in the U.S. to initiate block scheduling, which is practiced nationwide today. Some within the Christian Brothers community referred to it as the "free school."

"The spirit at that school from its very founding was marked by a sense of community and care and respectful nurturing of the individual student," Brother Jerome Gallegos says. "Everybody was on the alert to take the freest view to the rules and guidelines so the individual could be served. The person was more important than the rules. The human aspect was prominent. Everything was flexible. Rigidity was not a key in determining the course of action at De La Salle. Bob attached himself to that as he got exposure to it. He naturally became a leader in that manner of educating kids."

Brother Laurence Allen was the most influential teacher on campus at the time. He was young, handsome, and stood apart from the other Brothers. He skydived and once rented a motorcycle and rode it to Mexico. He loved anything to do with the outdoors, most of all whitewater rafting. He and a group of students once filmed themselves skateboarding down the twisting S curves of Lombard Street in San Francisco.

He stayed up late at night sipping wine and contemplating whether suffering was redemptive.

Brother Laurence was identified by his superiors as a brilliant educator early in his career and was on the fast track to becoming a principal. He was a gifted counselor, especially when dealing with drug- and alcohol-related issues. The druggies and stoners, as they were called, were Brother Laurence's boys. As dean of students, he meted out punishments that were appropriate for the crime.

"He had a different relationship with everybody," said Jack Henderson, who was Brother Laurence's favorite student. "He would kick guys out of school and they would come back and ask him for advice. They understood why they were booted out, but they were still friends."

Ed Hall had given Ladouceur one piece of advice after the rookie coach approached him at a clinic earlier that summer: Befriend Brother Laurence. It was something Hall had been unable to do.

Ladouceur gained Brother Laurence's approval without even knowing it. He and his coaching buddy Rob Stockberger were amusing themselves with the athletic department's public-address system that summer. They had recently seen the movie *One Flew Over the Cuckoo's Nest* and loved it. "Time for the medication, boys," Ladouceur said into the microphone one day, not realizing that his words echoed throughout campus.

Brother Laurence was walking through the main quad at the time and he almost doubled over with laughter. *One Flew Over the Cuckoo's Nest* was his favorite movie.

The young Brother took an active interest in Ladouceur and the football program from that moment forward, easing the new teacher's transition into the classroom and even helping sort through the mishmash of plastic sand-filled weights Ladouceur asked players to bring from home. Later, after learning how important weights were to the program Ladouceur hoped to establish, Brother Laurence gave his new friend a personal check for $1,000, which was a lot of money for someone who had taken a vow of poverty and was paid accordingly.

"I don't know where he got the money, but there was any number of people he could've asked who would've spit it up for him," said Brother Robb Wallace, who was also a close friend of Brother Laurence's. He had that kind of power.

There was only one condition. Brother Laurence wanted to keep his contribution confidential. Ladouceur kept the secret for twenty-three years.

∼

De La Salle players and coaches stood watching, mouths agape, when the Bishop O'Dowd Dragons took the field for the first Catholic Athletic League game of the 1979 season. "Mean Machine" was spelled out in yellow letters across their black jerseys, a reference to the prison football team quarterbacked by Burt Reynolds in the 1974 movie *The Longest Yard.*

They wore rain capes despite the ninety-degree heat, and players had painted their faces to resemble warriors from some distant tribe.

The Bishop O'Dowd players stood menacingly in the middle of the field staring down the Spartans as they stretched. It was an obvious attempt to intimidate the program that had been the laughingstock of the league. It infuriated Thomas, who responded by denting a locker with his fist.

"No one will admit it, but we were all scared to death before that game," Crespi recalls.

The teams that were supposed to beat De La Salle did, which was one of the reasons why the program garnered so little respect. But against Bishop O'Dowd players competed as fiercely as any De La Salle team before or since. The game was deadlocked 7–7 at halftime.

The Spartans were playing with newfound intensity. Thomas remembers watching Crespi register one of the most crushing blows he has ever seen on a football field—high school, college, or pro.

"He knocked a guy six feet back and then he turned around and had a look of pure glee on his face," Thomas said. "That was when we first started to punish people play after play after play."

Bishop O'Dowd led 13–7 and was driving for what appeared to be the game-clinching touchdown when Chuck Young intercepted a tipped pass in the end zone and returned it 104 yards for the game-winning score.

The biggest win thus far in De La Salle school history was followed by the loudest postgame celebration in school history.

"They should've creamed us," Ladouceur said. "They had so much more talent. Those guys fought their *asses* off. That was the first game where I felt guys played like Spartans. It was real impressive."

The East Bay Prep Writers Association had never ranked De La Salle before, but the Spartans were listed as an honorable mention selection on the strength of their 4–1 record and upset of Bishop O'Dowd.

"The Spartans will be hard pressed to improve their status," an accompanying article in the *Contra Costa Times* warned. "They meet fourth-ranked St. Mary's and ninth-ranked Moreau in the next three weeks."

∽

St. Mary's had won five of six games and was led by standout running back Reggie Mosley. They were 21-point favorites over De La Salle, but when the two teams met in 1979 it was the Spartans who bolted to a 21-point lead.

It was a rough and tumble game, filled with questionable calls and pushing and shoving by players on both teams. St. Mary's scored a token touchdown on the rain-soaked field with less than two minutes left. When the final gun sounded, the Spartans were tied with top-ranked Salesian for first place in the Catholic Athletic League, and the school community was rallying around the team.

Teachers who had never shown up for games in the past began to spend their Saturdays at Owen Owens Field. Parents began attending games even though they didn't have a son on the team.

"For the first time we had uniforms with something other than the number on it," Schuler recalls. "We started having pep rallies, and players were required to wear their jerseys on game days. People started showing up for games, people who hadn't been there in previous years. Nothing like that had ever happened at that school before."

The mighty Salesian Chieftans and their legendary coach Dan Shaughnessy were slated to host the upstart Spartans the following week in what was shaping up as the biggest game in De La Salle history. The Spartans had leaped to a No. 8 ranking in the 2A prep poll, and the winner of this game would have the inside track at winning the league championship.

"De La Salle a football power? You gotta be kidding!" was how *Contra Costa Times* sportswriter Don Peterson began his column that week.

"I really didn't expect us to be 5–1 right now," Ladouceur told Peterson. "But I did feel this team had potential. I think a lot of our kids wanted to win but didn't know how."

The Chieftans were the defending CAL champion and a regional power who had outscored opponents 198–6 the year before. They were 6–0 and led by standout running back Rodney Webster, who was coming off a 200-yard rushing performance against Moreau.

Shaughnessy's teams were hard-nosed and physical, and he was famous for always having a trick play or four up his sleeve.

114

"The aura and mystique around Shaughnessy and Salesian back then was pretty damned intimidating," Crespi remembers.

The junior varsity game dragged on forever as adrenaline seemed to leak out of De La Salle's varsity players with each additional minute they were forced to wait. Ladouceur was confident until he addressed his players in the tiny locker room minutes before the game.

"I could see fear in their eyes," he said. "It was the most obvious feeling I've ever gotten from a group of guys. I knew right then we weren't going to win. They were looking at me like I was going to give them something they needed. I didn't have anything."

Webster returned the opening kickoff for a 97-yard touchdown and the rout was on. When Salesian intercepted a Heaney pass and returned it for a touchdown moments later, the game was essentially over.

Salesian led 24–0 and was driving with less than two minutes left when a timeout was called. They eventually added a fourth touchdown against demoralized De La Salle and rubbed it in with a fourth 2-point conversion for a resounding 32–0 triumph.

"We weren't ready for the big boys yet, obviously," Heaney said.

It was a deflating defeat but there was still plenty to play for, especially with hated Moreau the next team on the schedule. Players had been talking about their "rivalry" with the Catholic school in Hayward ever since Ladouceur arrived at De La Salle.

"They're not your rival if they kick your ass every year," Ladouceur informed them. "They can't be your rival until you beat them."

De La Salle led Moreau 17–7 early in the third quarter after two touchdown runs by Heaney, but Moreau answered with scoring passes of 74 and 80 yards to the tight end over the middle. The Spartans regained the lead only to watch hated Moreau score the game-winning touchdown on a 45-yard run with 3:34 left in the fourth quarter.

The 26–24 defeat dropped De La Salle out of the prep poll heading into the season finale against St. Patrick's of Vallejo. Heaney played the best game of his career against St. Patrick's, completing 10 of 11 passes for 167 yards as the Spartans ended Ladouceur's initial season with a 42–7 win.

The Spartans finished with a 6–3 record, which was the first winning season in school history and good for second in the CAL. They played for the league title, and an unprecedented six players, including Heaney, Schuler, Young, and Crespi, received postseason honors.

"We had no athletes on that team," Crespi recalls. "Looking back on that year, I don't know how we won as many games as we did."

ST. FRANCIS
A Giant Step Backwards

t he St. Francis High School campus is similar to De La Salle's. An ancient oak tree shades the northwest corner of Ron Calcagno Stadium, which lights up like a birthday cake when the sun disappears behind the Los Altos hills.

It's an intimate setting for a high school football game, far removed from the pageantry and hype in Honolulu the week before, when the team played at Aloha Stadium. The yellow school bus that carried De La Salle coaches and players fifty-nine miles south to Mountain View idles through campus unnoticed. This nonconference game will be televised, but on a local cable access channel. The panel van doubling as the satellite truck looks as if it might have once delivered bread.

Nobody in the visitors' locker room complains when they have to take turns getting dressed in the cramped conditions. These facilities are more typical of the high school football experience than were the spacious accommodations at Aloha Stadium. Here, players sit on rows of benches outside the locker room door and beneath a dim street light waiting to stretch.

The victorious De La Salle players returned from Hawaii exhausted and sleep-deprived just as a heat wave gripped the East Bay. Players slogged through a week of practice every bit as uninspired as the workouts leading up to the season opener against Mitty. The feeling of urgency that fueled what Ladouceur would later call one of the toughest practice weeks in school history had been left behind in Honolulu.

"I don't have a good feeling about tonight," Ladouceur said while picking at a meat pie at a Concord deli early in the afternoon. "They do enough to keep the ball away from us. They hit well. They always play good defense. They know us. That coaching staff has been around forever. They have a lot going for them. Plus, whenever you play a Catholic school they have more fight in them, they're more disciplined. They just seem more courageous in a lot of ways. I don't know why that is but that's how it appears to me. They don't give up as easily."

The St. Francis Lancers have one of the most storied programs in the Bay Area and will not be intimidated by De La Salle. Ladouceur told his players early in the week about how the Spartans' 1998 team traveled to Mountain View after a 28–21 victory over Mater Dei, the biggest win in school history at that point. The Spartans came out flat and led 7–0 at halftime before prevailing 21–0, which is hardly a comfortable margin of victory for what has been the most dominant team in the state. St. Francis' willingness to schedule De La Salle every season makes it one of the greatest threats to The Streak. The school won 13 West Catholic Athletic League titles and 11 Central Coast Section championships in the twenty-four years that Ron Calcagno headed the program. Longtime assistant Mike Mitchell took over in 1996 and won three of the next four section titles. The Lancers won only six games in 2000–01, but they always play De La Salle tough.

"They can devise a game plan that's very dangerous to us IF you come out tomorrow flat and not ready to play," Ladouceur told his team at its Thursday night meeting, his voice echoing through the garage. "If that happens I believe in my heart of hearts that this team has an excellent opportunity to beat you."

Maurice Drew's ankle has improved steadily since the St. Louis game, but he will not play against St. Francis, not with the matchup with powerful Long Beach Poly just two weeks away. Ladouceur is curious to see how the team will respond without him, which means expanded roles for Gino Ottoboni, Jackie Bates, and even Willie Glasper, the talented junior cornerback who has been longing for a chance to run the ball. Center/linebacker Cole Smith is still recovering from the concussion he suffered against St. Louis, and Erich Faustman is on the sidelines in street clothes nursing a badly sprained ankle.

None of that seems to matter when Ottoboni runs for 20 yards on the opening play of the game. The senior is similar to Drew in that he makes up for his lack of size with quickness and power. He lacks Drew's game-breaking speed and elusiveness, but he would star for most other teams.

Bates might have scored on the next play if he hadn't dropped a perfect pass from quarterback Britt Cecil. The Spartans punted only once against St. Louis, and that was late in the game when they wanted to milk the clock instead of attempting a field goal. Another incompletion against St. Francis brings the punt team onto the field after the first drive.

Ladouceur's jaw muscles flex and relax in gum-chewing cadence. It's impossible to tell how his team is faring on the field by watching the expression on his face. He wears a mask of quiet intensity whether the game is tied or his team leads by 50.

Ladouceur says little on the sideline, sometimes communicating with a nod, sometimes with a frown. Sometimes it appears that he has lost himself in the crowd, which is in stark contrast to Eidson, who is always easily found.

A veteran *Contra Costa Times* photographer spent years photographing Eidson before realizing that Ladouceur was the head coach. It's an honest mistake.

"If you didn't know who he was, you would wonder what he was doing on the sideline," St. Francis coach Mitchell observes from across the field.

Joe Aliotti paces the sideline, a blur of motion, sometimes walking 10 yards out onto the field to shout instructions to players or to plead his case with officials. Ever the traffic cop, Aliotti is in charge of substitutions, waving one player off the field and waving in another. He helps manage the game, presenting Ladouceur with the information needed to make the ultimate decisions.

Mark Panella's eyes never leave the quarterback. He meets Cecil as soon as he comes off the field in his dual role of tutor and cheerleader. Mike Blasquez watches for the slightest sign of injury. Eidson signals in plays when De La Salle is on defense and offers advice when Ladouceur's offense is on the field.

Ladouceur's success has been attributed to many different things, and rightly so, but defensive coordinators know he's a gifted play caller. Perhaps it's that gift of spatial awareness. He has an uncanny ability to sense open spaces on the field, and he finds a way to get the ball into that space.

He wears khaki slacks, black cross trainers, and a Spartans green windbreaker, but no headphones or even a hat. There's no eye in the sky offering advice from above. He considers input but relies mostly on his own intuition.

"He always seems to have an answer," Mitchell said with a sigh. "I don't know if I'd say he's always a step ahead of you, but he's close to it."

On rare nights such as this, it doesn't seem to matter what he calls.

St. Francis running back William Taufoou worried Ladouceur all week. He was the sophomore of the year in the WCAL the previous season, and at 6', 235 pounds, he is the type of punishing runner that can allow Mitchell's team to control the ball and keep the explosive De La Salle offense off the field.

"You've got to gang-tackle him and hammer him," Ladouceur told his players while they were reviewing their checklist the night before. "Lay some hurt on that guy. Get him going sideways, that's when he's in trouble. If he's going straight up the field with a head of steam, good luck."

Cameron Colvin throws a reverse pass to De'Montae Fitzgerald on the second play of De La Salle's ensuing drive for a 37-yard gain. Cecil fumbles on the next play, however, giving the ball back to the Lancers at their 23-yard line. Colvin catches a punt after the defense holds, shakes a tackler on the far sideline, and outruns would-be tacklers back across the field before being tripped up at the St. Francis 40. But the scoreless quarter comes to a close with a busted play and a near interception that foretells more mistakes to come.

Colvin is developing into a big-time player, reminding some long-time observers of former De La Salle great Amani Toomer, who went on to Michigan and is now starring for the New York Giants. He lacks Toomer's otherworldly speed but has a knack for keeping his body between the defender and the ball. He wants to play major college football at a university far away, where nobody will know about his tragic family history. Then he wants to play in the NFL.

Every catch brings him closer to that reality. That's how he thinks of it, anyway. Every time he runs downfield, sees the ball in the air and hears the defensive back laboring to catch up, whenever he feels that ball fall out of the sky and into his waiting hands, he believes he is inching closer to his goals.

He stretches out parallel to the ground to make another spectacular catch for a 41-yard gain. An unblocked defensive end hits Cecil as he is pitching to Glasper on the next play, resulting in a fumble and a loss of nine yards. Cecil completes a pass to tight end Terrance Kelly over the middle for a 26-yard gain; Kelly fumbles the ball away after being hit from behind.

De La Salle often benefits from short punts because opposing coaches instruct their punter to kick the ball out of bounds rather than risk a long return. High school punters aren't asked to do this often, and the result can be a shanked punt that glances off the side of their foot, giving the Spartans the kind of field position the coach hoped to avoid in the first place.

That's what happens after St. Francis' next possession. A 14-yard punt gives De La Salle a first down at the St. Francis 34-yard line. Cecil hits Fitzgerald for a 19-yard gain and Bates, sure-footed in his size 11s, eventually scores on a 2-yard run for a 7–0 lead with 5:10 left in the second quarter.

It's not uncommon for an opponent to play tough for a quarter before a De La Salle touchdown opens the floodgates for more scoring. But the Lancers buck this trend with a slow, sustained drive that is kept alive when the usually reliable Parker Hanks jumps offside on fourth-and-2. Eidson looks as if he might spontaneously combust on the sideline.

Facing a third-and-long at De La Salle's 33-yard line, senior St. Francis quarterback Kyle Spraker avoids the rush of Erik Sandie and Chris Mulvanny and fires a perfect pass that sails through his receiver's hands in the end zone. The collective groan from the home crowd gives way to silence as the receiver lies motionless in the end zone, his hands on his helmet, knowing that a rare chance to tie De La Salle has just slipped through his fingers.

The Spartans go into the locker room leading 7–0. The game is unfolding just as Ladouceur has predicted. It is 1998 all over again.

The coaching staff has seen this coming since early in the week. It tried to shake the players out of their doldrums on Thursday night. By then, of course, it was too late. The week had already been wasted.

"Playing one good game against St. Louis of Honolulu in front of 30,000 people, that's not Spartan football," assistant coach Justin Alumbaugh said during an impassioned speech. "Coming back the next week when you're hurt, when you're not feeling good, and beating a team that wants to knock your dick off, now that's Spartan football. That's a big game. Anybody can get up for St. Louis. That's not the test of a true Spartan. Come back the next week and the week after that. This is a bigger game. We expected you to be ready for St. Louis. If you have any balls you'll be ready for St. Francis."

Alumbaugh is more like Ladouceur than anyone else on the staff. He is one of the most decorated athletes in De La Salle history but is unassuming, has the gift of perspective more often found in people twice his age, and has Ladouceur's ponderous gait. Most coaches would not want to succeed a legend. Alumbaugh's only fear is that he won't have the same impact on his players that Ladouceur has.

He knows this program better than anyone. Alumbaugh coaches linebackers and offensive linemen and therefore is the only coach aware of the intricacies of both the offensive and defensive game plans. Ladouceur and Eidson have worked together for so long and trust each other so completely that they are often unaware of the specific strategies the other has chosen to employ during a given week.

Alumbaugh's blond hair is parted down the middle and he has a long face, a lantern jaw, and an easy smile. He was a two-way star and a three-year starter who was so perceptive that he would often call out an opponent's play before the snap based on the formation. In ten minutes he could memorize a scouting report Ladouceur took ten hours to meticulously compile. By his senior year, there were times when he was doing as much coaching as playing.

"He's got a good heart, good sense of humor that you've got to have," Ladouceur says. "He doesn't take himself too seriously, which is good, yet he does, which is good. But the most important thing is he's got a feel for the game and he knows how to solve problems out on the field. He sees how it all fits together. His potential to know a lot about the game is unlimited. He could be a NFL head coach. He's that smart."

Alumbaugh was an all-state linebacker his senior year and had invitations to walk on at several Pac-10 schools, as well as scholarship offers from smaller Division-I programs. Like many De La Salle players, however, he felt dehumanized by the recruiting process and ended his college career before it started.

He remembers one incident in particular. He was practicing with the baseball team when Aliotti summoned him to meet with a UCLA recruiter. Alumbaugh had his heart set on going to UCLA, where his father had played guard in the 1970s. He didn't care if he played football or not.

The recruiter didn't bother to introduce himself when Alumbaugh extended his hand. Instead, he turned to Aliotti and said: "He's not 6'1"."

Nice to meet you, too, Alumbaugh thought.

Ladouceur called later that summer. The fall semester at UCLA didn't begin until October. Would he be interested in coaching until then? Alumbaugh had worked at Ladouceur's Championship Football camps but had never seriously considered a future in coaching. He would spend the next four years coaching at De La Salle before leaving for college. He was more surprised than anyone to learn that he was No. 1 on Ladouceur's list of eventual successors.

He will be leaving again this year, even though he has already earned a degree in history from UCLA. He plans to tour Europe with his brother, but has promised not to depart until after the Long Beach Poly game.

"When he leaves our team really misses him," Ladouceur said. "The last two years he was in tears and his guys were in tears when they said goodbye to each other. That's something special that you don't see a lot. He gives nonstop vigilant feedback on every play, whether players are doing the right job or the wrong job. Those kids appreciate that and miss it when he's gone."

The Spartans take a 14–0 lead over St. Francis on their first possession of the second half. A 57-yard scamper by Bates sets up Ottoboni's 5-yard touchdown run, but the offense resumes struggling after that. The Lancers' wishbone attack limits De La Salle to three possessions in the second half. A 47-yard touchdown pass to Terrance Kelly is called back because of a holding penalty. De La Salle tries to lure St. Francis offside later in the drive when Hanks jumps from his tight end position, forcing another Tony Binswanger punt.

Fortunately the defense, Chris Mulvanny in particular, is carrying the day. Mulvanny is wreaking havoc all over the field. He reads a screen pass perfectly and drops Taufoou for a 2-yard loss. He sacks Spraker to end a drive and makes three straight tackles on the Lancers' next possession.

Mulvanny had met with defensive line coach Geldermann on Wednesday. He was distraught over his performance in Hawaii and felt that problems at home were carrying over onto the field. His parents are divorced and his mom suffers from a medical condition that causes swelling in the lower legs, which can make it difficult to walk.

Her son was trying to ease her load by running errands and helping out around the house. Coming off the Honolulu trip, it had taken a toll.

"I bring my emotions to practice," he explains. "If I have an episode at home I dwell on it. I'm constantly thinking of ways to help my family."

Mulvanny has sandy blonde hair, piercing blue eyes, a boxer's nose, and the sculpted cheekbones of a model. He is one of the few players on the team who didn't enter the school as an incoming freshman. He attended Deer Valley High School in Antioch through the tenth grade and was carrying a 3.8 grade-point average. He had been called up to varsity midway through his sophomore year, and won the shot put and discus competitions at the junior varsity league track meet. But Chris Mulvanny felt unsatisfied, as if he were stuck in a routine. He wanted to do more.

He had always been infatuated with De La Salle and even once served as a ball boy. He made the inquiries himself. He filled out all the applications, asking his mother only for her signature, and was surprised to learn he had been accepted for his junior year. His mom sold their house in Antioch to pay for his tuition and moved with his brother and sister into a townhouse closer to campus.

"I wanted to go to De La Salle since the fifth grade," he said. "From what I saw and heard, De La Salle students were highly thought of because it takes a lot to go to that school and succeed. That's where I wanted to be."

His new teammates had already spent two years studying and working out together by the time he arrived. He didn't fit in. He spent his junior season on the scout team trying to figure out what it all meant. The alcohol policy, for example. Who enforced it? When he asked Ladouceur this question, the coach pointed his finger right back at him. That's what he didn't get. He didn't understand how they could be expected to police themselves.

On the field he had always relied on his instincts. It was a simple game. If someone ran with the ball, he would run after the person with the ball. The team concept at De La Salle was much more complicated; in fact, everything at the school he had always wanted to attend was much more complicated. It wasn't until the summer before his senior year that he realized he had to look inward to succeed.

"When I came in as a junior I was a cocky kid and very cavalier," Mulvanny recalls. "I had to learn true humility. I had to have more respect for other people."

Nobody knew what to do with Mulvanny when fall practices began. They didn't need him at linebacker or safety. Geldermann thought his quickness might make him an effective pass rusher as an undersized defensive end. The other coaches were content to let Geldermann deal with Mulvanny.

Geldermann rode him harder than anybody during fall practices. Mulvanny had unharnessed talent but was maddening to coach. You could tell him he was responsible for outside containment, drill it in his head, and he would take off after the quarterback like a retriever chasing a tennis ball.

John Chan and Cole Smith, who had the unenviable task of lining up against Mulvanny in practice, pulled him aside and encouraged him. He had the speed to be a dominant outside pass rusher, they told him. Use it. He had high expectations for himself but felt inadequate during his first two games. He threw himself into preparation leading up to the St. Francis game, studying film and memorizing his scouting report. So many emotions were festering. He wanted to show his teammates what he could do, which was why he stood up in Thursday night's team meeting and said what he said.

"I'm ready for this game tomorrow," he told his teammates. "I've been mentally preparing and physically preparing and I just want to unload on someone. I want to be one of the people who makes something happen."

It's moments like this that make the Spartans program so special, at least in Blasquez's opinion. He admires the way players stand up and call themselves out in front of their teammates. It takes guts. When several players are willing to do it, he knows the team is on the verge of something special.

Colvin and Drew called themselves out before the Hawaii game and delivered. Now Mulvanny was doing the same, but as Blasquez looked around the garage twenty-four hours before the St. Francis game, he wondered about everyone else. What was it about this team that made players so tentative?

Ladouceur had been asking himself the same question. It takes courage to stand up in front of your teammates and reveal what lies deep in your heart. But that's the kind of courage it takes to play for this team, which is what Ladouceur had said the night before. He had seen players call themselves out hundreds of times through the years, and what impressed him most was they almost always followed through. This team wasn't like that. This team played it safe.

Mulvanny is the exception, just like Drew and Colvin had been exceptions. Mulvanny is following through. De La Salle, held without a sack in its first two games, begins piling them up in the second half as St. Francis throws the ball to get back in the game. Mike Pittore flushes Spraker into Mulvanny for a sack on the first play of the next drive. Mulvanny later adds a third sack. He also has two tackles for a loss, 13 total tackles, and a fumble recovery.

"Good job coach, you saved us," Aliotti says to Eidson when clock expires. "We should make them walk home," he says of the offensive players.

The no-longer-suspect defense registers its second shutout in three weeks, but an offense that has averaged 40 points per game during The Streak musters only 14 points for the second time in three weeks. There are four fumbles. Even Colvin, who has played so well the past two weeks, muffs a punt. There have been near interceptions, busted plays, and uncharacteristic penalties.

"Jackie, man, we're going to have to work so hard this week," Colvin tells Bates after the game is over, knowing that the dispassionate performance by the offense will result in another brutal week of practice.

Fans crowd around the gate that leads to the locker rooms and slap De La Salle players encouragingly on the shoulder pads after their 14–0 win. "Keep that streak alive!" one man says. "Man, I'm bigger than these guys," says another. "Boy, you guys are really scary," a sarcastic voice calls out.

They have allowed the momentum they generated with the victory over St. Louis to stagnate. They came together in Hawaii only to come home and fall apart. Without Drew, this team was as vulnerable as it had been against Mitty.

The worst part is, the showdown with Long Beach Poly is two weeks away.

"The Streak is over in two weeks anyway," Eidson said quietly before boarding the bus. "There's no way we're going to beat Poly."

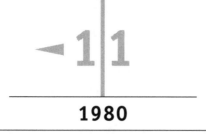

1980

THE SPIRIT OF BROTHER LAURENCE

brother Laurence Allen was the school's most popular teacher. He embraced the new football coach and religion teacher from the start, even convincing skeptical faculty members and students that the inexperienced Ladouceur would fit in. Unlike some other administrators, he believed in the importance of a football program as long as it embraced the philosophy of the school. He quickly became Ladouceur's friend and ally, but the new coach's first year at the De La Salle campus would be Brother Laurence's last. The dynamic young Brother planned to take a sabbatical next fall to pursue a Master's degree in substance-abuse counseling at the University of Arizona. He would be sorely missed by teachers and students alike.

"I patterned myself after him on just about everything," Ladouceur said. "I knew I could always go to him no matter what was going on, whether it was in the classroom, on the field, or in my personal life, and he would help me."

Brother Laurence had never felt closer to a group of seniors. He didn't want to leave until he and his students had one last adventure. He was an experienced whitewater rafter who had saved enough from his stipend to buy his own raft. He was the one who suggested going to the river. There had been a deep snowpack in the Sierra that winter. Conditions would be ideal. It would be the perfect way to end the school year.

Nineteen seniors, including numerous football players, and a junior left early one morning. Brother Laurence led the caravan in a pickup truck piled high with inner tubes.

The Mokelumne River snakes through the Sierra Nevada foothills three miles south of the former Gold Rush boomtown of Jackson. It's surrounded by rugged country dotted with granite rock formations, old-growth forests, and some of the best whitewater in the central Sierra.

Brother Laurence was as excited as his students when the caravan crossed the bridge and they peered down at the water rushing beneath it. It looked like a real adventure.

"It didn't look like a raging torrent from the bank," Mark Mullen said. "You couldn't tell how rough it was until you got in."

Runoff from higher elevations made the water even colder than they had expected. It didn't dampen their enthusiasm. The sun was warm as the first group waded into the clear blue water at midmorning.

Some wore wetsuits, others life jackets. Brother Laurence had neither. He warned them to get out of the river before they reached the bridge or risk the more perilous whitewater below.

Brother Laurence and Jack Henderson were the last ones in the water. They had developed a lasting bond during the previous four years. Laurence told friends that he had never felt closer to a student. Henderson decided to join the Brothers largely because of Brother Laurence's influence.

They talked all the way down the river, passing other groups of tubers until they were in the lead. Intermittent clouds blocked the sun and raised goose bumps on their arms. The water was ice cold and running fast. Everyone was relieved when they rounded a bend in the river and saw the bridge.

Between Brother Laurence and Jack Henderson and the end of the run stood a standing wave they couldn't avoid. They braced themselves but couldn't keep from flipping over. Henderson surfaced in the middle of the river and immediately saw Brother Laurence's head bobbing downriver.

He watched as Brother Laurence flipped his brown hair out of his eyes, sparkling droplets forming a high, arching rooster tail above the water.

Their tubes floated between them. Jack swam hard for the nearest one. He was kicking his way toward shore when the current pinned his leg in a tangle of submerged tree branches.

Mark Mullen played running back and outside linebacker for Ladouceur in 1979. He had seen Jack and Laurence flip and hoped to avoid a similar fate. He was freezing. He clutched his tube with both arms when he hit the same wave, but he couldn't keep from capsizing.

"The water was so cold it was hard to breathe," he said. "If I hadn't gotten my arm over my inner tube I would've been in trouble."

As he was struggling toward the shore, looking for a place to pull himself out of the current, he saw Henderson.

"The force of the water was crushing him against a tree," Mullen said. "He was stuck. We looked at each other. He was terrified. He had a look of absolute terror on his face."

Henderson couldn't free his foot no matter how hard he tried. His weight coupled with the current slowly dragged him under until he was eight inches below the surface and resigned to his fate.

He looked up and saw the sunlight dancing on the surface and sparkling silt rushing over him.

"I'm thinking I've had a good life and all that stuff," Henderson said. "I just stayed there looking at the beauty of the water and everything rushing over me. Then it was like, 'Fuck this.'"

He began kicking, desperately struggling, finally jerking his foot free, ripping a large piece of skin off the back of his heel.

John McKenna had not gotten out of the water before the bridge. He negotiated the first series of rapids before being pitched from his tube. He clung to a partially submerged rock but didn't know how much longer he could hold on. Students formed a human chain and rescued him.

"I felt very fortunate to get out of that river," McKenna said. "I didn't know which way to go underwater. It was all bubbles and murkiness. It was pretty terrifying. I felt I caught a break."

Mullen scrambled up the bank to help Henderson. His classmates had already formed a human chain and were fishing him from the water.

"After I could talk I said, 'Where's Brother Laurence?'" Henderson recalls. "Nobody had thought about Brother Laurence until I said that."

The thought occurred to them at once: Brother Laurence must have gone under the bridge. They immediately began searching the banks. A few desperate minutes later they realized they had to get organized, and they quickly split up into two groups and began a thorough search of both riverbanks. Laurence was young and a strong swimmer. Maybe he was just hiding somewhere, ready to jump out and scare them. It was something he might do. Or he could've hit his head on a rock and be lying unconscious somewhere.

Nobody wanted to consider any other alternative.

His injured heel kept Jack Henderson from joining his classmates. He drove a few miles below the first bridge until he came to a second bridge where two men were fishing. The fishermen said they hadn't seen anything in the water. Henderson believed them. The river was wide and calm. Anything floating past would've been easily spotted. Henderson then drove into Jackson to find help.

McKenna was searching the banks when he found what he thought might be a body trapped under a rock shelf in shallow water. The students, hearts pounding, formed another human chain. McKenna stood in the thigh-deep water trying to dredge the object from beneath the ledge with a long branch. Someone screamed as a bleached log floated innocently to the surface.

"I distinctly remember having some pretty awful nightmares," Mullen says.

Other students broke into a cabin overlooking the river to call for help. Still others found footprints leading up the riverbank. Perhaps Laurence was dazed and wandering.

Rescue teams arrived to comb the river. A search plane buzzed overhead. There was no sign of Brother Laurence.

"As the evening wore on and the light began to fade, we resigned ourselves to not finding him that day," McKenna said.

They never gave up hope. Monday was a school holiday. By Tuesday wild rumors circulated around campus. Perhaps Brother Laurence had amnesia and had been picked up along the road. Maybe he crawled into the brush and passed out. "We were thinking a lot of weird things at that point," Henderson recollects. "Jesus rose on the third day, too."

At noon on Wednesday a woman spotted a body near the second bridge, less than two miles from where Brother Laurence had last been seen. Their worst fears were realized. Students and teachers were devastated. Classes were canceled.

"I've never seen such a dramatic change on campus," linebacker Bob

Guelld says. "People were wandering all over trying to find a quiet place. Teachers were trying to help, but they were in the same place we were."

The prayer service planned for Brother Laurence at St. Mary's College chapel instead became his memorial service. The church was packed. Ladouceur remembers being as nervous as he has ever been before speaking at Brother Laurence's funeral that day.

"He was my mentor for just about everything," Ladouceur says. "He believed in me without even knowing me that well. The school lost a great educator and I lost someone who believed in me and helped me from the very start."

Brother Robb Wallace delivered the eulogy. He talked about how much Laurence cared for and worried about kids, how he believed that students must be allowed to arrive at their own conclusions. He spoke of his humor, his near-photographic memory, and his spirituality.

"When Laurence's Dad died a few years ago, I wrote him a letter. He answered and one line was classic Laurence Allen. It began, 'It seems to me loss is not the point. The point is the experience.'

"And the point here is not the loss of Laurence, it's the experience of Laurence. And I don't mean simply the experience we had of Laurence— the memories. I mean the experience now as we try to make sense of his death, as we try to understand the message of his life, as we rely on one another for strength, for comfort, for counsel...."

As the senior class moderator, Brother Laurence had been in charge of graduation. His room at the Brothers' residence was always a mess. His desk was usually in a similar state, which made seniors all the more surprised when they entered his office to take control of graduation ceremonies.

Every detail involved with the ceremony was laid out. There was a to-do list. There was a schedule for when the songs would be sung and reminders to pick up programs and trophies. It was all so out of character, so predetermined that some students were spooked. It was as if he were testing them.

The seniors had been rehearsing those songs for months with no improvement. They practiced together after the funeral and stood in teary silence after hitting every note. Brother Jerome heard them. He told them it had been like listening to the voices of angels. It was one in a series of powerful events in the wake of the seemingly innocent outing that would forever shape the lives of the participants.

"Right before we hit the wave he told me to stay in the center, but if I drifted to the side not to worry. The water would bring me back to the middle," Henderson said. "I've taken it as a life lesson. If I start to drift I don't worry. I know I'll go back to the center. It's the last thing he said to me, and it has been the guide to my life."

Students refused help offered by various faculty members. They had planned this ceremony together with Brother Laurence. Now that he was gone they would do it themselves. Only one adult could participate. They needed someone to hand out the diplomas.

Those who attended said it was one of the most impressive graduation ceremonies ever staged at the school. It was the first time Ladouceur saw the spirit of empowerment and accountability that Brother Laurence helped instill in his students. The ceremony was executed just as Brother Laurence planned it, except for the tears. Ladouceur was so impressed that he became determined to create that same spirit within his football program.

A memorial to Brother Laurence was dedicated at the school in 2000. Elsewhere on campus, a haunting reminder of his contribution to a football program that he would never see win the first of its many championships is stuck to the dusty bottom shelf of an all-but-forgotten equipment closet.

They are the words he wrote on a box while helping newly hired Bob Ladouceur sort the weights that students brought from home, the weights that Brother Laurence somehow found the money to replace. Those replacement weights served as a foundation to a program that emphasized strength training.

The first five letters of "worthless" have been ripped away, but you can read the rest in his bold, black script: "less Weights."

The school wasn't the same after the loss of Brother Laurence. Students and teachers scattered over the summer. When they returned, the pall remained.

"That school went through hell for the next few years," former graduate and long-time teacher Pete Kelly says. "We didn't know how to grieve, so we started focusing on winning football games."

12

LA COSTA CANYON
The Power of Commitment

| | | | | | | | | |

"**h**as anyone told Chris Biller he can't play?" Justin Alumbaugh asks in the upstairs office after a 2002 preseason practice.

His question is met with silence. It had been three weeks since Chris Biller hit Erik Sandie during the first full-contact practice and felt a tingling sensation in his arms, which was subsequently diagnosed as spinal stenosis. Biller remained hopeful that he would be able to return to the team, but the coaching staff had all but eliminated the possibility. There was no way Ladouceur would let the junior offensive lineman back on the field unless he had full medical clearance and his parents' approval. But two cervical spine specialists had recommended that Biller not be allowed to play contact sports.

Chris Biller felt as if he'd been ambushed. All he had wanted his whole life was to play football at De La Salle just like his older brother, who was now playing for St. Mary's College. His identity was wrapped up in the game. He was even counting on a small-school scholarship to help him afford college.

He had been so close to realizing his dream. He had worked hard during the offseason to pack muscle onto his stocky frame. He was confident he would get a chance to play, perhaps even start as a junior. Then, after his first full-contact practice as a varsity player, he was faced with the possibility of never putting on a helmet again.

Yet after a few days he felt fine. His narrow spinal canal hadn't been an issue in previous years. Why was it an issue now? He was as strong as anybody in the junior class. His short arms and legs rippled with thick muscles. He was in the best shape of his life, but all he could do was watch longingly from the sidelines.

Biller's teammates would look enviously at him while running gassers after practice, as if he were the lucky one, when all he wanted was to join them. It didn't matter how often his friends tried to include him— he didn't feel like part of the team because he wasn't playing.

Biller was beginning to accept his fate. He told his mother he was glad it was his career that was ending, and that this nightmare wasn't happening to someone like Jackie Bates, who would have a chance at a Division-I scholarship.

"It may force him to grow in another direction," Ladouceur said matter-of-factly. "It could turn into a positive for him."

Dr. Wilhelmy and trainer Mike Blasquez hadn't given up, but they didn't want to give Biller false hope, either. They consulted with numerous experts, including a Los Angeles-based spine specialist.

Dr. Wilhelmy found an exhaustive study of college and NFL football players which concluded that players with spinal stenosis ran a greater risk of quadriplegic-type injuries only in the specific case of spinal fractures. But the study also found that spinal fractures did not occur more frequently in players with spinal stenosis.

In other words, Biller might be more prone to the type of temporary symptoms he experienced after the collision with Sandie. If MRIs revealed no new injuries, however, he could safely return to the field after a sufficient recovery period.

"It's a situation where you have to ask yourself, 'What are the risks?'" Dr. Wilhelmy said, his gray hair dancing in the breeze as he stood on the sideline watching practice. "A boy who has spinal stenosis definitely is at a greater risk for temporary nerve palsy, but he's not at a greater risk for a quadriplegic-type injury unless he has a spinal fracture. The study of six years shows that the chance of him getting a spinal fracture is no greater than anybody else's in a football uniform."

Dr. Wilhelmy forwarded his findings to the leading specialists employed by Biller's health care provider. After reviewing the available data, the specialists agreed with Dr. Wilhelmy's opinion.

Biller was watching films at lunch during the week before the game against La Costa Canyon when assistant coach Joe Aliotti walked into the room wearing a smile on his face and holding a medical clearance form in his hand. They made a compromise. Biller wouldn't be allowed to play defense because that's where most head and neck injuries occur, but he could return to practice and would be allowed to play offense.

Chris Biller was a football player again.

"I was blown out of the water," his mother Sue Biller said. "I couldn't believe it. They took so much interest in him and went to such lengths to meet with the best doctors and experts. I was utterly amazed."

Biller's athletic rebirth came at an opportune time. The offensive line had taken another step back against St. Francis, although turnovers and penalties played an even more prominent role in the substandard offensive output.

John Chan and Erik Sandie had been so offended by the offensive line's lackluster performance in the season-opening win over Archbishop Mitty that they had a late-night phone conversation a few days later. How could this be happening during their senior year? They spoke for more than an hour and were both in tears when they finally hung up the phone.

They thought they had put the first game behind them with a solid performance in Hawaii. But after the St. Francis game, Ladouceur was harping on the same things he had harped on during the preseason, and the linemen knew he was right. They didn't understand what it took to play at the highest level. They weren't aggressive enough. They were making too many mental mistakes. They sometimes played as if the game were a burden. Where was the joy? Where was their passion for the game?

"It was so sad because we worked so hard during the offseason but we couldn't put it together," Chan said. "The aggressiveness wasn't always there. We weren't hitting, and that had never happened before."

Biller returned to practice on Wednesday before the La Costa Canyon game, filled with six weeks of pent-up frustration. He has a mean streak; that much was obvious when he dominated on the junior varsity level the year before. At 5'9", 205 pounds, he epitomizes the type of offensive lineman that has long served as the foundation for the De La Salle program.

He is strong and quick and has a low center of gravity. He can think on his feet and plays the game with aggression. He doesn't always make the smart play, but he seeks out contact. No one takes more pride in planting a defender flat on his back.

Biller fires off the ball with such ferocity on his first play back at practice that an opposing player's spit drips off his facemask. He ear-holes linebacker Terrance Kelly on a screen pass a few plays later.

"Biller has the most heart of anybody on that line," Chan said. "He gets it from somewhere and I wish I had it. He's got that spark that I never had because everybody else around me always had it."

Biller can't wait to get back in his stance for the next play. His enthusiasm is contagious. His linemates are breaking the huddle and racing up to the line. They are firing off the ball more quickly, holding blocks longer, and punishing the scout team. The offense is suddenly alive.

It is the best practice of the season, and Biller is the spark plug.

"He wanted to play so much," Sandie said. "He reminded everybody of what we were playing for. It wasn't about the coaches making us do it. It was about us wanting to do it."

Biller had slept little the night before. The long weeks of uncertainty have been emotionally draining. He is physically exhausted after his first full-contact practice in thirty-nine days, and his sleep that night is filled with strange, wonderful, delirious dreams.

Few have contributed so much in so little time to De La Salle football than has Steve Alexakos.

The former NFL offensive lineman was as intimidating as any coach in the program, save Ladouceur. Alexakos wears a beard and a menacing stare and has a deep, guttural voice that seems to emanate from within a dark cavern.

Technically he is a businessman. But he considers himself first and foremost a mentor to young men. He began coaching his sons in youth football and followed them to De La Salle before leaving the program in 1994 to become the line coach at his alma mater, San Jose State.

Alexakos spent a relatively short four years as an assistant coach at

De La Salle, but his legacy remains very much alive. He refined the techniques that help offensive linemen perform at increasingly higher levels. He spent his final summer at the school teaching Ladouceur everything he knew because Ladouceur insisted on coaching the offensive line himself. Ladouceur believes that a coach has to spend as much time teaching technique to each individual offensive lineman as he would with the quarterback. It was too important to trust anyone else with the job.

Alexakos introduced the numbering system that helps players identify where defenders line up and relay the information to the coaching staff. He also simplified blocking for the veer, teaching players to count the defenders in the "box," or those playing close to the line of scrimmage, from the outside in. That's one reason why De La Salle's linemen always have their heads up as they approach the line before a play. They're counting.

Alexakos was the junior varsity line coach in 1991 when Ladouceur called him up to the varsity staff. Alexakos initially refused the promotion.

He had made a commitment to his current players, he said, and he wasn't going to leave them in midseason. Finally Ladouceur spoke directly to the JV linemen, explaining how much Alexakos was needed on the varsity staff. They were the ones who urged Alexakos to do what was best for the program. He reluctantly agreed.

"When he came [onto the varsity staff] I realized how much I'd let these guys slide accountability-wise," Ladouceur recalls. "I wasn't even holding my coaches accountable. He was a breath of fresh air. He came in and said, 'Are we going to do this right or are we going to accept mediocrity?'"

The team was running gassers after practice one day when Ladouceur's new line coach told him that some of the players were cruising toward the finish line instead of running hard through the line as instructed.

Gassers are the most dreaded conditioning drill. Players run back and forth across the field five times within a prescribed time. Coaches tell players to run hard through the sideline but they often ease up, especially if they're finishing well ahead of the time allotted.

What was Ladouceur prepared to do about it? That's what Alexakos wanted to know. Was he going to accept that?

Ladouceur sighed. He didn't really want to deal with it at the time.

"Does that mean I have to punish them all?" he asked.

"That depends on whether you're going to allow it to become part of the expectation, or hold them accountable," Alexakos answered.

"He called me on everything and really made me think," Ladouceur says in retrospect. "It was good for me."

Alexakos' greatest contribution came in the form of the white index cards that De La Salle players always seem to be carrying around. The commitment cards Alexakos introduced became a staple of the program.

Ladouceur was accustomed to setting team and offensive and defensive goals, but it was Alexakos who demanded that each of his linemen set individual goals before every game.

The new varsity assistant had just arrived at the site of his second team dinner when Ladouceur asked him to lead the team meeting that night. "I knew he was very capable and had a presence about him and the kids would listen," Ladouceur says. "At that point of the season I felt the rest of the staff, me included, had lost the kids a little bit. They needed to hear from somebody different."

Alexakos is a big believer in collective visualization and told players to imagine they were going through a preflight checklist from the cockpit of an airliner or fighter jet. But since they were football players and not pilots, he wanted their checklist to apply to the upcoming game.

Point by point he took them through the game plan and scouting report. Then he talked about the importance of individual goal-setting.

"I wanted them to put some pressure on themselves," Alexakos said. "If you do it in public it's conceited. But if you do it to an intimate friend it's a commitment, and the power of commitment is bonding."

One of his offensive linemen stood up that night and promised a friend that he would execute a seal block that was critical to the success of one of their most basic plays. His friend promised to critique his performance during the game and hold him accountable.

"Lad couldn't believe the power in it," Alexakos recalls.

Ladouceur expanded the concept until every player was required to make at least one weight-lifting goal, one practice goal, and one game goal, which are then written on index cards. Players give the cards to a teammate or coach who is responsible for determining whether the goals have been fulfilled. The findings are reported to the team the next week.

"I added the practice and lifting goals so kids who don't get in the game could still participate and improve themselves and measure their progress," Ladouceur said. "I wanted them to be striving for something, too."

Commitment cards fit Ladouceur's program perfectly. They teach goal-setting and accountability and keep nonstarters from giving up on their seasons. Players have taken the concept to another level, making life commitments to each other. Ladouceur remembers when a former player showed up at practice one day to inquire about former teammate Anthony Vontoure, who had recently been suspended from the University of Washington football team. He reached into his wallet and pulled out a wrinkled commitment card with Anthony's handwriting on it.

Anthony had committed to being the best person he could be. His friend wanted to mail him the card to remind him of that commitment.

"I said, 'Whoa,'" Ladouceur said, smiling at the memory. "He said he had saved every one of his commitment cards. I've asked other kids if they kept their commitment cards and they all say they have."

Now, at the team dinner on the eve before the 2002 La Costa game, Ladouceur calls into question his players' commitment to their commitment cards. He lists their unrealized offensive goals from the previous game. They had been lofty—300 yards rushing, no sacks, no punts—but they were unrealistic because the players hadn't practiced well enough during the week to expect that kind of production.

No punts? That might be a worthwhile goal for an offense that is hitting on all cylinders and that has practiced well, but not for a team that had slogged through practice all week without its best player. De La Salle had been forced to punt on its first drive against St. Francis.

"I don't know what to tell you guys," Ladouceur says. "I don't want to set your goals for you, but obviously you have a diluted sense of what you've prepared for and what you're capable of doing. It doesn't match up. It borders on saber-rattling to me."

Senior running back Gino Ottoboni stands up to read quarterback Britt Cecil's commitment card. Cecil's goals for the St. Francis game included 100 percent ball security, making the correct run reads 95 percent of the time, and a 65 percent completion rate.

A lineman's goal had been to take the proper first step on every play. Ladouceur noticed after watching the film that he hadn't taken the proper step even once. This is unacceptable to a coach who preaches that taking the proper first step is the first step to success, both individually and collectively. Another of his linemen says that his present goal is to work on his technique off the ball. "I don't want that goal," Ladouceur interrupts. "What the hell is that? Does that mean you're going to keep your head up? Your ass down? I want to hear specifics. That goal means nothing."

Ladouceur hadn't planned on addressing the team that night. He was going to let Eidson speak instead. But now he has something to say, which is how it usually works. He never prepares notes for his Thursday night lectures, although he sometimes polls assistants to find out what they think needs to be said. Mostly he articulates what has been rattling around his head all week, as is the case now:

"What I have to say to you relates to tomorrow night and the rest of the season, and it stems from the goal cards. My piece of advice to you is this: Stop living off De La Salle's lore and reputation and carve a niche for yourself. You guys want to live this De La Salle dream of bad-ass football but you haven't put the grittiness in to do it yourself, and that starts with goal cards. Lifting goals are great. They're good. But let me tell you something, they're the easiest ones to get. You can work faster to get an extra set in or add another five pounds. The next easiest are your practice goals because that's when you have to step out there and slam into people and that's when it starts getting gritty and uncomfortable. The next step is the game goals. As you noticed, nobody is getting their game goals—very few. Practice goals? Some. Then most everybody is getting their lifting goals.

"My opinion of you guys is you don't want the blood and sweat and grit that goes along with [being] a great football team. That's the part you want to skip. It's not going to happen that way. You guys have to get tougher, mentally and physically. Your failure to attend to detail on this team—that's mental toughness. You totally missed the point of the goal cards as far as what's going to make us a better team. I can go through every single one of you and tell you

141

exactly what you need to work on, and if you don't understand it you haven't been paying attention to what these coaches have been telling you. . . .

"If you want to have De La Salle across your chest—We're No. 1— well, I've got news for you. You're not No. 1. Having you guys sitting at No. 1 in the *USA Today* poll is a sham. You don't deserve to be there, and if I ever talked to the guy who does that poll I'd tell him so. I don't even think you deserve to be in the goddamn poll, to be honest with you. You haven't earned it. You haven't lived up to your moniker, your mascot, the Spartan. . . . We have to take another jump, I'm telling you right now. We have to take a huge jump. I don't mean to bring you down or throw water on your fire, but if you guys think you've got a big fire going right now you're kidding yourselves. You're under-achieving as a team. Why the hell would I stand up here and tell you that if I didn't see it? Maybe I'm way off base. Am I way off base?"

He turns to his assistant coaches, who sit stone-faced in metal chairs behind him. He isn't being theatrical. He wants to know. Maybe he's wrong, maybe he was expecting too much from this group.

Eidson stops chewing on the drawstring of his hooded sweatshirt long enough to laugh silently and shake his head, his answer an obvious no. Blasquez frowns and shakes his head. "No, coach," says Aliotti, making it unanimous. Thus reassured, Ladouceur continues:

"As far as tomorrow's game, I really don't know what you guys are going to do. I don't even know what to tell you. I really don't. I don't know if these guys are going to come out and start knocking you around, making you look like shit. I don't know if you're going to come out and do what you have been trained to do and knock those guys around and make them look like shit. I have no idea. I'll tell you one thing. If you strut around like peacocks—I'm a De La Salle football player—you're going to struggle. Get that out of your heads. You have to earn that, and you earn it week to week with consistency, mental toughness, focus, the grind, and the grittiness of it. I don't know if you're earning it or not. We'll find out in the game. . . .

"That's where I stand. I've told you for the last three, four weeks.

Do you want a shot at Poly? Do you want a SHOT to beat them? You guys better get tough quick. Are you guys capable of beating them? I truly in my heart believe yes. It's not going to be easy, and you've got to pay the price. So quit living in a dream. We're the De La Salle football team. We're No. 1 in the nation. That's a joke. Last Friday I bet there were at least two hundred teams that could've beaten you.

"So forget about De La Salle's mystique or reputation. I don't think about that shit. I don't even think about the winning streak or any of that stuff. I heard somebody in the stands behind me during the St. Francis game mention the streak. No bullshit. I didn't give a shit if you guys lost the streak. I'm focused 100 percent on you guys as a team. I want you to become what you're capable of becoming. It has nothing to do with wins. In so many ways I wish you were the first team we had here. I really do. I wish we had no history whatsoever. That history has served some teams well, but to be honest with you I don't think it's serving you well. . . .

"I usually want to hear from you guys personally and emotionally, but I don't want to hear from any of you right now. It would be like me getting up here and telling you about my Vietnam War experiences. I've never been to Vietnam so it wouldn't mean much. So, I'll put it to you frankly and plainly: Dating back to when we started these meetings, not every meeting, of course, but we've had meetings where guys would have tears rolling down their faces as they spoke about playing next to each other and side by side with their friends. That's how much they were putting into it. It wasn't phony. For you guys to stand up and say something of meaning you have to go through the wars first, the battles, throughout the whole week, not just in the games, the whole week. We'll wait until there's something worth hearing. If when it's all said and done there's nothing to hear, this will be a sad season."

Darrin Brown always told his players they should never be afraid to play the best. The La Costa Canyon coach asked his athletic director to inquire about a game against De La Salle. He was surprised to learn that Eidson was interested.

Brown flew to the Bay Area from Southern California after the game was announced to research hotel accommodations, tour Owen Owens Field, and exchange game tapes. He was blown away by what he found.

"I did a lot to prepare the kids," he said. "I told them it's not a huge stadium, and that helped a lot. But when we got here there were still kids who were shocked by how small it was. A few of the kids just couldn't accept it."

Playing De La Salle had been a controversial decision. Many in Carlsbad, located thirty-one miles north of San Diego, wondered if their coach had lost his mind. His team was scheduled to play nearby Torrey Pines the following week. How would playing the No. 1 team in the country prepare them to beat their archrivals?

La Costa Canyon High School has a student population of approximately 2,600 and has only been in existence since 1996. The Mavericks traveled to Nevada in 2001 and handed Las Vegas High its only loss of the season, but the young team had never played an opponent such as this. As the game approached, however, excitement began to build.

Brown's team came to Concord sporting a 3–0 record and a No. 7 ranking in the San Diego Section. The big story surrounding the Spartans continued to be Maurice Drew.

The running back had returned to the starting lineup, although some thought he'd be better off not risking another injury the week before Long Beach Poly. If De La Salle can't beat La Costa Canyon without Drew, how can it beat Poly with him?

It makes little difference when De La Salle goes three-and-out on its opening drive for the second straight week.

Biller goes sprinting onto the field like an attack dog released from his chain before the next offensive series. Kyle Balough has played right tackle since Erich Faustman injured his ankle in Hawaii. Balough has filled in capably, but shows even greater promise as a defensive lineman.

The coaching staff is eager to get a look at Biller, especially after his performance in practice. He is sent in to play right tackle, and he has never been so excited. This is the opportunity he has been waiting for, the opportunity he thought he had lost forever. The offensive series begins inauspiciously and goes downhill from there. Drew recovers a fumbled pitch to Ottoboni for a loss of 13 yards. On second and long,

Cecil throws to Bates in the left flat. The junior sprints 51 yards for a touchdown that is nullified because of an ineligible receiver downfield.

Drew picks up five yards on a draw play. Then he collects a Cecil pass in the left flat and flashes down the sideline for another long score. Sandie and Chan are at the 7, mopping up the last defenders, when Drew crosses the goal line.

This time it's a clipping penalty that brings the play back. It doesn't take long to determine which De La Salle player is guilty. Biller is shaking his head in disbelief. There is no excuse for the right tackle to be penalized on a screen pass to the left side, and he knows it.

He ran downfield wanting to knock somebody to the ground but hit a defender in the back and is yanked from the game.

"Oh my God," he says on the sideline. "I feel so bad. I feel so bad for Maurice. It's my first game back and now I'm going to get ripped when we watch films."

La Costa picks up a first down before a fumble gives the ball back to De La Salle. Ladouceur shakes his head in disgust when Cecil keeps the ball on an option play, attempts to stutter-step a defender, and is dropped for a 2-yard loss.

On the next play Drew disappears between the tackles, blows through the secondary, and scores on a 29-yard run to give De La Salle a 7–0 late in the first quarter.

Kevin O'Connell is a strong-armed, 6'5" quarterback for La Costa Canyon who already is drawing interest from college programs Colorado, Washington, and Oregon. He has thrown nine touchdowns and one interception in his first three games.

A 30-yard pass early in the second quarter gives the Mavericks the ball on the Spartans' 6. O'Connell later scores on a 1-yard sneak to tie the score.

Assistant coach Mark Panella is standing silently on the sideline, his arms crossed, his face registering unfiltered disgust.

"We don't have that killer instinct," he says.

Or do they? Drew fields the ensuing kickoff near the left hash mark and heads toward a wall of blockers forming near the right sideline. Then he suddenly bolts up the middle. He avoids one tackler and cuts back again. Another tackler bounces off his massive thighs.

Drew cuts back again when defenders approach and is wrapped up from behind as another tackler smashes into him from the side. Drew is attempting a spin move at that precise moment and rolls completely over the defender, his legs continuing to pump. He pops up and sprints down the sideline for a 94-yard touchdown that immediately is declared one of the most amazing feats of athleticism ever displayed at Owen Owens Field.

"That kickoff really took the life out of us," Mavericks' coach Brown admits later.

There is a momentary hesitation as Drew crosses the goal line. No one is quite sure what to think. Everyone assumed that Drew had been tackled. But the official who was on top of the play rules that his knee never touched the ground. His momentum kept him upright. Game films later prove this, although no one would've blamed Brown for contesting the call from across the field instead of remaining composed.

"The kids have to win the game on the field," he says later. "What does bitching and moaning do for you? One of the refs threw his hands up like he was about to stop the play but I never heard a whistle."

Eidson had warned his players about the probability of a shanked punt earlier in the week. "Find the ball and then get out of the way," he told his return team. Now the La Costa Canyon punter, trying to angle the ball way from Drew, has it slip off the side of his foot and carom out of bounds after eight yards.

Drew blocks two defenders and Gino Ottoboni scores on a 28-yard run to give the Spartans a 21–7 lead with nine minutes remaining in the second quarter.

A leaping, twisting catch by Cameron Colvin for a 39-yard gain sets up another score, and Binswanger's ensuing kickoff sails out of the end zone. Two weeks after thrilling fans in Hawaii, he is putting on another show. The kickoff coverage team has always been one of the most tradition-bound units at De La Salle. By booming every kickoff out of the end zone, Binswanger is making it irrelevant.

His first kickoff sailed through the uprights. Each of his subsequent kicks landed in the end zone. He isn't finished. His punt from De La Salle's 31-yard line a few minutes later lands at the 20 and bounces through the end zone.

Kids scramble to catch his extra points and return them to the official. Binswanger's high, arching PATs keep driving the horde of eager young boys farther and farther back.

After Drew scores on a 9-yard run to make it 35–7 late in the first half, Binswanger's extra point clears the crossbar, the track, a row of oleanders on the east side of the field, and lands in the condo complex next door. Six boys throw their hands over their heads the moment the ball disappears into the night. It is football's equivalent of a ground-rule double. Binswanger's next kickoff caroms off the crossbar and bounces back to the 10.

There isn't much strategy to discuss at halftime. The score would be 42–7 if it weren't for the two touchdowns called back on De La Salle's first drive. Still, Eidson is scolding his defense. O'Connell kept rolling out and had plenty of time to set up and throw, which was precisely what the Spartans had prepared to defend.

"How's your ankle?" Ladouceur asks Drew, who nods affirmatively. It's fine. Ladouceur then strolls absent-mindedly into the training room, where he spots a carton of fried rice on Blasquez's desk. He doesn't know how long it has been there. He picks it up and sniffs it suspiciously, his raised eyebrow signaling his approval. Then he reaches into a nearby drawer for a plastic fork, sits down, and begins to eat.

"You've got to go there some time," Justin Alumbaugh tells Ladouceur as the head coach chews what was left of his assistant's dinner. "It only takes three minutes for carryout."

La Costa Canyon scores on the first possession of the second half on a crisp pass from O'Connell, prompting wild gesticulations from an outraged Eidson. "WHAT DID I TELL YOU?" he screams, indignant. "WATCH OUT FOR A SLANT PASS IN THE END ZONE!"

Joe McCormick stands on the visitors sideline, his fingers resting thoughtfully on his chin as he watches De La Salle answer with two quick scores to make it 49–14 in the third quarter. He is an economics teacher at La Costa Canyon and a close friend of Brown's who flew to Concord with approximately five hundred other parents, students, and fans of the program.

"I wanted us to be the team that snapped the streak," he says, never taking his eyes off the field, "but I'm just enjoying watching their precision."

The final score is 56–27. Brown leaves his first-string offense on the field until late in the game, resulting in a pair of fourth-quarter touchdowns. The headline in the next morning's San Diego Union Tribune reads: De La Slammed.

"It's flat-out their offensive line, period," Brown says when asked what separates De La Salle from other teams. "If you think for a second, they've got a touchdown. He puts out the best offensive line I've ever seen and that's the position he coaches, which tells you he's one hell of a coach. The fact that he can get that much out of his line means we can do better. Maybe he's God, but somehow we can do better."

The mood in the postgame locker room is as lighthearted as it has been all season. Smith returned to center after sitting out the St. Francis game with a concussion sustained against St. Louis. Biller played almost the entire second half after being flagged for clipping. The line has followed its best week of practice with its best game performance.

Offensively, the Spartans made early mistakes. But unlike the week before, they bounced back and blew La Costa Canyon away. Players sit around the locker room laughing and talking, waiting for the postgame talk. Eidson speaks first:

"Here's the bottom line: We knew from the very beginning, from the moment we walked off Veterans Stadium last year, that it was going to be Poly. Everything that we've done, in the back of our mind, we've been like, 'Is that going to get it done against Poly.' That's the bottom line. Up to this point that will be the best competition you will face this year. We all know that. You knew that last January when you got in that weight room, we knew it all summer, and we know it this fall.

"The only thing I can say to you about this week, and I'll only say it one time, so I hope you listen up: You want to do everything in your power as a student-athlete to get ready for this game. When you walk off that field at 4:30 on Saturday you want to be able to say, 'I did everything I could to prepare myself and I gave it everything I had.' That's all you can ask for. But you don't want to walk off that field and say, 'I could've done something more. I could've prepared better. I was too YOUNG. I was TOO IMMATURE.'

"You guys who played against them last year or were down there or watched it on TV know that none of the coaches cared what the score was. We knew from the opening gun to the very end that everybody gave it everything they could. We were going to live with it one way or the other. Those guys gave it everything they had. They even gave it everything they had earlier in the week. They watched film. They did everything they could to get ready. If you want to win this game you're going to have to do the same.

"For the first time all year you're going to be playing a team with better athletes. Across the board they have better athletes. But we're pretty good, too. We can do some things, but you have to concentrate all week. Against Poly do you think you're going to be able to have two touchdowns called back? Good luck. Do you think you'll be able to jump offside in critical situations? Good luck. Do you think you'll be able to turn the ball over three or four times? We're still going to make mistakes. But we have to be the best we can be. That's all there is to it.

"This is going to be a grind. This week is one of the most important weeks of your life as a football player. . . . We're going to watch film; we're going to get better. . . . I just want you to know that's all I'm thinking of. From this point on, I'm thinking about getting better and I'm thinking about Poly—Poly, school, school, Poly, Poly, school, Poly, Poly, Poly, Poly. This is it. Think about the time you put in. How many kids would love to play a game like this? It's a chance of a lifetime."

Ladouceur doesn't have much to add. Besides, he wants to sit down. La Costa Canyon kept throwing the ball in the second half and the game dragged on until he wished there was a director's chair on the sideline for him to sit on.

He congratulates players for their performance but tells them they will have to play even better in order to defeat the No. 2-ranked Jackrabbits:

"The coach is right about next week, and you guys who played last year will remember. There's a whole different demeanor to this week. It's total business, effort, and concentration. When we put in new plays, guys have to pick them up quick. That has to happen. We're not going to be able to come out strong right, strong left, and pound the ball on them. We're going to have to mix things up and be creative, slick and savvy. It's a big week—physically, mentally, and emotionally. Get ready.

"You put in a good week of work last week and it paid off. You're going to need another great week this week, and like Coach said, if you do that and go out and lay it on the line and play with a lot of heart—everything you've got—that's all any of us can ask of each other. You'll do it. I think you can find a way to win that game, too. I truly believe that."

The Lord's Prayer is a postgame tradition at De La Salle. Players join hands, bow heads, and recite the prayer in a reverential murmur.

"St. John Baptist De La Salle," Drew says, beginning the responsory.

"PRAY FOR US," his teammates answer.

"Keep Jesus in our hearts," Drew says.

"FOREVER," comes the familiar reply.

In the momentary silence that follows, players wait expectantly for the popular and long-standing post-prayer tradition. After the appropriate seconds have ticked away, Eidson throws his clenched fist toward the ceiling and screams: "AND DON'T FORGET, GOD'S A SPARTAN!" The corresponding cheer echoes off the cinderblock walls and cement floors.

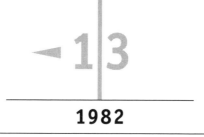

1982

TERRY EIDSON FILLS THE VOID

hey opened their presents on Christmas Eve. Christmas Day was reserved for the traditional six-hour drive from the Bay Area to Southern California. Every trainer, jockey, groom, and railbird in the state knew that Opening Day at Santa Anita fell on the 26th day of December.

"If you've never been down to Santa Anita, it's one of the most beautiful tracks ever," Terry Eidson says. "It's one of the best places to be in the morning when the sun comes over the San Gabriel Mountains. I always loved watching the horses work out at Santa Anita in the mornings."

Don Eidson sold legal books by trade but always had a small stake in several local thoroughbreds. His youngest son insisted on going to the track whenever one of his father's horses was scheduled to run.

Don Eidson traveled a lot, and Terry's two sisters and brother were older and off at school by then. Terry spent most of his time with his friends and the mother who doted on him. Lois Eidson took her son to Giants games and taught him how to play tennis on local courts, but the track remained in the background whispering his name.

His father always had a box near the finish line. They called Don the "Hat Man" because of the cowboy hats and fedoras he always wore. Terry loved it there, among all the familiar faces and voices and the smell of horses and sawdust. He loved the excitement and, later, the thrill of placing a bet, even if it was only a dollar.

"My friends would put fifty cents in. My dad would throw in a buck

151

and that's how we would bet," Terry said. "It wasn't about the money. It was about competition and the challenge of being right."

Don had a horse running the day of Terry's first Holy Communion. They took a picture of a smiling Terry standing next to the statue of Mary when the ceremony was over. Then they sped toward Bay Meadows Racetrack on the San Francisco peninsula.

They listened to the call of the race on the backside. They scrambled for the winner's circle when their horse won.

The horse already had been led to the barn by the time they got there, but they posed for a picture anyway: Terry, Don, and Lois, all dressed up for Holy Communion, smiling next to a jockey in silks. Terry still held his Bible in his hand. The horse paid $28. They didn't get a bet down.

He was an energetic, precocious child, intense even then. He wasn't a great athlete, but he understood competition. He organized baseball games in the middle-class neighborhood in Castro Valley, located southeast of Oakland. He called plays in the fall when he and his friends played football.

He always had opinions about who the best pitcher in baseball was, and why certain NFL quarterbacks choked under pressure.

"He has been a coach ever since he was a kid," said childhood friend Pat Hayes. "I remember him talking about how the game should be played in the fifth grade. He was managing the Giants when he was fifteen. He always knew when to run and when to pull the pitcher."

Baseball was his first love. He didn't play football until his junior year at Moreau High in Hayward, where Al Vermeil, the ultra-intense brother of NFL coach Dick Vermeil, was the coach.

Eidson was a good player, especially on special teams, but not a great one. He didn't get the coaching bug until he was enrolled at UCLA and found himself coaching co-ed softball and flag football.

He left UCLA with a degree in political science and a plan to enroll in law school. A member of the Christian Brothers whom he had gotten to know during summer retreats persuaded him to enter the prenovice program at Moraga's St. Mary's College in the fall.

Terry was intrigued by the idea of a life dedicated to forging extraordinary relationships with students, and he shared many of the core beliefs the Brothers held dear. Brothers must take a vow of celibacy, poverty, and obedience, and Terry could not imagine a future without a family. Still, he thought he should at least give it a try.

He isn't the type of person who likes being told what to do. He worried about fitting into the community but soon discovered it wasn't an issue—at least until football season started.

Terry grew up a rabid Oakland Raiders fan. There were no other Brothers who shared his passion for Jim Plunkett and Cliff Branch. Once a month the Brothers attended a local parish for Mass. They went in two cars. Terry told the driver of each car that he would ride with the other. Then he stayed home and watched the Raiders on TV.

It wasn't easy, but he managed to watch every game that season. "Desert Day" was a challenge. Brothers are required to spend one Sunday each month in solitude, prayer, and reflection. That meant no television.

Terry snuck down to the basement and watched the Raiders with the volume turned down. He turned off the set when he heard someone coming.

He was at the Brothers' retreat house when the Raiders met the Philadelphia Eagles in Super Bowl XV. They were to spend the weekend finding God through the arts. They watched "Ordinary People," attended a symphony concert, and went to a play. On Sunday, Super Bowl Sunday, they were to visit the Oakland Museum.

This was too much for Terry. How could they expect him to go to the Oakland Museum when the Oakland Raiders were in the Super Bowl? He argued with Brother Thomas Jones for two weeks. Brother Thomas offered to tape the game so Terry could watch it later. Terry knew he couldn't spend the day in football-crazed Oakland without inadvertently learning the score. Brother Thomas said the experience would be good for him.

"THIS IS NOT GOOD FOR ME," Terry answered. "This is not good for anybody. This will just piss me off. Trust me."

Terry passed packed sports bars en route to the museum. He refused to pose for a picture with the group after the museum tour—a sign of protest. Then the Brothers went back to St. Mary's to discuss what they had learned. Whenever the Raiders scored, cheering students and cowbells echoed through the Moraga hills. Terry was furious.

"I thought if I was a pain in the ass long enough I'd get my way," he said. "When I didn't I was completely turned off. I decided I had to split if they were going to be so unyielding about things that were important to me."

In some ways Eidson already had learned what he needed to from the Brothers. He had enough respect for their teaching methods and the Lasallian philosophy to know that he wanted to teach in a Christian Brothers school. He enrolled at St. Mary's and began working toward a teaching certificate and a Master's degree in theology.

The Brothers invited him to stay on campus with them during the summer of 1981, even though he was leaving the program. That was the summer he met Bob Ladouceur, although he didn't know it at the time.

Ladouceur also was taking classes at the college. Eidson had met Pete Kelly at the school and knew Kelly was an assistant coach at De La Salle. The Spartans had played for the league championship against St. Patrick's at St. Mary's Stadium in the fall of 1980.

Eidson watched from the stands as De La Salle scored what appeared to be the game-winning touchdown, only to see St. Patrick's return the ensuing kickoff 89 yards for a touchdown and a 24–21 victory. He told his friend Pete Kelly how the De La Salle head coach cost his team the game with a poor kickoff coverage scheme, not realizing that the silent presence walking with them across campus was the young coach he was criticizing.

"The first time I met Terry he pissed me off," Ladouceur said. "I figured he knew something about the game because he was able to pinpoint the most critical moment. But it was pretty presumptuous to pop off like that. He still hasn't stopped."

Eidson was offered a teaching job at his alma mater, Moreau. But he preferred to teach at De La Salle. Brother Jerome Gallegos found a position for him teaching religious studies and social studies and working in the campus ministry. Coaching would have to be done on his own time. Eidson gladly accepted. He was twenty-three years old.

His energy and passion filled a void on a campus still reeling from the death of Brother Laurence two years before. Eidson threw himself into his job. The school became his life. He helped Kelly with the junior varsity football team and assisted the freshman baseball coach.

"Brother Laurence was gone and then Terry came in and brought an enthusiasm and a real zest for life," Kelly says. "It was almost like a new beginning for us."

Eidson had a limited football background but was determined to learn what he didn't know. He overcame an awkward introduction to forge an immediate friendship with Ladouceur, picking his brain right away.

"Bob was talkative, outgoing, funny," Eidson said. "We just clicked. Then I came on campus and I realized I had gotten to know him more in one week during the summer than most people had in two years. I have never seen him the way most people see him unless we're around other people. He's never like that around me. Even now, the word around school is, 'only Eidson can talk to Ladouceur that way.'"

Eidson wasn't hired until school began, so he joined the junior varsity team as an assistant coach three weeks into the season. He was assigned defensive backs and receivers. It wasn't until the following spring that he learned Ladouceur was promoting Kelly to the varsity staff. That was fine with Eidson, but who would coach the JV team?

Ladouceur stared at him. Eventually, the reality sank in.

"ARE YOU KIDDING? I don't even know the offense," Eidson protested.

"You'll learn it," Ladouceur promised.

"I followed him around like a puppy all summer," Eidson said. "I was just trying to figure out how to run the offense."

There were some faculty members who chuckled at Ladouceur's decision. They didn't believe the first-year teacher had the temperament, background, or experience to be a head coach at any level. Eidson proved them all wrong by going 20–0 in his two years as the JV head coach. But the wins aren't what players remember most. They remember how he opened every game with a trick play.

Ladouceur used his offense to set up an occasional trick play. His new JV coach used trick plays to set up his offense.

He scribbled them down when he saw them on TV, collected them from other coaches, and invented some of his own. Every week another fumblerooski, flea flicker, or double-reverse pass was installed.

"You lose the element of surprise when the other team knows the trick play is coming," Ladouceur would point out logically.

"They know it's coming but they still can't stop it!" Eidson insisted, and he was right once more. His game-opening shenanigans almost always resulted in big gains or touchdowns. His players loved it.

The first play of the game had the urgency of the last, with opposing coaches screaming instructions to frantic players.

"That's when I knew he had a flair for it," Ladouceur said. "Those kids had a great time and got real excited about football."

Eidson had an uncanny knack for managing a game and the clock despite his lack of sideline experience. He was even more demonstrative then, even louder, if such a thing is possible. He stalked the sideline, destroying clipboards in fits of harmless rage.

"I don't want to say he was Bobby Knight. He wasn't that intense. But he was a close second," said Joe McNiff, his JV assistant. "He absolutely breathed Spartan football at that point in his life."

He picked songs out and played them to players if he thought they held special meaning for them, a practice he would later incorporate into team chapel services. Ladouceur preferred a low-key approach, but Eidson whipped his players into a frenzy before games.

It always came back to the trick plays. There was one game against Moreau, Eidson's alma mater, when the offense lined up in an I-formation with two tight ends instead of in the traditional veer.

On quarterback Mark Panella's signal, they shifted into a split-back formation. Then Panella retreated into shotgun position. The opposing coaches were pointing and yelling as bewildered defenders scrambled into various positions, unsure of what might happen next.

Panella handed the ball off to a running back, who pitched it back to Panella, who threw deep to a waiting receiver for a touchdown.

"The defense was chasing our guy downfield and Terry is on the sideline jumping up and down and screaming, 'I knew it would work! I knew it would work!'" Panella said, chuckling at the memory.

"That's how I'll remember him as a head coach. That was Terry in all his glory."

14 ▸

JUDGMENT DAY
The 2001 Long Beach Poly Game

| | | | | ⊥ | | | | |

t he scene stunned Bob Ladouceur. He knew his team was tired. He admitted as much during a quick television interview at half-time of the 2001 De La Salle-Long Beach Poly game. But he wasn't prepared for what greeted him in the locker room. He had wanted to make mid-game adjustments but now he wondered if his team could even finish the game.

Maurice Drew, the unexpected star of the first half, had to be carried by trainers into the locker room. Several other players had shed their pads and were lying on the floor in pools of sweat, chests heaving. Trainers twisted towels soaked with ice water over the heads and down the backs of overheated athletes. Ice was being packed under the arms and knees of All-American lineman Derek Landri to cool him down. Two other players needed intravenous fluids.

The visitors' locker room at Veterans Stadium in Long Beach, California, was no place to put an overheated football team. There was no ventilation inside the small and steamy locker room. Ice hadn't been provided for the visiting team. De La Salle assistant trainers had been forced to dash to a convenience store before the game, and their supply was now dwindling.

Outside more than 17,000 fans packed the grandstands from rail to rail, waving green and gold pom-poms and banging yellow Thunder-stix. Those without seats stood six-deep in the end zones. Thousands milled outside the gates trying to gain admittance. Streams of head-lights could be seen in both directions even after the crowd had swelled beyond the stadium's capacity.

Ladouceur had never felt so helpless. He wanted to talk to Mike Blasquez but the trainer was too busy tending to exhausted players, a group that seemed to include everyone. De La Salle led 21–15, but all of a sudden the score seemed irrelevant. Ladouceur didn't know how many of his players he could reasonably expect to play in the second half.

The game was announced nine months earlier, when The Streak stood at 113. Long Beach Poly boasted one of the most storied football programs in the country. It had sent thirty-nine players to the NFL, more than any other high school team. Its prestigious list of alumni includes former San Francisco 49ers star Gene Washington, former Dallas Cowboys receiver Tony Hill, and former and current NFL players Mark Carrier, Willie McGinest, Marquez Pope, and Omar Stoutmire. (Actress Cameron Diaz and rapper Snoop Doggy Dogg also are alums.)

The Jackrabbits had won thirteen Southern Section championships and had the second-highest number of wins (589) in state history. Having won or shared the past four Southern Section large-school titles, they had supplanted Mater Dei as the dominant team in the region. Being the dominant team in talent-rich Southern California means you are one of the elite teams in the nation. Poly boasted a 31-game unbeaten streak of its own at one point, and it had lost only once in its previous 59 games before meeting De La Salle.

It was the first time in history that the top two teams in *USA Today*'s Super 25 Poll had met—Poly was ranked No. 1, De La Salle No. 2. The schools were flip-flopped in the national *Student Sports Magazine* poll. The game was billed as the most anticipated high school football game in history and included every imaginable story line.

The matchup pitted a large public school with an enrollment of 4,600 against a small private school with 1,050 students. Poly, located in a dilapidated neighborhood in Long Beach, surrounded by liquor stores and faded hotel signs blinking vacancy, resembles an urban inner-city school. De La Salle is surrounded by $700,000 homes in a comfortable suburb. It was the discipline of De La Salle vs. the athleticism of Poly. It was first-year Long Beach Poly coach Raul Lara vs. a twenty-three-year head-coaching veteran who already had been inducted into the National Federation of High School Sports Hall of Fame.

Requests for media credentials were so great that the CIF Southern

Section stepped in to help relieve some of the burden from its member school. More than 120 credentials had been distributed to organizations as diverse as *The New York Times, Sports Illustrated,* and ABC's *World News Tonight.* NFL Films cameras were rolling on the sideline. Fox Sports Net was televising the game live and anticipated its highest Nielson ratings ever. Highlights would be shown during numerous college broadcasts and on ESPN's *SportsCenter.*

Rumors on the Long Beach campus had the Jackrabbits gracing the cover of *Sports Illustrated* if they snapped The Streak.

"You have to consider it a national championship game," television analyst Mike Lamb told his audience prior to kickoff. "You're talking about a school with the longest win streak in history and the school that has sent more players to the NFL than any other school in history. So if this isn't a national championship game for high school football, I don't know how you can put one together."

De La Salle already proved it could compete against Southern California's elite teams, having defeated Mater Dei four years running. Now it seemed the Spartans had to prove it all over again. Poly was not only considered the top team in the nation and state, but perhaps one of the most awesome collections of high school talent ever assembled.

It was the first prep football team to have five players rated among the nation's top 100 college prospects by major recruiting services. The so-called "Fab Five" referred to safety Darnell Bing, running back Hershel Dennis, offensive lineman Winston Justice, tight end Mercedes Lewis, and defensive tackle Manuel Wright. Twenty-four of the Poly players on the field that night would eventually land a Division-I college scholarships.

Long Beach Poly co-principal Mel Collins had marked the date on his calendar with a red felt-tip marker: The Streak Ends. His confidence reflected sentiment throughout the community. They were calling it "Judgment Day" in Long Beach. Placards bearing those words were posted all over town. The Spartans, despite The Streak and a star-studded lineup of their own—including quarterback Matt Gutierrez and All-American lineman Derek Landri—were considered underdogs.

The headline above a column in the *Long Beach Press Telegram* summed up the local sentiment: "Spartan streak will end tonight."

"They haven't played any teams near our talent level," the 6'7", 315-

pound Manuel Wright told the *Los Angeles Times*. "I think they're in for a big surprise."

Frank Allocco and Ladouceur went for one of their traditional pregame runs around the stadium and watched in awe as Poly players filed into the locker room in their muscle shirts.

Poly always has had skilled position players. "There's speed and then there's Poly speed" is how one college recruiter puts it. But they never had the size and strength along the offensive and defensive lines that they had in 2001. That's why many Poly insiders considered this the best team in the program's eighty-two-year history.

Long Beach's five offensive linemen averaged 275 pounds compared to 236 pounds for De La Salle's defensive line. The Spartans' offensive line averaged 231 pounds compared to 280 for Poly's defensive front.

"Bob and I were covering our mouths and saying, 'Oh my God,'" Allocco remembers. "It was the biggest football team I had ever seen, college or pro. It was unbelievable. Bob goes, 'Frankie, I'm scared.' We were both absolutely shocked at how big they were."

The game began as so many other De La Salle games do. Maurice Drew returned the opening kickoff 33 yards, then ripped off another 12 yards on the first play from scrimmage. Senior quarterback Matt Gutierrez led a six-play drive before being faced with third-and-8 at Poly's 25-yard line. He rolled right and threw a screen pass to Drew in the left flat. The junior dipped under two tacklers and somersaulted into the end zone to score the first touchdown Poly had allowed all season.

Drew had made a promise to Nate Kenyon and Alijah Bradley the night before. They were watching a college game in their hotel room when a punt returner had his legs taken out from under him and flipped into the end zone. If any of them were to score the first touchdown, it was decided, they had to promise to do the same.

Drew was flagged for an excessive celebration penalty.

"The coaches didn't say anything then," Drew said. "They were too into the game. But when we got home Coach Lad told me never to do that again. He told me we were not a celebrating team."

Poly coaches had been concerned about Drew, but as a defensive player, not as an offensive threat. They geared up to stop Bradley, who was averaging 12 yards per carry, and Kenyon. Drew, an unheralded junior who had excelled as a linebacker, had only rushed ten times for 140 yards in De La Salle's first three games, but it was quickly becoming apparent he would be the featured back against Poly.

Quarterback Brandon Brooks threw a bomb to sophomore Derrick Jones on the Jackrabbits' first play. Jones was a sophomore speed-burner whom defensive coordinator Terry Eidson had been intent on stopping. On this play he was wide open at the 25. The potential game-tying touchdown slipped through his fingers, however, prompting a groan from the partisan crowd.

"You know why he dropped that pass?" a De La Salle player yelled to his teammates on the sideline. "Because he wasn't pulling tires all summer like we were! That's why he didn't make the play!"

Regardless of what Jones and the Jackrabbits had or had not done that summer, the dropped pass bolstered the Spartans' confidence. They believed they made plays when other teams didn't because they worked harder. The mindset was that they deserved to win because they wanted it more.

It was fourth-and-4 near the end of the first quarter when Gutierrez faked a handoff to Drew and dropped back to pass. He looked quickly to his right and then immediately turned back to Drew, who was wide open down the left sideline. The play unfolded just as assistant coach Mark Panella had predicted after watching a Poly defender overpursue a few moments earlier. Drew had his defender beat by two steps, and Gutierrez hit him with a 29-yard rainbow to give the Spartans a 14–3 advantage. The lead swelled to 21–9 after Drew caught another 17-yard scoring pass late in the first half.

Drew hadn't practiced well that week and was surprised when Ladouceur told him that he would be a big part of the game plan. Still, he hadn't planned on this. Nobody had. Gutierrez knew the offense so well that he had been given free rein to call plays at the line of scrimmage. The quarterback was calling Drew's number more and more.

"We were waiting for him to break out," Panella said of Drew. "We were waiting for him his sophomore year, too. He needed a game like that to believe in himself. We knew he could do it, but he didn't know it. After that game he didn't have any doubts about himself."

A troubling trend was developing, however. De La Salle had the lead, but the momentum had swung to Poly. De La Salle didn't have an answer for running back Herschel Dennis, whose combination of speed and bruising power made him one of the top backs in the country. They had prevented him from ripping off huge chunks of yardage, but he was gaining 5 and 10 yards almost at will. Spartans defenders hit him with everything they had, but it usually took a second or even a third tackler to bring the USC-bound running back to the ground.

De La Salle was wearing down, just as experts predicted a team with so many key two-way players must. The Spartans couldn't stop Long Beach Poly as it marched methodically downfield and pulled to within 21–15 on a 12-yard touchdown pass to Lewis with less than a minute remaining in the first half.

First-year Long Beach coach Raul Lara called Spartan Derek Landri the best linemen he had ever seen on film. Landri had 80 tackles, 17 sacks, and had knocked down 12 passes during a dominating junior year. Now a senior, the 6'4", 280-pounder was breathing heavily and had to push himself to his feet after ranging downfield to tackle Herschel Dennis from behind on the final drive. He was going head to head with 6'7", 300-pound tackle Winston Justice on offense, and with 6'7", 315-pound end Manuel Wright on defense. Both were considered among the top prep linemen in the country.

"Television doesn't do justice to the size of these [Poly] guys," broadcaster Mike Lamb told the television audience late in the first half.

Landri was all over the field, splitting double teams, collapsing the pocket, and chasing Dennis from sideline to sideline. He was in the midst of a performance that would play a key role in his selection as *Student Sports Magazine*'s State Player of the Year.

He wasn't the only one feeling the pace. Drew had been almost as effective on defense as on offense, registering several big hits and even recording a sack, but his mouth hung open and he was sweating as if an internal sprinkler system were trying to douse a fire. Andy Briner, another standout two-way lineman, also was exhausted.

Ladouceur huddled with assistants Joe Aliotti and Mark Panella in the locker room in an attempt to solidify the offensive line. John Chan suffered a knee injury in the first half and was out. They didn't know if Landri and Briner would recover in time to play the third quarter, which meant that they needed to find replacements at three offensive line positions. Defensive tackle Javier Carlos was dehydrated and being given intravenous fluids. Since Briner and Landri also started on defense, they would need three backups along the defensive line as well.

They still hadn't plugged all the holes when it was time to take the field for the second half.

"I just remember sitting in the locker room with wet towels over my head trying to drink as much water as I could," Landri says. "I couldn't comprehend what Coach Ladouceur was saying because I was so beat. I don't even really remember what happened at halftime."

Allocco took it all in. He heard Ladouceur tell the backups to be ready. They were going to play. This was their night. This reminded the former Notre Dame quarterback of the time when USC scored 49 points in the second half against his former team in the famed comeback of 1974.

Allocco walked out of the locker room and spotted his long-time assistant coach Brian Sullivan. Allocco felt tears welling up in his eyes when he told Sullivan that The Streak would end that night.

"I told Brian, 'It's over. We cannot win this football game,'" Allocco recalls. "The momentum had changed. We were done, gassed, and they were coming on. Landri couldn't go. A lot of kids couldn't go. They couldn't even make adjustments at halftime."

Ladouceur pulled Blasquez aside as they left the locker room. Players refused to come off the field but were pushing themselves to the danger point, and he was concerned. He told the trainer to take control of all substitutions in the second half. He could assess players' physical condition better than Ladouceur could because of his background in sports medicine. Besides, it would allow Ladouceur to focus on the game, regardless of who was on the field.

"I remember walking back to the field thinking, 'I hope these guys don't blow us out in the second half,'" Ladouceur says.

De La Salle players wearing clean white jerseys ran on and off the field early in the second half, and it showed. Poly controlled the ball for almost the entire third quarter and outgained De La Salle 84–10. It didn't seem possible at halftime, when several players were on the verge of collapse, but the Spartans played harder in the second half, their sweat-soaked jerseys turning a shade of gray the manufacturers never intended. The backups slowed the Poly offense between the 20-yard lines before Blasquez sent the starters back in. The De La Salle defense held on fourth down twice in the scoreless third quarter.

The Jackrabbits, with their all-American running back, their UCLA-bound tight end, and their massive offensive line, couldn't score. Dennis would rush for 161 yards but never crossed the goal line.

Briner and Landri eventually recovered and spent more time on the field in the fourth quarter as De La Salle resumed control of the game. Although Poly was still ripping off moderate gains, it was the Jackrabbits who appeared to be wearing down.

Drew sealed his place in De La Salle lore by scoring the game-clinching touchdown, his fourth of the night, on a 22-yard run with 6:57 left. He finished with 157 yards of total offense and was as active as any De La Salle player, save Landri, on defense.

"We just wanted to lie down on the field and soak it up," Landri said. "We were glad we won but were too exhausted to celebrate."

It was a partisan Long Beach Poly crowd, no doubt about it, but there were many curiosity seekers who wanted a first-hand look at the De La Salle team they had heard so much about. When the game ended, Poly fans rose as one and applauded the effort of both teams.

"I tell people it has to be one of the top three things I've ever seen in athletics," Allocco said. "Bob and I talked afterwards, and he felt the kids pushed themselves to the point where they were in danger physically. I believe that. As a coach you dream of getting kids to that point. We always say you want to be picked up off the field and be able to say you gave everything. Well, nobody ever does that. As humans we always hold something back. There was nothing held back that night.

"If we had played Poly a hundred more times that year we wouldn't have beaten them again. On that night we found a way. It was an unbelievable thing. It was a marvelous, miraculous win."

Lara walked off the field convinced that his team could've won. De La Salle's team speed was better than he anticipated. But if the Jackrabbits could have converted those two fourth downs in the third quarter to keep scoring drives alive, if his sophomore receiver had caught even one of the three potential touchdown passes he had dropped.... It was a crushing loss for a young coach and former Poly graduate who had deep roots in the community.

Lara was a starting linebacker for Poly in 1983 and served as the defensive coordinator for longtime Poly coach Jerry Jaso for six years. When Jaso joined the staff at Long Beach City College, he handed the reins to his young assistant. Coaching Poly is a thankless task. When the Jackrabbits win it's because of their superior athletes. Poly is a magnet school that can draw the best students and athletes from a wide geographical area under the district's now-revised open-enrollment policy. Some Southern California coaches referred to the program as "The Long Beach All-Stars."

When the "All-Stars" lost, which wasn't often, it was because the coaching staff had been outcoached.

Lara's fourth game as a varsity head coach was arguably the biggest high school football game in history. His offensive and defensive coordinators also were new to their jobs. Now that they had seen De La Salle, they knew what to expect. Next year would be different.

"It hurts," Lara said that night. "I'll probably go home and cry."

A cool breeze blows down off the brown slopes of Mt. Diablo as the Spartans finish practice three days before the long-awaited 2002 rematch with Long Beach Poly. Rush-hour traffic backs up on Treat Boulevard, and a lone jogger sends blackbirds scurrying from her path as she circles the track. Thirsty players gulp water from hoses.

"I feel good about the game plan," Ladouceur tells assistants Nate Geldermann, Joe Aliotti, and Justin Alumbaugh as they stand in a circle in the middle of the practice field. "They understand what we're trying to do."

Ladouceur is as relaxed in the days leading up to the showdown with Poly as he was on edge the week before the game against St. Louis.

He didn't spend the summer watching Poly film the way he had while preparing for the Crusaders, but Poly's offense and defense haven't changed from the year before. Plus, he had gauged their speed and size while watching them destroy Kahuku in Honolulu.

He spent all day Saturday and Sunday engrossed in the long, tedious process of breaking down film and compiling a scouting report. Mark Panella stopped by his house on Sunday afternoon to make suggestions. Ladouceur studied more film with Alumbaugh and Aliotti early in the week before the game plan was finalized.

The 2001 Poly team may have been one of the most talented rosters ever assembled, but Ladouceur and his staff think the 2002 version might be a better team. The young, inexperienced receiving corps that dropped several passes the year before has matured. This group appears more selfless than the team dominated by the "Fab Five." Poly has outscored its four opponents by an average of 42–9.

The Sporting News has ranked Poly's defensive line No. 1 in the nation. De La Salle won the battle on the line of scrimmage the year before, but not by much. And that was with the departed Derek Landri and Andy Briner in the lineup. It's frightening to think that Poly's defensive line is superior to the line the Spartans faced last year.

Ladouceur added several wishbone plays before the 2001 game in an effort to fool the Jackrabbits. He won't do anything as radical this year. The only thing he'll change is blocking assignments.

De La Salle coaches have told their offensive linemen to double-team larger Poly players all the way across the line. The Jackrabbits' linebackers aren't as active as they were the year before. Drew, who breaks tackles himself, can gain enough yards to keep the chains moving. The coaching staff hopes the strategy will give their offensive linemen confidence against a defensive line that averages four inches taller and 38 pounds heavier per man.

"That's one of the gifts and curses of coaches," Ladouceur says. "They think they can control a lot of stuff. They want to be in control and be the difference maker. We get caught up in that sometimes. If I decided to run the same things we ran last week, I wouldn't feel like I was doing my job, even if last week's game plan seems perfect. We have to tinker and put our bit in. But it doesn't matter what I know. It only matters what the kids know. That's what gives me confidence. I'm seeing them understand what we want and perform it in practice. That's when I start feeling good about our game plan."

Ladouceur may not have installed any new base plays against a Poly defense that hasn't allowed a touchdown all season. He has added a few trick plays that he thinks might work in the right situation.

He likes using trick plays in big games because players seem to execute them better. They almost always go for scores or long-gainers. When they fail he blames himself, not his players.

"Against Poly you've got to be right on the money because those guys are so fast," he says. "You can fool them a little bit, but once they see it they recover quickly. Last year we caught them off balance on misdirection plays. We hit them three times, once for a touchdown and twice on critical third downs, to keep scoring drives alive. That's how you have to hit Poly. The slow-developing trick plays don't work. They may suck up but they'll turn around and catch you in a second."

The inattention to detail that plagued the offense and frustrated coaches for much of the season has subsided. They haven't had to harp on the team for mental mistakes this week. The players have put together back-to-back solid practice weeks, and they haven't had to be reminded of plays and techniques introduced a few days or weeks ago.

"In order to beat Poly they have to truly elevate their game, which they have not done yet," Ladouceur says. "But I get the feeling they're on the cusp of that. We've prepared these guys as well as we can. At this point in the season they have probably come along as far as they can. Are these guys good enough to beat Poly? I don't know. I really don't. They may not be. But I feel that in the last few weeks they've put themselves in a position to beat them. If they carry that through and play hard, I'll be proud of them no matter what. I really will."

He has pushed this team harder than he has pushed teams in recent years. Now it's time to build its confidence. Aliotti has been hammering that point home all week. It's right out of Coaching 101. If you tell players they're not good enough all week, they probably won't be good enough in the game. Ladouceur knows it's true.

"You guys can do this," he tells his team after Wednesday's practice. "You can put up 28 to 35 points on these guys if you get off the line, protect the ball, and run the option. But you have to believe. You have to believe in a game like this—not wish, believe. That's how we've always approached big games like Mater Dei, Merced, and Bakersfield. Those teams believed and that was the difference."

Poly has destroyed its first three opponents with long passes to speed receivers and a potent running game. Defensive coordinator Terry Eidson wants to make the Jackrabbits earn their points, which they haven't had to do thus far.

He watches tapes of six different Poly games before formulating a defensive plan based on stopping the run and the long pass. He wants to force Poly to complete intermediate throws, which is difficult for high school quarterbacks to do, even with talented receivers.

After a few incomplete passes and stalled drives, he hopes that Poly players will become frustrated. Everything has come easily for the Jackrabbits thus far. He wants to make it difficult.

"In every film we've got they score so quickly," Eidson says. "When a team is used to scoring so fast, being patient can be extremely difficult for them. Since summer passing leagues, they have been scoring and attempting to score in the same way. We want to change their coordinator's mindset and force them to move the ball down the field. We want to see if they can do that. I don't think they've been practicing for it. They definitely haven't had to do it in games."

Eidson and Ladouceur are preparing for the biggest game of the season with a skeleton staff. Panella is out of town on business but will return in time for the game. Geldermann will be at his twin brother's wedding when the De La Salle-Long Beach Poly game kicks off. Even Aliotti, in his role as dean of students, will be out of town later in the week to attend a mandatory Christian Brothers conference.

Alumbaugh works with offensive linemen on their new assignments and preps his inside linebackers while packing for his long-awaited trip to Europe. His brother and several of their friends are meeting him in London for a journey that will mark the end of their college years. Alumbaugh has lived with his parents and waited tables since graduating to save money. It's an opportunity of a lifetime, something he may never get a chance to do again, especially on a De La Salle teacher's salary. Still, he has mixed emotions.

"I'm used to leaving every year, but it's a lot harder this time because I've been here so much more," he says. "It's amazing how much time these kids put in. They're here all the time. That's why I keep popping in film and coming earlier and earlier. I want to help them succeed. I don't want to let these kids down. They have put in so much work that if I don't do these things I couldn't look them in the eye."

The pregame hype isn't as intense as it was the year before. Requests for media credentials have dropped from 121 in 2001 to 69, but camera crews have still descended on the school, and out-of-town reporters are leaving numerous phone messages. Drew is the focal point of the media. Everybody wants to interview him about his four-touchdown performance the year before. He won't catch the Jackrabbits by surprise again. Stopping him is their No. 1 priority.

The *Long Beach Press Telegram* covers Poly football as if it were a college or pro team. "Drew won't sneak up on Poly again," reads the headline on one of the numerous articles published in the newspaper in the days leading up to the game.

"All anybody wants to talk about this week is Maurice Drew," Ladouceur says loud enough for Drew to hear before a midweek practice. "Everybody wants to do a story on Maurice. I just tell them, 'He'll be there Saturday. We'll see what happens.'"

~

The faculty lounge is abuzz Friday morning. Teachers sip coffee at long tables and discuss a quote from Brother Christopher Brady that appeared in a front-page article in the *Contra Costa Times*.

"It's hard to say I want them to lose," the De La Salle principal told reporter Joe Stiglich. "But losing is part of the game. We just haven't experienced it. There's a lot to be learned from finishing second or third and not having the score in your favor."

Several players approach Ladouceur that morning. It almost seems to them that their principal is rooting for them to lose. They want an explanation. Ladouceur isn't sure what to tell them.

Brother Chris is tall, thin, and bald. He's forever bustling around campus, his black robe billowing around his ankles. He knows a little about the mentality of a football player. His nephew, Tom Brady, is the Super Bowl-winning quarterback of the New England Patriots.

Ladouceur bumps into him in the main office later that morning.

"The kids are mad at you," Ladouceur says matter-of-factly.

"Why?" Brother Chris asks, surprised.

"Because of what you said in the paper," Ladouceur says.

"What did I say?"

"Did you read the paper?" Ladouceur asks.

"Yes," Brother Chris replies.

"The kids feel like you're rooting against them."

Brother Chris has made similar statements during his two years as principal. In this case it's the timing that has created the uproar. It's not as if he wants them to lose, he tells Ladouceur. But there are valuable lessons to be learned from losing.

"I know what you mean," Ladouceur says. "But I don't know if the kids do."

Later, after relaying the conversation to his assistants—several of whom, Panella in particular, are irritated by the quote—Ladouceur grumbles: "I don't like to have to defend the principal to the kids."

"To think that a principal would want his team to lose in order to experience what that means is ludicrous," Brother Chris would later say. "I was speaking to a much larger audience than De La Salle football players. I'm about as supportive of the program as I can be, but a loss is inevitable and I think our players are well-equipped for when that does happen, whether it be this week, next month, or whenever."

Ladouceur hopes Brother Chris will say as much to his players, although he never vocalizes the desire. Brother Chris doesn't believe that any explanation is necessary.

"My thinking is that if they want to talk to me about it, they should be the ones to initiate the conversation," he said. "If they have a concern about what I said, all they have to do is walk into my office, sit down, and say, 'Brother Chris, what did you mean?'"

The subject has come up before. The only lesson the football program doesn't teach student-athletes is how to lose. That's one popular perception, anyway, but Eidson says that's not true.

"There's no great lesson in losing," Eidson claims. "The lesson comes with the effort you put into it. These guys lose at things all the time. They lose every day in practice. Cameron Colvin lost his mother. The daily life of a teenager is one of trauma with girlfriends and friends. The one tangible thing in life is they can play a sport and control the outcome a little bit through their work ethic.

"You have to remember that we may win as a team, but individually we have a lot of losses out there. We don't look at the scoreboard. It's about individual commitment and effort. Anybody who doesn't understand that doesn't understand our program. It's not results-based. You need someone with a unique perspective on winning and losing to keep something like this going. If it was about wins and losses we would've lost a long time ago."

The game against Long Beach Poly is drawing interest around the state and nation. Tickets are selling briskly in the small campus bookstore, but there is no visible evidence of big-game fervor at De La Salle save a lone sign—Drop Dead Bunny Rabbits—that hangs over the school's theater. Teachers are talking about the game more than the students are.

Students from all-boys De La Salle and neighboring all-girls Carondelet mix in small groups in the parking lot after school. Others skateboard or wait for parents to pick them up. Two sophomores sit at a picnic table discussing their weekend plans.

"My grandpa is, but I'm not," says one of the students when asked if he plans to attend the game. "I've got a project due."

"For any other school in the country this would be a pinnacle event in the history of the athletic department," says Lou Ascatigno, a De La Salle graduate, long-time teacher, and the football team's public address announcer. "To me it's sad that we're not getting more psyched up. But at this school it isn't the cool thing to do."

The student body got excited about its football success in the early years. Winning, however, has long since become a foregone conclusion. The low-key approach is now part of the tradition. It's a shame. How often does a high school football team play for a national championship? With De La Salle ranked No. 1 in the country by *USA Today,* and Long Beach Poly ranked No. 2, that's what this game boils down to.

Then again, when De La Salle played Mater Dei in 1998 for its first national title, there wasn't a pep rally, either.

"This school tries hard to keep things in perspective, but sometimes we go overboard," Eidson says. "There shouldn't be a rally before every game, but with this type of event you would think there would be more of a buzz. I can't really explain it."

Late in the week rumors circulate that a pep rally has been planned for lunchtime Friday. Erik Sandie, wearing a black T-shirt, sits on a brick wall near the main quad, eating corn chips in the warm sunshine, when Ladouceur, wearing a white golf shirt and a charcoal vest sweater, sits next to him.

The leaves on the small trees lining the courtyard are tinged yellow, one of the first visible signs of the changing season. Sandie is not wearing his jersey like many of his teammates, but his thick chest and wide shoulders are impossible to disguise. The marks on his protruding forehead can only be the result of wearing a football helmet day after day.

"I don't like to wear my jersey," he shrugs, chewing. "I don't like to be singled out as a football player. It's uncomfortable, too."

Most students don't bother to look up from their brown-bag lunches or interrupt their conversations when a student who has smeared his torso and face with green body paint chases another student wearing rabbit ears through the quad. Water balloons are flung from the roof of the theater and it's over before most students realized it began.

"The rallies sure have gone downhill at this school," Sandie says, chewing.

The student covered in green paint, obviously pleased with his performance, approaches Ladouceur, who has taken in the scene indifferently.

"Hey, Big Daddy," he says, referring to Ladouceur by his nickname.

"Hey," Ladouceur answers dryly. "When are you guys going to crank things up here?"

"We're already finished," the boy says.

"I let the kids out of films for this?" Ladouceur says, slowly rising to his feet and beginning to make his way across the quad, his words trailing behind. "I don't understand this school sometimes. There should be a rally for these kids."

~

Players file into the campus chapel after school on Friday, drop their backpacks, and slip off their shoes in the foyer before lying down on the soft blue-gray carpeting and closing their eyes.

Sun splashes through the narrow marbled windows on each side of the room. Jesus' body is twisted in pain as it hangs on the cross above the altar. Eidson is as quiet and calming in this setting as he is easily incensed on the practice field. Listening to him talk about relationships as he moderates these sessions, about mistakes he has made and what he learned from them, makes it easy to envision him in a black robe and white collar counseling the boys of his parish.

He always was the most spiritual person in his family. His older brother wasn't surprised to learn that he was considering becoming a Christian Brother after graduating from UCLA. What surprised him was when Terry left the Brothers.

Now, all these years later, he calls him the "High Priest of Football."

"From this point on it's just us and getting ready for this game," Eidson says. "Clear your mind. We all have distractions in our lives, but now it's time to focus on your role. What are you going to do? I'm giving you permission to do just one thing. That's nice. It can be a very freeing experience. So relax and get yourself ready to go."

Eidson's love of heavy-metal music serves him well when he is helping seniors pick out an appropriate song for chapel. John Chan and Erik Sandie have helped him select "Rooster" by the heavy-metal band Alice in Chains. The song has been played during the pregame chapel service in each of the past two years. They all three feel that its chilling lyrics are appropriate this week.

Ladouceur is lying face down on the floor with his eyes closed when the tribute to a Vietnam soldier's life begins.

Matt Drazba is a meaty 6'2", 250-pound junior lineman. He lives one mile from Pinole Valley High School in west Contra Costa County, twenty-three miles from the De La Salle campus. He drives himself, his sister, and two other students to school every morning in a Plymouth Voyager minivan.

De La Salle students take classes at Carondelet, and Carondelet students take classes at De La Salle. Drazba was walking down a hallway at Carondelet when he noticed several motivational passages taped to the wall above a row of lockers. He found one passage especially poignant and stuffed the paper in his pocket.

"It really hit home to me because a lot of people said Poly is bigger and faster and will be out to get us after we beat them last year," Drazba says. "People thought Poly was going to kick our ass. We needed confidence. You won't win if you don't believe you will win."

173

He rises from the floor and walks slowly to the podium as "Rooster's" haunting guitar riffs fade into silence. He shares the quotation from author and self-employment expert Barbara J. Winter:

"When you come to the edge of all the light you know and are about to step off into the darkness of the unknown, faith is knowing one of two things will happen: There will be something solid to stand on, or you will be taught how to fly."

"I chose this reading because faith is believing what you can't see," Drazba says. "It's just like I have faith we'll win tomorrow based on the hard work and sacrifices we've made this season."

There is a momentary pause as players absorb this. The only sounds are the soft clearing of throats or rustling of paper.

"I think that's one of the more profound things we've heard in chapel," Chan finally says, breaking the silence.

"I'd like to talk about the song," Sandie says a bit later. "It's appropriate for us. They're doing what they need to do to defend themselves, and that's the same thing we're trying to do."

Chan prepares to read a poem written by De'Montae Fitzgerald, who is in a tutoring session and therefore unable to attend chapel and read his own poem.

Fitzgerald has always written poems on little scraps of paper. This time he wanted to create something that defines his experience at De La Salle. He started thinking about it during summer workouts and put pen to paper for the first time before the trip to Hawaii.

Chan clears his throat and begins to read:

MOTIFS OF A SPARTAN
Months of blood and sweat
Tears and fatigue, laughs and cries
Pain and relief, struggle and progress
Commitment and dedication
Excellence and perfection
Persistence and repetition
Technique and strength
Bonds and brotherhood

Teaching and learning
Speaking and being heard
Courage, pride, and endurance
Respect and honor, respect and honor, respect and honor
Fundamental stance and demeanor
Sacrifice and determination
Never arrogant
Always modest
Always humble
Never takes more than needed
But always gives what is possible of giving
Always exceeds expectations
And forever will remain a tool of inspiration
Months of blood and sweat
Tears and fatigue, laughs and cries
Pain and relief, struggle and progress
A lifetime of brotherhood

"It's not about victories. It's about the De La Salle way," Eidson says softly when Chan has returned to his spot on the floor. "This poem reflects that. It's an honor for all of us to be in a situation like this. It's an honor to be able to play. It's an honor to coach you. That's why I take the sign of peace so seriously, because it's a sign of commitment to your teammates. It's being honorable. With that in mind let's offer each other that sign of peace."

The players walk in a circle around the chapel and embrace each other. "Peace be with you," they say after every sincere embrace. Eidson and Ladouceur hug the players, too.

It wasn't until years after the fact that former De La Salle running back Patrick Walsh, now the head coach at Serra High School in San Mateo, fully realized the power of this weekly ritual.

"Lad creates an environment where you can cry in front of your friends and tell them you love them," he said. "What do they do at the end of chapel service? They hug. Do you know how hard it is to get high school kids to do that? It wasn't until my first chapel service at Serra that I learned that love is the key to everything they do."

The 1980s

A NEMESIS NAMED SHAG

dan Shaughnessy was being hailed as "The Genius" in the pages of *Catholic Voice* long before Bob Ladouceur saw the article announcing Ed Hall's resignation at De La Salle. The long-time Salesian High School football coach celebrated his 100th coaching victory before Ladouceur completed his first season at De La Salle.

Shaughnessy is a barrel-chested, bantam rooster who is affectionately referred to as "Shag" by his legion of former players. His many competitors throughout the years have known him by other names, not always as affectionate.

When nobody knew who Bob Ladouceur was, Shaughnessy was the dean of the Catholic Athletic League, a now defunct former high school sports league made up of Catholic schools in the Bay Area. Their teams met for the first time in 1979 with the league title at stake. Shaughnessy's team won in a romp, 32–0.

They didn't know it then, but that was the beginning of a beautifully contentious rivalry.

That rivalry presented the first of many obstacles Ladouceur had to overcome en route to achieving the highest winning percentage in high school football history. It was by far the most imposing. Before his Spartans won their first league or North Coast Section title, before they could be crowned mythical state or national champions, they had to beat Shag.

He has been Ladouceur's only nemesis, the only coach to defeat Ladouceur more than once. In fact, Shaughnessy beat De La Salle three times in Ladouceur's first five years.

"He had a spell on everybody in the league," Ladouceur said of Shaughnessy. "He had everybody intimidated. I didn't know him and didn't care, but his legend extended to the kids. They were all spooked by what he might do. I was never intimidated. I was like, 'Who is this guy?' It pissed me off was what it did."

Shaughnessy was born in Oakland and raised in Berkeley. His father worked as a machinist in the shipyards. His mother stayed home and took care of him and his eight brothers and sisters.

He grew up playing football at the local playground. He would go to Memorial Stadium to watch Pappy Waldorf coach the University of California Golden Bears. He still remembers watching his first college game. He was a freshman in high school and saw Minnesota's famous single-wing do-everything halfback Paul Giel.

He played football at St. Mary's High School, Santa Rosa Junior College, and then at Utah State. He was the first of the nine Shaughnessy kids to graduate from college. Shortly thereafter, he met Diane on a blind date. They got married when Dan got out of the Army.

There was no football field at Salesian when he took over the fledgling program. The Chieftains played home games at a local park before Shaughnessy was able to organize volunteers to build Selway-Martin Field on a patch of land where farmers once grew sugar beets.

Shaughnessy was a fierce competitor who stormed up and down the sideline and swore more than a Catholic school coach should. He trolled for every possible psychological advantage. The Chieftains' home field was hard as concrete, which was precisely how Shaughnessy liked it. Opposing players choked on the clouds of dust kicked up after every play.

"He was very personable and you found yourself liking him, but at the same time you wanted to kick his butt," said former De La Salle athletic director Chuck Lafferty. "There were a lot of characters in the CAL back then, and he was the biggest character of them all."

Shaughnessy wore a hat to protect his freckled head from the sun after his curly red hair slowly turned white and began to thin. There were golf hats and even a white knit hat he found on the sideline. But mostly he just wore a baseball cap with "Shag" on the front. There was always a dollop of white sunblock on his nose.

Salesian's enrollment dwindled to 375 students at a time when De La Salle's student population was steadily rising. Shag taught English I and II, P.E., and driver's education. At different times he was assistant principal and dean of students. He coached football and track, was chairman of the P.E. Department, and also served as athletic director.

"He was a one-man band," said former Salesian quarterback Geoff Toretta, who transferred from Pinole Valley to Salesian because future major-league baseball player Dale Sveum had the quarterback position locked up at the public school. Geoff's younger brother Gino starred at quarterback for Pinole Valley before going on to the University of Miami, where he would win the Heisman Trophy.

"He did everything from getting kids to come out for the program to scouting. He had assistants, but you always got the feeling he could do it all himself. He had the ability to motivate guys who weren't as good; he made them think they were good and he had wacky ways to do it."

Shaughnessy got tired of hearing coaches complain about not seeing their families during the football season. He surrounded himself with his.

Diane hired babysitters on Friday nights and scouted high school football games with her husband. She only missed two games in his forty-year coaching career. The first was to see Oregon star Eugene "Choo Choo" Young, a former Chieftain, play Cal at Memorial Stadium.

The other was when she gave birth to their daughter Susie on game day. The four Salesian captains in the game her husband coached later that afternoon became Susie Shaughnessy's godfathers.

She was a mother to more than just her own children. Diane kept statistics, sold programs, took tickets, did whatever needed to be done to help her husband's program be successful. She hosted parties after big wins. The Salesian team bus would pull up right in front of the house.

Shag's four daughters were a constant presence on the sidelines. He called them ball girls and tee girls and sometimes invented things for them to do. His son Jake grew up following his dad around on game day, unlocking the gates and setting up the end zone pylons. Jake eventually joined his father's staff as the freshman coach.

The entire family went scouting together. They saw four games one weekend, including Salesian's game on Saturday afternoon. Shag asked who was coming along to scout a game later that night. It was one of the rare instances when he got no takers.

"I didn't know much about college or pro football other than it existed," Jake Shaughnessy recalls. "The team I followed and loved was the Salesian Chieftains. For a kid it was the coolest thing ever."

Shag's teams ran what he still calls a "horse-and-buggy offense." The Chiefs combined a punishing running game and hard-nosed defense with trick plays that their coach may as well have drawn up in dust.

By 1979 he was the godfather of CAL coaches and would soon begin referring to himself as "The Old Man." Salesian was the team that every other CAL team wanted to beat. St. Mary's was the Chieftains' traditional rival, but the rivalry with Moreau heated up when Al Vermeil arrived.

Then came Ladouceur and the rivalry with De La Salle.

"I never saw an arrogance from Ladouceur or De La Salle—never," Shaughnessy said. "But their fans could be arrogant as hell."

After being thoroughly defeated in 1979, the Spartans came into the Salesian game the following year fresh off an upset of St. Mary's, the No. 1-ranked team in the 2A East Bay Prep Writers Poll.

They retained their No. 1 ranking and avenged the previous season's 32–0 loss with a 16–8 win over Shaughnessy's Chieftains.

Salesian was ranked No. 1 and De La Salle No. 2 when they played the following year in the CAL opener for both schools. De La Salle quarterback Jay Jordan provided the Chieftains with all the extra motivation they needed when he was quoted in a *Contra Costa Times* article as saying: "We're going to win" and "After we go out and beat Salesian we'll have to take the rest of our games one at a time."

"Honest to God, that was so out of character for me," Jordan said in retrospect. "I never said those types of things. I always liked Joe Namath. Maybe that had something to do with it. I don't know. I was just a kid."

Jordan's quotes weren't what bothered Shaughnessy. What bothered him most was a quote attributed to Ladouceur in the same article.

"If Jay has a good day we can take them apart," Ladouceur said.

"I got pissed off over that," Shaughnessy admitted. "I told our kids it's about respect and they don't respect us very much. I told them I was

179

going to take that article and give it to Ladouceur when we shake hands in the middle of the field after we win."

Ladouceur and Shaughnessy are alike in many ways and different in many others. They are both taskmasters who teach fundamental football. They both believe in discipline, toughness, and outworking their opponents. Neither believes that film is a substitute for live scouting, and both keep the best interests of their players at heart.

Shaughnessy always has been extremely superstitious—every penny he finds on the ground on game day is another touchdown his team will score. Ladouceur doesn't believe in luck.

Shaughnessy thought it was important to let kids express themselves individually. He let players put anything they wanted on their helmets—stickers, nicknames, whatever. One player wrote "Chili" on his headgear. When the coach asked if that was his nickname, the player said no. Chili was his favorite food. Shag just laughed.

Ladouceur never allowed single-digit numbers because they draw attention to the individual and players fight over them. Former players are stunned and sometimes even disappointed to learn that he now allows names to be printed on the backs of jerseys.

Personality-wise, the two coaches are polar opposites. Shaughnessy is gregarious and animated while Ladouceur is quiet and detached.

"Shag appealed to the macho in kids," Chuck Lafferty said. "Bob appealed to the human in kids."

Shaughnessy knew he needed an edge heading into the 1981 game. It finally struck him. He would have his players paint their faces like wild Apache warriors, and instead of walking calmly through the gates when they took the field they would climb over the fence whooping and hollering like "wild-ass Indians."

Diane nixed that idea. The tactic would look awful silly if her husband's team lost the game, she warned.

The day of the game was stiflingly hot. De La Salle players had taken refuge under a weeping willow tree. Salesian players were walking past when one of them put on his helmet, lowered his head, and ran headlong into the De La Salle bus as the Spartans watched wide-eyed.

"He left a big dent in the fender," Shaughnessy said, chuckling at the memory. "I figured it would cost us a couple hundred bucks, but it was worth it. That was worth two touchdowns right there."

De La Salle led 17–7 early in the fourth quarter only to watch Shaughnessy's running game kick into high gear behind fullback Leo Mouton. The Chiefs took a 21–17 lead late in the game, then recovered a fumble on the ensuing kickoff when De La Salle's Greg Genovese suffered what appeared to be a serious neck injury on the return.

Genovese lay motionless on the field for fifteen chilling minutes before he was finally taken to a nearby hospital in an ambulance with what was later diagnosed, much to everyone's relief, as a sprained neck.

"He was down on the field for fifteen minutes and he wasn't moving," Jay Jordan remembers. "It cast a pall on what was already turning into a very bad day."

Shaughnessy fulfilled his promise when the game was over. He claims he only gave the article to Ladouceur. Others say he shoved the article in Ladouceur's face. Whichever, the incident almost sparked a brawl at midfield between coaches and players from both teams.

What Shaughnessy didn't realize was that many of his players were behind him yelling, "Take it home, coach!" to Ladouceur, which sent De La Salle players scrambling to defend their coach.

"When he turned around and saw his kids it shocked him, too," Ladouceur said. "He said, 'I don't want this,' and started pushing them away. I thought it was going to blow into a full-fledged riot."

Afterward, Shaughnessy made it sound as if he were only trying to mentor the young coach by teaching him a little humility. Ladouceur was infuriated. "He shoved the article in my face," he snapped to a *Contra Costa Times* reporter after the game. "It was totally unprofessional."

"What I should've done is taken him aside," Shaughnessy said twenty-two years later. "I shouldn't have done that in front of the kids. I'm real ashamed of what happened. I'll say that until my dying day."

Both coaches were called in front of the Catholic Athletic League's rules and sportsmanship committee, and Shaughnessy was reprimanded.

"Basically, what they did was chew my ass over that," Shaughnessy said. "The principal at Salesian loved to win. I remember we were driving back to school after the hearing and he said: 'They can say what they want but they can't change the score.'"

Shaughnessy knew his team was in trouble heading into the season finale against Ladouceur's Spartans the following year. The Spartans of 1982 already had thumped two teams from the supposedly superior

Diablo Valley Athletic League, outscored opponents 377–56 and were one win away from the first undefeated regular season in school history.

In addition, Shag noticed throughout the year that there was a De La Salle scout at almost every one of his team's games.

"They knew us better than we knew ourselves," he said.

A victory over Salesian would give Ladouceur's team its first-ever league championship and its first North Coast Section playoff bid. A loss would mean that the Spartans would share the conference title with the Chieftains, and Salesian would go to the playoffs on the strength of its head-to-head victory.

The game was hardly a game at all. The Spartans scored on six of their first seven possessions and outgained the Chiefs 389–60 in a 48–0 whitewashing.

De La Salle players celebrated the football program's first championship in thirteen years by giving their young coach a Marine-style crew cut in the locker room after the game, cashing in on Ladouceur's pregame promise.

"If anybody would've told me the final score would be 48–0 I would've said they were crazy," Shaughnessy said afterward.

That De La Salle team went on to accomplish something a Shaughnessy-coached team never did—win a North Coast Section title.

The seesaw rivalry continued in 1983 when De La Salle committed nine turnovers and watched Salesian end the Spartans' hopes for an unbeaten season. The Spartans turned the tables the following year. An offense led by quarterback Mark Panella exploded for five second-half touchdowns en route to a 42–7 win that would serve as a springboard for the program's second NCS 2A title in three years.

That, however, was Shaughnessy's final season at Salesian. He never wanted to leave. He considered himself a Chieftain for life. It still brings tears to his eyes to discuss the philosophical differences with the Salesian principal that resulted in his leaving the school where he had taught and coached for seventeen years.

He took over at St. Mary's the following year, but his new team appeared to be no match for the Spartans of 1985, the most talented team Ladouceur had coached in his seven years at De La Salle.

The Spartans had won thirteen straight games by an average score of

45–9. Their offense was averaging 440 yards per game but couldn't score a touchdown in the first half against Shaughnessy's new team. St. Mary's led 13–3 at halftime, its first touchdown coming on a 68-yard pass and the second coming on a play that was pure, unfiltered Shag.

It was a halfback pass. His strong-armed halfback Paul Howard took a pitch and appeared to be sweeping the right end when he stopped and threw a pass all the way back across the field to Shon Page, who was streaking down the left sideline. The 20-yard pass traveled 40 yards in the air.

De La Salle coaches noticed something else during the first half. It almost seemed as if the St. Mary's defense knew what was coming. Players reported that Shaughnessy knew what play they were going to run and was telling his players before the snap.

"THEY DON'T KNOW OUR PLAYS," Eidson kept insisting.

"So I'm wandering around in the end zone late in the second quarter and I see them stealing the walkie-talkie plays," said former De La Salle basketball coach Steve Coccimiglio, who was doubling as the student supervisor that night. "Blair Thomas was calling the plays down to Lad, and their coaches were on the same frequency. These were real cheap walkie-talkies. They had a couple guys standing in front of another guy who's got a walkie-talkie and they're stealing the plays."

Ladouceur took Coccimiglio's eyewitness account seriously enough to call the tight-end middle screen, a play he hadn't run in three years and therefore a play Shaughnessy couldn't possibly have anticipated. When they saw Shag running up and down the sideline screaming, "Tight-end screen!" Ladouceur took off his headset and threw it to the ground, disgusted.

He hasn't worn a headset since.

Shaughnessy admits they were intercepting De La Salle's plays, but claims it was only for a short while and only after they accidentally tripped across the frequency. To ignore such a stroke of luck, after all, might seem ungrateful.

"I should've just gotten on the bus and left when it was 13–3," he said. "I could've just said, 'Oops, I thought the game was over.'"

De La Salle scored 47 points in the second half—crossing the goal line seven times in less than seventeen minutes—to win 50–13. As the touchdowns piled up Shaughnessy could be heard yelling across the field, "How many touchdowns do you need, asshole?"

"CHEATER!" Eidson screamed back, shaking his fist.

Coccimiglio and others claim that was the only time they ever saw Ladouceur leave his starters in for the entire game. Ladouceur denies running up the score that day—or any day.

"Shaughnessy is Shaughnessy," Ladouceur said. "Did that surprise me? No. Did that anger me? No. That's just him. I don't think he's a bad guy. I think he's a good guy. He's done a lot for kids. He's built programs up and given kids a sense of pride. He's done wonderful things as a coach but Shag is Shag. I never wanted to stick it to him. I loved beating him but I never wanted to humiliate him because you're not just humiliating him, you're humiliating kids. I don't humiliate kids."

That was the last time Ladouceur and Shaughnessy met head-to-head. The Catholic Athletic League was disbanded when the North Coast Section realigned member schools, and their two teams ended up in different leagues.

Shaughnessy retired after the 2000 season with a 254–118–6 record, 16 league championships, and 14 NCS playoff appearances. Perhaps his greatest claim to fame is a 3–4 record against Ladouceur.

"It's easy to take shots at him because he was so out front and visible, but I'm pretty confident I knew where his heart was," Lafferty says of Shaughnessy. "He loved his kids and would do anything for them."

LONG BEACH POLY 2002
Britt Cecil's Redemption

t he thought had never occurred to Britt or Rick Cecil. It was assumed that Britt would attend the local high school. Then during the fall of his eighth-grade year, he and his father watched a De La Salle football game on television.

"Hey, wouldn't it be cool if I could go there?" Britt asked his dad. Rick Cecil was intrigued, but the conversation ended there. Later, without his son's knowledge, he began to investigate the possibility.

Rick Cecil spent eight years as an electronics technician in the Navy before becoming a systems specialist at the Oakland Air Traffic Control Center. He moved his family to Livermore, an eclectic town of 75,000 that is home to nuclear scientists, winemakers, cowboys, and commuters. A knee injury prevented Rick from playing high school football himself, but he and his wife Paige, a former cheerleader, took a keen interest in their son's athletic career.

Britt was always a natural athlete, delighting his parents. He was a perennial all-star shortstop in Little League. Mostly he wanted to play football.

When Rick and Paige spotted a banner hanging from an overpass announcing the upcoming youth-league season, they signed Britt up immediately and watched every practice and game. They already were wondering if Livermore High School's football program was the best place for their son. Then Britt suggested De La Salle all by himself. Rick and Paige were fascinated by the idea.

They had applied for Britt's admission into De La Salle when they saw an ad for Ladouceur's Championship Football Camp. Rick was curious to see if Britt could withstand the scrutiny of high-level coaching. Most of all, he wanted to know just how good Britt really was.

"Is this kid as good as I think he is?" Rick wondered. "I'm his father, so it is hard for me to know. Is he as good as other people say? It's one thing to be good in Livermore, but it's different at De La Salle."

Rick and Paige took a week off work and attended every camp session. Each player receives a written evaluation when the week-long camp ends. Rick and Paige were thrilled when Britt was named the camp's most valuable player.

"That struck us," Rick said. "We were sitting there thinking, 'God, no, he couldn't possibly be the MVP.' This is the preeminent coach in the country and he's saying all these wonderful things about my son. It was crystal-clear validation to us about why we came to this camp."

Britt's future at De La Salle was sealed when he attended an open house at the school and heard a graduating senior speak. The motto of Lasallian schools is: Enter to learn, leave to serve. That was the message of the speech, but it was the delivery that convinced Britt he wanted to attend De La Salle.

"He didn't play sports, but he talked about what it was like to be a Spartan," Britt recalls. "I was blown away. The guy was eighteen and he sounded like he was forty. When we walked out I said, 'Wow, I really want to come here.'"

Livermore lies in northern Alameda County, some thirty-five miles from De La Salle's campus. The commute, which takes anywhere between forty-five minutes and two hours depending on traffic, would be a twice-daily chore. Paying the then $7,100 for tuition meant that the Cecils wouldn't be able to purchase the new home they coveted.

Britt's acceptance letter was displayed on the wall of his bedroom. Britt entered school that fall with Ladouceur's glowing words resonating inside him.

It would be three years before he would hear such praise again.

Britt was the starting freshman quarterback when he pulled a back muscle during the fourth game of the season. He missed the next game and wasn't immediately re-inserted into the lineup when he received medical clearance.

He had been unable to find a niche on campus, and now he felt betrayed by the coaching staff. De La Salle was different than other schools he had attended. Students came from all over the county and formed cliques with students from their hometowns. This was especially true among incoming freshmen.

Britt missed his old friends, his old life. He hung out mainly with the few kids he knew from Livermore. They were the ones who suggested he blow off practice one day. He readily agreed. He felt as if he were stuck in an endless routine of early mornings, long car rides, classes, practices, and homework.

Everyone said that high school was supposed to be the best time of your life. If that was the case, why shouldn't he have some fun?

He jumped in a car with his friends and drove to a nearby strip mall. Somebody produced a baggie, and soon a pipe was being packed and passed. Thick marijuana smoke filled the inside of the car with its acrid aroma.

The news spread fast. Britt's friends boasted about what they had done and soon the whole campus knew. Britt still believed his secret was safe when Ladouceur appeared as he stuffed books into his locker the next morning.

"Where were you yesterday?" Ladouceur asked.

"Doing homework," Britt replied, quickly. Too quickly.

Ladouceur nodded. "Did you tell your coach?"

"No, I had a teammate tell Coach," Britt answered honestly.

"That's not acceptable," Ladouceur said. "Talk to your coach yourself."

Britt exhaled when Ladouceur was gone. It wasn't until he and the other boys were summoned to Joe Aliotti's office that reality sank in.

"It was pretty intimidating," Britt said. "We 'fessed up."

The dean of students wields great power at De La Salle. There is no school board. The Spartan Life Handbook explains rules and potential consequences. Aliotti is free to use his discretion within the boundaries provided. He metes out suspensions and expulsions on a case-by-case basis. Parents may appeal to the principal, but few cases are overturned or reversed.

The policy states that possession, transfer, or being under the influence of any controlled substance can result in immediate suspension. The student may also be placed on "contract," which can include drug counseling and/or testing and requires strict adherence to the other rules outlined in the handbook.

Aliotti will immediately suspend and often expel a student caught selling drugs. A student caught using is put on contract, which can be binding for the remainder of the student's career, or terminated on Aliotti's whim.

Britt Cecil was suspended for two days and not allowed to participate in athletics until Aliotti decided otherwise. That wasn't the worst part. The worst part was what Aliotti told him when he pulled him aside after the meeting.

"How does it feel to lie to Coach Lad's face?"

Britt felt the nausea rising in his stomach before the words were out of Aliotti's mouth. He had lied to the man he wanted to impress more than anyone. Ladouceur had known when he questioned Britt earlier that morning.

Britt wanted to run, to cry. He felt unworthy, dirty. He respected Ladouceur so much and was convinced that such respect would never be reciprocated, not after this. Who was Britt Cecil to Bob Ladouceur? His mind raced. Why would Coach Lad respect any freshman, let alone a freshman who had smoked pot and then lied about it?

He rode home from school with the mother of a friend who also had been suspended. Paige was devastated. She wanted to withdraw her son from De La Salle. Why spend all that money on private-school tuition if Britt was going to get into the kind of trouble they were trying to shield him from?

Rick was enraged. He had sacrificed time and money to enroll his son at De La Salle, and this was how Britt was repaying them?

"I hope you're happy," he told his son.

Britt spent the rest of the day in his room, where he could hear his parents talking in subdued tones. He overheard his father on the phone, inquiring about the possibility of Britt transferring to Livermore High.

The threat of expulsion hung in the air. Rick and Paige met with Aliotti and were relieved to learn that he and other faculty members were forgiving.

"I was interested to see if De La Salle wanted to wash their hands of him or give him a chance at redemption," Rick said. "They were willing to give him a second chance, but he had to prove it, not just say it."

Aliotti didn't believe that drug testing or counseling was necessary, but he made it clear that if Britt made one more mistake he was gone.

"I was looking forward to transferring to Livermore at first," Britt said. "I talked to my parents and they were so disappointed. They didn't want me to give in that easily. I went back to De La Salle for my parents first. It wasn't until later that I realized I'd done it for myself, too."

Britt was the talk of the school when he returned. He didn't think he would ever be able to escape the black cloud that hovered over him. He didn't know it then, but it would shadow him until the summer before his senior year.

"It's unfortunate, but it will always be with you," Aliotti told him. "You made that choice to do that; now people are going to say, 'Look at that quarterback, he's a dope-smoker.' People do things like that because of the choices you make. People are going to think Britt Cecil is a dope-smoker. You're going to have to prove to everybody that that's not the way you are."

Britt went out for the freshman basketball team even though he would not be allowed to participate in the games. He set his alarm clock for 4:30 A.M. so he could attend 6 A.M. practices. Rick dropped him off on his way to work, and Britt waited in the predawn darkness for the gym door to be unlocked.

He traveled with the team to all the games and watched in street clothes. He received the news in December. Aliotti was satisfied. Britt could play.

"I wasn't sure they were paying attention to me," Britt said. "Them giving me permission to play made me realize they were watching my progress and were curious to see which way I would go. I wanted to prove to them that I would go the right way."

He still felt like a parolee. The incident lowered the ceiling on his expectations. He had lied to Coach Lad, after all. As far as he knew, he would carry the stigma across the stage on graduation day.

Britt was too humiliated to face Ladouceur. Rick wondered if Britt could work out with the varsity during the summer between his freshman and sophomore seasons, but Britt didn't feel that he had even earned the right to ask.

"Lad is a mysterious man," Britt says. "You never know what's going on with him. I wanted to know what he would do. He didn't do anything. I wanted to know what he was thinking, but there was no way to figure that out."

∼

Britt was getting pulverized in the first half of the first junior varsity game during his sophomore year. His offensive line wasn't picking up blitzing defenders. Britt got up more slowly after every hit, his body language telling everyone that this wasn't his fault.

De La Salle trailed Buchanan 16–0 at halftime when Ladouceur walked into the locker room. "Where's the quarterback?" he demanded.

Britt raised a tentative hand from the back of the room and was summoned to the front, where he was admonished in front of the team.

"What are you doing in the back? Sit in front. You're the quarterback. You're supposed to be the leader."

Britt nodded but said nothing.

"Are you hurt?" Ladouceur asked.

Britt mumbled, "No."

"Then why are you getting up so slow?" Ladouceur asked.

Britt remained silent.

"Get out there and lead the team in the second half," Ladouceur told him.

Britt was shaken by the exchange but engineered two second-half scoring drives to pull the Spartans to 16–14. Two potential go-ahead touchdowns were called back because of penalties.

De La Salle trailed by two with 12 seconds left in regulation. Britt dropped back near Buchanan's 30-yard line and threw a pass over the middle to De'Montae Fitzgerald, who was pushed out of bounds at the 1-yard line as time expired. The JV team didn't lose another game. Britt threw for 900 yards that season and rushed for nearly 500 more. He bounced up whenever he got knocked down.

"At first it scared me," Britt said, recalling the scolding. "But then I realized he was watching me. That's what I most wanted to know."

As a junior Cecil began his first year under Ladouceur's direct tutelage with no aspirations beyond being the third-string quarterback behind Matt Gutierrez and Brian Callahan. He would get out of his season whatever he put into it. He wanted to redeem himself for the mistake he made two years before.

His enthusiasm waned as the season dragged on. There was no pressure, no urgency given his status with the team. He was the long snapper for punts and field goals and the scout team quarterback. He kept his head down and mouth shut, avoiding Ladouceur at all costs, which wasn't difficult given his role.

"When I was suspended it set a boundary for me, or at least that's what I thought," he recalls. "I didn't know what I was allowed to say to him or what I could ask."

Britt joined his teammates when the offseason conditioning began in January, but he soon found himself in Aliotti's office once again. Graduating seniors had been making life hard for the new geology teacher, and Britt had joined in the fun. Ladouceur was made aware of his behavior.

"What now?" Ladouceur wanted to know. "When are you going to snap out of it and become the quarterback of this team? We've got guys behind you who can step up and do the job. Let us know what you want to do."

That was the problem. Britt didn't know what he was supposed to do. He was supposed to act like the varsity quarterback, but what did that mean? He didn't know what was expected of him and was too intimidated to ask.

"All I was getting was negative feedback and no shove in the right direction," Britt says. "I didn't know what steps I needed to take. I knew I had to be like Matt Gutierrez, but I didn't know how to get there. He was a three-year starter. How do I get to that level of maturity and respect?"

Rick and Paige didn't believe that Ladouceur was offering enough support or guidance. Ladouceur admitted as much in a meeting with them. He should've told Britt that he was forgiven for the mistake he made as a freshman.

Britt's parents were told that their son needed to become a leader on and off the field. Britt was unsure of how to assume the role. Given his past, wasn't it hypocritical for him to tell others how to behave?

Ladouceur wanted Britt to figure that out for himself.

"He's not a very approachable guy, even for an adult," Rick says of Ladouceur. "He's got such a presence. But it was a much more relaxed conversation than I expected. When I walked out of there I felt comfortable. He gets it. Looking back on it, maybe some placating was going on. There may have been some psychology to it, but that's fine by me."

Britt buckled down, separated himself from class clowns, and his GPA rose from 2.5 to nearly 3.0. He called a team meeting when offseason workouts weren't progressing to his satisfaction. He worked hard. It seemed that whenever his teammates saw him he was watching film or studying the playbook.

"I don't think Ladouceur does anything that's not calculated," Rick said. "The proof is in the pudding. The kid is growing up. It was a fantastic lesson for him. We couldn't have planned it better. It will serve him well."

~

The last practice of the week is always the most carefree, and the Friday walk-through before the 2001 Poly game is no exception.

Players laugh and talk as they stretch by themselves, wearing only their game jerseys and shorts. This is Eidson's day, which explains why there are no other coaches on the field. The first third of practice is dedicated to special teams. The day before a game also is the day that the Cobra persona makes his weekly appearance. Given the magnitude of the upcoming game, there is little doubt that today's encounter will be memorable.

Players begin chanting at the first sight of Eidson in his silver-studded, black leather coat, black sunglasses, black slacks, and black zip-up boots. "Cobra! Cobra! Cobra!"

Cobra ends his act by pulling out a stuffed rabbit pilfered from his daughter's room, soaking it with lighter fluid, and setting it ablaze in the end zone, prompting wild cheers as flames engulf the bunny.

"Cobra! Cobra! Cobra!"

The broadcast team that will televise Saturday's game visits with Bob Ladouceur before practice and watches from the sideline as Tony Binswanger is called to the middle of the field for field goal practice.

This is the kicker's defining moment of the week, the one time he's on the field with his teammates in a competitive practice situation. It's also a time when he'd rather be anywhere else.

The team gathers around him, shouting, "Hook it! Miss it!" before every kick, trying to simulate the pressure he might encounter in a game. Eidson and Aliotti, who are forever organizing faculty-wide pools, pull cash out of their pockets and wager, or at least pretend to, on every attempted field goal, which makes the stakes that much higher. Eidson and Aliotti are always organizing some faculty-wide pool. The cash goes under the kicking block until the bet is decided. Eidson will stoop to pick it up if the kick is good. Aliotti will claim it if it's wide or short.

With his teammates screaming in his face, with Eidson and Aliotti bent over at the waist, hands on knees, watching intently, and with the Fox Sports television crew looking on, Binswanger shanks a 40-yarder.

"BINSWANGER, WILL YOU FOLLOW THROUGH AND KICK IT, FOR CHRISTSAKES!" Eidson screams as he moves the block to the opposite hash.

Aliotti makes a show of licking his finger and slowing counting his winnings, a huge grin on his face. Eidson searches his pockets for more cash and comes up empty. He retrieves a credit card from his wallet and places it under the block—double or nothing.

"KICK THROUGH THE BALL AND KEEP YOUR HEAD DOWN!" he yells at Binswanger, who would've crawled under the bleachers and stayed there if he could. "YOUR COACH IS GOING TO BE BROKE."

Much to his and Eidson's relief, Binswanger nails the next one.

"IT'S 41–40 POLY," Eidson shouts as he repositions the ball in the middle of the field. "LAST PLAY OF THE GAME RIGHT HERE. IT'S ALL ON YOUR SHOULDERS!"

Players are behind their kicker now, chanting, "Nail it! Nail it!" The snap comes back and the ball goes down. Binswanger is mobbed by his teammates as the ball sails cleanly through the uprights.

"WE WIN!" Eidson shouts, holding his arms up in triumph.

Later, deep shadows are cast as the sun dips behind the trees in the northwest corner of the field. Practice is running long. Equipment manager Chris Rodriguez's four children are playing in the bleachers while he tightens facemasks and pumps air into helmets.

John Chan slaps his arm, then his calf, then his arm again.

"I hate this time of day because it's when all the mosquitoes come out," he says.

Someone screams, "DE LA SALLE SUCKS!" from a passing car. Chan rolls his eyes.

It's the only goal Ladouceur hasn't reached in nearly a quarter-century at the school. He remembers hearing people shout insults as they drove by during his first season and thought how nice it would be to elevate the program to the point where the heckling would stop.

It never has, although now people hurl insults for much different reasons than they did in 1979.

"Now practice can end," backup receiver Chris Kinsel says. "We've heard our 'De La Salle sucks' for the day."

Players finish eating the night before the Poly game and are inside watching television while coaches finish their linguine with pesto and ziti with sausage on the back deck of Matt Kavanaugh's family's house.

"Give your two favorite run plays, your favorite pass plays, and the pass play you think will go for big yards," Ladouceur says.

Ladouceur's assistants all give their input while he sits there, chewing, listening intently and straining to hear as if he can't wait for the information to make its way across the table.

He nods as each coach speaks in turn.

"The key to the game will be turnovers," says Aliotti, eying an ice cream bar. "We've had fifteen fumbles in five games."

"You're not going to say that, are you?" Ladouceur asks, incredulous.

"What?" Aliotti answers, defensively.

"This isn't time to hammer them," Ladouceur says, revealing the joke and making Aliotti smile. "We've got to build them up."

Aliotti rolls his eyes before pointing his thumb at Ladouceur by way of explanation. "That's what I've been telling him all week," he says.

Paula Kavanaugh sets a huge tray of brownies on the table next to a plate of Rice Krispy treats. Ladouceur picks up a Rice Krispy treat, holds it three feet above the table before dropping it, then nods his approval. Paula rolls her eyes and walks away.

The Rice Krispy treats were dry and hard at a team dinner the year before, and Ladouceur teased one of the moms about it. Ever since, he has made a show of dropping a treat on the table as a test, the height of the corresponding bounce revealing the confection's moisture content.

"Wouldn't it be nice to have just one of their kids?" Aliotti asks, referring to Long Beach Poly's roster.

"No. 60's twelve-year-old brother could start for us," Alumbaugh says, as if repeating a well-known fact.

They break into groups then. Poly has outscored its four previous opponents by an average of 42–9 thanks largely to a potent passing attack that features senior quarterback Leon Jackson and junior receiver Derrick Jones, who wants to redeem himself after dropping three potential touchdown passes against De La Salle in the 2001 game.

De La Salle cornerbacks Damon Jenkins and Willie Glasper are fast, but they aren't as fast as Jones, who has been clocked at 10.3 seconds in the 100 meters and is averaging 38 yards per catch through the first four games.

"In all their games I've never seen these guys drive it down the field," Eidson tells his secondary. "Last year, we hung in there, and the longer they were out there the worse their blocking got. This is where your conditioning will pay off. It won't show up on the first three downs of the drive, but the longer the drive goes, the more your conditioning will show up."

Eidson is the first to speak after players assemble in the garage, a stuffed deer's head looking down upon the assemblage. Fishing poles and skis rest on rafters. A metal locker filled with canned goods sits along a wall next to a dartboard.

He tells the team that Poly has yet to acknowledge that De La Salle had been the better team the year before. Everything he heard and read from the Jackrabbits after the 2001 game focused on missed opportunities, how they would've won if they had just converted on a few of those fourth downs and caught a few more passes. Not once, Eidson says, has he heard anybody from Poly acknowledge that the better team won.

He calls Poly a "numbers team." That's all they care about, according to Eidson: how many players go on to play for Division-I colleges or the NFL. All people talk about is how fast they run, how much weight they can lift, and how many yards they average per carry and catch.

"... This is not the impossible dream. That's how they act down there. It has to be a miracle or something. Bullshit. It doesn't have to be a miracle. They want miracles, go to the Vatican—that's where miracles happen. This is something that can and should happen.

"If you guys play with heart, we'll be fine. It's just a matter of executing tomorrow. That's what it comes down to. If we drop the ball and give those guys great field position, and we keep our defense on the field all game like we did in the second half last year, we're going to run into problems. If we don't cover on special teams, we're going to run into problems. I knew this team was going to get progressively better. I think you're primed offensively and defensively to put it together....

"Keep your wits about you. We could get behind tomorrow. That's a definite scenario. We could get behind by two touchdowns. That COULD happen. Don't panic. Stay together. Don't get intimidated if something goes wrong because I know the one thing we've got going for us that they don't have—and I don't care what they say—they don't have the grit and desire that you have. They have not put in the time that you have.

"Personally, I don't think they care as much as you. They talk about how they do but I don't buy it, not one bit. You'll beat them tomorrow and they'll go, 'Ah, we've got the Southern Section to win, that's our goal.' They've got their excuses ready. This game means more to you than it does to them. I'll always believe that.

"It's always about their accomplishments later. They've got thirty-nine guys in the NFL. Great. This is a high school football game. We're not trying to beat them in the NFL. They would beat us in an NFL game. Congratulations. But we're not playing in the NFL tomorrow, and we're 1–0 against them in high school. This game isn't played on video. It won't be played on the back of a football card. It's played on the field.

"It's a great opportunity. I don't know what more you'd want as a high school football player. This is a dream come true. It's déjà vu all over again. It's another great game. It's the talk of the country. *Sports Illustrated, ESPN the Magazine, USA Today*—they're all going to be there for this game. That shows you the interest. You get to play a great game. I suggest you go balls out and enjoy every minute of it."

Everybody is waiting to hear what Ladouceur will say. This is the biggest game of the year, an even bigger game than last year if for no other reason than De La Salle is not as talented.

There is great anticipation, even among the assistant coaches, as Ladouceur rises to speak. He starts by reminding players to check their equipment. He doesn't want them coming out of the game because of a loose facemask or because the strings holding their shoulder pads together have broken. They had better attend to those details before the game because the equipment is going to get some wear. No excuses.

"Two things I want to mention tonight, just two.

"I don't know if I agree with Coach Eidson. I agree with a lot of what he said but I don't know if I agree 100 percent with what he said. Some of the things I've read in the paper indicate that this team may be a little different than last year's team. Last year all those guys fought for attention, to get the ball, and they complained when it didn't happen for them. Some of the things I read gave me the indication that they have come together more as a team. They say they don't care who gets the carries. I don't know if it's true or not. We'll see.

"One quote in particular I paid attention to. Someone off that team actually gave you guys a compliment and that was [Freddie] Parish. It was an offhanded compliment. They essentially said, 'They weren't intimidated by you guys at all.' But Parish said, 'They play differently. Their hearts are as big as their chests.' I thought that was a real compliment coming from a Poly player. That indicated that they understand something they didn't understand previously. That kind of concerns me because I think they're going to take you seriously tomorrow, a lot more seriously. What concerns me most is, is he talking about last year's team or is he talking about you guys?

"Is your heart actually as big as your chest? That's a good question you have to answer tomorrow. Is he correct in that assessment? Tomorrow is the test for that. The test for that isn't against Clayton Valley or Liberty, it's against Poly. That's the test for that.

"The other thing I want to say tonight is this. You guys are all going to have to individually—I'm not talking collectively, I'm not talking as a team—individually you are going to have to make a decision tonight. The decision is, are you willing to play through the discomfort to play a great game tomorrow? Playing a great game individually isn't going to be easy. It isn't going to be comfortable.

"You're going to be tired, you're going to get fatigued, you're going to get hit, you may even get your bell rung. You may get an ouch here and a hurt there [he points to his thigh, his elbow] and a pop in the back. It's not going to be easy and you need to make the decision tonight. Can you live with that and can you work through that?

"That's the scare factor of football. That's what I remember from the game, that I had to individually decide, how am I going to play this game tomorrow? Am I going to look for chances to take plays off? Am I going to look for chances to rest on a series or when the play is going away from me and I can get away with it? All those things present themselves in a game, and you guys have to decide how you're going to do that before you get on the field. You have to search your own heart.

"In a certain sense, it's like walking on hot coals. You know it's coming, you're not going to like it. You know it's going to be uncomfortable, going to hurt, and all that other shit but you still have to do it if you want to play well. The sooner you decide I can go through this, I can do it, the more prepared you're going to be and the better you're going to play. . . .

"If you're a one-way player and you're not out there kicking ass, that's a crime. There's no excuse for that. I don't care if you're playing against King Kong, if you're a one-way guy, with the training you've had and the condition you're in, you ought to be killing people out there. . . . There's no reason why any of you should be dragging your ass the way [Andy] Briner and [Derek] Landri did last year. Those guys were two-way players. They went in and they didn't come out. Or they came out when they were totally gassed. Make that decision now. Don't be riding over to Memorial Stadium wondering what kind of effort you're going to give today. To answer the question, you have to live up to what they already think of you. It's a great question. Are their hearts as big as their chests? I read that in the paper today, and I thought, damn, what a compliment, but is it true? You'll have to prove it with your play.

"Anything I said about the streak still holds true. I don't give a shit about the win or the loss. I do care about how you play, with passion, desire, heart, intensity, grit, determination, do not give up, do not let up, that's what I care about. That's all you should care about, too. So, if we win it's like, yes! We earned that son of a bitch. And if we lose, you say fuck it. We did the best we could. We move on. That's how it's got to be, because you'll regret it later if it's not."

They go through the offensive and defensive checklists, with even more attention to detail than usual. But it's getting late, and because kickoff is scheduled for 2 P.M., Ladouceur doesn't want the meeting to run long. He wants players to get their rest.

"I still think I'm improving," Cameron Colvin tells his teammates. "I haven't proven anything yet. You guys can depend on me."

The coaches hope Gino Ottoboni will be the X factor, much like the unheralded Drew had been the year before. With the Poly defense keying on Drew—they aren't going to let him sneak up on them again—Ottoboni will play a more prominent role in the offense.

"I feel like Cameron does, like I really haven't proven myself yet," Ottoboni says. "I've never rushed for 100 yards and that's disappointing. Tomorrow afternoon I may not rush for 100 yards but every yard will be hard-fought. I'm not going to let you guys down because I know you guys are going to be doing the same thing."

"I don't expect you to go for 100 yards," Ladouceur tells Ottoboni. "I expect you to score a touchdown and pick up some first downs."

John Chan talks about how he hurt his knee in the second quarter of last year's game and watched helplessly from the sideline when his teammates needed him most. He feels that he never proved himself against Poly, but vows that will soon change.

"It seems like Poly underestimates me, and I don't blame them because

I haven't done anything yet," Cecil says later. "I look at this as an opportunity to make big plays."

"They haven't learned yet," De'Montae Fitzgerald says. "They think we're choir boys who can't hang with all their talent. They haven't learned about our hard work and commitment."

"I haven't done anything," Chris Biller says, the disappointment registering on his face. "I want you guys to have faith in me."

Ladouceur looks at his watch. It's getting late. He asks if anybody has anything to say that can wrap up the night.

Aliotti rarely addresses the team in these situations but makes an exception tonight: "In a game like this, everybody has to take care of their job," he says. "If everybody takes care of their job and works hard and works together, it will be hard to stop you. Do YOUR job well and you'll be successful. YOUR job."

~

Memorial Stadium on the University of California-Berkeley campus was opened in 1923 and named to honor soldiers who perished in World War I. It remains one of the most spectacular settings in college football, even if the weathered wooden benches are filled with splinters and curling strips of paint hang from its cement walls.

The old bowl sits in picturesque Strawberry Canyon, with the pine-tree-covered Berkeley hills to the east and a panoramic view of Oakland, San Francisco, and the bay to the west.

De La Salle players and coaches are led to the Big Game room, which is packed with memorabilia honoring the Cal-Stanford rivalry. Players are getting their ankles taped, reviewing scouting reports, checking their equipment, and listening to music when a crisis arises.

Binswanger has forgotten his helmet.

"Sorry, Coach," he tells Eidson, who keeps his cool. No problem, he tells Binswanger. There are two hours before kickoff, enough time for someone to drive back to school and pick it up.

"We can expect a few shanks now," Eidson whispers to Aliotti as they discuss whom they should dispatch to fetch the helmet.

Ladouceur paces around the silent room as kickoff approaches. He walks onto the balcony, near where legendary Cal coach Pappy Waldorf once addressed swelling masses of fans as if he were a presidential candidate. De La Salle fans are tailgating in the parking lot. The mothers of several players join hands in a pregame prayer.

A floor fan drones in the front of the room, drowning out the nervous coughing and throat-clearing. Ladouceur shares a joke with Blasquez before slowly making his way to the front of the room and closing the sliding glass door to the balcony, which clanks shut with the finality of a cell door. He turns off the fan. Players wait expectantly.

"You guys enjoy this day and have fun," he says at last, breaking the silence. "The fun begins when you start making plays out there. It's a special day for De La Salle football. It's a special day for high school football, and you guys are part of that. You should enjoy that and be proud of that. It takes a lot of work to get to this point where we are right now, and it will take a lot more work to put us over the top in this one. I know you guys are going to do that today."

Long Beach Poly players can be heard chanting "LET'S GO PO-LY!" through the closed locker room door as they prepare to take the field. It's unnerving.

"Don't panic," Ladouceur resumes, louder now. "Don't worry about making mistakes. Mistakes are going to be made. They're going to make plays today. We've got to make more plays than they do. You do that with execution and by getting after them. Be smart on special teams. Get good field position for us. Don't clip. Don't let a punt roll. If it's a bad punt take it on a good hop, get in front of it and have fun. This is what you guys do as football players. We're at that game. So go out and glorify yourselves personally and collectively, and I mean that in a very spiritual way."

Strangers slap them on their helmets and shoulder pads as they walk silently through the locker room door after kneeling in prayer. "Put a hurt on them," one gray-haired man says. Players hold hands as they walk solemnly down two flights of stairs, through the low stone tunnel, and into the brilliant sunshine. The grass is an almost electric green in contrast to the deep blue sky. "California" is spelled out on a backdrop of blue and gold diamonds in one end zone. "Golden Bears" adorns the other.

Stadium workers have roped off seating in both end zones of the 75,000-seat stadium. The De La Salle side is packed from top to bottom, end to end. The pregame reception for De La Salle alumni and supporters was packed. The whole day feels like a big reunion.

Poly fans, seated in the blinding sun, fill up about one-fourth of the visitors' side. The final attendance will be announced as 15,000; the crowd appears much larger than that.

Freddie Parish was a two-way standout during his sophomore year at South Torrance High School but sat on the bench behind All-American free safety Darnell Bing during his junior year at Poly. He was so physically impressive at recruiting combines during the offseason that he collected fourteen scholarship offers before starting his first game for Poly. He already has committed to Notre Dame.

A De La Salle teammate points it out during warm-ups—Parish has a picture of Drew on the pad that protects his lower back. On the left side of the picture is the word "Drew," and on the right side, "Who?"

Television cameras focus on Britt Cecil as the De La Salle offense takes the field in their home green jerseys. It is duly noted by broadcasters that the senior quarterback has yet to throw his first touchdown pass of the season.

Drew, who returns the opening kickoff 25 yards, runs up the middle for two more on the first play of the game before being hit hard by Parish. The Poly defense isn't as massive as it was the year before, but this still looks like a college team. Poly players, in their white jerseys with green numbers, gold helmets, and gold pants, tower over the De La Salle offensive linemen.

Ottoboni gets the ball next and is swallowed by the Poly line. The senior has never been so nervous before a game. The defense will be preoccupied with Drew, and he hopes to play the role that Drew played the year before. He has gotten more repetitions in practice, and Panella told him this will be his breakout game.

Cecil drops confidently back on third-and-8 and hits Cameron Colvin for an 18-yard gain. On the next play, Chris Biller, starting at right tackle, fires off the ball and straight into the team highlight film.

Biller is matched against 6'5", 250-pound defensive end Junior Lemau'u, who is ranked the No. 2 defensive end in the West by one recruiting service. Lemau'u received scholarship offers from USC, Oregon, and Washington after bench-pressing 185 pounds thirty-five times at a recruiting camp during the summer.

Biller, five inches shorter and 45 pounds lighter, buries his helmet in Lemau'u's chest and drives him 10 yards into the secondary. Then he knocks Lemau'u off his feet and falls on him.

It is easily the most dominating block of the year, and it helps Drew pick up 17 yards to the Poly 35-yard line.

"Besides the fact that it was a great block, it said a lot about what we do," Ladouceur says later. "It shows a lot of the belief and courage our kids have, that they can take out guys who are bigger and stronger than them. They have the ability to rise above size and ability difference by sheer determination. It stood for something besides a great block."

Ottoboni picks up five yards, and 15 more are tacked onto the end of the play because of a facemask penalty on the Jackrabbits.

Drew disappears into a scrum in the middle of the line on the next play before popping out the other side. He absorbs a ferocious hit from a Poly defensive back but somehow spins away, dropping his hand to the turf to maintain his balance. He keeps his legs churning and dives to the 1-yard line as the De La Salle crowd goes wild.

Cecil scores on a sneak and Binswanger, who received his helmet with time to spare, adds the extra point to give the Spartans a 7–0 lead with 9:07 left in the first quarter.

Sandie runs up and down the sideline, distributing high fives. Panella is in Cecil's face as soon as the senior walks off the field, congratulating him for the game-opening drive. Biller wears a Cheshire grin as he walks the sideline, his hair clipped in military style.

Eidson expects Long Beach to throw deep. He wouldn't be surprised if left-handed quarterback Leon Jackson throws a bomb to Derrick Jones on the first play from scrimmage, repeating the Jackrabbits' opening play from the 2001 game.

"We've got fast guys, but we don't have anybody as fast as Derrick Jones," Eidson said earlier in the week.

Dwayne Washington picks up a yard on first down before recovering his own fumble. Spartans' linebacker Terrance Kelly pops Lorenzo Bursey after a 3-yard gain before Jackson finds receiver Alex Watson wide open over the middle for a 26-yard gain. It's an impressive across-the-field throw. If given time, Jackson can deliver the ball to his receivers in the blink of an eye.

"There's got to be a safety back there," Aliotti points out on the side-line. "I KNOW THAT!" Eidson screams, signaling in the next play while intermittently hiking up his pants.

Jackson's scrambling ability worries Eidson. He and Defensive line coach Geldermann have emphasized the importance of defensive line-men staying in their lanes all week, even if it means sacrificing a pass rush. It is a lot to ask, considering that the average Poly lineman is 6'4", 284 pounds, and De La Salle's defensive front averages 6', 225.

It means that the Spartans line will be forced to rush straight up the field against a much bigger opponent on almost every play, which could help give Jackson the time he needs to find receivers downfield.

He finds Watson open over the middle again, but the pass is high and Watson is unable to hang on. Two plays later, Poly punts.

Eidson's strategy appears to be paying off as the first quarter continues. The Jackrabbits are unable to run the ball, and Jackson is growing frustrated. After a short completion on third-and-long ends Poly's second drive of the game, the quarterback, who doubles as the punter, stands on the field shaking his head in disgust.

He shanks a punt off the side of his foot for 13 yards on the next play, giving the ball to De La Salle near midfield.

Ottoboni gains 21 yards on the fifth play of the next drive, but the gain is nullified because of a holding penalty. Still, Ottoboni is central to the game plan, which becomes even more obvious when he runs a draw play on third-and-9 from the Long Beach 27-yard line.

He tries to spin off a hit in the middle of the line when a defender lands on his lower leg, bending his knee and ankle at an unnatural angle. The ball pops loose and a huge pileup ensues. Poly linebackers Mark Washington and Tracy Mimms signal that their team has recovered the fumble as officials wade into the pile.

It takes several minutes to sort everything out. Officials rule that Ottoboni's forward progress had been stopped before the fumble occurred, and therefore De La Salle maintains possession. Players begin to back away. Ottoboni remains on the ground. Soon Blasquez is at his side. Replays confirm the gruesome tale. Blasquez and assistant trainer Josh Quintero help the senior running back off the field.

Television cameras focus on Sue Panella, Mark's wife, standing in the crowd, her hands pressed against her face in obvious concern.

Ottoboni lies on a stretcher on the sideline with ice bags on his left knee and ankle, his arm draped over his eyes to block the sun and hide his tears. He felt that his De La Salle career would be defined by his performance in this game. None of the scenarios he had played out in his mind during the past week prepared him for this.

"This could've been my opportunity, my chance," he thinks to himself as he lies there. "This was supposed to be my game."

A trend is developing defensively for De La Salle. Poly isn't running the ball effectively, and Jackson has nowhere to run and no open receivers to throw to. Poly offensive players are bickering. They are reacting precisely the way Eidson anticipated.

"They're getting tired already," Panella observes from the sideline.

De La Salle coaches never considered Cecil a classic passer but predicted that he would be more a classic option quarterback. It hasn't evolved that way. Cecil gained positive yards through the first four games but has not established himself as a running threat. He has quick feet that help him elude tacklers, but he doesn't have the raw speed to break big runs.

He drops back to pass on third-and-5 on the Spartans' next drive. When he can locate no open receivers, he tucks the ball under his arm and runs around the right end for six tough yards and a first down. He keeps the ball again on the next play and picks up eight more before almost being decapitated by Parish. Cecil leaps to his feet and bangs helmets with a teammate to show he's not hurt. In fact, he's as fired up as he has ever been. He wants more.

It's third-and-1 at midfield one play later when Cecil fakes the handoff up the middle and runs down the line, stringing defenders out. Then he spins back to the inside, picking up two yards where none existed, and De La Salle has another critical first down.

It wasn't the start of the next play that people will remember. Cecil bobbles the snap, almost allowing the ball to drop to the ground, before he drops back and surveys the field.

Cameron Colvin is streaking down the seam, a full step ahead of a Long Beach Poly defender. Ladouceur has been waiting to match up his 6'0" receiver against Poly's 5'6" cornerback. Colvin puts his hand on the trailing defender's chest while the ball is in the air. It's not a push, but the defender can get no closer.

Cecil is hit as he throws, but the 46-yard pass is on the money. Colvin catches it at the 3 and runs untouched into the end zone before pointing to the sky to honor his late mother. He hadn't planned the tribute. In fact, he didn't even think of it until he crossed the goal line and heard the Memorial Stadium crowd erupt in a deafening roar. Back near midfield Britt Cecil jumps to his feet when the realization hits him: That's his first touchdown pass.

"When I saw it was a perfect spiral I knew it was a touchdown," he would later say. "I just hoped he didn't get tangled up with the cornerback."

The defender burned by Colvin redeems himself by blocking the extra point, making the lead 13–0 with 3:18 left in the half.

A sack by Chris Mulvanny helps De La Salle get the ball back with just enough time to mount one more scoring drive before the half ends.

"Hey, Garth, what goals do I have so far?" Mulvanny asks Garth Gorrall while taking a quick breather on the sideline. Mulvanny knifed through the line to drop a running back for a 1-yard loss earlier in the quarter and is now beating his man to the outside.

"You've got your sack and you're keeping outside contain," says Gorrall, remembering what Mulvanny wrote on his commitment card. "The only thing you haven't done is clamp down on the tight end."

Mulvanny nods and turns to watch the offense.

The Spartans move the ball downfield until they are at the Long Beach 27-yard line with 13 seconds left in the first half, well within Binswanger's extended range. Ladouceur calls for a quarterback throwback instead. He thinks Poly is set up for the trick play he has wanted to run all week. But it is doomed from the start. Bates has no time to throw after taking the pitch and cuts back inside instead. He doesn't get out of bounds and therefore doesn't stop the clock. The precious final seconds tick away.

Eidson wasn't eager to kick a field goal in the first place. The Spartans went for it on fourth-and-7 at the Long Beach 25 late in the first quarter instead of attempting a field goal.

It has nothing to do with Binswanger forgetting his helmet. His headgear was delivered more than an hour before the game, and he was once again booming kickoffs into the end zone.

The problem is with the protection. Poly sent a defender flying off the end of the line and nearly blocked the first extra point. The second was effectively blocked. Eidson can't fix the problem on the sideline because too many of the players he needs to talk to are always on the field.

He doesn't want to risk another attempt until he can fix the problem at halftime. The last thing he wants is for the game-turning play to come on a blocked field goal attempt.

As the players walk off the field, a number on the scoreboard seems to flash like a beacon. Long Beach Poly, with its tremendous size advantage and three backs who came into the game averaging more than eight yards per carry, gained only one yard rushing.

"We found something out," Eidson says at halftime as the junior varsity coaches carry Ottoboni up the stairs and into the locker room. "They're not gods. We can wear them down but they're not going to quit. If they score one touchdown their momentum will skyrocket."

"They're tired up front," Panella tells them. "We have to keep pounding. We're in better shape than they are. They're giving you great blocking surfaces. They're standing straight up."

The halftime scene is radically different than it was the year before, when the players were physically wiped out. Blasquez tailored his offseason conditioning program so that players would be in peak physical condition for this game.

Unlike 2001, players can't wait to get back on the field. They feel as if Poly is ready to crumble. Ladouceur warned them that this will be a dirty job. Now it's time to finish it.

"We all expected Poly to play better than they had in the first half," Cecil said later. "I kept waiting for them to do something."

De'Montae Fitzgerald broods as minor adjustments are made and fluids are consumed to guard against cramps.

"What's wrong with De'Montae?" Ladouceur whispers to Aliotti.

"I don't know," Aliotti responds. "It looks like he swallowed a lemon."

Fitzgerald is hungry for his opportunity. He wants to contribute.

There isn't anyone in uniform who cares more about the people in that room. He desperately wants to make a difference.

"You guys played hard in the first half," Ladouceur says. "You guys did a great job on defense and offensively, too. You guys are moving the ball a little bit. We've got to move it again in the second half and get two more scores. We've got to keep plugging away. I think these guys are getting a little tired. They're not as good as they're cracked up to be. But you have to get after them to make it happen. So, there it is. You've played half of this game. You guys can do this. You jumped on them and now you've got to finish them. We're kicking off, and you've got to hold those guys and get the ball back. If we take it in one more time we're in good shape. Make that happen."

Binswanger's kickoff sails out of the back of the end zone to start the second half.

The first drive of the second half is an extension of the first half for the Jackrabbits. The smaller, quicker, perhaps even stronger De La Salle defensive line stuffs the run and pressures Jackson.

Jackson throws deep to Jones, but he is surrounded by Colvin, Drew, and Bates. Poly salvages some momentum when Jackson's 51-yard punt is downed at the De La Salle 1-yard line.

If the Spartans are going to score on their opening possession of the second half, as Ladouceur urged them to do at halftime, they will have to march 99 yards against one of the nation's top defenses.

A quarterback sneak gains two yards and gives the offense some breathing room. Bates is stopped for no gain, setting up a critical third-and-8 deep in De La Salle territory.

If De La Salle is forced to punt here, Poly will have great field position and the momentum that has eluded it to this point. This is the biggest play of the game thus far, and Ladouceur bends at the waist, hands on his knees, watching nervously as Cecil takes a short drop and throws a quick slant to Fitzgerald, who is blanketed by a Poly defender. Cecil has thrown the ball high and to the inside of his receiver to reduce the possibility of an interception. Fitzgerald leaps and reaches high above his head with both hands to somehow make the catch for a critical 15-yard gain.

It's the best catch of the year, better even than Colvin's juggling catch against St. Louis, especially considering the circumstances.

"That's the play of the game," Panella tells Aliotti.

A few plays later, Cecil rolls left on third-and-13 from the De La Salle 26-yard line and completes another pass to a wide-open Fitzgerald at the 45. Fitzgerald cuts back to shed the free safety and is all alone, galloping over a seemingly endless field of green.

It is the greatest feeling he has ever experienced in his life, running free and clear toward the end zone, not hearing a sound despite all the clamor. Receiver Aharon Bradley holds his block on a Poly defender at the 3-yard line for several seconds, clearing the path for Fitzgerald to score a 74-yard touchdown to cap a 99-yard drive.

Cecil crosses the goal line on a keeper for the 2-point conversion and a commanding 21-point lead. At that point, the Spartans would gladly have played through the day and deep into the night.

Fitzgerald, it turns out, had heard a Poly defender tell his teammates not to worry about No. 24 before he caught the slant pass for the first down. He was just a possession receiver, the defensive back had said. Colvin was the only De La Salle receiver they had to concern themselves with.

"That's what people thought of me," Fitzgerald would later say. "I was just a possession receiver. I don't want to be known as just anything. That says I'm incapable of other things. It limits my capabilities."

Mulvanny is 85 pounds lighter than the offensive tackle assigned to block him, but he continues to make plays. He drops a Poly running back for a 2-yard loss. Sandie hits Jackson as he throws two plays later. Jackson throws deep over the middle on third-and-6 but his receivers have run the wrong routes and nearly collide. Poly eventually turns the ball over on downs.

"They're not that big but they're not that little, either," said Lara, who spends the game pacing the sideline in his white coaching shirt, green hat, and wrap-around sunglasses. "Everybody is making it sound like they have little tiny guys playing on the line. They're not little tiny guys. They're short, stocky, strong guys who get it done. The discipline part helps them, the strength, the conditioning. Once again, we thought we were going to take the third quarter but they continued to execute."

Drew hasn't found the end zone yet but will finish with 161 yards on 19 carries. He is always able to turn the corner, even against Long Beach Poly, one of the fastest teams in the nation. Not only can he get up the sideline but once there he runs straight upfield and is a blur of helmet, shoulder pads, and pumping thighs.

"We knew about Drew this year and focused on tackling him," Lara said. "He's a phenomenal athlete. We couldn't bring him down. I thought that was the difference, Drew."

Drew picks up nine yards on a sweep left before Cecil rolls right and throws a shallow crossing route to tight end Terrance Kelly. Kelly catches the ball in midstride, outrunning the linebacker assigned to cover him, and cuts up the sideline where Aharon Bradley is preparing to make another key downfield block.

Bradley is the younger brother of Alijah Bradley, whom Poly had geared their defense to stop the year before. He played basketball as a junior and decided to try football during his senior year, even though he hadn't put on a helmet and shoulder pads since he played youth football.

"Let's give Aaron some props," Ladouceur had said during the team meeting the week before. "I like the way he practices." His teammates clapped and howled, applauding his effort against the first-team defense. Bradley smiled, proud, and looked at the floor. "He's got a great attitude. He hits and he's not afraid of the defense. He doesn't get shit for blocking half the time but he's got some guts. He's got some guts. I admire that. I'm glad you're on the team."

Cecil holds his arms over his head in triumph as Kelly crosses the goal line. De La Salle leads 28–0 with 3:26 left in the third quarter. Cecil began the game with no touchdown passes as a varsity quarterback. Now he has three.

He has never worked so hard in his life. He told himself early in the week that if he played poorly it wouldn't be because he had failed to do everything humanly possible to prepare himself. He had watched film with the team and watched more film at Panella's house Wednesday night.

He knew it had paid off after he completed that third-down pass to Colvin on the first drive of the game. He was so well prepared, he didn't have to think. He just knew. The game was unfolding slowly, even if this was the fastest defense he had ever played against.

He finishes the game with 12 completions in 17 attempts for 237 yards.

He throws for three touchdowns and runs for another. He picks up first downs at critical moments and does not turn the ball over.

Britt Cecil was supposed to be a caretaker, not a playmaker. He was expected to hand the ball off and run occasionally. It was his job to not lose games. Nobody expected him to win them, especially in the biggest game of the season, or so it seemed as the season began. But he no longer can be considered an unknown, or worse, a liability. He played a more prominent role against St. Louis because of Drew's injury, and he delivered. Now this. He has played the best game of his life in one of the biggest games in school history.

Coaches will later agree that there has never been a De La Salle player who improved so much in such a short time.

Matt Gutierrez threw for 300 yards and six touchdowns against Mater Dei in 1999. Mike Bastianelli averaged 9.6 yards per carry during the 1994 season and threw 13 touchdown passes, but Ladouceur will later call this the greatest performance ever by a De La Salle quarterback.

Despite the many newspaper articles that will trumpet Britt Cecil's performance all over the state the next day, those words, coming from Ladouceur—after all they have been through—mean the most.

"It didn't dawn on me at first, but slowly and surely I thought about not just what it meant to me, but what it meant to De La Salle history," Cecil says. "I wasn't a quarterback who just kept the streak alive. I really contributed to it."

The Jackrabbits have a first-and-goal at the Spartans' 1-yard line after driving the length of the field on their next possession. Drew lines up outside the defensive end like a sprinter ready to explode from the blocks. There is no one there to stop him.

Drew flies in from the side and drops the running back for a 1-yard loss to set up second-and-goal from the 2. Jackson fumbles the exchange on the next play. Drew scoops it up, and for a brief moment it appears that he will return it all the way, scoring on a 98-yard fumble return that will serve as a stunning exclamation point to a two-year sweep.

But at the last moment, just when he is breaking away, a Poly player grabs Drew by the ankle and hangs on for dear life.

There's no one on the field who is having more fun than Chris Biller. He is hustling downfield and blindsiding Poly defenders on pass plays,

211

more than holding his own against Lemau'u, and grinning in the huddle in anticipation of the next play.

The call from the sideline is "38 power," one of the playbook's basics, a play that every offensive lineman who ever played for Ladouceur can still recite down to the most minute detail. Biller pulls down the line, stands up the linebacker and is pushing him back when another Poly defender falls onto the back of his legs. Biller crumples to the turf and bites down hard on his mouthpiece, the worst pain he has ever felt exploding like fireworks up and down his left leg.

It is later diagnosed as a hairline fracture of his left fibula. He knows the injury will sideline him for weeks, perhaps the entire season, but he is too happy to feel sorry for himself.

"I wasn't thinking about the rest of the season," he said. "I was just happy with the way the game was going. I was grateful to have played. I went from out for the season to starting and playing pretty well in the biggest game of the season. I felt satisfied with that."

The final score is 28–7, and Ladouceur has never been so emotional after a game. He calls it the greatest win in school history. He knows how vulnerable his team was earlier in the year, how players doubted themselves. Later, he will admit that this is his crowning achievement as a coach.

In many ways, Britt Cecil's story is a microcosm of the team as a whole. Ladouceur has never coached a team that came this far, this fast. This team is no longer living off De La Salle lore. It has created its own.

There have been games during his career where Ladouceur looked out on the field and felt inspired by his players' performance. He felt that after the 2001 Long Beach Poly game. He feels it again in 2002.

Ladouceur has to swallow hard to hold back the tears. After watching Long Beach destroy Kahuku in Aloha Stadium he didn't know if his team was capable of beating the Jackrabbits again.

"They played way beyond expectations," Ladouceur said later, when given time to reflect. "They put together an almost perfect game, and Britt Cecil led the charge. I would've never dreamed he would've had a game like that. There were heroes all over the field. I feel that game embodied the spirit of our program in a lot of ways."

Poly players wander around the field in a daze while others cry or lie on the field with disbelieving looks on their faces. This game has been a focal point since the last loss to De La Salle. They were convinced it would be different this time. Instead, it has been much, much worse.

They can't point to dropped passes or a lack of execution. This game couldn't have gone either way with a break here or there. This has been total domination in all phases. De La Salle rushed for 237 yards to Poly's 45. De La Salle passed for 237 yards to Poly's 213. The Spartans had four sacks and allowed none. Poly committed seven penalties, true, but the Spartans overcame eight of their own.

"They execute everything," linebacker Mark Washington tells reporters. "They're almost on a college level. Their coach has them ready for every situation."

"Their hearts were bigger than ours today," Parish says.

They may not have as many blue-chip athletes as the year before, but Lara is convinced that this is a better Poly team, a more unselfish team. He was criticized for being outcoached the year before. Why didn't he run Herschel Dennis more? Why hadn't he gotten UCLA-bound tight end Mercedes Lewis more involved in the game?

Lara has never prepared so thoroughly for a game. He and his assistant coaches were calling out De La Salle's plays on the sideline. That was the frustrating part. The Poly team was bigger, faster, and deeper. They knew what was coming and they still couldn't stop it.

Lara walked off the field the year before dejected, but knowing that he would have another shot at De La Salle. That isn't the case this time. De La Salle's schedule is full and offers are pouring in. Lara knows he might never again be in position to win a game as big as the two he has lost to De La Salle in back-to-back seasons.

"It's not about having the best athletes," he says. "It's about playing together. You have to be mentally prepared to beat them. Whoever beats them has to understand that, because they're into the game the whole way. That's what I learned this year."

De La Salle players finally wander back to the Big Game room after hugging parents, girlfriends, each other. They mill about inside the spacious interior, laughing, talking. Colvin and Fitzgerald stand out on a balcony watching the departing crowd below.

"Did you ever hear about the legend of Pappy Waldorf?" Fitzgerald is asked. He is then told how alumni and fans would mass under a similar balcony to hear postgame comments from the great Cal coach. He shakes his head. He doesn't care. He replies with a question of his own:

"Did you ever hear about the legend of Bob Ladouceur?"

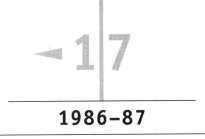

1986–87

OLD FRIENDS ON A COLLISION COURSE

t he high school football community was clamoring for it, but it wasn't going to happen. The teams weren't going to play each other. No way. The programs were too intertwined. There was too much at stake. It had nothing to do with football. This was about close friends and family.

Rob Stockberger and Bob Ladouceur met in the summer of 1972 while working for the San Ramon Parks and Recreation Department. Rob had been introduced to his future wife at the Ladouceur home on Broadmoor Drive. Bob and Rob roomed together at San Jose State and drove home together on weekends.

Bob didn't realize that his future was in coaching until he helped Rob with the junior varsity team at Monte Vista High School. Rob helped Bob land his first paid coaching job at the school a year later.

Bob was twenty-four when he got the head coaching job at De La Salle in 1979. Rob was twenty-five when he was named head coach at Monte Vista in 1981. By 1986 they had built two of the most prominent football programs in the Bay Area, if not all of Northern California. They shared the same philosophies and middle-class values. They started out coaching youth baseball together and now they were ushering in a new era in Bay Area prep football.

Their training techniques, offseason conditioning programs, and practice plans were so similar they were almost mirror images of each other. The two coaches even scouted for each other. Monte Vista played on Friday nights. De La Salle played on Saturdays. Ladouceur would scout Monte Vista's upcoming opponent on Friday night, and Stockberger would return the favor the next day. Then they would swap scouting reports.

"Rob started his coaching career before me and set a standard for me to shoot for," Ladouceur said. "I used to go and just watch Monte Vista games. I was a big fan of theirs. I admired the way they executed and the way the kids responded and the heart they played with. I really admired those teams. I wanted to bring our teams to that level."

De La Salle emerged as local power in 1982, Ladouceur's fourth season. With an offense led by quarterback Rich Pelletier and a defense led by 175-pound all-state noseguard Pat Oswald, the Spartans outscored opponents 425–56, finished 12–0, and won the school's first North Coast Section 2A football championship.

Stockberger's Mustangs won the 3A title that same season, on the same night. It was a memorable evening, with De La Salle and Monte Vista winning championships in back-to-back games at the Oakland Coliseum.

There was a big party afterward. Half of the cake that Bob's mother cut was decorated with red and white frosting for Monte Vista. The other half was green and white in honor of De La Salle.

The Spartans won the 2A title again in 1984 but weren't viewed as a regional threat until they thrashed longtime Bay Area superpower Bellarmine of San Jose 37–14 in the 1985 season opener.

That got the attention of *USA Today*'s Dave Krider, who became an overnight high school football king-maker when his national rankings were introduced in the "nation's newspaper" in 1982. None of the other publications that featured national prep rankings and all-American teams had the reach of *USA Today*. Krider's rankings became the gold standard for prep sports, spurring interest and controversy in every state in the nation and making the accomplishments of a humble private-school team in Concord, California, nationally known.

De La Salle went undefeated again that year, outscoring opponents 567–138, and finished the season ranked 23 in the Super 25 High School Football Poll. It was the first national recognition for the program.

Monte Vista experienced a parallel ascent to power. The Mustangs had never won a league championship when Stockberger was elevated to head varsity coach in 1981. His first team not only captured the East Bay Athletic League title, but upset Ygnacio Valley and respected coach Kent Robie to win the NCS 3A crown.

Bob and Rob piloted the top private school and public school football programs in the East Bay and were often asked about the possibility of a nonconference matchup. They both flatly refused. They were young and proud. Someone would walk away disappointed, and they didn't wish that on each other. There were enough quality teams to play.

Then in 1986 the Catholic Athletic League was dissolved, De La Salle was elevated to 3A status, and the decision was out of their hands. From that point on, Stockberger and Ladouceur were on a collision course.

It would've been simpler had it just been those two. They had enough mutual respect for one another to realize they had nothing to prove. But their staffs were interlaced with family connections.

Tom Ladouceur, Bob's older brother, was Stockberger's assistant at Monte Vista. De La Salle's defensive coordinator Luke Wurzel was married to Stockberger's sister, Linda.

Rob, Tom, Bob, and Luke all lived within a mile of each other in San Ramon, and the families socialized often. The Stockbergers lived across the street and one house down from the Wurzels.

George Cockerton had been the defensive coordinator under Fred Houston at San Ramon when Ladouceur played there, and he was a valuable resource early in Ladouceur's coaching career. Now he was the defensive coordinator at Monte Vista. De La Salle assistant Blair Thomas married Suzy Ladouceur, Bob and Tom Jr.'s sister.

There were skeptics who believed that De La Salle would be humbled at the big-school level. Stockberger was not among them. There was no chance the two teams would face each other during the regular season: the Mustangs were an established power in the East Bay Athletic League, while the Spartans had been realigned into the Golden Bay Athletic League. But they could meet in the playoffs.

Such a meeting appeared more and more inevitable as the two teams steamrolled one opponent after another during the 1986 season. Both teams finished undefeated and were the top seeds in the playoffs. Tom Jr., who bears a striking resemblance to his brother even with a thick, frowning mustache, tried to break the mounting tension by carrying a sign to scout his brother's team in the playoff semifinals: "God rides with the Mustangs," it read.

"In the back of our minds we were rooting for that game," Tom recalls. "Deep down we all wanted to know how we would do."

The matchup came to pass. There were storylines galore, and Bay Area newspapers ate them up. It was the first time in nine years that both 3A finalists were undefeated. Both programs were vying for a fourth NCS title. "Goliath vs. Goliath" was how one newspaper described the matchup in a bold headline.

At least one article detailing the family ties angle was published in every paper. The *Contra Costa Times* pictured the four coaches on the front page of the sports section, but not even that image could illustrate how interwoven these two teams were.

The De La Salle roster included ten players from the greater Danville community that Monte Vista served. Many of them had attended grade school and played Little League with Monte Vista players.

The grade school that Kirk Pulver attended looked out on the Monte Vista practice field. He didn't think that high school football games got any bigger than the rivalry between Monte Vista and nearby San Ramon.

He was a starting offensive lineman for the Mustangs as a sophomore before his parents insisted that he transfer to De La Salle for his junior year. He had let his grades slip, convincing his parents that he needed more discipline and a more demanding academic environment. His Monte Vista teammates offered to try to talk his father into reconsidering the transfer.

"What was really good about the Monte Vista program, which made it easier when I transferred, is they expected similar things on and off the field," Pulver said. "It wasn't quite as exacting as De La Salle, but it was pretty darned close."

Mike Wakeman had been Pulver's best friend since childhood and their families still lived across the street from one another. Wakeman played tight end for Monte Vista. Pulver was an outside linebacker. The friends and neighbors would go head to head in the championship game.

Both coaching staffs prepared intensively for the big event. So did their extended families.

Tom Sr. followed Bob's coaching career closely and even shouted advice from the stands. With his oldest son, Tom Jr., on the Monte Vista staff, he joked that he and his wife Mary would have to sit in the end zone so they wouldn't show allegiance to either team. Stockberger's dog often crossed the street to visit Luke Wurzel. When Rob whistled for Buddy to come home one day that week, his retriever walked into the house dressed in a De La Salle T-shirt.

"An NCS Championship game in and of itself is a huge emotional event," said Stockberger, who wore the same walrus mustache as Tom Jr. "It's huge. Add to that the whole family dynamic and it was pretty big, pretty emotional."

A record crowd of 12,228 showed up at the Oakland Coliseum for the game, many of them expecting the established 3A power to break the gaudy 32-game winning streak the upstart Spartans carried into the showdown.

Monte Vista took a 7–0 lead after picking off a De La Salle pass on the first possession of the game. "It looks like these guys have finally met their match," said a Monte Vista sideline observer after De La Salle went three-and-out on its second offensive series.

The Spartans defensive backs, coached by Terry Eidson, called themselves the "No Passing Zone," which was what the Los Angeles Raiders defensive backs were calling themselves at the time. They were led by standout Tuan Van Le, who would later play at Stanford.

Van Le outjumped a Monte Vista receiver for an interception late in the first quarter, and Greg Pron later scored untouched on a 23-yard run to tie the score.

De La Salle took a 14–7 lead when quarterback Chris O'Rourke threw a 41-yard touchdown pass to Van Le. The Spartans scored yet another touchdown before the half, setting it up with the type of trick play that had long been Stockberger's trademark. Pron took a pitch from O'Rourke and threw a halfback pass deep down the sideline for Mike Salvemini. One of the two Monte Vista defenders covering Salvemini tipped the pass into the air, but Salvemini never took his eyes off the ball. His diving catch set up another score that gave De La Salle a 21–7 halftime advantage.

Monte Vista hadn't given up 21 points in a game all season.

The Monte Vista offense entered the game averaging 413 yards per game. The De La Salle defense confused Monte Vista's offensive linemen by shifting from even- to odd-man fronts before the snap. It was a technique Ladouceur learned years ago from his San Ramon coach, Cockerton. The Monte Vista offense finished with 143 total yards against De La Salle.

The Spartans added a second-half field goal to make the final score 24–7. Mustang quarterback Stewart Hansen had thrown only one interception all season. He threw four against De La Salle.

Ladouceur had expected the game to go down to the wire. He walked off the field surprised by how easy it had been.

Stockberger knew that in the future he could count on returning players Stewart Hansen and standout running backs Steve Abrams and Schon Branum, who had combined for nearly 2,500 rushing yards and 32 touchdowns as juniors. He walked off the field thinking he had 365 days to prepare for the rematch.

"None of us liked the taste of that loss," Abrams recalls. "It was in the back of everyone's mind. We knew we would play them again."

Those who thought the jump to 3A would derail De La Salle were wrong. In the Spartans' first year of competition in the large-school classification they won the NCS title over one of the most established programs in the area. They also won their first mythical state championship when *Cal-Hi Sports* magazine put them atop its statewide 3A poll.

There was no party after the championship game. The coaching staffs went their separate ways, but the extended family would spend time together over the Christmas holiday. Rob and Bob avoided the topic whenever possible and joked about it when the subject was unavoidable. There were no hard feelings. They both realized there was more to life than football.

De La Salle's win streak was the big story as the 1987 season grew near. The Spartans had won 33 consecutive games and three straight NCS titles. To maintain the state's longest win streak, however, they would have to negotiate the toughest preseason schedule in school history.

The two teams—De La Salle and Monte Vista—were ranked No. 1 and No. 2 in the East Bay heading into the 1987 season. The Spartans defeated powerful Bellarmine 32–7 in their season opener. Quarterback Brad Heyde's 53-yard touchdown run with 2:52 left in the game provided the winning margin in a 29–23 victory over St. Francis, then ranked No. 6 in Northern California.

A troubling trend was developing, however. The Spartans trailed at halftime in each of their first four games. The team was committing too many penalties and was prone to mental lapses.

"When a team makes that many errors, it's a direct reflection on the coaching staff," Ladouceur said. "I think a coach should be able to break a team of those things. I really do. I just didn't feel like the team had the mental discipline and I blame myself. I don't blame the kids."

Monte Vista began the season without starting quarterback Stewart Hansen, who broke his fibula during preseason practice. But with or without Hansen, this was the most explosive offense in school history. Schon Branum rushed for more than 100 yards in each of the Mustangs' first seven games and broke the EBAL record for career rushing yards. Steve Abrams scored 16 touchdowns in the first six games. Hansen returned to the Mustangs in time to play in what was then considered to be the greatest game in EBAL history, when Monte Vista edged Foothill 36–35 in a game that featured 764 total yards, 36 first downs, and 10 touchdowns.

Spartans quarterback Brad Heyde missed two De La Salle games with a sprained ankle at about the same time Hansen was returning to action for Monte Vista. Without Heyde, De La Salle eked out a 24–21 win over Kennedy of Richmond. It was the narrowest margin of victory since the streak began.

De La Salle assumed the nation's longest active winning streak—43 games—after defeating Rancho Cotate of Santa Rosa in a first-round playoff game.

"That's when we started to realize that we were achieving on a level that hadn't been done before," De La Salle linebacker and tight end Jim King says. "That was an emergence. It was a new level of validation. We really learned we were doing something special."

De La Salle beat undefeated Ygnacio Valley, a team ranked ninth in the state, 34–7 to clinch a spot in the NCS 3A finals. Monte Vista, meanwhile, defeated Foothill 42–6 in one rematch, setting up another.

"In the back of our heads we knew how good they were and how many guys were coming back," De La Salle running back Rob Forester said. "We figured we'd end up with a rematch against them at the Coliseum."

As had been the case the previous year, the lives of many of the players who would compete for the title were hopelessly tangled.

Spartans quarterback Heyde and Monte Vista linebacker Jim Coleman grew up playing football together on Woodbriar Drive—in Toledo, Ohio. The families both moved to the San Ramon Valley before the boys entered high school. Heyde's parents had chosen De La Salle, while Coleman attended his local public school. Now the old friends would be playing against each other in the biggest football game of their lives.

Tom Jr.'s stepson had starred for De La Salle's 1985 team. His stepdaughter was a Carondelet student and a De La Salle cheerleader who was dating Rob Forester as the big game drew near.

When it arrived, De La Salle seemed unprepared. Forester returned the opening kickoff 35 yards, but a clipping penalty brought it back. De La Salle was flagged again on its first offensive play.

Heyde had been a backup running back as a sophomore when Ladouceur saw him throwing crisp passes on the sideline in practice and moved him to quarterback. Heyde kept the ball on an option keeper, cut inside, and scored a 72-yard touchdown on the next play. But once again penalty flags littered the field. The lack of discipline De La Salle showed earlier in the season was resurfacing at the worst possible time.

The two teams were evenly matched and battled to a scoreless tie at halftime. Every play began with two quick lines slamming into each other and ended with a big hit as rugged running backs from both teams absorbed blow after blow. The game was played ferociously, with players always seeking out contact, even if the play was going the other way. Monte Vista's white jerseys soon turned the same deep brown color as the dirt from the baseball infield.

Stockberger and Cockerton had revamped their defense after talking with then-Oregon offensive coordinator Bob Toledo during the offseason. Toledo made a recruiting visit to the school, and Stockberger asked him how Oregon teams had defended the Houston veer. Toledo told them that instead of assigning the defensive end to the quarterback and the outside linebacker to the pitch back and so on, defenders should be schooled to attack the first threat.

For interior linemen that meant the dive back. The defensive end and outside linebacker played the quarterback. That left the pitch back for the cornerback, safety, and whomever else was in the area.

It was Monte Vista running back Abrams who made the new scheme work. He was determined to play running back in college and showed little interest in playing defense during the regular season. But he was pressed into duty for the playoffs when the starting free safety went down with a shoulder injury. His impact in the game was apparent from the outset.

The Spartans' Rob Forester and fellow running back Craig Pruski lacked the raw speed of De La Salle running backs in future years. They were rugged runners who gained most of their yards after the initial contact. Abrams' speed allowed him to roam from sideline to sideline, uncoiling on De La Salle ball carriers and knocking them out of bounds.

"We didn't have him pegged as someone to watch for, but as the game went on he was making a ton of tackles," Forester recalls.

Cockerton provided halftime inspiration in the Monte Vista locker room, recounting a story about how a De La Salle player's father had bumped into the son of a Monte Vista coach that week. "It should be a great game," the boy said. The De La Salle father strongly disagreed. He predicted the Spartans would win by 40 points.

Players had already heard of the slight—news travels fast in a small town—but it served as a rallying cry nonetheless.

"We were appalled when we heard that story," De La Salle linebacker Jim Hinckley said later. "It wasn't as if we didn't respect them."

De La Salle finally broke the scoreless tie when Heyde threw a touchdown pass to Andre Butler in the right corner of the end zone. A Monte Vista defender had slipped on the wet grass and fallen, leaving Butler wide open.

Monte Vista fought back. Branum collected a screen pass from Hansen late in the third quarter and ran 36 yards to the Spartans' 12. Abrams scored from there. De La Salle blocked the extra point, preserving a one-point lead.

Stockberger's team had practiced the fake punt all year but had never run it in a game. On fourth-and-7 midway through the fourth quarter, Stockberger called for the play.

"Everyone was holding their breath," Abrams says. "There was excitement on the sideline but nobody wanted to give it away."

The Mustangs lined up with two upbacks behind the guards and in front of the punter's personal protector, just as they always did. At the snap, the punter leaped high into the air, as if the ball had sailed over his head. Instead the ball was snapped to the personal protector, who placed the ball between the legs of the right upback while the left upback screened defenders from the deception.

Then the personal protector, the punter, and the upback without the ball all ran to the right side of the formation while the upback with the ball remained hunched over with his elbows on his knees, waiting.

After pausing for eight seconds, little-used running back Chris Musseman started running down the left sideline, barely avoiding the tackle of one of the few De La Salle defenders who hadn't been fooled.

Eidson was going nuts on the sideline. He had attempted to run a clever trick field goal attempt earlier in the game but it had been nullified by a penalty. He and Ladouceur saw this one coming. They had both seen San Ramon run the same play years before. Eidson had even suspected trickery and signaled for his punt return team to guard against the fake at all costs. Not all his players heard the instructions.

Jim King was an outside linebacker who also returned punts for De La Salle. He suspected Monte Vista would try a fake and tried to alert his teammates before the play began to unfold. Then he saw Musseman racing down the left sideline and started streaking across the field after him.

His first thought was disappointment over his teammates having been tricked. Now the Mustangs would have great field position. His second thought was that he was going to make Musseman pay with a hit that would be replayed for years to come. King was a good open-field tackler. He never even considered the possibility of Musseman scoring.

He was flying across the field, running as hard as he had ever run, determined to knock Musseman into the third row of seats. Based on his angle of pursuit, the collision would occur at the 5-yard line.

"When I went by him I got the feeling you get when a glass slips out of your hand but hasn't hit the floor," King recalls. "I knew it was going to be a hit everybody would remember. It never occurred to me that he would juke me. I didn't think he had a cutback in him."

He did. Musseman avoided the tackle, and was mobbed in the end zone after a 40-yard touchdown run that gave Monte Vista a 12–7 lead. Stockberger wasn't satisfied. He sent his offense back onto the field to attempt a 2-point conversion that would give his Mustangs a more comfortable seven-point lead.

Mustang Stewart Hansen was a three-year starter for one of Northern California's most prestigious programs. He was the EBAL's all-time highest-rated passer and had thrown for more than 3,000 yards with 26 touchdowns and nine interceptions during his career. But he had thrown an uncharacteristic four interceptions and played his worst game against De La Salle the year before. He was determined to redeem himself in his last high school game.

Kristian Hansen (no relation) had filled in for Stewart Hansen when the starting quarterback broke his leg earlier in the season. Kristian Hansen lined up in the left slot on the 2-point conversion attempt before motioning back to the right and taking a pitch from Stewart Hansen.

Kirk Pulver hadn't played in De La Salle's regular-season finale or the first playoff game because of an injured knee. But there was no way he would miss the matchup against his former friends and teammates. He was responsible for outside containment. But when the tight end crashed to the inside he took a step in that direction. By the time he realized that the quarterback was running a pass pattern toward the end zone to collect the halfback pass, it was too late.

"It was a panicked feeling," he recalls. "I knew I couldn't get there fast enough no matter how hard I tried. I remember seeing the ball released and me turning and running toward Stewart. He jumped for the ball and got both hands on it and then I heard the roar of the crowd. He had run right past me. I felt I just lost the game."

There were still more than seven minutes left, and the Spartans weren't about to quit, especially after Forester returned the kickoff 38 yards to the De La Salle 40. Rugged running by Forester and Pruski resulted in a first down. Pruski converted a fourth-and-1 from the Monte Vista 30 with a

225

4-yard run, keeping the potential game-winning and streak-saving drive alive.

Ladouceur had no choice but to go for it again on fourth-and-6 a few plays later. Heyde rolled right with two Monte Vista defenders in pursuit, closing fast. At the last moment he threw a jump pass to Forester, who had seen Heyde in trouble and stopped in the middle of the field, losing the linebacker who was covering him.

The play netted 15 yards and gave De La Salle a first-and-goal on the Monte Vista 7 with less than two minutes left. Heyde gained two yards on a keeper, then Forester barreled in from five yards out to pull De La Salle to within 14–13 with just over one minute left.

The frenzied pace of the game left players from both teams exhausted. Forester was breathing heavily in the huddle on De La Salle's final drive and was thankful for the timeout that gave him and his teammates a brief rest before the deciding play.

Ladouceur could either decide to kick the extra point in an attempt to force overtime, or try to win the game with one bold stroke. He sent the field goal unit onto the field before calling timeout and sending his offensive players back out. Both teams were on the verge of collapse. He didn't want to extend the game. He thought his best chance was to try to win it now.

"I was so glad we went for it because I was exhausted," says Jim Hinckley, who played five different positions for De La Salle that season before going on to Stanford. "I haven't been that tired before or since. Just standing up straight was pure agony."

The play was called "lead at 9" and had been an offensive staple for years. It was designed for two receivers to line up on the right side, which would pull the free safety—in this case Abrams, who already had 13 tackles in the game—away from the middle of the field. The quarterback would run left with Forester in tow. He could either turn upfield himself if he saw a hole, or pitch if necessary.

"That play shocked me," Abrams remembers. "They had been running it all day long. I thought they were going to do a pop pass to the tight end over the middle or something. I was really surprised by the call."

Heyde collected the snap and ran down the line. Inside linebacker

Shad Hansen, who would end up at BYU, sliced through a gap in the line and was closing with speed that defied his 6'1", 212-pound frame.

Heyde's pitch was a little behind Forester, forcing him to turn his torso to collect the ball against his right shoulder pad. Hansen continued to pursue relentlessly, diving at Forester's heels and almost tripping him up.

Forester had the ball cradled in his left arm and was running for the left corner of the end zone when he spotted Abrams out the corner of his right eye. He had two options. He could try to cut back and hope no one else was pursuing from the backside, or he could lower his shoulder and drive for the pylon. He chose the latter.

"He had the weight of the world on his shoulders, not to mention a 44-game winning streak," Hinckley said. "He did everything he could do to get into the end zone."

Ladouceur has always used receivers to shuttle in plays. In the momentary confusion on the sideline only one receiver had gone into the game. The other two stood next to Ladouceur on the sideline as the play unfolded. He didn't notice until he watched the film that the receiver who was supposed to line up to the far right to draw Abrams toward that side of the field had not gone into the game.

It was the most crucial play of the game—the most crucial play of the streak—and the Spartans only had ten men on the field.

Paul Still was playing guard for De La Salle. He came off the ball hard and fast and ended up face down in the end zone.

"I heard a roar from the crowd and I thought, 'OK, I made a mistake but we still won,'" Still recalls. "Then I heard another roar from the Monte Vista crowd and everybody was arguing with the ref."

Officials are taught to retreat out of bounds on goal line plays in order to be in position to determine whether the ball crosses the plane of the end zone. In this case, the head linesman retreated up the sideline and was standing at the 6-yard line when Forester and Abrams collided in the most controversial ending in NCS playoff history.

Forester reached across the goal line, the pylon deflecting off his left forearm as Abrams' hit sent him careening out of bounds. The ensuing seconds seemed to unfold over hours to those on the field.

De La Salle players threw their hands in the air, anticipating the touchdown signal from the official. Monte Vista players jumped up and down, convinced that Forester had been knocked out of bounds.

When the official indicated that Forester had stepped out of bounds before the ball broke the plane, Monte Vista players rejoiced.

"There was no way he could've seen the ball crossing the plane because he wasn't on the plane," Hinckley says. "He was looking at Forester's back. From his angle, [Forester] probably did look out of bounds."

The play would be reviewed from a dozen different angles in the ensuing days, but each angle was as inconclusive as the next. It was impossible to determine whether Forester stepped out of bounds before the ball crossed the goal line. Those who were there debate it to this day.

"I remember rolling over and staring at the ref and he was waving it off," Forester said. "All these emotions hit me like a Mack truck. I knew that was it. We weren't going to get a chance to get back down the field. All that hard work, the streak, was rushing through my head."

Monte Vista recovered the onside kick and a brief fight broke out on the field. Stockberger and Ladouceur tried to keep players from leaving the sideline to join in the fray. Moments later the clock expired, and Tom Jr. and Stockberger embraced on the sideline as fans from many different schools spilled out of the crowd and started running onto the field to join the celebrating coaches and players.

"All these people rushed the field and you saw all these different letterman's jackets and they were all congratulating us," Abrams recalls. "They kept saying, 'It's about time somebody beat these guys.' To have guys you played against celebrating with you was weird."

North Coast Section commissioner Paul Gaddini describes what he witnessed in the aftermath of that game as the greatest single moment in De La Salle history. The Spartans had been defeated on two gadget plays and the most controversial of calls. Players were sobbing as Monte Vista players celebrated and fans swirled around them.

"It was their ultimate moment of athletic grief, but they remained on the field and paid tribute to the team that defeated them," says Gaddini. "To me, that was impressive. That was the defining moment in educational athletics at De La Salle High School."

Stockberger had felt good about the game all day. When Tom's wife offered him a carnation, he did something completely out of character. He accepted it and pinned it proudly on his black-and-red Monte Vista windbreaker. He tried to hug each one of his players when the game was over, the carnation getting mashed with every heartfelt embrace.

He had never given any indication that the two games against De La Salle were more important than any other games. It wasn't until the second one was over that his players realized what it meant to their coach.

"He may have been worried that he had been outcoached in the first game," Monte Vista linebacker Jim Coleman said. "He had a strategy the second time."

Stockberger stunned the Monte Vista community when he resigned after the 1989 season to become an administrator. Tom Ladouceur left the program at the same time and later became an administrator himself.

Perhaps the greatest testament to the mutual respect the two programs had for each other occurred long after the celebration ended. De La Salle tackle Brad Thompson roomed with Monte Vista's Steve Abrams during a postseason All-Star game. The two became fast friends.

Soon players from both teams were hanging out together and going to the same parties, as if the two hard-fought games they played against each other made them members of the same elite club.

They have kept in touch over the years, and phone calls and e-mails fly back and forth to this day. Rob Forester and Steve Abrams, whose collision on the goal line remains one of the great moments in the history of Bay Area high school football, are especially close.

They attended each other's weddings.

"That last game was so indecisive, it's hard to say there was a loser," Coleman says. "But it's those relationships I really value. When we draw off that experience together it's pretty powerful."

18

LIBERTY AND FREEDOM
The Private School-Public School Debate

| | | | | | | | | |

d e La Salle's latest resounding victory over Long Beach Poly in 2002 may have changed the way the school is perceived on a regional or national basis. The program's rise to national prominence has even lessened the animosity directed at the program locally.

For the most part, however, the Spartans remain the perceived scourge of the East Bay. They are more than dominant—they are the catalyst for an intense, ongoing debate over the competitive equity between private and public schools.

This is a debate that rages wherever public and private schools coexist. Public schools bemoan the fact that private schools have no attendance boundaries. This allows private schools to draw students from a wide geographic area, giving them, theoretically, an unfair advantage over public schools that must draw students from within district boundaries.

Private school supporters counter that the high cost of tuition and the lack of government-subsidized transportation to and from campus make it more difficult for them, theoretically, to attract students. Besides, private schools point out, many local public school districts began operating under open enrollment policies in the 1990s, allowing those programs to draw athletes from outside their boundaries.

Nowhere is the practical aspect of this debate more hotly contested than in the East Bay Area, where the unparalleled success of De La Salle's football team has contributed to two sweeping realignments.

The first came in 1986, when the North Coast Section decided to break up the Catholic Athletic League, citing concerns over competitive balance. De La Salle opposed the breakup, preferring to remain in a league comprised of private schools that share similar philosophies.

In fact, most CAL coaches and administrators opposed the idea and fought desperately to keep the league together. De La Salle even hired lawyers to oversee an appeal.

"We were adamant about protecting our right to maintain our history, but we never took it to court," said Brother Jerome Gallegos, the De La Salle principal from 1981 to 1992. "We didn't want to become so ideological that we would make ourselves outcasts."

The league eventually was disbanded and member schools placed in public school leagues based on enrollment and geographic location. De La Salle was placed in the new Golden Bay Athletic League with teams from eastern Contra Costa and Alameda counties. It was a less-than-ideal arrangement. In fact, under the new plan, the Spartans were required to travel longer distances to compete than almost any other school.

"It was an honest effort to do what was right," said Paul Gaddini, the North Coast Section commissioner for twenty-eight years. "It would've been easy for us to leave the Catholic schools alone, but we didn't do that. We set our criteria and we applied it. I believe it was a major step toward competitive equity given the resources we had."

As part of the realignment, De La Salle was reclassified from 2A status to 3A status. To some, the reclassification seemed punitive.

"They were trying to teach De La Salle a lesson because we had started to win," said Brother Thomas Jones, who represented De La Salle in meetings along with Brother Jerome. "The whole idea was they would put us in with larger schools and that would teach us a lesson."

It didn't. De La Salle continued winning at the 3A level. In 1988 the school was subject to another realignment. The new Bay Valley Athletic League was considered the premier football conference in Northern California and was made up of schools much closer to De La Salle's Concord campus.

Pittsburg High School had one of the proudest traditions of any team in the state. Antioch and El Cerrito fielded rugged teams year in and year out. Pinole Valley produced Gino Torretta, who would go on to the University of Miami, where he won the Heisman Trophy in 1992.

Although the Spartans played many competitive games against Pittsburg, Antioch, and Pinole Valley, the vast majority of their games were lopsided affairs. Their only conference loss—in fact, their last conference defeat—was a one-point loss to El Cerrito in 1989.

Nobody was more adamant about the inequity of De La Salle's ongoing dominance than Liberty principal Gene Clare.

De La Salle outscored Liberty 196–28 in the first four games of the series between the schools. The controversy came to a head after the Spartans outscored six BVAL opponents 326–27 during the 1996 season.

Clare and three other Bay Valley Athletic League principals threatened to forfeit games against De La Salle in 1997 unless the North Coast Section agreed to hear their concerns about competitive equity between public and private schools.

Clare referred to the NCS mission statement, which said that all competition should be "wholesome, equitable and fair."

Few were better equipped to preside over the debate than Gaddini, whose background gave him keen insight into the public-private issue.

As a teen growing up in Santa Rosa, Gaddini was in danger of flunking out of a public high school when his parents sent him to board at St. Mary's in Berkeley. His grades rose immediately and he went on to attend St. Mary's College, run by the Christian Brothers.

He was a non-practicing Catholic who coached under Dan Shaughnessy during the legendary coach's first stint at St. Mary's. Gaddini wrote a sports column for the *Catholic Voice* newspaper and later served as the commissioner of the Catholic Athletic League, the same league he was criticized for disbanding while NCS commissioner.

"Ideally, public schools and private schools should compete amongst themselves," he said. "But that just wasn't practical."

Longtime BVAL commissioner John Nules, a former track and football coach at El Cerrito High, had little sympathy for the schools threatening to forfeit games to De La Salle. He thought having the school that owned the national record for consecutive wins gave the BVAL a measure of prestige that other conferences didn't have.

"They have a hell of a coach," Nules said. "How much did they dominate before Lad got there? They have it rolling and the pendulum has swung, but I think it would swing back in a hurry if Lad left."

The NCS held numerous public hearings over a ten-month span. The realignment and classification committee studied the public-private debate, and possible solutions were considered. A proposal to pit the biggest schools in the area against De La Salle in a football-only league was ultimately defeated when several of the proposed members complained about being placed in such a strong league for football.

De La Salle officials explored the possibility of joining the Western Catholic Athletic League for football only, but there were several potential pitfalls with this arrangement as well. The nearest WCAL school was thirty miles away, which would require additional travel costs. Plus, WCAL schools were members of the Central Coast Section, which meant that De La Salle would compete for a league title in one section while participating in another section's playoffs. This would require approval from both governing bodies.

De La Salle officials weren't necessarily advocating the status quo. High-powered programs from around the state had made inquiries about future games, but Eidson had little flexibility because of a BVAL schedule that obligated him to play nine conference opponents each season.

He and Aliotti were watching a Pac-10 Conference game at Aliotti's home in Pittsburg when the idea first occurred to them. Pac-10 teams didn't play every other league member each season. They played teams on a rotating basis. Why couldn't De La Salle do the same?

The arrangement gave De La Salle quasi-independent status. The Spartans would play five games against BVAL opponents and would be free to play the other five regular-season games against teams of their choosing.

Pittsburg wanted to continue to play De La Salle every year, as did Clayton Valley, which was coached by ex-Pittsburg coach Herc Pardi. The other three teams would be selected via a lottery system.

That compromise was approved by a vote of 31–0 and ended almost a year of hearings on competitive equity.

"On behalf of the ad hoc committee, thank God," said College Park High School principal Bud Beemer when the compromise was finally passed.

BVAL Commissioner Nules kept bullet casings from a starter's pistol in a coffee can, which he used to determine lane assignments when he was the track coach at El Cerrito. BVAL coaches selected casings from the can. Those who selected a casing with a smiley face taped to the side would not have to play De La Salle during the upcoming season.

The Spartans would no longer compete for the league title but would instead apply for an at-large berth into the NCS playoffs. Spartans players would remain eligible for postseason league honors.

The compromise satisfied everybody at the time. BVAL schools that didn't want to compete against De La Salle were only required to do so once every three years. Eidson was free to begin scheduling games against powerhouse teams such as Mater Dei and Bakersfield.

"De La Salle's success is certainly a problem in an environment where you want to have competitive equity," Gaddini says. "But it was hard not to respect their decision to leave the BVAL. Their proposal didn't come at anyone else's expense—it came at their own. They put the onus on themselves to find teams to play."

Five years later many still considered it an imperfect solution. In essence, BVAL teams were required to "service" De La Salle, or provide the school with enough games to fill out its schedule. Head-to-head competition between the Spartans and league schools would not count in the official BVAL standings. It was basically a practice game. The disparity between De La Salle and BVAL teams grew wider than ever before.

As De La Salle continued to improve, the league was deteriorating, resulting in scores that were more lopsided than ever. The Spartans beat Pittsburg 60–12 in 1998, scored 71 points against Ygnacio Valley in 1999, and defeated Freedom 55–7 in 2000. In back-to-back weeks in 2001, De La Salle beat Antioch 64–0 and Liberty 65–0.

Liberty High School is located in the east-county community of Brentwood, an agricultural town that has turned into one of the fastest-growing cities in the state.

It has never been a football school. The Lions always struggle to compete in the Bay Valley Athletic League, but in 2002 they are 3–2 overall and tied for the league lead on the eve of their home game against De La Salle.

Liberty coach and athletic director Mark Stantz is a large, red-haired former Marine machine-gunner whose attitude toward De La Salle reflects the sentiments of many past and present BVAL coaches.

"You go into it saying they have to lose sooner or later and you try to fire the kids up, but in the same breath you're thinking, 'Why do I want to do this?'" he says. "It's not a good situation for me. I don't want my kids to get hurt. Every time you step on the football field you have an opportunity for injury. Here I am playing a meaningless game against a team nobody wants to play that has an advantage over all of us. Why am I doing this—because they have to play football? Well, what about me? What about my kids? What about my school, my spirit? My hat is off to them. I wish them well and I hope the streak continues forever, but not at my expense."

A week after defeating Long Beach Poly for the second time in two years, De La Salle players step off the bus in Brentwood and see a soggy field that looks as if it hosted a tractor pull the night before. De La Salle coaches suspect that the quagmire is an attempt to slow down their team. It's a tactic that has been attempted by various teams over the years.

Stantz blames it on an erratic sprinkler system that has inadvertently soaked the field in the days leading up to the game. The ankle-deep mud doesn't slow down Maurice Drew. The senior running back and kick returner runs the length of the field untouched to score on the opening kickoff.

The Spartans sweep Liberty's defensive line down the field, allowing Drew to scamper 22 yards to score another touchdown, again untouched, on De La Salle's second possession.

"Maurice Drew should be going to Antioch or Deer Valley," Stantz growls. "Their quarterback should be at Livermore. That's a pretty big attendance area and we have to compete against that. I guarantee you if those players went back to those schools, those schools would be on top. They would be competitive schools in their leagues. That's the kind of athletes they are. But instead of that one athlete playing for Livermore and one athlete playing for Antioch, they get them all. They're getting the cream of the crop from every school."

It's the most common complaint by local public school coaches. De

La Salle robs them of their best players, which makes the Spartans' program stronger while at the same time weakening the competition.

"It's one thing if a kid moves to Sacramento. It's another thing when you have to play against that kid year after year," said former Antioch and Deer Valley coach Mike Paul. "In high school football a couple kids can make a huge impact on your program."

Opposing coaches frequently complain about De La Salle not having a defined area from which to draw students. To listen to some, however, it's almost as if they don't deserve to have any area at all.

Drew is the perfect example. He grew up in Antioch but attended Saint Peter Martyr Catholic Grammar School in the neighboring town of Pittsburg. The closest Catholic high school is De La Salle.

If De La Salle isn't even entitled to students who attend the area's Catholic grammar schools, what students is it entitled to?

Erik Sandie knocks the defensive lineman he is assigned to block 10 yards into the secondary before falling on him in the second play of De La Salle's next possession. Drew runs up the middle and is in the clear once again. Liberty defenders give up the chase when he reaches the 10-yard line. Drew's 54-yard run gives De La Salle a 21–0 lead with 2:06 left in the first quarter.

"A lot of years when teams go down to us, I walk away thinking they got what they deserved," Ladouceur says. "They never show us any respect or say anything nice about us in the paper. They approach the game the wrong way, and it starts with the coaches. They're always complaining about how it's unfair or they're making excuses. Rarely does a coach say, 'These guys are a good team. We're going to have to play our best.' I don't want them to kiss our ass or anything, but if I were in their shoes I would approach it much differently.

"First of all, I'd coach my kids and put them in a position where they had a chance. It's the same way I approach the Mater Dei or Long Beach Poly games. It's a win-win situation. It's an opportunity. These guys are really good, and we're going to take our best shot; and if they win, they're better than us and we'll come back next year. Instead, it's always pissing and moaning. I don't like it. It's a poor example of the kind of message a coach should send to his team."

Ladouceur has heard about De La Salle's "advantages" before, of course. In his opinion, most of his so-called advantages are the result of stability, success, and the collective effort to outwork opponents. He doesn't feel the need to apologize for that.

He believes that high school football today is in crisis. He sees a decline in the quality of coaching and quality of play. Head coaching positions are no longer coveted and often are filled by well-meaning off-campus coaches who are unable to put in the necessary time. Administrators don't support coaches the way they once did, and coaches are unable to hold players accountable in an increasingly litigious society.

"There's a lot of incompetence out there, and the finger gets pointed at us for it," Ladouceur said. "I don't see us as geniuses. I don't see it that way at all. We're vigilant and we know technique and that's all you really need to be successful at our level. The solution to the De La Salle problem is not to get rid of us but to elevate their own programs and put in the kind of time we put in here. If they can't get that type of dedication and commitment from their kids, I don't know what to say. I don't know what to tell them. It's possible."

Stantz begins substituting en masse early in the game. He prepped his team for De La Salle but has kept his focus on the next league opponent. His goal is to bring a rare BVAL championship to Brentwood. He won't risk suffering an injury to a key player just so he can keep the final score respectable. He will substitute liberally for the rest of the game, giving everybody on his roster a chance to play.

In other words, the game is over.

De La Salle scores on its first five possessions. Jackie Bates scores on a 15-yard run to make it 28–0. Parker Hanks catches a pass from Cecil over the middle and turns up the sideline to score on a 55-yard catch and run to give De La Salle a 35–0 lead with 8:33 left in the second period. There is no reaction from the Liberty stands. It is eerily silent after both touchdowns are scored.

The final score is 48–0. De La Salle finishes with 220 rushing yards to Liberty's 14. The Spartans have 386 yards of total offense. Liberty finishes with 112, most of which come in the second half when both teams are substituting freely.

"They better win," Stantz grumbles. "That's what I tell people. He better win with the setup he's got."

~

Freedom High School coach Kevin Hartwig approaches his matchup with De La Salle much differently. When he was hired before the season, he told his players that his goal was to build the best program in the area. De La Salle is going to get beat sooner or later, he tells his team in the days leading up to the game. Why not by us?

He has prepared his team well and it shows. He has a tough, hard-nosed roster led by seniors Stuart Gobble, Chris Bodishbaugh, Nick Ostlund, and junior Michael Neal. Many De La Salle opponents are defeated before they take the field. That isn't the case on this night. Freedom comes to Owen Owens Field determined to give De La Salle its toughest test of the year, regardless of the final score.

"Everybody thinks they're good, but everybody thinks they're overrated, too," Gobble said. "They can be beat. It's not impossible."

An interception and 35-yard return by Willie Glasper sets up De La Salle's first touchdown, a 1-yard sneak by Britt Cecil. Freedom isn't about to cave in, however. Gobble is all over the field on defense and picks up hard-earned yards as a running back on offense.

Cecil throws a pass deep on De La Salle's third possession. Drew is covered on the play but manages to tip the ball to himself for a 32-yard gain on third-and-19. De La Salle fumbles on the next play, however, and Freedom takes over with a renewed sense of purpose.

Bodishbaugh scrambles for 10 yards before being smacked out of bounds by Drew. He throws a 10-yard pass to Neal on the next play and then rolls left, cuts back inside, and picks up 18 more on a scramble.

"You guys are missing tackles, not getting off the ball!" Geldermann shouts at his linemen.

"Not only that," Ladouceur says, almost indifferently, "they keep biting on pump fakes."

A pass interference penalty against De La Salle on fourth-and-4 keeps the drive alive. Gobble plunges into the end zone from a yard out to knot the score at 7–7 with 8:53 left in the first half.

Kickoff was moved up to 7 P.M. to accommodate ESPN2, which is televising highlights of the game throughout the broadcast of the Friday night college game between Hawaii and Fresno State.

With the score tied, the network's timing seems impeccable.

The Spartans score quickly when Cecil throws a 43-yard touchdown pass to tight end Terrance Kelly. Gobble blocks the extra point to keep it 13–7 and then makes a touchdown-saving tackle on Drew's 50-yard run on De La Salle's next possession. Glasper scores on the next play for a 19–7 lead. Binswanger later adds a 27-yard field goal that would've been good from 47 yards away to give his team a 22–7 lead as ESPN cameras film De La Salle running off the field at halftime.

Eidson didn't anticipate Bodishbaugh being a running threat and makes adjustments that don't go unnoticed on the opposite sideline.

"We made them change," Hartwig said. "That was a big accomplishment by us. The kids didn't recognize it and the fans didn't recognize it, but as a coaching staff that meant a lot to us."

Ladouceur writes "44" on the markerboard at halftime. It's Gobble's number. "That guy is chewing you up," he says.

Meanwhile, Eidson is addressing defensive players across the room: "YOU'RE MAKING THAT QUARTERBACK LOOK LIKE MICHAEL VICK!"

There are puddles of water on the locker room floor left from when junior varsity players took showers. Discarded athletic tape, chunks of dirt, plastic bags, and empty Gatorade bottles are strewn about.

"I told you they were seniors," Eidson scolds as Ladouceur adjusts blocking assignments for the veer. "I told you they were tough. I don't care who they have played. It's not just about your heart. It's about their heart also. THIS IS MITTY ALL OVER AGAIN!"

Drew returns Freedom's first punt of the second half 71 yards for a touchdown. Cameron Colvin catches a 37-yard pass from Cecil to set up a Jackie Bates touchdown, making it 35–7 when Rich Sjoroos runs under the goalpost hoping to catch the extra point.

Sjoroos is in town on a business trip of sorts, having convinced two other members of the Juneau-Douglas Crimson Bears football coaching staff to make the long journey down from Alaska. The three out-of-towners spent the week watching practice and talking with Ladouceur and Eidson while their wives shopped in San Francisco.

"I expected to see a slew of 26-year-old Tongans who ran a 4.4," said Eddie Brakes, Juneau's junior varsity defensive coordinator. "I'm comparing these kids to our kids and thinking we could physically compete with them. But it's the system. It's a program and a half."

There are no roads in or out of Juneau, which has a population of more than 30,000 and is located amid the fjords of Southeast Alaska. The Crimson Bears' nearest conference game requires traveling 750 miles—or a one hour and 25-minute plane ride. They have to pay to fly teams in from Anchorage to play on a field of glacial silt carved out of the Tongass National Forest. Players walked the field picking up glass, nails, and rocks before every practice until Adair-Kennedy Memorial Field was finally covered with artificial turf. The stands are covered to protect fans from the near-constant rain.

As a result of the remote location and high travel costs, the Crimson Bears are one of the few high school programs in America that rely on private funding. The program is actually an extension of the town's youth football league. Players must pay for their own uniforms, secure business advertising for the team's programs, sell raffle tickets, and do odd jobs around the community to help raise the funds.

"The biggest difference is the sureness of everything," says Juneau varsity head coach Richey Reilly of De La Salle's football team. "They play at a higher level than even I thought it would be, and I thought they would be bigger. I imagine everybody thinks that. But they're the fittest group I've ever seen."

De La Salle leads 43–7 at the end of the third quarter. Eidson sends Binswanger onto the field to attempt a 47-yard field goal in the fourth quarter with hopes of drawing the attention of college scouts. Several schools are expressing interest in Binswanger, but none has yet to offer a scholarship. The ball clears the goal post and the track. It would've been good from 55.

The Juneau coaches leave the sideline to join their wives in the stands as PA announcer Lou Ascatigno congratulates the Spartans on their 132nd consecutive victory. The scoreboard reads 46–7 as players mingle with their parents beneath a spectacular harvest moon. Two kids ask Maurice Drew for his autograph and he dutifully signs, smiling all the while. Another young boy asks Cecil for his sweatbands. The quarterback smiles and says, "Sure." Toddlers wobble about, carrying balloons as the White Coats roll up tarps on the sideline.

"Tonight was our homecoming," Eidson tells players in the locker room at halftime. "Next week will be a homecoming for [Pittsburg] Coach [Vic] Galli. He's a friend of mine but that doesn't prevent me from wanting to kick his ass all over the football field. I know he feels the same way, too."

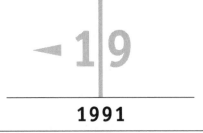

1991

PITTSBURG'S CLAIM TO FAME

| | | | | | | | |

Joe Aliotti kept a notebook and pen on his bed stand because X's and O's often played chess in his dreams. That's how the idea came to him. The more he thought about it, the more sense it made.

He had seen Dennis Erickson's Idaho teams run the same offense when he was at Boise State. He had even planned to incorporate it into his playbook had he been named head coach at Pittsburg High School before the 1991 season.

The job had gone to Herc Pardi instead. Many in the community had supported Aliotti, who had been one of the best quarterbacks in school history before starring at nearby Los Medanos Junior College, then leading Boise State to the Division I-AA national title.

He came from a coaching family. His brother Nick was an assistant coach at Oregon who would later become an assistant coach for the St. Louis Rams before returning to Oregon as defensive coordinator. Joe spent five years coaching at Boise State and Oregon State before moving his family back to Pittsburg, where he became a teacher at his alma mater. He eventually rose to vice principal.

Pardi also was a Pittsburg boy, even if he had grown up in Clayton and attended Clayton Valley High School. His father and uncles starred for the Pirates in the late 1930s. As a child Herc Pardi attended every Pittsburg High game, home and away, and was drawn to the rich tradition that played out under the bright lights at Pirate Stadium on Friday nights.

He got the job based on his 72–17 record at the junior varsity level, where he won five league championships and went unbeaten during his last two seasons. Aliotti had college playing and coaching experience but had never been a head coach at any level.

Pardi—stout, fit, and equipped with the authoritative voice of a talk-radio host—was a master organizer. Aliotti swallowed his pride and became Pardi's offensive coordinator. His brother-in-law Jerry Haflich was named defensive coordinator. Pardi took on the role of a CEO. He let his coordinators do most of the coaching while he organized a vast network of boosters.

Pittsburg players were provided with fruit and juice before the first practice during double days. They were served lunch at school between workouts. It was all provided free of charge, thanks to Pardi.

"Pittsburg loses a lot of good athletes because they're out selling dope," former player Derrick Huffman said. "That's what Herc kept us from."

Pittsburg coaches didn't take the Spartans lightly when De La Salle joined the Bay Valley Athletic League in 1988. Former Pirates coach Larry Rodriguez scheduled scrimmages with De La Salle twice in the early 1980s. The first scrimmage was fairly even. De La Salle dominated the second, and Rodriguez and his assistant left the field with newfound respect for the private school from Concord.

De La Salle defeated Pittsburg 28–21 in the BVAL's first year, finishing the season undefeated and winning the North Coast Section championship. The Spartans whipped the Pirates 43–18 the next year on their way to another perfect season. Pittsburg didn't fare any better the third year, getting trounced 49–14 in 1990.

Pardi, Aliotti, and Haflich realized that Pittsburg was one of the few schools that had superior talent to De La Salle. But the Pirates kept losing. The only logical explanation was that they were being outcoached, but they didn't believe that, or they didn't want to believe it.

Beating De La Salle quickly became an obsession.

"Joe and I desperately wanted to beat those guys," Haflich says. "We thought we were good coaches, but to be considered good you had to beat the boys over the hill. You had to beat De La Salle."

The Pirates finished a disappointing 5–5 during Larry Rodriguez's final season as head coach, but the team Pardi inherited was dominated by a close-knit senior class that had come up through the program together. Nine of the eleven offensive starters for the 1991 varsity team had started for the 1988 freshman team. The junior varsity teams defeated De La Salle in back-to-back years by scores of 31–7 and 19–7.

The Spartans had won three straight NCS title games by scores of 42–0, 41–6, and 49–24, and they were the fourth-ranked team in the nation when they met Pittsburg during the 1991 regular season. But Pardi and his staff were convinced they finally had a team that could beat them.

Their team wasn't intimidated by the De La Salle mystique. There was a unity among this group that hadn't been present in previous years. If Pittsburg was ever going to beat De La Salle, this was the team — which made the 28–16 loss in the 1991 BVAL opener all the more painful.

Pittsburg's standout running back Percy McGee scored on a 78-yard run late in a hard-fought game to make the final score somewhat deceiving. The Spartans racked up 261 rushing yards on the most basic play in their playbook, the dive. Still, the Pittsburg staff was encouraged. McGee had run for 208 yards. They'd have to iron out some problems defensively, but at least they knew they could move the ball on a De La Salle defense that has always been tough against the run.

"We'll see you in December," Pardi told Ladouceur after the game.

Ladouceur believed him. He fully expected the two teams to meet in the NCS 3A championship game later that season.

"I just felt they were capable of more," Ladouceur said of that first 1991 meeting. "As I watched them throughout the season, I knew they were getting better. They were gaining momentum."

The momentum came in the final game of the season against hated Antioch. The neighboring communities had maintained a fierce rivalry for seventy-three years. The annual game between college rivals Cal and Stanford is called the Big Game in California. The season-ending showdown between Pittsburg and Antioch has long been known as the Big Little Game among locals and is marked by parades, pageantry, and standing-room-only crowds.

It was a matchup of Antioch's league-leading defense and Pittsburg's league-leading offense. Percy McGee made a fingertip catch in the end zone to give the Pirates a 26–20 overtime win and a playoff berth.

"Antioch was a stepping stone, but our sights went well beyond Antioch," Pittsburg's two-way lineman Jon Buxton said. "De La Salle was our world. They were the archenemy. That's what may have made the Antioch game as close as it was. Our sights were set on De La Salle."

While Pittsburg was gaining momentum, De La Salle was losing it. Quarterback Alli Abrew was continually harassed and sacked three times during a 13–9 win over Ygnacio Valley in the second-to-last game of the regular season. The Warriors had a chance to snap De La Salle's 30-game win streak after driving to the Spartans 42-yard line with 5:00 left. The Spartans' Brian Souto made an interception to seal the win.

"That was disgusting," De La Salle receiver Tyler Scott remembers. "That's when we realized we had to do some soul-searching because we weren't as good as we thought we were."

Actually, trouble had been brewing all season. Nothing major, but little things that, when added up, gave Ladouceur reason for concern.

There were divisions on his team, especially between the junior and senior classes. The coaching staff also was in flux. More of Luke Wurzel's time was being taken up by his contracting business. The long-time assistant was having trouble getting to practice on time.

Ladouceur replaced Wurzel with junior varsity line coach Steve Alexakos, the father of the commitment card, midway through the season. Still, there was something missing.

"Sometimes as a coach you have the realization that you're in trouble as a team," Ladouceur said. "When that happens it usually means you've been in trouble for a long time. There was an intangible missing, and it was hard to pinpoint what it was. It didn't seem like that team respected each other like good teams do. There were two camps, and they pulled against each other all season. That's not like us. We usually mix real well but that team was divided. It was a season that was slipping between our fingers and we didn't even know it was happening."

Both teams rolled through the playoffs, inching ever closer to Pardi's prediction. The Pittsburg coaching staff sensed De La Salle's vulnerability and remained convinced it had a team talented enough and determined enough to upset the Spartans for the first time in school history. But the Pirates needed something else. They needed an edge.

"Joe kept talking about how we had to have something for them,"

Haflich said. "We were well aware that we needed a Plan B, C and D because they always did. Joe kept saying we have to have a plan."

Aliotti talked to other coaches who had had some success against De La Salle. Pinole Valley's Jim Erickson told him they needed to come up with some new plays to run in the second half so De La Salle wouldn't be able to make adjustments at halftime.

It came to Aliotti in a dream. He scribbled it down on Monday night and thought it through for two full days before calling Pardi on Wednesday night, three days before the championship game.

It wasn't the Spartans' athleticism that had been the deciding factor in previous victories over Pittsburg. It was their discipline, precision, and execution. If Pittsburg could surprise them, find a way to match its athletes up against De La Salle one-on-one, it might be able to create indecision and undermine that cohesiveness.

Players were excited when Aliotti introduced the spread formation during practice on Thursday. They would wait and unveil their secret weapon in the second half, employing one-back or even no-back formations with multiple receivers instead of their split-back scheme.

Multiple-receiver formations would spread the De La Salle defense out and allow Pittsburg's quicker skill position players to make plays. The Pirates had never run anything like this before. De La Salle coaches couldn't prepare for something they didn't know was coming.

Aliotti had the personnel to make it work. Pittsburg was loaded with talented skill players and a quarterback savvy enough to pull it off. Chris Shipe was the only quarterback who had ever been allowed to call audibles as a freshman. He had broken nearly all the Pittsburg passing records Aliotti had once held during his two and a half seasons on the varsity and would end the season with a 26–2 touchdowns-to-interceptions ratio.

McGee had run for 1,163 yards and 16 touchdowns in the regular season, both single-season records at Pittsburg. He was twinned in the backfield with Derrick Huffman, an equally capable runner who would move to receiver in the spread formation.

Greg Quesada would go on to break junior college pass-catching records at Los Medanos before playing for the Washington Huskies.

Mike Gargalikis and Aaron Alatorre also were capable receivers who could make plays if matched in single coverage with defensive backs.

De La Salle's linebackers were big and physical and dominated at the line of scrimmage, but it was hoped they would struggle defending quick passes on the perimeter. Forcing them to line up farther outside should open up the middle for McGee to run traps and draws.

"Our goal was to keep it close in the first half so they couldn't make adjustments," Aliotti said. "De La Salle makes the best adjustments. Their kids have always understood quicker for some reason. At halftime you can talk to all of them, but during the second half you can't because some are playing offense and some are playing defense. That was the idea, to keep them from making adjustments."

Coaches have spent years trying to answer the perplexing question of how to beat De La Salle. First players must believe they can win. Many teams are defeated before they step on the field.

An opposing coach must also find a way to negate the Spartans' get-off—easier said than done. You have to keep them from jumping out to their typical big lead and capitalize on their mistakes while making few of your own. Big plays: That's another time-tested answer. To beat De La Salle a team has to keep the ball away from the Spartans' offense while also scoring on quick strikes.

Most people fail to mention the common thread in the Spartans' past four defeats. In each of those games the opposing coach has saved something for the second half—something the Spartans weren't prepared for.

Skyline held on for a 22–21 win in 1984 after coach Tony Fardella ran a fake field goal and a fake point-after-touchdown late in the game.

El Cerrito edged De La Salle 14–13 in 1989 after coach Frank Milo pulled dusty plays out of a file cabinet. His teams ran variations of the I formation at the time but practiced a series of wing-T plays for four weeks before debuting them in the second half against De La Salle.

Rob Stockberger followed the same formula while preparing for Monte Vista's rematch against the Spartans in the 1987 NCS championship game. He built his game plan around some plays the Mustangs used only sparingly and others they had practiced for the first time that week.

A quick pitch to the halfback, for example, resulted in several key gains. Stockberger also used two trick plays to provide the winning margin—a variation of the "fumblerooski" out of a punt formation, and the quarterback throwback on a 2-point conversion.

"They are so good at halftime adjustments that as a coach you have to have something for the second half that they didn't see in the first half," Milo said. "You have to do something different."

Pittsburg's new offense, which was quickly dubbed "Pirate," was only half the equation, however. The Pirates had to keep the game close for it to work. They not only had to stop the veer, but preseason All-American receiver Amani Toomer, who would go on to star at the University of Michigan and for the NFL's New York Giants.

Haflich had consulted with various college and high school coaches about the best way to stop the veer. He designed a 4-4 defense precisely for that reason and dedicated all of spring practice to shutting down De La Salle's quick-strike running attack.

That defense gave up 451 rushing yards in a tie against Lincoln of Stockton during the nonleague season. After it surrendered 261 yards in the loss to the Spartans, Haflich moved 6'1", 215-pound middle linebacker Jon Buxton to noseguard and put sophomore linebacker Charlie Ramirez in his place. Now instead of a four-man front they had five twisting, stunting linemen occupying blockers and therefore freeing up the linebackers to make the majority of the tackles.

The improvement of the new "fifty-two" defense was dramatic.

"For whatever reason it clicked with those kids," Haflich said. "From that point on they learned it and owned it."

Toomer had the speed and athleticism that made it obvious he was destined to eventually play in the NFL. He was in his third year as a varsity starter and was being recruited by every major college. At 6'2", 180 pounds, he was the fastest man on the field and equally dangerous as a receiver and kick returner.

He was the best athlete to ever come through the school, such a force that Ladouceur predicted he would be a major college star as a sophomore. His game-breaking ability prompted Ladouceur to incorporate the passing game into his offense more than ever before.

"Defenses were so focused on Amani that sometimes there wasn't a cornerback or even a weak-side safety on my side," said Tyler Scott, one of two Spartan receivers who lined up opposite Toomer during his senior year.

Scott remembers a game early in the 1991 season when he was wide open in the middle of the field. Junior quarterback Alli Abrew still threw deep for Toomer, who was triple-teamed. Toomer made a leaping catch over three defenders for a touchdown.

"There was no one within 20 yards of me, but what was I going to say? Amani made an amazing catch," Scott says. "He was that good. He deserved to have the ball thrown to him every time."

Thousands of Pittsburg fans showed up in the Oakland Coliseum parking lot for a pregame barbecue, which came as no surprise since the visitors' bleachers were usually packed when the Pirates played on the road.

There were more than 40,000 seats at the Coliseum then, so there was no fear of the event being sold out. Most fans bought their tickets on the day of the game. Thanks largely to eager Pirates fans, however, the 2,600 presold tickets for the 1991 title game marked an unofficial record for an NCS championship event.

The Pirates wore their black jerseys with orange numbers and black helmets with an orange "P" on the side. They went through their pregame drills under threatening skies on a damp, chilly late afternoon in Oakland. They were convinced they could win, their confidence bolstered by the new offense they had practiced all week.

The Spartans wore white and performed their pregame routine as if the matchup were more of an obligation than an opportunity.

"We went into that game hoping we'd win and not confident we would win, and that's very unlike De La Salle," Ladouceur recalls.

The opening kickoff sailed high to Toomer, who slipped and fell on the wet field while trying to make a cut at the 20-yard line.

Dyshun Beshears was celebrating his eighteenth birthday that day, and becoming a legal adult took on added meaning for the senior from Pittsburg. He had been placed on juvenile probation after arrests for fighting with Antioch kids and members of a local Mexican gang. He already had made many changes in his life, thanks largely to the help of a Pittsburg counselor who took an interest in him. His probation ended on his eighteenth birthday. It felt like the first day of a whole new life.

Beshears sacked Abrew on the second play of the game; De La Salle was forced to punt after Scott dropped a pass on third down. It was the first pass Scott had ever dropped in a game.

"Once we stopped them on that third down, our confidence level went way up," Pittsburg linebacker Anthony Shipe remembers.

Pittsburg scored first, on a 25-yard reverse to lightning-quick Eric Alston. It was the first time De La Salle had trailed all season.

The De La Salle offense featured two prototypical veer backs in senior Damian Vallis and junior Patrick Walsh. They both were compact, strong, quick runners who were perfectly suited for the offense.

Walsh picked up 13 yards on the first play of De La Salle's third series, but Beshears registered two more sacks on the drive, the second of which came on fourth-and-5 at the Pittsburg 38-yard line.

De La Salle tied the score early in the second quarter when Abrew sprinted to his right and threw back to Walsh running down the left sideline. Walsh had hesitated for a moment, pretending to block, losing himself in the scrum near the line, before releasing into the pattern.

Ladouceur installed the play earlier in the week and it worked just like he had drawn it up. Walsh caught the ball on the Pittsburg 35-yard line and outran the secondary to the end zone.

Chris Shipe (Anthony's cousin) was the epitome of a field general. He was tall and lanky with black hair and wore a serious expression. There was no doubt who was running the offense when he crouched behind center.

He dropped back on third-and-12 at the Pittsburg 27 and looked quickly to his right before throwing deep for Quesada down the left sideline. Quesada had a step on cornerback Chris Vontoure and hauled in the perfectly thrown pass for a 56-yard gain. On the next play, Shipe found Beshears in the end zone for a 17-yard score that made it 14–7.

De La Salle responded with two quick touchdowns—one after a 27-yard catch by Toomer—to take a 21–14 lead with 2:13 left before halftime. The Pirates, however, weren't content to run out the clock and go into the locker room down by seven points. Big runs by Percy McGee and Derrick Huffman put the ball on the 50-yard line with 35 seconds left.

That's when Shipe threw the best pass of his career. He took a quick two-step drop and side-armed a floater down the left side. Huffman had released from the backfield and didn't have to break stride as the ball dropped into his arms. He made one defender miss at the 10 before finally being tripped up and pushed out of bounds at the 1.

McGee scored on the next play as De La Salle fans looked on in disbelief. The score was 21-all at the break, which meant that the Pirates had accomplished their first goal. They kept the game close.

Now they could unleash "Pirate" in the third quarter.

"They were tired but I had never seen a team more alert at halftime," Pardi says. "They were so into it. They were ready to go back on the field. They couldn't wait for the second half."

De La Salle team members played the first half as if they couldn't wait for the game to be over. Their body language told a tale of impending defeat. They trudged back to the huddle with slumped shoulders and an almost robotic glaze in their eyes.

Toomer was one of the more flagrant offenders. He had caught only one of the four passes thrown to him in the first half and was increasingly frustrated after slipping several times on the field.

"We were playing on the baseball infield part of the time and I wasn't used to that," he said years later. "My cleats were an issue."

The Spartans wandered about the sideline in disinterested groups while waiting for the second half to begin. Pittsburg players, meanwhile, were bursting with energy. Nobody can explain the Spartans' lack of enthusiasm that night, even all these years later.

"We had a horrible meeting the night before," Abrew recalls. "People wouldn't say anything. Nobody was committing. Lad wanted to hear the seniors, and those guys weren't talking. It was silent."

"I thought we needed stronger senior leadership," Ladouceur said. "I don't remember them talking about winning a North Coast Section championship. I don't know if it was something they felt passionately about. Maybe I didn't motivate them the right way. I believe firmly that if a team is not motivated it goes right back to the coaching staff. I fell down in that area. I should've motivated them better."

Pittsburg unveiled "Pirate" early in the third quarter. The offense lined up in its usual split-back formation with three receivers on the left. Then Huffman went in motion and lined up as a receiver on the far right. McGee slid over until he was behind Shipe.

The confusion was immediate. De La Salle players were pointing and shouting. After two plays, Eidson called a timeout.

"I could see there was concern over there," Pardi said of the De La Salle sideline. "It was kind of a stunned look. They were back on their heels and the excitement was building on our sideline."

"They didn't know what to do," Huffman said. "As disciplined and well-coached as that team was they were very, very confused."

This game has been elevated to mythical proportions in Pittsburg, where the details become more blurred with every retelling. One common misconception is that the "Pirate" formation allowed the Pittsburg offense to roll over the Spartans defense in the second half.

Not true. Eidson did an excellent job of getting players in the proper positions during the timeout. The mismatches that Aliotti and Pardi had hoped would result in receivers running free up the seam never materialized. There were no game-breaking plays, no passes to wide-open receivers streaking down the sideline.

The "Pirate" formation wasn't a turbocharged version of Pittsburg's already potent attack. What it did was allow Pittsburg to put together a methodical 82-yard drive that gave it a 28–21 lead midway through the third quarter and milked 6:24 off the clock.

Shipe called plays based on where the Spartans lined up. He completed short passes to Alston, Quesada, and Huffman to set up quick-hitting trap plays and draws to McGee up the middle.

"They surprised us," Ladouceur said. "It was nothing fancy but it forced us to spread out the second-level guys, and when we did that we were vulnerable to the trap. We couldn't take everybody off the field to make an adjustment, and you can't do it during a timeout."

There was still a lot of football to be played, and it wasn't as if De La Salle had been unable to move the ball. Walsh was 5'7", quick, powerful, and determined. He and Damian Vallis had been picking up steady yards on the ground.

Ladouceur quickly identified a weakness in the Pirates' defense and began exploiting it. Their stunting, five-man defensive front was vulnerable to play-action passes over the middle, especially on first and second down. Tight end Andrew Freeman already had caught passes for

12 and 17 yards when Abrew threw him another on the second play of the next series. The 6'3", 185-pound junior rambled 47 yards before being hauled down from behind as the third quarter expired.

Freeman caught another 10-yard pass before Walsh scored on a 2-yard run. The extra point sailed wide left. With 9:35 remaining in the fourth quarter, the Spartans trailed 28–27.

Percy McGee had been an all-league linebacker as a junior but played defense only sparingly during his senior year because of nagging back and ankle injuries and recurrent "hustle violations."

If a Pittsburg coach saw a player giving less than 100 percent on film, the player was given a hustle violation. An excess of violations resulted in that player being benched, even if he was as talented as Percy McGee.

Haflich knew he had to contain Spartan Andrew Freeman if Pittsburg were to cling to its lead. He grabbed McGee on the sideline sent him into the game.

"I told him he had to stop the tight end over the middle," Haflich said. "He had to make sure that guy didn't get open. I needed somebody to make a play. That's why I picked Percy McGee."

De La Salle's Ryan Christie missed a 47-yard field goal attempt with 4:34 left. The Spartans forced a Pittsburg punt after three plays. The Pirates' sophomore punter, who was trying to keep the ball away from Amani Toomer, had the ball glance off his foot and squirt out of bounds two yards downfield. The Spartans had the ball on the Pittsburg 30-yard line with plenty of time left on the clock to score the game-winning points.

The play went bad at the snap of the ball. It was almost as if the center and the quarterback were the only two people aware that the ball had been snapped. The rest of the linemen and backs were still in their stances when Abrew began rolling to his left.

Abrew was waiting for the whistle. He didn't know if the play was live or if an illegal motion penalty would be called when he made an awkward fake to Damian Vallis. On the Pittsburg sideline, Chris Shipe was screaming for the officials to call an illegal motion penalty and back De La Salle up another five yards. On the De La Salle sideline, Ladouceur could see the play falling apart.

"Don't throw the ball!" he shouted. "Don't throw the ball!"

Beshears was closing quickly on Abrew from behind when the quarterback looked toward Andrew Freeman, who had been open all night.

"I ran a corner route to the back of the end zone," Tyler Scott said. "I knew I was going to be open. I thought Alli was looking at me and not Andrew. I thought I was going to catch the game-winning touchdown."

Instead, Abrew threw a short pass to Freeman. McGee stepped right in front of him and made the interception at the 21-yard line. Abrew threw himself at McGee but couldn't make the tackle. Walsh missed him, too.

"I can still feel his legs ripping out of my arms," Walsh says.

De La Salle players knew what was at stake and pursued McGee up the sideline, running hard. He broke two more tackles before Pirate Regan Upshaw appeared, running stride for stride, looking to make a block.

Upshaw was a junior offensive tackle and defensive end who would be named to the Parade All-American team after his senior year. He eventually went on to play for the University of California and was later a first-round draft choice of the Tampa Bay Buccaneers.

He was just who McGee wanted most to see. McGee was running down the sideline with the ball under his arm, each step taking him a little closer to history, pointing at the potential tacklers he wanted Upshaw to block.

Meanwhile, Shipe was no longer hoping the officials would throw a flag. Now he was screaming for them not to.

McGee scored, returning the interception 79 yards, prompting a big pileup in the end zone as Pirates' players jumped on one another in celebration. The Pittsburg sideline was in hysterics. De La Salle players lay where they had fallen, exhausted.

"As soon as I scored I knew we had won the game," McGee said.

The initial euphoria would be short-lived. Pittsburg led 35–27, but there were two minutes and 15 seconds left and the Pirates had to kick off. That meant Toomer would likely get at least one more opportunity to touch the ball.

"We kept waiting for him to take over," Freeman says. "Amani was notorious for that. If he gets past you once, he breaks the game open."

Pirate Leif Hall had hardly played as a junior but was one of those players who improved during every practice. He was a quiet kid who had gained confidence while playing against Toomer in a summer passing league game, a game the Pirates had won. He held Toomer to three catches for 38 yards in their regular-season matchup.

Toomer had just three catches for 40 yards when De La Salle huddled for what the Spartans hoped would be the first play of a game-tying drive.

"Considering Amani Toomer's talent and what he had done to other teams, for Leif Hall to really shut him down was huge," Pirates' lineman Jon Buxton recalls. "That helped eliminate their passing game."

During the summer, Ladouceur had told his talented receiver not to show up for some passing league games because the offense had become overly reliant on him. But it came to rely on him just as much during the season. For the first time since Ladouceur and Blair Thomas introduced the veer, the Spartans lacked an offensive identity.

"We were always a pound-it team that knocked people back," Ladouceur said. "I definitely did not feel that way that season."

Abrew threw to Toomer for a 15-yard gain on the first play of the final drive. Toomer made a leaping catch on a middle screen on the next play, and for a brief moment it appeared that he might split two defenders and take it all the way. He was unable to summon his usual burst of speed on the wet field, however. It had been obvious all night. Even when he wasn't slipping on the turf he seemed unsure of his footing. He got knocked off his feet after a 22-yard gain.

Abrew threw to Toomer again on the next play but Hall was right there and the pass was incomplete. Toomer caught the next pass for a 25-yard gain to give De La Salle a first down on the Pittsburg 24-yard line with 25 seconds left in the game.

Beshears knew he was having the game of his life. This was just the beginning of his career, not the end. He would go on to be a four-year starter at Humboldt State and a Division I-AA All-American.

He sacked Abrew on the next play and the ball came loose. Pirate Regan Upshaw picked it up and began a circuitous path toward the end zone before being pushed out of bounds, where he was mobbed by his teammates.

A celebration that would last for several months, with parades and community dinners in the team's honor, spilled onto the field. Aliotti ran frantically up the sideline, trying to find Shipe to explain that he had to take a knee before the clock could run out and the game could officially end.

Long-time Pitt athletic director Al Bonanno kissed Pardi's bearded cheek when the clock finally expired. Pittsburg players celebrated while De La Salle players wandered around the field dazed and disbelieving. They looked like fish in a tank, cattle in a pen. They had to remain on the field for the trophy ceremony but didn't know what to do or how to act.

Toomer hurled his helmet in frustration.

The same team that had rushed for 261 yards against Pittsburg less than three months earlier ended the game with nine consecutive pass attempts. Walsh, who had rushed for 157 yards in De La Salle's regular-season victory, had only two carries in the second half.

"If they hadn't passed to Amani Toomer as much as they did, they would've won the game," Anthony Shipe says. "I know he was The Man. But they had another man in the backfield. Walsh was a horse."

Ladouceur took an emotional inventory when he finally got to the locker room. Many of his players were in tears. He remembers thinking that it was more emotion than he had seen out of his seniors all season. Junior leaders Abrew and Walsh seemed to be taking it hardest.

Critics point to scenes such as this as an example of how too much emphasis is placed on winning at De La Salle. You should've seen their players after they lost to Pittsburg, they'll say. They were devastated. Is that really what high school football should be about?

Ladouceur's program is based on the belief that if you do everything precisely right, if you make a commitment to your coaches and teammates and sweat through all the grueling hours of workouts, and bond with your teammates and play for them and not for yourself, winning just happens. It's a byproduct. But in the end the byproduct isn't as important as paying attention to the details.

Those players knew in their hearts that the celebrating Pittsburg players had attended to the details better than they had. The Pirates had out-De La Salled De La Salle. They had been a tighter, more disciplined group that played as a team while De La Salle relied on an individual.

They knew they hadn't bonded the way previous Spartans teams had. Deep down they knew why they had lost. The truth stung.

"I can look back now and say it was just a high school football game," Abrew says. "But that's why we win. We win because we all know it's about much more than just a high school football game."

Ladouceur told them that sometimes you can do all the right things and you can still lose a football game.

Tyler Scott raised his head and looked into Ladouceur's eyes when he heard those words. "You don't mean that," he thought to himself.

PITTSBURG

A Homecoming for Two Ex-Spartans

usty boxcars rattle down the track beyond the vine-covered fence that separates the Pittsburg High School practice field from the railroad siding. Bent electrical poles lean over the tracks.

The steel mill and chemical plant that have employed generations of football players dominate the horizon, a reminder of what the future holds for young men in this blue-collar town.

A rusty backstop stands silent vigil over a neglected baseball diamond so barren you have to imagine where the infield ends and the outfield begins. A dirt pile sits on the edge of the parking lot, a remnant of a long-forgotten improvement project.

Potato chip bags cartwheel across the practice football field, more visual reminders of the difference between a public high school in a tough town and a private high school in the white-collar suburbs.

A baby-faced youth pushes a baby in a stroller through a hole in the fence and across the rutted ground as first-year Pittsburg High football coach Vic Galli arrives wearing an orange golf shirt, black nylon pants, and sneakers. Being from Pittsburg carries a special connotation, an attitude that says: "Don't mess with me. I'm from Pittsburg." Vic Galli is Pittsburg to the core. His coal-black hair is slicked straight back and he wears a street-wise smirk.

"I have a lot of pride in being from Pittsburg," Galli says as he unlocks the sturdy padlock and pulls the thick silver chain that secures the door. "I'll never live anywhere else."

Pittsburg is unique in a region filled with nondescript bedroom communities and sprawling suburbs. It is a town of nearly 60,000 that sits on the banks of the San Joaquin-Sacramento River Delta. It has remained insular despite the insurgence of commuters drawn by low-income housing and defiantly proud despite blight and crime rates more often found in inner cities.

This is one high school town where football has been king since before John Henry Johnson wore the orange and black, then went on to a future that included professional fame as a member of the San Francisco 49ers' "Million Dollar Backfield." This is a town where for generations the high school football coach has been considered keeper of the third most important job in town, behind the mayor and the police chief. If a player is talented enough, he might even be inducted into the Pittsburg High School Football Hall of Fame.

"Football has always been the heart of Pittsburg and it still is," says former Pirates coach Larry Rodriguez. "That's this town's glory. Players may not find glory anywhere else, but they can find it on the football field in front of the hometown fans on a Friday night."

For generations being from Pittsburg was synonymous with being Italian. But the city is now one of the most ethnically diverse communities in the entire East Bay. Many of the city's most historic family surnames still end in a vowel, however. The Galli name reaches deep into the city's history and has long been associated with the Pittsburg High football program.

Vic Galli's father and uncles played here. His great-uncle George Galli was a star for the Pirates before going on to play in the Rose Bowl for USC. George returned home, like most Pittsburg natives do, and coached the Pirates in the 1960s and '70s. Another great-uncle, Charles, is the unofficial historian of Pirate football.

Vic grew up longing to spend his Friday nights on the field inside Pirate Stadium. He played in Pittsburgh's Junior Football League, which was established as a feeder system for the high school team, but he never realized his dream of wearing the black and orange. His mother was determined to send him to De La Salle.

He didn't want to attend the Catholic private school "over the hill" in Concord. He wanted to stay in Pittsburg with his friends. But he had attended a Catholic grammar school in Pittsburg and his mother insisted he continue his education at a parochial high school.

She sat in the De La Salle principal's office and cried when her son wasn't admitted initially. Finally, the principal relented. Twenty years later Galli still has mixed feelings.

"I'm sorry I didn't get to play here, but I still had all my friends here," he says, slurping from a bowl of Cocoa Krispies in the coaches' office. "I remember going to the Pittsburg games and wishing I could be out there playing with my friends, but you know something? I got to be on the foundation of one of the greatest stories of all time. I played for De La Salle's first championship team and got to play for Coach Lad. I scored a touchdown on an interception at the Oakland Coliseum and they actually showed it on the news. It was a great experience. Now, as much as I love Pittsburg, I'm glad I went where I did. I wouldn't trade it for anything in the world."

He is a native of Pittsburg and a product of De La Salle. He always has been caught in the middle, suspended somewhere in between. He still finds himself defending De La Salle to his Pittsburg friends and defending Pittsburg to his De La Salle friends.

His two worlds are about to collide. The Spartans host Vic Galli's 2002 Pittsburg Pirates on Friday night at Owen Owens Field.

"People hate De La Salle and they don't know what they're talking about," Galli says. "I don't hate De La Salle. I don't have anything bad to say about De La Salle, but people want me to say those things."

Every game against De La Salle is a big game if you're the head coach at Pittsburg High. But this is more than that. No other school or community has been impacted by the Spartans' rise to dominance as much as Pittsburg has, because no other community's identity is as directly linked to the success of its only high school football program.

The Pirates were a regional power before De La Salle came along. They ended De La Salle's 35-game winning streak with a 35–27 victory in the 1991 North Coast Section championship game. The celebration lasted several months. In many ways, it has never stopped.

The team bus took a victory lap all over town that night, people waving and whistling and cheering wherever it went. Proclamations were presented, and various civic groups organized dinners in their honor. Congratulatory messages, telegrams, flowers, and even a banner flowed in from schools all over Northern California. For that one night, it seemed, Pittsburg represented every public school that had ever lost a game to "The Green Machine."

It was a big win then and it gets bigger every year. They root for De La Salle in Pittsburg now. The town that ended the Spartans' last streak doesn't want the current streak to end. Every win that's tacked onto The Streak makes what Pittsburg accomplished in 1991 more significant.

It has become the program's claim to fame, even if the Pirates have been outscored by the Spartans 430–89 in fifteen games since.

"You find yourself hoping Poly doesn't beat them and St. Louis doesn't beat them because who would ever talk about Pitt?" said Pittsburg junior varsity coach Aaron Alatorre, a wide receiver on the 1991 team. "When someone else beats them, we'll be forgotten."

In other ways that victory has turned into a cruel joke. No one knew it at the time, but that game represented Pittsburg football at its absolute peak. De La Salle has built the nation's longest winning streak in the eleven years since while competing against some of the most powerful teams in the nation in some of the biggest games in the history of high school athletics. The Pirates have been on a long, slow downhill slide since that night.

"I'm getting letters in the mail from people I don't even know on ways to beat them," Galli says. "I don't know if everybody gets those letters. Everybody is waiting for The Streak to end."

Galli is convinced that his program is on the rise. The community's commitment is evident by the transformation of the old girls' gym into a football-only facility. It's not much to look at now, with a hot-water heater sitting where the weight benches will eventually be and stepladders leaning against unfinished walls, but you can glimpse Galli's vision for the future of Pirate football.

Two-thirds of the old girls' gym will be a state-of-the art weight room. The remaining third will serve as a team room for film review and study halls. The assistant coaches' office is three times the size of the office at

De La Salle. Galli's office has plywood walls now but soon will be a work-space befitting a man of his stature, with a window overlooking the new weight room.

Players currently store their equipment in moving boxes with their names scribbled on the side. At this time next year this will be a plush locker room with orange and black carpeting with a "P" in the middle.

Pittsburg football is on the rise, all right. This building will be the envy of every high school football coach in the area.

Galli has grand visions, as most thirty-seven-year-old coaches do. He is taking what Ladouceur taught him and applying it to the team that is his family's legacy. It will take time and there will be challenges, no question. These kids aren't De La Salle kids, most of whom come from well-to-do families who have the time to devote to year-round football training.

Many of Galli's players come from single-family homes and have more pressing concerns than football, like working in order to make enough money to feed themselves, or babysitting a brother or sister until their mother gets home from work.

"They're not dealing with all the same issues we're dealing with here," Galli says. "They have kids with family problems over there too, but they're isolated issues. We have massive issues."

This community has long been a prime breeding ground for foot-ball talent. This is the only team that plays De La Salle regularly that can claim to have equal and often superior athletic ability. The Pirates may not be as polished or as devoted, but the raw athleticism is always here.

Athletes and opportunity—that's why Pittsburg is the single great-est threat to The Streak. While other schools have threatened to forfeit games against De La Salle in the past because of concerns about com-petitive equity, Pittsburg has volunteered to take on the Spartans sea-son after season, loss after loss. Every year the hope returns. Maybe this will be the year Pittsburg rises up and slays De La Salle again.

Optimism is as high as it has been in recent years. The Pirates have a popular new coach, a Pittsburg boy, and who is better equipped to defeat De La Salle than the former De La Salle player and coach?

"They don't have a perfect program," Galli says. "They make mis-takes, but they have a hell of a blueprint. I have that blueprint. I've been on the inside. Other people want to do what De La Salle does but they don't know how because they haven't been there. I've been there."

Galli was supposed to have gotten this job four years ago. He had the unflagging support of long-time athletic director Al Bonanno and was the choice of the hiring committee, but was passed over by the school board because he was not a school district employee.

He was crushed. Bonanno, a Pittsburg native who taught at the school for more than thirty years, resigned over the flap and later did what many in his hometown still consider the unthinkable. He followed Galli to De La Salle as a member of the junior varsity staff.

That's just one example of how intermixed the two programs have become. Joe Aliotti was a hometown hero in Pittsburg and a head coach in waiting. He was the assistant principal in charge of discipline who came from one of the most recognized families in town. Coming to De La Salle was as easy as switching fingers, he jokes. Instead of raising his middle finger at the Spartans, he holds up his index finger instead: "We're No. 1!"

He laughs now, but some still consider his defection a treasonous act, even if a fractious school board and small-town politics prompted an exodus of many long-time Pittsburg teachers.

"People still call me traitor," Aliotti said. "But that's narrow-minded and not understanding of what's best for my family. People who understand that say it's a great move. They understand my family is number one and this is a different challenge, a better place for me."

It's stories like this that add another level of intensity to this series. The men in green jackets who'll be standing on the opposite sideline on Friday are Galli's friends and former teachers, people who know him as only a select few do. He knows the faces of the players behind the silver facemasks as well, if not better, than he knows the faces of his own players.

This is personal, although not for the reasons you might imagine. There is no bad blood here, even if there always was friction when Galli was coaching under Ladouceur.

Galli did things his own way, which didn't always endear him to the man who created a program in his own image. The brash assistant ordered jerseys with single-digit numbers, something Ladouceur had never done because he didn't want to promote the individual, and because he didn't want his players arguing over them. Galli ran an offense that didn't always resemble the offense the varsity ran. "Ever hear of the veer?" Ladouceur grumbled when he passed his JV coach at the end of a game against Clayton Valley one year.

Ladouceur even began to call his JV team the Pittsburg Spartans.

"Vic always was and always will be a Pittsburg guy," Ladouceur says. "That means he's very loyal to the community and his roots there, which is fine. It told me too that he always wanted to go back there and he never 100 percent bought into what we were doing here. He treated athletes a little differently than I did. He cared about the kids. I like that. But I never felt he wanted to be the head coach here. I never felt that or felt he was preparing for that."

"I wouldn't want the De La Salle job for two hundred grand a year," Galli admits. "I feel sorry for the next guy who takes it. If you lose you're the asshole who ruined the program. If you win you will never get the credit because it's Ladouceur's program to begin with."

This game is personal for Galli, but not only for the obvious reasons. It's personal because his life has been defined by football and because he will measure his success against his ability to beat his mentor under the lights on a Friday night. It's personal because he's convinced that fate has chosen him to finally end The Streak.

All these common strands create internal conflict in Galli and make him want to win this football game more than any single thing he has wanted in his life. He can't help but think that given his background, beating De La Salle is precisely what he was born to do.

"Everybody has been talking about it since I got the job," he says, the words coming in rapid-fire bursts. "De La Salle, De La Salle, De La Salle. I didn't want to talk about De La Salle. We've got to win football games, and when we get to De La Salle we'll talk about it. Now there's a buzz around town. We're 5–2—we should be 6–1—but people are getting excited and now this game comes up. You know something? We've got athletes that will match up with them. We're not like other teams. We've got home-run hitters. We've got guys that can go the distance. We can hit home runs against De La Salle. We have athletes. Anything is possible. Nobody expects us to win, but we're capable of shocking the world. It's not an impossible thing.

"I had a good experience there playing and coaching, but nobody wants to beat them more than I do. It's going to happen, whether it's this year or next year or the year after that."

His assistant coaches are trying to come up with new ways to stop De La Salle's veer, something Pittsburg coaches have attempted to do with precious little success for fifteen years.

But Galli has a secret weapon. He has something no other Pittsburg coach has ever had. He's got the greatest veer quarterback in De La Salle history on his side.

∼

Mike Bastianelli has never felt so uneasy. He is standing in the De La Salle parking lot, shifting nervously from foot to foot, his hands buried deep in the pockets of his Navy pea coat, waiting for the Pittsburg bus to arrive.

He still moves with the fluidity and grace of an elite athlete. His smile still lights up his dark Italian features. The only difference between the way he looks now and the way he looked ten years ago, when he was knifing through the line at the last possible second and bolting upfield to score yet another De La Salle touchdown, is the flecks of premature gray in his short black hair.

He is striking, charming, and in many ways an unwittingly tragic figure. Between his own fallible instincts and fate's cruel hand, he keeps winding up in odd situations, places where he doesn't seem to belong.

"In a way I feel like a traitor—not a traitor, but uneasy, like gosh, here I am coaching against the school that gave me everything, gave me the world," he says quietly. "I want to give back and I feel I can by taking what I learned somewhere else. They don't need me. Lad and Terry have everything wired. This is my way of giving back."

He had a storybook high school career. He not only was the best veer quarterback the school had ever known, he also kicked and punted and returned kicks and played safety while guiding the Spartans to back-to-back undefeated seasons in 1993 and 1994. Not once in his four years at De La Salle did he taste defeat at any level. He left with a record of 39–0.

He always will hold a special place in the hearts of his former coaches, and it has nothing to do with him rushing for 938 yards with 22 touchdowns as a senior. It goes far beyond his 54 percent completion rate and his 14 touchdown passes.

There's a flicker of tragedy, an inherent goodness, and a sense of long-ing in his sparkling brown eyes that make people care about Mike Bas-tianelli. Few have cared for him more than Terry Eidson and Bob Ladouceur,

"It shaped me," Bastianelli says. "Without De La Salle I would've gone the other direction. Eidson was huge in my life. He was my father fig-ure. I am who I am because of him."

He can't help but feel that he has failed them. He has yet to earn his college degree. He is divorced and separated from his daughter, who means more to him than anything. He is working as a day laborer until he could get hired on at the steel mill.

Everybody knew he had been with former USC teammate Darrell Russell the night Russell and two others allegedly drugged a woman at a San Francisco nightclub, then videotaped themselves performing sex-ual acts with her at Russell's home. It didn't matter that Bastianelli had not been so much as questioned by the police when they arrested Rus-sell the next morning. It didn't matter that Russell and the two others were eventually acquitted. Bastianelli knew that Ladouceur and Eidson didn't approve of his friendship with the former Oakland Raiders defen-sive tackle, even if all they knew about Russell was that he had twice been suspended for violating the NFL's substance abuse policy.

Bastianelli knew how some would view this series of circumstances. He knew how it would look through the eyes of Ladouceur and Eidson. They would think he was everything they feared he would one day become. All this is swimming in his head, making him look nervously over his shoulder, when the Pittsburg bus hisses to a stop and Vic Galli appears wearing his own nervous expression.

"You got something for me to wear?" Bastianelli asks his boss.

Vic takes off his orange and black "Pirate Football" windbreaker and throws it to Bastianelli, who sheds his pea coat and puts it on, leaving no doubt about his allegiance in this upcoming drama. They are De La Salle graduates and Ladouceur disciples, but here they are, on this famil-iar campus, pitting themselves against the man and program they revered.

This is going to be awkward for everybody.

"I guess I don't need to show you around," says White Coats President Tom Bruce, extending his hand. Vic smiles his sideways smile. "I guess not," he says, shaking hands.

Galli was Bastianelli's freshman coach at De La Salle, but they became more like brothers. The young coach recognized the young student's athletic ability right away. But there was something else that drew him in, something someone born and raised in Pittsburg understands intuitively.

"Everybody thinks De La Salle is full of rich boys, but Mike didn't have the greatest family," Galli says. "He was more like a Pittsburg kid."

Bastianelli never met his father, a reputed organized crime figure who was only recently released after serving an eleven-year term in a minimum-security Illinois prison. Mike took the last name of his stepfather, who divorced his mother when Mike was nine. He loves his mother dearly, but her struggles with alcoholism eventually forced him out of her house.

Nancy West and her three sons lived in San Diego, Oklahoma, and Phoenix before moving to Walnut Creek. Mike's best friend planned to attend De La Salle. Bastianelli's mother was running a successful advertising company at the time. She could afford the tuition, so Mike decided he also would attend De La Salle, even though the local public school coach tried desperately to change his mind, even having a jersey made with the teenager's name printed across the back.

Mike moved in with his girlfriend's family when his mother's drinking made his home life too chaotic for him to bear. He moved in with Galli when his mother moved to Oklahoma City. He always felt he was among kindred spirits in Pittsburg, even if he played for De La Salle.

"There were times when I wasn't there for Mike, and Lad and Terry were," said the since-remarried Nancy West-Marr. "I was going through another divorce and I couldn't stop drinking for long. They took Michael off and made him a star. They treated him like their own son."

Bastianelli played on a Rose Bowl team during his freshman season at USC. He started the last seven games at receiver during his sophomore year and finished the season as the team's third-leading receiver. He was suspended for two games during his junior season after it was discovered that an athletic department employee wrote part of a term paper for him. His senior year was full of more disappointments as his playing time dwindled.

When his girlfriend got pregnant, he did what he thought was the right thing and married her. The baby girl he loved more than he thought possible was born with a visual impairment.

Galli drove him to training camp after the 49ers signed him to a free-agent contract following his senior year at USC. By that time Bastianelli had so soured on football and was so distraught over being separated from his daughter that he wasn't sure he wanted to play.

He blew off a practice. Later that night he was arrested for driving with a suspended license. Team officials bailed him out and eventually cut him from the team.

"He's his own worst enemy," Galli says, sighing. "He's a decent kid who will be the first to tell you when he screws up. He regrets some of the things he's done."

Bastianelli was working as a grip in the TV movie industry when his marriage fell apart. He felt lost in Los Angeles and came back to the place that felt like home, if for no other reason than there were people there whom he knew cared about him. The first person he called was Galli.

"In a way De La Salle is a fantasyland," Bastianelli says. "They won't let you mess up. You get out on your own and you mess up and your mistakes are your mistakes."

He's standing in the back of the end zone watching a junior varsity game and feeling like a stranger when Nate Geldermann smothers him in a warm embrace. The former teammates have been joined by Mark Panella when Bastianelli spots Ladouceur trudging up the home sideline.

He walks toward his former coach and gives him an awkward hug. They have barely exchanged pleasantries before Ladouceur turns serious.

"What are you doing hanging out with Darrell Russell?" he asks.

"Coach, I've made a lot of bad choices and done things I'm not proud of, but here I am," Bastianelli replies, holding his arms out from his sides, looking Ladouceur in the eye.

Bastianelli is chewing sunflower seeds and pacing nervously as Pittsburg players stretch in semidarkness behind the stadium during the fourth quarter of the junior varsity game. Galli is checking his watch for the umpteenth time when Joe Aliotti walks across the track, through the gate, and shakes Galli's hand just as the Pittsburg JV team scores to pull to within 43–7.

268

"Hey, look, we scored," says a Pittsburg student equipment manager, amazed.

Aliotti has spent the afternoon three miles up the road scouting a critical Bay Valley Athletic League game between Clayton Valley and Freedom.

"Clayton beat Freedom, 20–14," he tells Galli. "You're in it."

"You're shitting me," Vic responds, his jaw dropping.

"No, Clayton beat Freedom," Aliotti repeats firmly.

"Why are you talking to a guy from De La Salle?" a Pittsburg ball boy demands of Galli after Aliotti walks away.

"Did you know that is the greatest quarterback in Pittsburg history?" Vic fires back, impatiently. "Did you know he was offensive coordinator the last time we beat them? So shut up."

It's obvious the boy knows none of this. "He's with De La Salle now," he offers weakly.

The Freedom team that played so valiantly against De La Salle in the first quarter the week before came unplugged against a Clayton Valley team that had lost five straight. Coach Kevin Hartwig's team had had several key players banged up against the Spartans.

The loss came as no surprise to Liberty coach Mark Stantz, who believes that placing too much emphasis on beating De La Salle undermines a team's chances in its next game.

"My hat's off to Kevin Hartwig," Stantz would later say. "He got seven points on the board. Good for him. I wasn't willing to sell out. I wasn't willing to sell out my team for a score."

It is a huge break for Pittsburg. Tonight's game against De La Salle will have no impact on the BVAL standings. If the Pirates beat Liberty and archrival Antioch in their next two games, they will claim their first outright league championship in twenty-two years.

"I've got to stay healthy," Galli says, clapping his hands together, delighted. "Shit!"

He groans when he hears that the final score of the JV game is 50–7. His good mood is ruined. "Welcome home, Galli," someone shouts from high atop the home stands.

"Tonight is a beautiful night for football," he tells his players minutes before they take the field. "Just think, you're in high school, you're facing the No. 1 team in the country, and they're not invincible—believe me, they're not. This could be the greatest night of your life, something you will never forget. Will it be a night you want to forget, or the greatest night of your life?"

"There is so much I want to say," Bastianelli tells them when Galli is finished. "I wish I could play with you guys tonight. That's what I wish."

The Kansas City Chiefs have a bye week, allowing NFL rookie Shaunard Harts to return home to California and watch the Pittsburg team for which he once starred take a shot at ending The Streak.

He wears a sweatshirt, baggy jeans, a backward Chicago Cubs hat, and cradles a video camera in his right hand as Pirates players bounce up and down in the end zone before introductions.

"We're done talking," Harts shouts, a menacing scowl on his face. "We're going to talk with our pads tonight. LET'S MAKE HISTORY TONIGHT. IT'S TIME TO GO TO WAR. WE'RE GOING TO WAR. ARE YOU ALL READY TO GO TO WAR?"

"HELL YES!" several players shout in reply.

"IT'S TIME TO GO DOWN IN HISTORY. YOU CAN GO DOWN IN HISTORY, FELLAS. YOU CAN GO DOWN IN HISTORY TONIGHT. BE PROUD. WEAR THOSE JERSEYS WITH PRIDE. YOU REPRESENT PITTSBURG. YOU REPRESENT YOUR WHOLE COMMUNITY. YOU REPRESENT YOUR FAMILY. YOU GOTTA REPRESENT!"

"LET'S GO!" fired-up players shout. "IT'S A WAR. IT'S A WAR, BABY."

Pittsburg players begin to learn the difference between hope and false hope when the Spartans score on their first possession. Cameron Colvin throws a 31-yard reverse pass to tight end Terrance Kelly. Maurice Drew scores the touchdown on a 15-yard run.

Pittsburg's athleticism worries Ladouceur, especially the way his offensive line performed against Freedom the week before. The Pirates have talent, particularly on offense. They take advantage of a muffed punt and march to the Spartans' 25-yard line on their next drive. An incomplete pass on fourth-and-6 gives the ball back to De La Salle.

Spartan Jackie Bates sweeps the right side and glides down the sideline for a 46-yard gain. Drew eventually scores untouched from 10 yards out for a 14–0 lead with 1:57 left in the first quarter. Galli stands stoically on the visitors' sideline, arms crossed, gnashing his gum.

A bad snap sails over the head of the Pirates punter and out of the end zone for a safety to make it 16–0. "They ran that same play in the junior varsity game," a member of De La Salle's chain gang cracks before Bastianelli quiets him with a glare.

Bates takes an option pitch from quarterback Britt Cecil and finds himself so in the clear that he cuts back, even though there's no reason to. Pittsburg coaches grab their hair and scream, "No! No! No!" as Bates crosses the goal line. The 2-point conversion makes it 24–0.

"Don't y'all want to win?" screams a middle-aged woman in a Pittsburg jersey who is hanging over the string of flags that keeps spectators from wandering onto the visitors' sideline.

Pirates running back Brian Robinson gains 12 yards on a draw play. "They ain't shit!" a Pittsburg player screams on the sideline. Quarterback Vince Seeno completes a pass to Alex Toeaina, who makes a one-handed catch for a critical first down, sending the Pittsburg crowd into hysterics.

Seeno drops back on fourth-and-goal at the 14 and throws a pass to a receiver positioned near the left pylon. Damon Jenkins makes the interception at the 1 and races up the sideline in front of disbelieving players and coaches en route to a devastating 99-yard score.

"Don't let them do you like that!" the woman on the rail screams loud enough for players to hear. "Y'all look bad, real bad."

Galli remains focused on the action on the field, directing players, shouting instructions, communicating to his assistant coaches. Bastianelli stares off into the night, as if imagining himself anyplace other than the visitors' sideline at Owen Owens Field.

Pittsburg gets the ball back with 1:09 left in the half. After a completion for a 12-yard gain, an incompletion, and a failed reverse, Eidson calls a timeout to stop the clock and give his team a chance to return the punt before the halftime clock expires. As if the play were scripted, Drew returns the punt 46 yards for a touchdown with 14 seconds left to make the score 37–0.

Bastianelli is furious at what he considers to be a blatant attempt to run up the score and confronts Eidson as the teams exit the field at halftime.

"It's 30–0," he shouts. "Why are you trying to score?"

The confrontation surprises Eidson.

"HOW LONG HAVE YOU BEEN COACHING?" he shouts over his shoulder, immediately attributing Bastianelli's outburst to naiveté. "THREE WEEKS?"

De La Salle often was accused of running up the score in the 1980s, a charge Ladouceur flatly denies. More often in recent years, opposing coaches appreciate his restraint.

"I always think the first half of a game is open," Eidson says later. "I don't know of many teams that can't play a half of football. If the team is completely overmatched it's another thing."

"They should show some class," Bastianelli, still angry, mumbles to Galli outside the weight room at halftime.

"You know what?" Galli says. "That's football."

"It's not right," Bastianelli shoots back, refusing to concede.

"Let them do what they do," Galli says, trying to calm him. "Every dog has its day. Ours is coming soon."

"I'm pissed," Bastianelli says.

"I'm pissed too, but calm down," Galli tells him.

"We're 6−2," Galli says, more to himself than to Bastianelli. "Fuck this game."

Galli marches into the weight room, as if the statement helps him make up his mind. Players follow him with their eyes as he paces back and forth, composing his thoughts.

"Things are not going our way tonight," he tells them. "These guys are good. They're a good football team. We've got a ways to go, but we have a good football team in here. You know what? We got a gift tonight because Clayton Valley beat Freedom. I wanted to come and try to win this game, but we need to stay healthy. If we win the next two games we win the league. So right now, everybody's going to play in the second half. We're going to get everybody in. If you go in, you need to keep fighting. I just don't want you guys to quit. Play hard. No pouting. Write this one off. When the time comes maybe we'll see these guys again later this year."

Vic's halftime speech does not sit well with many of his players. The grumbling begins as soon as they leave the locker room.

"The coaches say we'll get the subs in the second half," one player shouts as they make their way back to the field. "Fuck that. This ain't over." Others nod in agreement. Still others repeat the mantra as they try to fire themselves up for the second half.

"This ain't over," they scream again and again, while slapping each other on the facemasks and shoulder pads. "This ain't over."

Britt Cecil throws a bomb to Cameron Colvin down the right sideline on the first play of the second half. Colvin leaps high in an attempt to make the catch but the pass falls incomplete.

Galli and his coaches immediately recognize the play for what it is. Colvin is from Pittsburg. Ladouceur wants to give him a chance to make a play in front of friends and family.

The irony occurs on the next play, when Bates takes an option pitch and runs down the sideline, right in front of Bastianelli, who has his hands in his pockets and is still shaking his head in disgust and dismay, en route to a 59-yard touchdown that makes the score 44–0.

"If you don't want us to run up the score, let us throw the ball in the third and fourth quarter," Eidson says. "Throwing the ball isn't our strength, especially with the second and third unit. If we run the ball it's not considered running up the score, but that's how we score all our points. If we throw the ball with our backup guys you're going to get sacks, incompletions, you're going to get the ball back. If I was coaching against De La Salle I would say keep throwing it, it's fine with me, because I know they're not going to score that way. But nobody looks at it that way."

De La Salle keeps the ball on the ground and soon the lead balloons to 51–0 and, a few minutes later, 58–0.

"They ought to have a completely different fucking league for these guys," mutters an observer in a black leather jacket standing on the Pittsburg sideline.

Bastianelli is still fuming about Eidson's timeout as he kicks the grass with his hands in his pockets, at times talking to former De La Salle players who come out of the stands.

"I've never seen it before," he says, referring to the Spartans running up the score. "What are they teaching over there? Aren't they supposed to be teaching sportsmanship and class? How can you do that when you know the other team is clearly outmatched? I'm still pissed."

Bastianelli makes a point to hug Eidson after De La Salle's 65–6 win.

It's more of an expression of appreciation for all Eidson has done for him than an apology for the confrontation. "It starts in January, not June," Eidson says. Bastianelli knows exactly what he means. In order to have any hope of defeating De La Salle, a team must first match the Spartans' commitment to their offseason training program. Bastianelli nods.

"I don't know if I struck the wrong chord with some guys at halftime," Galli tells his players a few minutes later. "We came here to win this game tonight. In no way am I telling you guys it's OK to quit. Things didn't go our way. I wanted to beat these guys in the worst way. It wasn't our night to shock the world. It will happen. But you know what? We've got a bigger goal. Once things weren't looking good for us I had to do what's right for our football team. I want, and I know you guys want, to win the title. We win the next two games and we're BVAL champions. Keep your heads up. Monday we go back to work. Tomorrow we've got films and we'll take a look at this mess. Get your stuff. Let's get on the bus and get the hell out of here."

Deep down Galli didn't expect to win this game. But he didn't expect to lose by 59 points, either. He's mystified as he boards the bus for the long, quiet ride back to Pittsburg. He coached those De La Salle kids. He knows his current players. How can they be that much better?

"That was fun to watch," Eidson tells his players in the De La Salle locker room. "Those De La Salle graduates were pretty sheepish walking across the field after the game tonight. There's a lesson to be learned from this game and I think they learned it tonight. You can't wish it and hope it. It takes hard work and dedication. You guys proved that. You reminded the guys who played here—and they knew it, deep down inside—what Spartan football is all about."

Shades of Gray

THE RECRUITING CONTROVERSY

the allegations have dogged Bob Ladouceur his entire career. By all accounts, his personality renders him incapable of what he is frequently accused of. He finds the idea of recruiting so contrary to his nature that he turns down offers to work at the college level, where success is determined by a coach's ability to sell himself, his program, and his school.

Tom Ladouceur may have been a slick enough salesman to buy a house with a five-dollar down payment. His youngest son is not.

Bob is a reluctant celebrity. He never had the desire to walk into a room and have strangers slap him on the back and call him "Coach." Alumni mixers, booster luncheons, and recruiting visits are his private definition of hell. To him, they have no real meaning.

"He doesn't want to go into someone's home and tell parents how great their son is when he knows the only reason he is there is because the kid is 6'4" and runs a 4.4," said Steve Coccimiglio, a former De La Salle basketball coach and a close friend of Ladouceur's. "He won't do it."

De La Salle recruits. It's a simple deduction, the easiest way to explain the school's success and dismiss The Streak. The accusation permeates the public school community and is repeated so often that it's assumed to be true, even though nobody can show conclusively damning evidence.

Rumors have swirled around the program for decades. De La Salle offers financial enticements. Players take steroids. Star players are given automobiles and other bonuses. A rumor several years ago held that Ladouceur drove a Lexus, when in fact his battered Nissan had more than 120,000 miles on the odometer at the time.

"The accusation of recruiting has been here from the beginning," said former De La Salle principal Brother Jerome Gallegos. "The gossip has always been there. We're constantly trying to prove we're innocent. It's hard enough to prove you're not guilty, let alone innocent. People end up shrugging their shoulders and saying, 'Yeah, we know.'"

A De La Salle basketball coach was fired for recruiting two student-athletes from Oakland in the mid 1970s. Other than that, school officials past and present insist there has been no disciplinary action taken against a coach or faculty member for recruiting.

But the charges became so persistent in the late 1980s and early '90s that Gallegos carried cards bearing the name and phone number of Paul Gaddini, the North Coast Section commissioner at the time. He presented the cards to accusers and urged them to forward any evidence to the NCS office so a full investigation could be launched.

Gaddini and current NCS commissioner Tom Ehrhorn say they never see enough evidence to warrant an investigation.

"They [De La Salle staff] do everything by the book," says Ehrhorn, who has been the NCS commissioner since 2000 and involved in NCS governance for a decade. "They are very sensitive to accusations of recruiting and go to great lengths to make sure that doesn't happen."

People either love De La Salle or loathe the school. They either are convinced that recruiting takes place, or certain that it doesn't. There are very few fence-sitters in this debate. People want to believe this issue is illustrated in black and white, when in fact it is cast in so many shades of gray.

How each student arrives on this well-swept campus is a saga in itself. Many come because their parents can afford it. Others are there for the prep school curriculum or Catholic values. Parents send their boys to De La Salle because they perceive it to be safer than public schools.

There is no doubt that some are attracted to the football program.

"I know some coaches over there are out hustling," says Clayton Valley assistant coach Jerry Coakley, who has coached in the area for forty years. "I know it. The kids have told me."

There have been numerous instances in which eighth-graders boast that they were recruited by De La Salle. Gaddini investigated a recruiting charge that did not involve De La Salle while he was commissioner of the Catholic Athletic League.

photos by Bob Larson/Contra Costa Times

Bob Ladouceur brings a smoldering intensity and an obsession with the game's most minute details to every De La Salle practice.

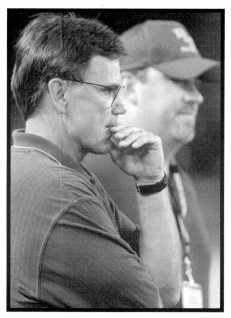

Ladouceur shows little emotion on the sideline but opposing coaches say nobody makes quicker in-game adjustments.

Bob Ladouceur reviews his game plan before his team's 99th straight victory in 1999.

Ladouceur inventories equipment at the beginning of the 1999 season.

Pulling tires across the parched practice field during summer workouts has become part of the tradition at De La Salle.

Former players claim the conditioning program at De La Salle is more demanding than anything they endured in college or even the NFL.

Ladouceur gives strength coach Mike Blasquez much of the credit for the program's rise to national prominence.

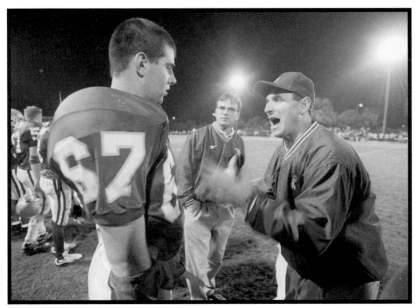

Ladouceur watches assistant coach Joe Aliotti make his point during a game at Owen Owens Field at 1999.

Bob Ladouceur watches as his players fire themselves up before a home game at Owen Owens Field in 1999.

Offensive linemen huddle on the field in the twilight after another grueling practice leading up to the program's 100th straight victory.

Cameron Colvin, De'Montae Fitzgerald, and Britt Cecil (left to right) look longingly at the aqua waves of Waikiki Beach during the team's trip to Hawaii during the 2002 season.

(left) De La Salle players walk through the hotel lobby on their way to the bus that will take them to practice at Aloha Stadium.
(right) Assistant coach and athletic director Terry Eidson performed with Polynesian dancers during a beachfront luau. He didn't know that television footage would be aired in the Bay Area.

Bob Ladouceur described the practices such as this in Honolulu as some of the most intense in the program's history.

Tackle John Chan and his teammates toured the USS Missouri while visiting Pearl Harbor.

Guard Erik Sande addresses his teammates during a critical meeting in the team hotel the night before De La Salle's game against St. Louis.

The locker room was eerily quiet before the Spartans took the field against St. Louis.

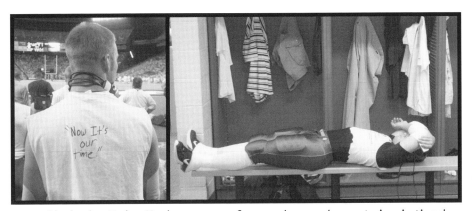

(left) Linebacker Parker Hanks was one of many players who wrote inspirational messages on their T-shirts before the game. (right) Running back Gino Ottoboni listens to music in the locker room at Aloha Stadium to prepare himself for the biggest game of De La Salle's young season.

Cameron Colvin taped a picture of he and his late mother to his locker at Aloha Stadium.

(left) Maurice Drew and Britt Cecil lead the Spartans onto the field before a crowd of 30,000 at Aloha Stadium. (right) Assistant coaches (left to right) Terry Eidson, Joe Aliotti, and Justin Alumbaugh celebrate a De La Salle touchdown.

Drew gives the "Hang Loose" gesture after scoring a second-quarter touchdown against St. Louis.

Britt Cecil hugs his mother Paige after playing a crucial role in a game many wondered if De La Salle would win.

Tackle John Chan holds up his helmet in triumph after a 31–21 victory over St. Louis.

Team meetings are held in garages and are integral to creating a bond between players that makes them greater than the sum of their parts.

Players relax after dinner during a Thursday night meeting in 1999.

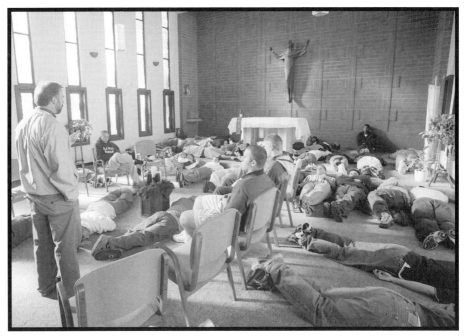

Defensive coordinator Terry Eidson is as loud and demonstrative on the practice field as he is calm and reassuring during chapel services.

De La Salle players embrace after every chapel service. Former players agree that the key to the program's success is love.

Players gather in either the training room or the weight room to watch films during their lunch hour during the season.

A feeling of brotherhood permeates the program, as displayed by (left to right) Mike Pittore, Terrance Kelly, and Erik Sandie in a game against Clayton Valley during the 2002 season.

(left) Erik Sandie loses his helmet but sacks the Clayton Valley quarterback. (right) A muddy field couldn't slow down Maurice Drew.

Nate and Jason Geldermann were two of the fiercest defenders to ever play for Ladouceur at De La Salle.

(left) Mike Bastianelli was the best veer quarterback in school history. (below) Patrick Walsh celebrates a touchdown in the 1991 North Coast Section Championship game. It was the Spartans last loss.

Players recite the Lord's Prayer before kickoff against Long Beach Poly.

(above) Players return to the locker room after pregame warm-ups at the University of California's Memorial Stadium before the 2002 rematch against Long Beach Poly.
(right) Bob Ladouceur and Terry Eidson devised the game plan that defeated a much larger Long Beach Poly team.

2002 captains De'Montae Fitzgerald, John Chan, and Cole Smith join hands and stride to the middle of the field for the coin toss before the game against Long Beach Poly.

(left) Cameron Colvin's touchdown catch gave De La Salle a 14–0 lead in a game that many predicted they would lose. (below) Maurice Drew picks up tough yards against the Jackrabbits.

Britt Cecil, Chris Biller, and Terrance Kelley (front row: left to right) relax during halftime of the Long Beach Poly game.

(above) Quarterback Britt Cecil played the best game of his career in the biggest game of De La Salle's 2002 season. (right) Erik Sandie and John Chan celebrate a 28–7 wind over Long Beach Poly in 2002.

The student burst into tears as soon as they were left alone in a room. He'd never been recruited, he told Gaddini. He just thought it made him look better to his friends.

"I think that happens more than we would like to know," Gaddini comments.

Justin Alumbaugh was a senior at De La Salle when he was approached by a middle school student who puffed out his chest and told him that Bob Ladouceur offered him a football scholarship. He wanted to know what kind of financial enticements Alumbaugh received.

The senior captain knew he should've set the kid straight, but he couldn't resist a tease.

"I got a Lexus," said Alumbaugh, then the proud owner of a 1988 Chevy Celebrity with 131,000 miles that he'd nicknamed "The Beast."

"They'll say, 'De La Salle offered me a full ride,'" said Pittsburg High coach Vic Galli, a former De La Salle player and coach. "I hear it all the time. They swear they got a letter, but there is no letter. Kids like to talk."

Few blame Ladouceur and Eidson directly. They believe that a network of former players, alumni, parents, and sometimes even assistant coaches scour the region for the top football players and funnel them to De La Salle, even offering financial assistance.

De La Salle has no more formal control over its alumni than any other private school. Former players who cherish their football experience at the school may see nothing wrong with encouraging others to do the same. Such testimonials can be interpreted as recruiting and in extreme cases may even fall under the North Coast Section definition of recruiting.

The section defines recruiting and undue influence as "any act, gesture or communication performed personally or through another, which may be objectively seen as inducement, or part of the process of inducing a student, or his parent or guardian, by or on behalf of a member school, to enroll in, transfer to, or remain in a particular school for athletic purposes."

"I don't think Bob recruits," said former Pittsburg coach Bill Cockerham. "He's above that. But there are no alumni rules in high school like there are in college. I think from time to time his assistants recruit, and there's no question that alumni do."

The school's teachers and coaches have become hyper-sensitive to the accusations. For years it was taboo for faculty members to even mention the word "recruit" on campus. Eidson forwards all inquiries to the athletic office directly to admissions.

Ladouceur believes that if the school is guilty of anything, it is over-vigilance. He doesn't believe that teachers and coaches should recruit kids, but he thinks they should be able to talk about the school to prospective students who express an interest in attending.

Even that has been discouraged in recent years.

"I found very little recruiting by public and private schools in the section when I was there," Gaddini said. "What I saw a lot of was school shopping, where parents wanted to showcase their kids who had talent in a given area. That's not recruiting. That's human nature."

Ladouceur and Eidson maintain that their program creates athletes. They describe Derek Landri as a chubby kid with little athletic potential when he first arrived on campus. Ygnacio Valley coach Mike Ivankovich admits that Maurice Drew probably would not have been a Division I-caliber athlete if not for four years of Blasquez's ultra-demanding strength and speed program.

"They've been harangued," said De La Salle's first football coach, Ed Hall, who went on to a successful junior college and college coaching career. "Ground zero for their success is Bob and his philosophy and vision and the standard he sets. People are jealous of others who have success. They don't recruit. They are the hardest-working football program in America. People don't want to admit that."

No one denies that The Streak sells itself. No other team has its games televised regionally on a regular basis. Bay Area newspapers and television stations cover the Spartans extensively. The local paper, the *Contra Costa Times*, assigns a reporter to cover the De La Salle beat.

"They don't have to recruit anybody," said former Antioch and Deer Valley coach Mike Paul. "If you are a great high school football player, why wouldn't you want to play there?"

Both sides offer compelling, albeit circumstantial evidence.

For example, former Pittsburg High running back Percy McGee was the player perhaps most responsible for De La Salle's last loss. McGee returned an interception 79 yards for a touchdown to provide the winning score in Pittsburg's 35–27 victory over De La Salle in the 1991 North Coast Section championship game. He claims he was recruited. A De La Salle assistant coach allegedly approached McGee in the stands while he was watching a junior varsity game between the Spartans and Pittsburg High during his freshman year in 1988.

McGee's mother confirms the story, saying she received a phone call from a man who tried to persuade her to enroll her son at De La Salle.

She told him no, her son would attend Pittsburg High, just as his uncle had. She said she hung up the phone before asking the name of the caller or inquiring about his position at the school. Percy refuses to name names, saying only that it was a well-known assistant coach.

Like most people, Tyler Scott assumed that De La Salle recruited. His father urged him to attend the school, but Tyler resisted. He planned to attend College Park High School with his friends—until he participated in Ladouceur's Championship Football Camp during the summer of 1988.

Some consider the camp a recruiting tool, which Ladouceur calls absurd. Twenty-nine of his varsity players did attend the camp, and some parents like the Cecils use the camp to see how their son stacks up against other future De La Salle players.

Almost every successful high school football program has a summer camp of some sort. Ladouceur has always invited numerous public school coaches to work his camps, which fill up in a matter of hours. Parents somehow get Ladouceur's unlisted home phone number and beg him to let their sons attend.

"They get kids from all over the county that go to that camp," said former Pittsburg coach Larry Rodriguez. "It's a good way to get kids on their campus. Is it unethical? No. I don't believe it is. They are there to teach kids to play football. If they are there to get kids to come play football it would be unethical, but I don't believe Bob does that."

Tyler Scott got a taste of what he describes as "the De La Salle way" at the camp. He was only five feet tall and weighed 96 pounds, but he decided during the camp that he wanted to play football for the Spartans.

His father scheduled a meeting with Brother Jerome Gallegos. Tyler was an outstanding student. Although it was late in the admittance process, space was available in the freshman class. After a long discussion Gallegos welcomed Tyler into the De La Salle community.

"I just have to ask you, Tyler," Brother Jerome said at the discussion's end, "I find it coincidental that you made the decision to come to De La Salle right after attending the camp."

Gallegos' demeanor changed from accommodating to deadly serious.

"I'm curious if any coach led you or guided you or pressured you in any way into coming to De La Salle."

Tyler told the truth. He was impressed by the quality of coaching, how everything they were asked to do had a purpose. He liked the way the coaches talked about being a champion not only in football, but in life. He wanted to be a part of it.

"I'm relieved," said Brother Jerome, turning affable once again. "If you had said yes and explained what happened, I would've had to fire one of my coaches, even if that coach was Bob Ladouceur."

"After we left the office we were stunned," said Scott. "We looked at each other said, 'Geez, I guess they don't recruit.'"

Many of the public school coaches who believe that De La Salle recruits admit that they themselves recruit, especially if a quality player in their district is considering attending De La Salle. It's not uncommon for parents to seek out a school based on its athletic department, even moving to another town or another region when it suits their needs.

It's also not uncommon for public school coaches to attempt to convince talented eighth-graders to transfer to their high school.

"There's recruiting at public schools too," said former Pittsburg and current Clayton Valley coach Herc Pardi. "I'd be a hypocrite if I said there wasn't."

Patti Rains has taught at Glenbrook Middle School in Concord for fourteen years and makes no apologies for steering students such as De'Montae Fitzgerald and Damon Jenkins away from local public schools and to De La Salle, even helping them with the application process.

She's convinced that she's acting in the best interests of her students. She estimates that she has sent twenty students to De La Salle in those fourteen years. Seven played football with varying degrees of success.

"There's not a high school in the Mt. Diablo School District that compares to De La Salle," she says. "There's not the same support system. I don't want my kids to go down the tubes."

Students in the Mt. Diablo School District are free to apply to any high school within that district. Rains says that she has seen numerous public school coaches attempt to recruit athletes from Glenbrook but never a De La Salle coach.

Many of those who level the accusations know little about the private school's policies on admittance. Sixteen primary Catholic feeder schools put intense pressure on De La Salle to enroll their students.

Prospective students must take a test. They must go through an interview process with the admittance committee; athletic department employees are prohibited from sitting on that committee.

Of the 443 prospective students who applied for admission into the freshman class for the 2002–03 school year, only 270 were accepted.

"Admissions is absolutely a loaded hot potato because there are criteria we apply that are not hard and fast but take into account a whole laundry list of issues," said current principal Brother Chris Brady.

Boys from the primary Catholic feeder schools are prioritized. Some applicants, from both public and private schools, have fathers or brothers who attended De La Salle, or sisters or mothers who attended Carondelet. The school also tries to accommodate those families.

Typically 15 to 20 percent of the student population is non-Catholic. This is for the sake of religious diversity. School officials believe that a non-Catholic student population enlivens class discussions and offers students differing points of view.

Ethnic diversity is another consideration. Many within the De La Salle community, including Ladouceur, are disturbed by the lack of minorities accepted to the school in recent years.

"We take a lot of Catholic school kids, and rightfully so, but in the past we reserved slots for public school kids and kids that have economic or academic needs," Ladouceur said. "Now it seems like we take as many Catholic school kids as we can take, which puts us at the whim of our feeder schools' admissions policies, which tend to be, from what I can see, anybody who can afford to go there. So we get a preponderance of white middle- and upper-class kids and we lose diversity. I've always been on the other side of the fence. I don't care if they play sports or not. The more diverse your school is, the greater the educational opportunities on both sides."

St. John the Baptist de La Salle founded schools in France in the seventeenth century for the purpose of educating the underprivileged. That remains a fundamental principle of Christian Brothers schools today, even if it appears that they now primarily educate the privileged.

Financial aid is available to students who qualify and is based on need only. Financial aid applicants send their information directly to a financial aid clearinghouse in the Midwest that the school employs, which determines whether that student qualifies for assistance; if so, it gives qualifying families a corresponding number. When the financial aid form is returned to the school, the family is identified by number, not name. This makes it impossible for the clearinghouse to know what students have been admitted, and for school officials to know which students receive financial aid until after they have been admitted.

"We have an independent firm that validates our financial aid process," Brother Chris said. "We don't do it to prove to others that we're legitimate. We do it because it's the right thing to do."

It was widely believed that D.J. Williams, the most dominant athlete to ever play at De La Salle, was not only recruited to the school but was given a full scholarship. The North Coast Section office was even urged by a public school coach to open an investigation but could not unearth enough evidence to justify such an inquiry.

"People said I was recruited," says Williams, now a preseason All-American linebacker at the University of Miami. "I never took any benefits from the school. Nobody talked to me. I took a test like everybody else. I got financial aid, but it's available to everybody."

Far from being recruited, Williams said he had the opposite experience. He attended a game between De La Salle and Pinole Valley during his eighth-grade year; he later approached a De La Salle coach on the field and told him that he was interested in playing football for the Spartans.

"He shooed me away," Williams said. "He wasn't very welcoming."

Sherri Gonzales, D.J.'s mother, has heard it all before. She wanted her son to attend private school because she didn't like the boys he was hanging out with in their middle-class neighborhood in Hercules. She knew D.J. would be running with the same kids if he attended Pinole Valley High School.

She investigated De La Salle but ruled out the possibility because she didn't know how she would be able to get her son to and from school every day. When she discovered that two boys who lived nearby had enrolled and were willing to car pool, the aspiration became slightly more realistic.

Still, she and her husband couldn't afford it. It was only after they had applied for and received financial aid that sending her son to De La Salle became anything more than a remote possibility.

Williams qualified for a large grant, but his mother still paid as much as $1,930 and no less than $1,430 in annual tuition, according to financial aid records released by the school at her request.

It was difficult for her to make the payments even with the financial aid. At one point she sold baked goods door to door to raise the money she needed to make her son's monthly tuition payment.

"What bothers people is I wasn't making a lot of money," she said. "They wondered how I was doing it. I did what I had to do to get him where he needed to be. I wish they did give out scholarships."

De La Salle awarded $827,130 in financial aid to 174 students during the 2002-03 school year. Ninety-seven of those students, or 56 percent, participated in athletics. According to a 2002-03 Western Association of Schools and Colleges student survey, 63 percent of De La Salle students self-reported that they participated in extracurricular athletics at the school.

The average grant for student athletes was $2,444. Yearly tuition is $8,400.

"The misperception is that kids come here with no strings attached, for free, and grades don't matter," Ladouceur said. "It's not true. Even if you get financial aid you have to pay something. What you did in grammar school matters. If he's not a good student we don't even want him. He's only going to get into trouble here."

Several years ago Ladouceur narrowly avoided a physical confrontation with a fan who accused him of recruiting while he was scouting an upcoming opponent with his assistant coaches.

He jokes about it now. All the De La Salle coaches do.

"And they say I recruit," Ladouceur said on the first day of practice one year while watching his freshmen, who all appeared either fat or skinny. "If I am, I'm sure doing a lousy job."

~

Marlon Blanton remembers standing at the bottom of the stairs, holding his little sister's hand, watching his mother's boyfriend punch her in the face again and again until he thought the angry fist would drive her head through the floor.

He remembers the needle sticking out of his mother's arm when he surprised her in the bathroom. His mother approached him and his friends on the streets, begging money for heroin. He would come home to an empty house, an empty refrigerator, his mother having disappeared again—for days, maybe even weeks.

His grandmother took him and his cousins in, as many as five at a time, doing the best she could. But she struggled with her own demons—alcoholism and mental illness.

Marlon Blanton was recruited. That's what they believe in Pittsburg. Some hold Blanton up as conclusive evidence that De La Salle recruits football players to the school. It's not that simple. Nothing about Marlon Blanton's childhood was simple.

"I'm stuck with two last names," he said. "I joke about it. I don't even know my own real last name."

According to his birth certificate, his surname is Hamilton. When Marlon was in third grade, he learned that his biological father's last name was Blanton. He began writing "Marlon Blanton" on the top right corner of his homework assignments. As soon as he turned eighteen he went to the county courthouse in Martinez and legally changed his name.

He tried to have a relationship with his father. He would stop by his father's house and talk to him when they met on the street. He even tried to find out more about what kind of man his father was after his violent death, but what he learned frightened him.

When his childhood got too crazy, Marlon sought refuge at the home of his buddy Charles Williams. Charles was the kind of friend a guy could count on. They met one day when Marlon was jumped by two older boys in front of school. Someone rushed into the fight to help Marlon, someone he didn't even know. It was Charles. The two became very close, even calling each other brothers.

Marlon sometimes called Charles in the middle of the night, when he couldn't stand it at home anymore. They would meet at a canal halfway between their houses. It wasn't uncommon for Charles' mother Dorothy to wake up and find Marlon sleeping peacefully on the floor of her son's room.

"Thank God for her," Marlon says today. "I would go to her house every weekend. It was a stable home. She didn't drink. She didn't do drugs. She had it together. She welcomed me with open arms."

Marlon played on Pittsburg's freshman team before his mother took him with her to Los Banos midway through his freshman year. They lived there with her boyfriend. Marlon considered himself a Pittsburg boy. He missed his friends. He had nowhere to go, nobody to hang out with, no trouble to get into. The agonizing solitude was good for his grades—his GPA rose from 1.9 to 3.0.

It was hell on his psyche, however. He remembers walking home through the athletic fields behind his school, the empty baseball diamond to his left, the endless grass. "I was more outgoing before I went to Los Banos," he said. "I turned inward to survive. I was a complete loner. I remember always being alone in that field, always."

His mother brought him back to Pittsburg before his sophomore year. Then she disappeared again. The bank was foreclosing on his grandmother's house in town. Marlon moved in with his aunt in Pleasant Hill, just a few miles from De La Salle's campus. This was when Vic Galli informed him that he would attend the private school.

Galli was Marlon's coach in Pittsburg's Junior Football League. Their relationship developed into something deeper. Galli looked out for the kid, picking him up for practice and driving him home. He often took Marlon home with him and made sure he got fed.

"I always looked old for my age," Marlon recalls. "I had a beard in the eighth grade. Vic Galli taught me how to shave."

Galli grew up in Pittsburg but graduated from De La Salle. He was in no way affiliated with the school when he picked up the application, filled out the necessary paperwork, collected Marlon's transcripts, and talked to people he knew at the school on Marlon's behalf.

He didn't want Marlon going back to Pittsburg, where nobody was around to tell him to go to school, to get good grades, to keep out of trouble. He didn't want him hanging out on the streets with his cousins and old friends. He wanted to help give Marlon a chance.

"I introduced Marlon to De La Salle and talked to some people over there," Galli says. "He was a good kid who needed a break. I didn't send him there to make De La Salle a better football team. He needed to be in a different environment. I don't care if people say I recruited him. I know I did the right thing."

Marlon trusted Galli. Whatever Galli thought was best, he would do. If Galli wanted him to go to De La Salle, he would go to De La Salle, even if he had never considered it an option before.

He wrote a paper explaining why he wanted to attend private school, took the necessary entrance exams, and enrolled in a summer-school program before he was admitted as a sophomore.

Marlon applied for and received financial aid as an independent. Since he had no official income he qualified for a large grant but still had to work in the library and at fundraisers. Unbeknownst to Marlon, several teachers, after getting to know him and learning his story, wrote checks to help cover his remaining tuition. None of those teachers were athletic department personnel.

"What kind of world are we in if we can't help kids?" said one of Marlon's secret benefactors unapologetically.

Galli did what he believed was in the best interests of the boy but it didn't play well in Pittsburg. Marlon Blanton was one of the two best players in the Junior Football League during his eighth-grade year. The Pittsburg High coaches knew he had a chance to be a special player, even if he was only 5'7", 160 pounds. They had lost players to De La Salle before, but this was different. The Spartans were placed in the Bay Valley Athletic League—which was being called the "Super Conference"—before the 1988 season. Pittsburg also was a member.

The Pirates didn't mind playing De La Salle every year. They looked forward to it, actually. The mentality at Pittsburg was always to take on all comers. But Blanton was one of the Spartans' starting running backs during the first-ever meeting between the two schools. Not only was he not playing for the Pirates, he was playing against them.

"That's what people didn't understand," Charles Williams says. "They thought Marlon was over there trying to shove it in their face or something. I kept trying to tell them he had the option. It's a private school. Anybody could go there and better themselves if they wanted."

The De La Salle experience wasn't without its challenges. Marlon never felt like he fit in among all the white faces from upper-middle-class families at the school. He kept his family history to himself.

De La Salle students often take classes at neighboring all-girls Carondelet, and Carondelet students take classes at all-boys De La Salle. A Carondelet teacher stopped Marlon as he walked across campus on his first day at school. She wanted to know what he was doing there. He tried to explain that he was a student, but she didn't believe him. Finally, the dean of students from De La Salle had to come over and straighten things out.

"I did everything I had to do at De La Salle," Marlon said. "I followed all the rules, but I really felt all alone."

De La Salle beat Pittsburg in that first-ever meeting, rallying from a 21–7 deficit to win 28–21 at Owen Owens Field in 1988. Marlon wasn't the featured back on offense that year and wasn't much of a factor.

The 1989 game was at Pittsburg. It was a homecoming for Marlon, and it nearly pitted him against his best friend. Charles was a football player, too, but he had injured his ankle as a sophomore. His mother Dorothy wouldn't let him play football as a junior. Instead of competing against Marlon, Charles sat in the stands and cheered him on.

Marlon can still hear the sing-song taunts of the crowd before he took the field—"Mar-lon, Mar-lon." He can still remember the silence after his 95-yard run in the second quarter of what would be a 43–18 rout. Marlon rushed for 148 yards on 14 carries in the game.

"I remember reading an article that said Blanton was recruited," Marlon said. "I began to understand there was serious resentment, and it was because we were successful. It wasn't until we started beating them that I started to get in fistfights about it."

If he was ever going to go to college it would be on a football scholarship. At least that's what Marlon thought. He was small, but a quick, hard runner who was being recruited by several small colleges. Then he tore the medial collateral and anterior cruciate ligaments in his knee midway through his senior season.

Football was the only thing he ever had. The game was the only thing he ever felt he had any control over. Now it was gone. He was extremely bitter and increasingly distant. He wanted to quit school. He wanted to hang out with his friends in Pittsburg.

"If you want to be a nobody, go ahead," Eidson told him.

"He was despondent," said longtime De La Salle college career counselor Nancy Jokerst, who shepherded Marlon through that tough time. "But deep down he knew what he needed in life. He knew he needed an education and he wanted to help kids."

It took a near-death experience for Marlon to regain his resolve. He got a phone call from some friends. Some kids from Antioch had been talking trash, calling his friends "niggers." Marlon drove his pickup truck to where the fight would take place. He and his friends were waiting there when the first shots were fired.

They hadn't anticipated guns. They thought it would be a fistfight. Instead, muzzle blasts and gunshots filled the night. His friends took off. Marlon jumped into his truck, but in his haste his foot slipped off the clutch and the engine stalled.

Charles was across the street, running as fast as he had ever run, hearing the bullets whistling past his head, when he turned and saw the man approaching Marlon's truck with a pistol in his hand.

Marlon hid under the dashboard. He saw the man looking in the window, heard the shots fired from point-blank range breaking the windows and ripping holes in the upholstery. He heard the retreating footsteps and the excited words: "I got him! I got him!"

"At that moment I knew that wasn't what I wanted," he said. "I had great people at De La Salle telling me to go to college. They didn't care if I got a scholarship. They just kept telling me that I was going to college."

The small-school college recruiters that were courting Marlon disappeared after the knee injury. Jokerst enrolled Marlon in classes to prepare him for the SAT. He would join her family for dinner and she would personally drop him off and pick him up after the class.

She knew of a new tutoring program at St. Mary's College that was geared toward helping incoming minority freshmen bridge the gap between high school and college. She wrote and collected letters of reference and got Marlon into the program.

Blanton said he would've never gone to college without her.

"I had a great deal of admiration for Marlon, not because of his childhood but because he was such a good human being," Jokerst says of that time period. "I just liked him. He was so gentle and kind. He really wanted to do something good with his life, and I watched him do that."

He worked at a golf course, in a cafeteria, and took whatever coaching jobs he could find to help put himself through college. He graduated with a degree in health, physical education and recreation.

He started subbing at De La Salle and coaching the freshman "B" basketball team after college. He worked his way through De La Salle's football program, starting as a freshman assistant and eventually becoming the head junior varsity coach in 1997. He was hired as the head coach at St. Patrick's in Vallejo the following year.

"I was very angry about losing Blanton to De La Salle," said former Pittsburg coach Larry Rodriguez. "Later on someone explained to me he wasn't getting the education he wanted at Pitt, and that was a better place for him to evolve. As a person who cares about kids, I thought about that. And I thought, well, maybe that's what's most important."

Blanton doesn't know where he would be today or even if he would still be alive if Galli hadn't made the decision to go to De La Salle for him.

"Knowing who I am, knowing where I came from and what I saw," Blanton asks now, "how could anyone say what Vic Galli did was wrong?"

22 ▸

CLAYTON VALLEY AND YGNACIO VALLEY
Foes and Neighbors

| | | | |⊥| | | | |

t he bus carrying the No. 1-ranked high school football team in America pulls into the parking lot at Concord's Clayton Valley High School at 1:30 on a Friday afternoon after the five-mile drive from De La Salle. Students hanging outside a classroom behind the school barely notice.

Dark, fast-moving clouds reach down and almost touch the tops of the goal posts. De La Salle players, wearing green game pants and carrying shoulder pads and helmets, walk from the bus to the field, skirting standing water on the cinder track and admiring the geese and gulls feeding in the puddles behind the visitors' bleachers.

Bob Ladouceur walks straight onto the field, the saturated ground squishing under his black sneakers, mud soiling the cuffs of his khaki slacks. "It's sloppy, but not real muddy," he tells Mike Blasquez after he has walked over the field and examined the playing surface.

Erik Sandie stands on the sideline looking longingly out onto the field where the grass gives way to black ooze between the hash marks. The smell of earth and mud and impending rain fills his nostrils.

"This is a childhood wet dream," he says, grinning.

The players stretch on a cement pad beneath an aluminum roof which, when finished, will become the Clayton Valley High baseball team's new batting cages.

"Let's go! Thirty-five minutes until kickoff," Blasquez shouts.

Teams often struggle when playing in the unusual afternoon games at Clayton Valley. Freedom coach Kevin Hartwig maintained that the early

290

kickoff played a key role in his team's loss to Clayton Valley the week before. Ladouceur told his players cautionary tales about teams that weren't prepared to play their best so early in the day.

It's obvious why players could fall victim to uninspired play. There's no pageantry to be found. Clayton Valley students have yet to be released from classes. There's no sign of the red and blue-clad Clayton Valley Eagles. Five fans dressed in rain gear huddle under the press box on the home side of the field.

It starts raining, and the way it comes down—incessantly and in big, cold drops—makes it seem as if it might never end. De La Salle fans, who outnumber their Clayton Valley counterparts two to one, open umbrellas and hold garbage bags over their heads as Fred Astaire's "Singing in the Rain" crackles over the public address system.

A dozen De La Salle players relieve themselves on a vine-covered fence that separates a gravel lot on school property from the backyards of residential homes. The place they choose is down a slight incline from the field, providing good cover.

An irate homeowner is immediately on the scene, walking hurriedly, windbreaker flapping in the breeze. Blasquez and Mark Panella try to placate him, but he ignores them and demands to speak directly to the head coach. Joe Aliotti intercepts him, apologizes, and tries to act as an intermediary. The man blows past him with a determined stride.

He finally locates Ladouceur walking down the sideline to where he will address the team. The man obviously is upset, his large meaty hands gesticulating purposefully, his white hair dancing in the wind.

Ladouceur is diplomatic but he keeps walking, forcing the man to hustle to keep up. The words "Those kids should know better" are picked up and carried by the wind. Ladouceur apologizes again.

"But suppose I hit you in the mouth and said I was sorry," the man says in a thick European accent. "What good would that do?"

"What?" Ladouceur asks, baffled.

"It was like something out of a Fellini movie," he would later say. "We were wrong. There were outhouses on the opposite end of the field and we could've used them, but that's one of the things that bothers me about Clayton. They don't provide a locker room or a place to go to the bathroom. When I played, I had to go every five minutes."

Terry Eidson was delayed by a meeting at school and shows up just in time to don rain gear and hustle to the sideline before kickoff.

"What do you want to open up with?" Ladouceur asks Panella as Eidson gives last-minute instructions to his kickoff team.

"How about a stretch?" Panella answers, referring to a running play out of a single-back formation that requires the quarterback to get the ball to the running back as quickly and as deep in the backfield as possible so the runner can pick his own hole.

Ladouceur scowls. "I opened with a stretch against them four years ago and got nothing," he says.

"He's unbelievable," Panella comments when Ladouceur is gone. "He'll remember a play we scored on in 1994. He's got a great memory, but then he's also always watching film, so he's constantly reminding himself."

De La Salle wins the toss but defers, content to let the Eagles try to move the ball on the soggy turf first. The rain stops as abruptly as it began, but threatens to start again at any moment.

Clayton Valley gains two yards on its first two running plays and then completes a six-yard pass. Damon Jenkins muffs the punt, but the Spartans recover and Erik Sandie bounds onto the field with the offense.

Maurice Drew runs off tackle and slips after gaining three yards.

"Maybe we should try running something OUTSIDE where it's not so MUDDY," Eidson says, loud enough for Ladouceur to hear.

Eidson knows that his unsolicited advice annoys Ladouceur and his offensive assistants. Ladouceur doesn't mind getting Eidson's feedback as long as it's done tactfully, not in a way that undermines his authority among the players. Eidson has been better about this in recent years, but when he's sure he's right he can't help himself.

The Eagles recover a De La Salle fumble at midfield on the next play. Linemen are sliding around in the muck. A promising pass play is foiled when an open Eagles receiver slips and falls on his back before the ball reaches him.

"No dancing today. Just get upfield," Eidson tells running backs and receivers on the sideline.

Drew squirts through a hole and rambles 61 yards before being caught from behind late in a scoreless first quarter. Players look at each other with puzzled expressions. Nobody can remember the last time a healthy Drew got caught from behind. He scores three plays later.

The Spartans lead 6–0 when teams switch ends of the field at the conclusion of the first quarter. The song "Splish Splash" plays from speakers mounted on either side of the press box.

Panella approaches Ladouceur on the sideline early in the second quarter. Lad's hat, as always, is pulled low over his eyes.

"Are you going with the sprint draw?" he asks.

"Yeah," Ladouceur says dryly.

Panella nods, spits, and watches as Jackie Bates takes an inside hand-off, cuts to his left, and finds himself running down touchdown alley. A 50-yard run and the ensuing 2-point conversion make it 14–0.

Spartan center Cole Smith is running downfield moments later, chasing Drew, who is en route to a 54-yard touchdown, when Smith is nailed in the back by a defender, prompting an unsportsmanlike conduct penalty on the Eagles.

"That's the third time they've done that," a disgusted Panella shouts at the officials. Aliotti pulls John Chan, Sandie, and Smith together on the sideline as the defense takes the field.

"I told you they would do that," he tells them. "It's a cheap shot. Let it go. If you retaliate you're out. Let it go. If they spit in your face or call you names just tell the referee."

"I told the ref and he told me to shut up," says Sandie, who is covered in mud and has blood streaming down his right calf.

"Then I'll tell him," Aliotti says before turning to confront the official.

A shanked punt nets minus-5 yards for Clayton Valley. Britt Cecil connects with a wide-open Terrance Kelly on a 25-yard touchdown on the next play to make it 28–0 late in the first half.

Sandie loses his helmet during a mad-bull rush into the backfield but still grabs the quarterback and throws him down for a sack on the final drive of the first half. He's having the time of his life.

"Putting up 28 points in the goo is good," Ladouceur tells Blasquez as players file into the locker room at halftime.

Players sit atop rows of chest-high lockers. There's not much to discuss. They're dominating the game on both sides of the ball. The score would be even more lopsided on a dry field.

The sound of clacking cleats, voices, and players banging their heels against the metal lockers echoes off the cement walls and makes it impossible to hear Eidson's horse whisper.

"I understand your frustration with cheap shots," he says. "It's the lowest point of humanity. But we've talked to the refs and now they're looking for it, so if you retaliate you'll get tossed and you won't play next week. If you're a senior that means you won't play in your final home game. Turn the other cheek. That's the way it goes."

De La Salle coaches maintain that their players are the target of cheap shots from frustrated and resentful opponents. Some opposing coaches think that the aggression Ladouceur demands results in the Spartans playing overzealously. The issue came up after the first game of the season. Archbishop Mitty coach Dave Brown was surprised and upset by what he considered dirty play by the Spartans and the officials' reluctance to flag them for unnecessary roughness. He even promised to send a tape highlighting the infractions to the officials' organization.

"If that's what it takes to be the No. 1 team in the nation, I don't know if I'd want my kids going there," Brown said a few days later. "I was expecting something different. I was so disappointed."

Ladouceur noticed the plays in question while reviewing film with the team the morning after that game, and he castigated his players for it. The three players guilty of late hits or unnecessary roughness were required to write letters of apology to the player they fouled and to the opposing coach before they could return to practice.

Now Ladouceur holds a marker board in the Clayton Valley locker room, but there are only a few adjustments to make. The line is blocking well, the backs running hard, the defense controlling the game.

Players spend the rest of halftime talking among themselves.

"If you get pushed or shoved and guys are talking to you, it's part of De La Salle tradition not to retaliate," Ladouceur says in the way of last-minute instructions. "You're talking on the field right now with your blocking and tackling and running. That's what this game calls for. If it continues like this, they will get more frustrated, and that's the only way they know how to retaliate because they can't do it on the scoreboard. Keep playing De La Salle football. Let's go."

You can't see the scoreboard from the parking lot at Clayton Valley.

More fans are showing up now, and those in blue-and-red jackets carrying seat cushions under their arms walk briskly, hopefully, until they can peek at the scoreboard. Then they sigh and slowly make their way up the bank of metal bleachers. Some stand on either side of the end zone to watch the game and visit with each other.

"HAS CLAYTON VALLEY BEEN CALLED FOR ANY PENALTIES TODAY OR HAVE THEY ALL BEEN ON US?" Eidson yells at the officials after the teams have returned to the field.

"Clayton has been called for illegal motion, illegal block in the back, offsides,..." one official recites calmly.

"OK, OK," Eidson concedes.

The wind turns cool and blustery but, amazingly, there is no more rain as the third quarter comes to a close. There is a lot of talking on the field, and De La Salle players constantly complain about Clayton Valley players pushing and shoving after the whistle.

A De La Salle second-string lineman is called for a late hit on the Clayton Valley sideline. There are offsetting unnecessary roughness penalties on another play as the officials attempt to maintain control.

"These refs would get somebody hurt in a real game," cornerback Damon Jenkins says while standing in a puddle of water on the sideline. "We keep telling him they're cheap-shotting us, and he says he's not going to call it unless he sees them get in our face."

The Eagles reserves are driving early in the fourth quarter when Ladouceur walks up the sideline toward the Porta Potties. As soon as he closes the door behind him, the Clayton Valley running back fumbles and Spartan Matt Kavanaugh picks up the loose ball, anticipating a long return.

An opposing player grabs him by the ankles, however, and Kavanaugh goes down still trying to yank his legs free. A moment later a Clayton Valley player punches Kavanaugh in the facemask. The De La Salle sideline erupts in protest and grows even more animated when the official rules the whistle had blown and signals that the Eagles will maintain possession.

"Calm down or I'll throw the flag!" the official tells complaining players and coaches, many of whom have taken several steps onto the field and are continuing to argue the call.

Moments later the flag lands at Eidson's feet. He quickly spins around, banishing every player who isn't in the game—which includes every starter at this point—to the track, far away from the field of play.

"I'm in shock," Kavanaugh says. "The guy takes a swing at me and the ref is right there and we're the ones who end up with the penalty."

The door to the Porta Pottie swings open and out steps Ladouceur. He has missed the entire sequence.

An elderly gentleman in a black leather jacket and powder-blue fishing hat approaches Ladouceur moments after the De La Salle coach has officially recorded his 270th career victory, moving him into the top five all-time in the state's career victory list. Ladouceur won't realize this, however, until he reads it in the paper the next morning.

The man explains that he has driven a thousand miles just to see the Spartans play. There's a private school in the Seattle area that he would like to see on their schedule. "You're a legend in Seattle with all the coaches," he adds. Ladouceur is courteous but unimpressed. The man's loafers have disappeared into the slop.

The teams shake hands at midfield without incident. The person running the scoreboard changes the score to Clayton Valley 99, De La Salle 0. "At least somebody has a sense of humor," one Eagles assistant coach grumbles. Then Clayton Valley Principal John Neary addresses the team, telling players to be proud despite the lopsided 42–0 final score.

"You played hard like I knew you would," defensive coordinator Jerry Coakley tells them. "I'm proud of each and every one of you."

Coakley is a leather-faced former Marine who has spent the past forty years coaching various sports in the area, mainly football. As he turns away from his players he spots a reporter standing on the edge of the crowd.

"Fuck them," he says, motioning to the De La Salle sideline. "Write that."

～

Seniors are preparing for their final game at Owen Owens Field, sorting through feelings of finality.

The sorting begins at the chapel service, held Friday after school. The seniors want to give something back to the program, to pass the torch to the juniors. Reinforcing the theme, senior lineman Garth Gorrall passes out lyrics before playing the Queen song "The Show Must Go On."

Cole Smith reads a column by *Sports Illustrated*'s Rick Reilly about a retarded football player who practiced every day with the Northwest High School team in McDermott, Ohio, but was not allowed to play in a game.

Jake Porter made national headlines when the Northwest coach and the opposing coach agreed to let him run the ball with five seconds left in a 42-0 game. The opposing coach told his players to get out of Porter's way and let him score. A grinning Porter ran the length of the field for a touchdown as players and fans from both teams cheered him on. His coaches and teammates told Porter that he had scored the winning touchdown .

"This football team is about being successful and putting plays together, but it's also about much more than that, things like brotherhood and community," Smith says, explaining why he chose the reading. "Letting Jake score was about more than football. The message of today's Chapel is passing it on to the juniors. That's what you guys have to do. It's not just a game. It's much more than that."

"I liked Cole's reading because it wasn't about football," Matt Drazba says. "It's about being a human being and doing the right thing."

"The game of football alone is so stupid when you think of it," Erik Sandie says, following Drazba. "But there's so much more to it. It's all the things you do to get there that make it so great. There's a lot more to football that people just don't understand."

No one has felt the yoke of responsibility that comes with being a senior at De La Salle more profoundly than John Chan. He has taken his role as captain seriously—too seriously, some of his teammates believe. They often try to get him to loosen up, to have some fun. But Chan has put so much pressure on himself to have an outstanding senior year, to lead this team, that joking and having fun with his teammates has become a foreign concept.

When he and his offensive linemates struggled early in the season, he put even more pressure on himself. Chan hasn't been as dominant as he hoped to be, and it is gnawing at him as he steps carefully over the bodies of his teammates on his way to the lectern, where he clears his throat before reading the poem "Success" by Ralph Waldo Emerson:

> To laugh often and much; to win the respect of intelligent people and the affection of children; to earn the appreciation of honest critics and endure the betrayal of false friends; to appreciate beauty; to find the best in others; to leave the world a bit better, whether by a healthy child, a garden patch or a redeemed social condition; to know even one life has breathed easier because you have lived. This is to have succeeded.

Ladouceur sits on a wooden pew in the back of the chapel and is touched by the words. When players share such sentiments and assign a value to them, he refers to it as a "victory" for De La Salle.

"The readings you guys brought in today were well done," he says. "A lot of times I go out in the community and am asked to talk about the secret of De La Salle football. I have run down many reasons for our success. I say the kids know how to make a commitment. When they say yes to playing football at De La Salle, they say yes to entering into a relationship with the coaches and with each other, and with that comes a lot of responsibility. "I hear it all the time: 'Does so-and-so play for you?' I say, 'Yeah,' and they say, 'He's such a great kid.' The assumption is that you all are. But we don't do things so we look good to other people, but because our mission is to be better people, players and coaches."

The chapel service typically ends with players embracing in the sign of peace. Eidson has a new twist since tomorrow night is seniors night. The seniors will offer each other the sign of peace first. Only then may the juniors approach the seniors for an embrace. The juniors, however, will not embrace each other this week.

"This is symbolic," Eidson explains. "This is a way to thank the seniors for all they've done. We always talk about playing for yourself and for each other, but this is their last home game. You juniors need to think about that, too."

The seniors' embraces are emotional and heartfelt. This team hasn't shown much emotion this season, but it's starting to surface here, which bodes well for tonight's team meeting. The juniors wait quietly for them to finish, then they approach the seniors one by one for another round of embraces and hushed thanks.

Then Eidson and Ladouceur hug each senior as well.

~

A thin layer of fog hangs in the air above the field on an otherwise clear night beneath a three-quarter moon. The moisture makes stadium lights at Owen Owens Field glow and soaks up the sound. It's the last home game of the year, but it's strangely quiet.

Seniors and their parents are introduced over the public address system. A cheerleader gives each player a rose. Players carry the rose with them as they jog to midfield, where their proud mothers and fathers are waiting.

Mothers wear their sons' jerseys and tears puddle in their eyes as they give their sons loving hugs. Fathers offer a quick handshake or an awkward embrace in a uniquely American scene that is played out every season on high school football fields throughout the land.

Andrea Drew includes her parents Maurice and Christina Jones in the ceremony as an expression of her gratitude for their willingness to shuttle Maurice to school before he had his driver's license.

Ygnacio Valley players wait patiently on the visitors' sideline. The Warriors have won four straight BVAL championships but enter this game with a 4–5 record. They are out of contention for a fifth crown.

They wear white jerseys and yellow pants, and their helmets are almost identical to those worn by the University of Michigan. They are always a tough, physical team. No school wants to beat De La Salle more than Ygnacio Valley. The two schools share a common boundary, their campuses divided only by a weed-infested canal and a cyclone fence.

For De La Salle seniors, the focus this week has been the beginning of the end of a four-year journey. That's not to say that they don't hold the Warriors in high esteem. No opponent is ever taken lightly. The scouting report for this game is as thick as it was for Long Beach Poly.

That they will win their regular season finale, sweep through the playoffs, and play for a North Coast Section title for the twentieth consecutive season is an unstated yet foregone conclusion. It's not a matter of "if" so much as "how" they will finish their season and how they will be remembered.

That was Ladouceur's theme for the team meeting the night before.

"Do you want to go out in a flurry, or do you want to struggle? If you are what you say you are and what you brought to the prayer service today, it will reflect on the field and on how you end your season because you'll play not just for yourselves but for your school and each other. That's how all the outstanding teams we've had ended their seasons. They went out like bulldozers, mowing people down. And they did it for each other as a group. 'This is who we are.' It was something they could look back on and say, 'What a season, look what we could do.'

"You're down that home stretch, just past the fourth turn. Here we go. It's exciting because you've put yourself in position. We're playing good football right now. You've trained well, you're in great shape, you're practicing well. It's all mental from here on out. How much do you mean to each other? Are you what you claim to be, a team, a real team? It's been a long journey. We've had ups and downs. We started out going, 'What's going to happen with this group?' We all thought that. We don't think that anymore. We're headed in the right direction, no doubt.

"This is it for you seniors. Done. Three weeks. Over. Some of you won't play anymore. Some of you will, but you may not finish your college careers. It won't be any fun. You won't want to play anymore. Some of you will have four-year college careers, or five. Not many. If you talk to any one of our guys who have gone on to play college football or pro football, they'll say their most memorable football experience was at De La Salle High School, without a doubt. I'm giving you a heads up on that. You're going to get involved with so many more important things than what you're doing right now—I hope. You better be. But you'll want to look back someday and say, 'Those were the days.' It's fun when you've got all forty-eight guys doing it together. No one is going to touch you. No way. But you have to be thinking and feeling the same way. You have to be thinking and feeling as one to do it."

Ygnacio Valley runs a variation of the antiquated double-wing offense. The double-wing incorporates a deceptive combination of fakes, laterals, and pitches and creates a mass of humanity along the line of scrimmage. This is football in its most basic form, linemen fighting over a few inches of sod. This is rugby with helmets and shoulder pads.

Maurice Drew takes a handoff deep in the backfield on the third play of De La Salle's first possession and races 51 yards for a touchdown. When senior Matt Kavanaugh, the holder on field goals and extra points, can't field a low snap, he runs around right end for two more points to make it 8–0 with 9:04 left in the first quarter.

Senior Tony Binswanger's kickoff hits the crossbar.

"Hey, get it over," Aliotti teases.

The double-wing incorporates simple blocking rules and unbalanced formations that force the defense to constantly adjust. When executed properly it produces the type of long, time-consuming drives that Ygnacio Valley coach Mike Ivankovich believes is essential if a team is to have any hope of slowing down a juggernaut such as De La Salle.

"The only way you can stop them from scoring is if they don't have the ball and you don't turn it over," he said matter-of-factly.

The Warriors put together a nine-play drive that consumes much of the first quarter but nets only 35 yards before Erik Sandie recovers a fumble. The score remains 8–0 at the end of the first quarter. Britt Cecil makes it 15–0 with a 3-yard run early in the second.

"We all joke about how we're going to have all this free time when football is over, which is something we haven't had for four years, but the reality is we're just going to watch TV," Cecil told his teammates the night before in a rare display of emotion from the senior quarterback. "I know that's going to get old after about a week, and we're going to realize how important this four-year period was. I just want to make the last three weeks a great memory because in three weeks this team will be a memory, and that's the scariest thing for me."

Cecil sat down and leaned forward in his chair, his face in his hands, crying softly. Drew, sitting next to him, rubbed his teammate's trembling shoulders comfortingly.

In the crowd tonight, the parents of seniors are laughing and cheering and holding up letters that spell out the words: Spartans We Love You.

The Warriors manage to put together another time-consuming drive, a few yards at a time. They are moving the ball but are no threat to score. Another nine-play drive ends 25 yards from where it began.

Binswanger misses a 43-yard field goal attempt wide left late in the first half as parents use cardboard letters in a vain attempt to spell out another message to their sons on the field. The words are all jumbled, however, and a few are even upside down. You can hear them laughing and teasing each other all the way down on the sideline.

"THEY'RE RUNNING HARDER THAN WE'RE TACKLING!" Eidson yells at his players at halftime. "THIS OFFENSE GETS YOU COMPLACENT. THEY DO THE SAME THING OVER AND OVER. IF THEY HAVE SUCCESS THEY'LL START BLOCKING HARDER. FOOTBALL IS ABOUT MOMENTUM. WE'VE GOT TO GET IT BACK."

Ladouceur is on the other side of the room, talking to his linemen. "Why aren't the counters working?" he asks, curiously.

"BECAUSE WE'RE NOT GETTING OFF THE BALL AND HITTING ANYBODY!" Eidson shouts from across the room. "IT'S OBVIOUS."

Ladouceur ignores his longtime assistant. He is tinkering with blocking assignments when several players begin noticing that their lockers have been ransacked during the first half.

Aliotti alerts assistant dean of students Bob Guelld, who is in charge of security on game nights. A former De La Salle student who now attends Ygnacio Valley is apprehended before halftime ends.

"WE'VE PLAYED HORRIBLE AND WE'RE STILL SHUTTING THEM OUT," an exasperated Eidson tells his defense at the end of halftime. "COME ON, I KNOW WE DON'T SEE THIS OFFENSE OFTEN, BUT WE'VE SEEN IT FOR AN ENTIRE HALF. I SHOULDN'T BE THE ONLY ONE WHO'S FRUSTRATED HERE."

Eidson's temperament is in stark contrast to the night before, when he stood in front of players in a four-car garage adjoining another two-car garage housing two Plymouth Chargers in various stages of restoration and a cherry 1972 Ferrari. Two-big screen television sets sat on the floor across from a large tool bench. Eidson spoke from the heart:

"The thing I liked about the prayer service today is I think you truly understood what the program is about, especially you seniors. This program is not about what you do on the football field. It's about the journey you take. The game is secondary to what goes on through-out the whole process. That's a very important lesson. I know what that's like. I was a very average athlete in high school. That was OK. For me it was about having an experience with my friends and doing something that I knew brought out the best in me. My self-esteem was never tied up in what kind of player I was. I learned that at a young age. My self-esteem was tied up in what kind of person I was. It was a gift I had when I was younger, and it stuck with me. Hope-fully, it will stick with you, too.

"As you guys talk about tomorrow night's game and what it means to you, don't talk about how you could've done this or that. I per-sonally believe that none of you went downhill at De La Salle. I truly believe you all worked as hard as you could and really maxed out. You had some plays here and there where you could've done better, but you guys came along great. You reached your ability. Maybe you wanted to be better and do this or that, but hopefully that doesn't mean your experience has been negative. You've all done as much as you could do to be the best you could be, and that's what life's about. That's the type of life lesson that you will carry with you. Like Coach said, hopefully, this will not be the highlight of your life. I don't want anyone in this program saying the greatest time of my life was when I was seventeen years old. If that's true, you've missed the point of this program."

De La Salle played a penalty-riddled first half, and the trend contin-ues on the Spartans' first offensive series of the third quarter. A holding penalty negates a 10-yard reverse by Cameron Colvin. Another holding call is declined after Cecil throws incomplete to De'Montae Fitzgerald on the following play. An Ygnacio Valley defensive back gets in Fitzgerald's face after the ball sails over his head.

"Hey, Chan, are you going to get your act together tonight?" Ladouceur shouts at his senior captain in a rare outburst. Then, sar-castically, he adds: "You're having a *hell* of a game."

Chan doesn't need to be told that he's having the worst game of his career in his final home game. He was responsible for the first holding penalty and struggled throughout the first half.

Drew runs off left tackle on the first drive of the next series and is knocked back three yards after a loud collision with an Ygnacio Valley defender. He miraculously manages to keep his feet, spins away, and sprints down the sideline for what would've been a 50-yard touchdown run if it weren't for another holding penalty on Chan.

Cecil drops back to pass on the next play and is hit hard a split-second after throwing an incomplete pass intended for Colvin.

"That's you, Chan!" Aliotti shouts from the sideline, as if Chan isn't aware that it was his man who almost decapitated the quarterback.

"I love watching the JV game before our game in the afternoon, and watching the sun go down and the lights come up," Chan said the night before. "But I could care less where I'm playing as long as I'm playing for my teammates, my friends, for people who work as hard as we have."

Cecil rolls out to the right and hits Fitzgerald, who slips a tackle and gains 28 yards before being driven out of bounds by the same cornerback who was in his face earlier. There has been a lot of talking going on between the receivers and the Ygnacio Valley defensive backs, as is often the case when these two teams meet.

"You can't stop me," Fitzgerald tells him; another flag is tossed onto the field, this one for unsportsmanlike conduct.

De La Salle scores after Cecil throws a 20-yard pass to Drew and walks in from two yards out on the next play.

"Why do they keep throwing that yellow thing, Daddy?" a little girl asks her father on the sideline.

"I'll explain later," he says, his eyes never leaving the field.

Cecil throws a 41-yard touchdown pass to Colvin to make it 28–0 early in the fourth quarter. The Ygnacio Valley offense has picked up only one first down in the second half when Damon Jenkins hammers a receiver to the ground after a short gain.

It's easy to forget how good Jenkins is because opponents rarely throw to his side of the field. They prefer to test junior cornerback Willie Glasper, who has made them pay with four interceptions this season.

Then Jenkins steps up and makes a play, like the 99-yard interception return against Pittsburg, or a big hit, like the stunning fumble-inducing blow he delivered against St. Louis, and you are reminded why Ladouceur calls him the best cornerback in school history.

The last game at Owen Owens Field is meaningful to Jenkins because his eight-year-old half-brother is in attendance. Jenkins puts an immense amount of pressure on himself to perform well when the boy is watching because he knows how much his brother looks up to him.

Jenkins is guarded outside his circle of friends, which made what he said the night before at the team meeting resonate throughout the garage.

"Growing up in Oakland I had my favorite coaches, but this group of coaches is my favorite," he said. "I really don't have a father figure in my life. I look at this coaching staff as father figures because I've learned so much from each one of you guys."

This team meeting is an emotional night for the coaches as well. Nate Geldermann coached this group of seniors as freshmen and has grown especially close to several players. He tells them that his wife recently asked him if he was disappointed because they hadn't had a boy.

He told her no. He already had forty-eight boys at De La Salle.

Mark Panella spoke when Jenkins was through.

"When I graduated and came back and had the opportunity to coach, it wasn't about the money. What Damon had to say, that validates it for me. That's why I make the sacrifice. That's why I coach."

Aliotti runs up and down the sideline early in the fourth quarter, trying to find seniors who haven't played tonight.

Being a backup at De La Salle has its advantages. The reserves take a beating playing against the first-team offense and defense during the week, but they get more playing time than they would at most schools because De La Salle games are often blowouts by halftime.

Some of the more heartfelt sentiments expressed during Thursday night's meeting came from players who rarely take the field until midway through the third quarter, after the game has been decided.

Matteo Richie fractured his skull when the fork fell out of the frame of his bike while he was riding to school in the seventh grade. He received an uncontested settlement from the manufacturer and told his parents that he would pay his own tuition during his senior year.

An undersized offensive and defensive lineman, Richie got beat up daily in practice during his junior year and seriously considered dropping out of the football program rather than endure another season.

"Then I thought about who I was becoming because of it," he said. "I was a jerk when I was a freshman. I wasn't a good person at all. My character has changed, and I realized it was a direct result of the football program. I saw the benefits and the good that has come out of it and decided to stick it out, and I'm so glad I did...."

Chris Bizot didn't have grand illusions about becoming a star during his senior season. The 6', 180-pound defensive back had one goal: to earn a Cobra Corps T-shirt for special teams play. He was awarded the prize for his all-around special teams play before the game against Freedom.

"Last year at this time I was real happy because the only thing that was driving me was that the season was almost over," he said. "I felt like an outsider. I didn't have any friends on the team. I feel totally different this year. I just want you guys to know that even though I don't play a lot, I couldn't be happier about my role on this team, and there's no one in this room I don't consider a friend."

Fittingly, tonight's game ends with two more big plays from seniors. Aharon Bradley, whose downfield blocks contributed to two long touchdowns in the Long Beach Poly game, scoops up a fumble and returns it 30 yards for a touchdown. Then cornerback Dan Fujimoto gets his first career interception with nine seconds left and is mobbed by his teammates on the sideline as parents chant "FU-JI! FU-JI!" from the stands.

De La Salle players pose for pictures with their parents on the field after the 35–0 win. Ygnacio Valley players do the same before trudging away after another loss to their hated rivals.

"I don't like them, but you have to give them respect," one Ygnacio Valley player tells a teammate.

"I hate losing here," his friend replies. "Losing here is the worst, and it happens every goddamn time."

Not every senior has made his final game at Owen Owens Field memorable. Chan is distraught on the sideline in the fourth quarter, his helmet tipped back on his head and his hands on his hips.

"When you're responsible for 35 yards in penalties and you almost get your quarterback killed, it doesn't feel so good," he says.

But as Ladouceur said in his summation the night before, there's something that can be learned from that as well.

"Some of the best lessons we learn in life are through adversity and disappointment. At least that's how it's been in my life. You don't have to be crossing the goal line all the time to learn and feel value, especially to learn about yourself. The most I learned about myself is when things were falling apart. So when you guys talk about your season not working out the way you wanted it to, don't piss and moan about it; look for the lesson in it. How do you grow from that? That's when you become a real man. When you're riding the crest of the wave and you're having a great time, that's fun, that's great. But when shit starts falling apart on you and things don't work out like you want, that's your opportunity to really become a man. You can't be a little boy to do it. I just want to reiterate: Follow through with what you say you are and what I believe you are. What you said tonight was inspiring. The way you've been practicing has been inspiring. The way you're coming together as a team is inspiring. Follow it through. Finish it right."

1992

THE STREAK BEGINS

t he record books will forever indicate that The Streak began with a 34–14 season-opening victory over Merced High School in 1992. The record books weren't in on the true ground floor. The greatest winning streak in football history was born during a confrontation in the weight room on a suffocating summer day several months after the loss to Pittsburg in 1991.

Juniors such as Alli Abrew, who threw the game-clinching interception during Pittsburg's 35–27 upset victory in the 1991 NCS championship game, and running back Patrick Walsh, who took that loss harder than many of the seniors, were determined to learn from mistakes made the year before.

Bob Ladouceur was moved to re-evaluate his program. He realized that he had been too lax, allowing players to come out late and coaches to leave early. That wouldn't happen again. From that point on he demanded total commitment from everyone. They owed each other that.

Offensive line coach Steve Alexakos introduced his own high level of accountability into the program. He was brought up from the JV staff midway through the 1991 season. His first words after the loss to Pittsburg were a rallying cry for the program:

"Monday, we go back to work," he said.

It was the end of a streak and the beginning of "The Streak." It was a painful loss, sure, but it also was an awakening.

"That game was a defining moment in our program's history," Ladouceur says. "The kids showed a tremendous amount of character after that game. It was a turning point for our program."

Players already had made "Leave No Doubt" their rallying cry for the upcoming season. They took it upon themselves to ratchet up the intensity during offseason workouts, pushing each other well beyond previously established limits, calling each other out when someone skipped a repetition in the weight room or coasted during sprints.

Their dedication extended well beyond the field. Team leaders knew that three players violated the no-alcohol policy over the summer. The offending players were cornered in the weight room and told they could either match their teammates' commitment level or leave the team.

When the three players wavered, they were escorted out of the weight room. Ladouceur didn't even know about the forced resignations until much later. When he learned of the confrontation he agreed wholeheartedly.

"That was a huge turning point," Patrick Walsh recalls. "That was when the team finally took itself over. It has been on automatic pilot ever since. Coach Lad is almost like a guidance counselor."

Quarterback Alli Abrew blamed himself for the loss to Pittsburg the previous year. The offseason was the worst time of his life. He vowed to carry that sense of responsibility on his shoulders until he redeemed himself as a senior. Walsh was just as devout. Without a size advantage, he propelled himself over and around would-be tacklers by the sheer force of his indomitable will.

Many believe that Patrick Walsh was the best high school football player—not the best college prospect, but the best high school football player—in De La Salle history. He rushed for 2,032 yards and 38 touchdowns during his senior season and embodied the ascendant spirit of the program.

"Patrick Walsh is the most passionate person I have ever met, and he was able to channel that tremendous passion into high school football like nobody I've ever seen," says Tyler Scott, a senior wide receiver on the 1991 team that lost to Pittsburg.

The 34 points the Spartans put up in their season opener was the fewest they would score in any game all season. They went on a rampage through the regular season, outscoring opponents by an average of 50–8, including a resounding 44–7 victory over the Pittsburg team that ended their 34-game win streak the year before.

In that game Walsh turned in one of the most dominant individual performances in De La Salle history. A standing-room-only crowd filled Owen Owens Field. Fans stood twelve deep in the end zones. They watched Walsh rush for touchdowns of 77, 35, and 20 yards, catch a 51-yard touchdown pass from Abrew, and throw a 62-yard touchdown pass.

He finished with 224 rushing yards on 14 carries, four touchdowns, one touchdown pass, and 360 yards of total offense.

"That was an angry team," Eidson remembers. "Every game was a personal affront to them. We kept waiting for them to settle down and they never did. We've never had a team like that. Every game really mattered."

Walsh taped newspaper articles above his bed trumpeting Pittsburg's upset victory the year before. Every night for a year he heard those articles rustling in the breeze generated by the fan in his room. It was an annoying, grating sound that made it difficult to sleep, but he refused to take them down. He wanted to remind himself of that loss every night when he went to bed.

He told his teammates this story during the meeting the night before the rematch with Pittsburg in the 1992 NCS championship game. He was in tears when he finished. The whole room was in tears.

After the Spartans defeated the Pirates 41–6 the following day, Walsh took the articles down and slept peacefully.

"That team taught me about the program," said Mike Blasquez, who was a first-year trainer in 1992. "It wasn't like they lost a game and had to work harder. It wasn't as simple as that. They examined the relationships and the intangibles that would make them a tighter group. They talked about how the seniors the year before didn't love each other and didn't watch each other's backs and how that was the reason they had lost. They wouldn't let that happen. They were going to do everything right. It goes back to Bob's initial dream: to create a program that teaches life skills at all costs, that teaches players how to do things right at all costs. It had nothing to do with football."

That team set the standard for every De La Salle team since. Juniors on the 1992 team saw the personal accountability that seniors demanded and followed their example. It became less of a coach-driven program and more of player-driven program.

"People always wonder what will happen when De La Salle finally loses," Walsh says. "I know what will happen. It will be a rebirth."

~

In only a handful of games has The Streak been in serious jeopardy. Only once could it be legitimately suggested that fate intervened.

The Streak was still in its infancy when De La Salle traveled to Pittsburg for the sixth game of the 1993 season. The crowd of 6,500 that packed Pirate Stadium was delirious late in the fourth quarter.

Pitt coach Herc Pardi was bent over at the waist, hands on his knees, head down, praying, during the final minute of regulation.

His quarterback, Cy Simonton, had engineered a flawless five-play, 66-yard drive to pull the Pirates to within 20–19 with less than a minute left. The De La Salle defense had numerous breakdowns on the drive, and Eidson was fuming on the visitors' sideline.

He told his players to watch for the reverse. He shouted it again and again as loud as he could before the 2-point conversion. When the reverse came, his defensive players were out of position. Lu Hearns, the Pirates' standout wide receiver and defensive back, crossed the goal line with 45 seconds left to give Pittsburg a 21–20 advantage.

"I remember talking to God after we scored," Pardi recalls. "That's the wrong person to talk to when you're playing a Catholic school."

The crowd began celebrating what would surely be Pittsburg's second win over the Spartans in three years. De La Salle fans, meanwhile, started to file out of the stadium.

"The game was over," remembers Pittsburg quarterback Cy Simonton. "They were a running team. If they put the ball in the air, we had the athletes to knock it down so they couldn't score. There was no way they were going to beat us."

There were 39 seconds left after Mike Gallagher returned the ensuing kickoff 21 yards to the De La Salle 38-yard line. There were 23 ticks left after quarterback Mike Bastianelli connected with Chris Del Santo for a 16-yard gain to the Pittsburg 46.

Bastianelli faked a handoff right and then rolled out to the left on the next play, looking for Robert Portis in the flat.

This wouldn't be the game-winning play, not in Bastianelli's mind. He also was the team's kicker. He was just hoping to throw a safe pass to Portis so the quick-footed running back could slip out of bounds and move the offense that much closer to field goal range.

The Pittsburg defense double-covered Portis in the flat, forcing Bastianelli to search for a secondary receiver. He found tight end Nate Geldermann running a deep drag pattern over the middle and let the ball fly, hoping he hadn't made a game-ending mistake.

Geldermann would later accept a scholarship to Cal, where he excelled as a defensive lineman despite devastating injuries. He was a legitimate Division-I athlete, but not someone who would outrun the Pirates' fleet secondary. Bastianelli knew he would gain positive yards but worried about the clock. Geldermann would catch the ball in the middle of the field. It would be difficult to get out of bounds.

Tony Lupoi was watching from the Spartans' sideline. He was the starting tight end before an emergency appendectomy ended his season.

"I was watching Nate on every single play," Lupoi says. "When he started dragging across the middle I said, 'Holy shit.'"

Geldermann made the catch at the 35 and swerved at the last moment to avoid the head-hunting Lu Hearns. They were screaming at him to get out of bounds on the De La Salle sideline. When he veered toward the left sideline they screamed for him to keep running.

Another defender dived at his feet at the 10 but Geldermann stepped out of the tackle. When he reached the end zone after a 46-yard play, giving De La Salle a 26–21 lead with 11 seconds left, the celebratory atmosphere had been replaced by a stunned silence.

"Everything about De La Salle football is so precise that nothing is left to luck," says Lupoi. "But that play right there, it seems like somebody was guiding us along."

"They practice that play every day," Pardi said of what was by far the most gut-wrenching loss of his career. "That wasn't luck."

The Pittsburg and De La Salle coaching staffs were the only ones who recognized the irony amid all the heartbreak and jubilation.

The winning touchdown had been scored on a power pass, a play so fundamental to the De La Salle offense that it is a staple of the freshman playbook. It was the same play Ladouceur had called in 1991 when Abrew's pass, intended for tight end Andrew Freeman, was intercepted by Percy McGee and returned 79 yards for a touchdown that provided the winning margin in Pittsburg's 35–27 victory.

"It was a very, very quiet bus ride home," Lupoi said of the trip back to Concord after the last-second win in 1993. "Most teams would celebrate a victory like that. We're not most teams. That was a bruise. To put yourself in a situation where you have to win in the last minute meant so much had gone wrong there was nothing to say."

The Streak isn't a string of unparalleled and glorious triumphs, immune to failure or impervious to human tragedy. There have been losses along the way—terrible heart-wrenching losses that took place far from the field.

The story of the Vontoure brothers is the most tragic tale in school history. Chris and Anthony Vontoure were two of the great individual athletes to play for Ladouceur. But the story doesn't begin with Anthony, or even Chris, the older brother he adored. It begins with Mike Jr., the oldest of the three Vontoure boys.

Mike Vontoure was a basketball and track star at De La Salle. Eidson is convinced he could've been an all-state-caliber defensive back if he had chosen to play football. Mike went on to play basketball for St. Mary's College in Moraga.

Chris followed Mike to De La Salle and was a standout in football. As a sophomore on the basketball team, he could execute the type of 360-degree dunks you see in the NBA.

He was a member of De La Salle's undefeated North Coast Section champion football team in 1992 and helped the basketball team win an NCS championship during the 1992-93 season. He was a gifted athlete who struggled in other areas. He was kind-hearted, soft-spoken, and always made his teammates laugh. But Chris Vontoure also could be volatile and temperamental.

He was the first student-athlete that Mike Blasquez took a real interest in. Blasquez had been a trainer at the school for only a year, but he was coming to understand the type of relationships commonly formed between teachers and students at De La Salle.

Chris was a kid who needed constant monitoring. Blasquez thought if he could help Chris rid himself of the drama that always surrounded him and convince him to dedicate himself in the weight room, he could tap his potential as an elite athlete.

They spent a lot of time together. Chris expressed a desire to go camping, to get out in the wilderness, away from it all. Blasquez is an avid hunter and outdoorsman. They struck a deal. If Chris worked hard during the January-through-June phase of the conditioning program, Blasquez would take him camping and rafting at a place his family often visited in the wilderness northeast of Clear Lake.

During their first day at the lake they fished and rode Blasquez's ATV over fire trails. The next day the temperatures reached into the 90s. They decided to take a two-man raft up Cache Creek and have a cool, relaxing float back to camp.

Blasquez had been tubing the river since he was five. The creek was the width of a three-lane highway, gently flowing water gurgling around partially submerged rocks. When the river widened the water became so shallow that it often was necessary to pick up the raft and carry it to deeper water.

They hiked up into the hills above the creek, enjoying the day. They both were strong and in good shape and were pushing each other. They reached a point that was as far upriver as Blasquez had ever been. They decided to push on past one more hill to make the trip back to camp even longer and more relaxing.

They lost sight of the creek behind the hill. When they reached the other side they jumped in the raft and pushed off.

"What we didn't realize was that the area we couldn't see was the only treacherous part of the waterway," Blasquez said.

The creek wound between two steep cliff faces, the river getting narrower, the water rushing faster, until they saw it crashing against a giant boulder completely blocking their path.

Chris was in the front of the raft when it capsized. He grabbed onto an exposed log that was pinned under the rock. "Hold onto that and climb out!" Blasquez shouted before he was sucked feet-first beneath the boulder.

It was like being squirted through a garden hose. It was cold, black, and full of murky bubbles that made Blasquez feel as if he were in a deep underwater cavern. He was about to give up when he saw a glimmer of light and fought hard for the surface.

He was so exhausted he barely made it back to shallow water. Then came the panic, followed by the horror and grief.

"I was spending so much time with him and we were doing so many positive things and then our worlds came crashing down," Blasquez recalls, disbelief still registering in his voice years after the incident.

Chris' body was found five days later in nearby Yolo County, nine miles downriver from where the accident occurred. He was less than a week away from celebrating his seventeenth birthday.

The De La Salle community was grief-stricken, bringing back memories of Brother Laurence's death in a similar incident thirteen years before. Nobody took it harder than Blasquez, who still finds it difficult to summon the words to describe his feelings of responsibility.

"The Vontoures embraced me, supported me, they knew I was doing something good for Chris," he said. "I don't even understand how they could be that way after losing their son, but they found it in their hearts to help me through it."

No one would've blamed Blasquez for quitting. Some even thought it best. It would've been understandable if the school had let him go. It wasn't as if he were a long-time faculty member. He was a twenty-three-year-old first-year athletic trainer at the time.

But the De La Salle community stood behind him. Blasquez dedicated himself to the program, even framing Chris' No. 23 jersey and hanging it in the training room where he was sure to see it every day when he came to work.

"Kids have a tough time and want to blame somebody," he said. "They want to be able to say why something happened. They want an answer. There were some kids who felt he never should have been up there with me and that he never should've been in that water. You never get closure on something like that."

Chris died in June 1993. Anthony Vontoure entered the school as a freshman two months later. Anthony, who was thirteen when Chris drowned, was devastated by his brother's death. In fact, some believe he never completely recovered.

Anthony never blamed Blasquez for the tragedy. In fact, they soon fell into a similar relationship. Like Chris, Anthony was a gifted athlete. Like Chris, he was capable of extraordinary compassion and dark rages. He was a leader, someone whom his teammates respected. Yet he also could be volatile and at times even disrespectful to the coaching staff.

Anthony found comfort in the tight-knit community of the football program and thrived on the field as a senior, racking up 100 tackles and returning four kickoffs for touchdowns.

During the spring of his senior year Anthony was arrested after he was involved in a fight at a party. He spent part of the summer at a boys' camp. He already had accepted a scholarship to the University of Washington, where he later led the Huskies with six interceptions during his sophomore season. He was an All-American candidate the following year when it all began to unravel.

There had been several incidents at Washington, each a little more troubling than the last. He forgot to do his laundry and asked a student trainer for a jock strap. When his request was denied, he smashed a window and was suspended from the team. He rejoined the Huskies in time for the Rose Bowl but missed a practice and played only sparingly in the game.

He later was either dismissed from the team or left on his own accord, depending on which story is to be believed. He planned to continue his career at Portland State.

Then came September 11, 2001, which changed his life forever. Anthony became increasingly disillusioned in the wake of the terrorist attacks on New York City and the Pentagon. He didn't feel that his coaches and teammates were reverential enough and immediately withdrew from his teammates, watching 24-hour news channels rather than attending practice.

Anthony still hoped to play in the NFL someday. He came back to De La Salle often, using the campus and familiar faces as touchstones, not unlike many of the school's graduates. Then in May came the death of a former Huskies teammate and close friend who had been paralyzed in a game against Stanford during the 2000 season.

Anthony was living in an apartment complex in a Sacramento suburb when several of his roommates were awakened in the early morning to strange sounds downstairs. Anthony was babbling incoherently. Little green men in masks were trying to get him, they recalled him saying. When his friends were unable to restrain him they reluctantly called police and described Vontoure as having a violent, bipolar episode.

Sacramento County Sheriff's officers arrived at the scene and used handcuffs to restrain him. They planned to take Anthony to a mental health hospital, according to a Sacramento County Sheriff's spokesperson and an initial police report. The sheriff's office later stated that Anthony kicked officers and tried to break free when they approached the squad car.

Three more officers arrived at the scene. Anthony's breathing became shallow during the ensuing struggle. Officers removed the handcuffs and began performing CPR. By the time paramedics arrived, Anthony Vontoure, six weeks shy of his twenty-third birthday, was dead.

"It brought it all back," Blasquez said of Anthony's death. "It was like both of them died at the same time. It was terrible. I hate to think what Mike and Emma were dealing with."

Mike and Emma Vontoure were divorced when Anthony was three. They both suspected police brutality and hired a prominent civil rights attorney. The preliminary autopsy report found cocaine in Anthony's system. University of Washington officials would later tell the *Seattle Post-Intelligencer* that he had been prescribed medication after being diagnosed as bipolar; this was consistent with the traces of what they believed was a psychiatric drug found in Anthony's body. The diagnosis was news to Mike and Emma Vontoure, whose quest for answers only produced more questions.

"Anthony's life was like a flash of brilliance, a lightning streak across a darkened sky—we all looked up and took notice...," Ladouceur said in his eulogy. "The price for heightened awareness often can be pain and disillusionment. Anthony had this heightened awareness. I knew it. I think we all knew it."

The game itself was not unlike the 72 games that preceded it. There was little doubt which team would prevail. The College Park High Falcons had size up front and speed in the backfield. They were coming off an impressive upset victory over Clayton Valley. They didn't deserve to be cast in the role of sacrificial lamb.

But that's the position in which they found themselves on November 7, 1997. The standing-room-only crowd spilled out of the stands. Fans stood in the end zones and hung over the fences lining the field. The sidelines were crowded with reporters. Photographers peered through telephoto lenses. A TV news helicopter landed on College Park's practice field across the street. TV satellite trucks were illuminated in the background, generators humming.

"I remember standing in the middle of the field before kickoff," said former De La Salle defensive back and running back Nick Walsh. "I remember looking at the faces of the College Park kids, seeing the fans and feeling the electricity. I had never been so excited."

For the most part, The Streak had been incredibly boring, the games laughably predictable. There were rare exceptions: the last-second win over Pittsburg in 1993, for example. More typical was the game between the Spartans and Pirates two years later. The Pirates were ranked 12th in the nation by *USA Today* when the two teams met again in 1995 before the largest crowd in the history of Pirate Stadium. De La Salle won 28–7 for consecutive win No. 44.

After the Spartans conquered Dan Shaughnessy's Salesian Chieftains to achieve dominance in the Catholic Athletic League, they were presented with a series of obstacles, all of which they negotiated with ease. They were realigned into one public school league and then another, each one posing a stiffer challenge than the one before. They won the league championship every year. They were bumped up in classification from 2A to 3A and finally to 4A and responded with undefeated seasons and North Coast Section titles.

The difference between De La Salle teams of the 1990s and their predecessors was speed. Ladouceur's teams always fired off the line and ran the veer to perfection. They always left every ounce of effort on the field. Now the school was attracting elite athletes. This no longer was a grind-it-out offense. Their veer became supercharged.

De La Salle continued to rise when the rest of the Bay Valley Athletic League was beginning a long, slow decline. There were many factors involved, from new schools skimming players from traditional powers to coaching instability. The gap between the Spartans and their opponents grew so wide that blowouts became a foregone conclusion.

Freshmen entered the school, seniors graduated, and The Streak went on, week after dominating week, the undefeated seasons piling up like cordwood. The novelty wore off and people became numb to the Spartans' success. "I'm sick of De La Salle" became a common refrain.

"I lost interest in the program for the past ten years," said De La Salle's former all-state defensive lineman Pat Oswald. "It gets to a point where you pick up the paper not to see if they won or lost, but to find out how wide the margin of victory is."

Cardinal Newman of Santa Rosa held the state record for consecutive wins with 47 from 1972 to 1977. De La Salle won its 48th straight game with a 41–8 victory over a powerful James Logan team in 1995. It wasn't until The Streak reached the mid-60s that Ladouceur became aware of another approaching milestone.

Hudson High School in Hudson, Michigan, won 72 straight games under legendary coach Tom Saylor between 1968 and 1975. As the national record came within reach, the media attention exploded. Ladouceur and Eidson realized that their pursuit of the record would be a national story, but they never imagined that The *New York Times*, *Sports Illustrated*, CNN, ESPN, and countless regional and local media affiliates would descend upon their school in the weeks and days leading up to the potential record-breaking game against College Park.

Ladouceur never underestimates kids. He had seen his players rise up and shock him with their tenacity and level of play. He expects the same from opposing teams, although he's almost always disappointed.

That's why he prepped for College Park as if it were the biggest game of the year. Between his class schedule, coaching demands, and media obligations, he was so exhausted by midweek that he started napping on an old mattress in the coaches' office.

"I just didn't want to do anything to mess it up for those kids," he said. "We were extremely prepared for them. I worked very hard all week to go over every detail and every scenario. If we screwed it up it wasn't going to be because I cut a corner."

No team before or since was more perfectly suited to breaking the national record. Nine players on the roster had older brothers who went through the program. They grew up attending De La Salle games and even serving as water boys. They understood that The Streak was an inheritance, something they prolonged and passed along.

"I was on the field when they lost in 1991," said Nick Walsh, whose older brother Patrick was one of the greatest running backs in school history. "I remember seeing how heart-broken my brother was. I remember the mission he and his teammates went on that summer.

"Those of us who had older brothers who had been part of the streak could feel their presence and a link to something really special even though they weren't on the field."

D.J. Williams was the fastest if not the strongest player on the field even in 1997 as a sophomore. He picked up some blocks, shook some potential tacklers after fielding the opening kickoff, and had crossed midfield before he fumbled after being hit from behind.

The crowd gasped as a College Park player scooped up the ball on the 29 and ran for the end zone—the wrong end zone. Confused Spartans players finally tackled him from behind at the 13, preventing further embarrassment.

From that point, the game unfolded predictably. Williams ran untouched for a 38-yard touchdown on De La Salle's first official play of the game. He scored again on a 54-yard run to make it 14–0 at the end of the first quarter. By halftime the score was 35–0 and the competition had turned into a coronation.

"We could've probably had a lousy week of practice and still beaten College Park," linebacker Matt Costello said. "But Lad made us believe that if we didn't play our best game, we could lose. He convinced us that if we took the wrong first step on 13 veer, we wouldn't break the record and everybody would go home disappointed."

Ladouceur hadn't talked to his team about The Streak until the week leading up to the record-breaking game. He and Eidson had prepared them for the media and let them know what to expect, but they hadn't tried to put the number 73 in perspective.

There was no avoiding the issue as the game approached. Ladouceur told his players they would never have this opportunity again. This was a chance to not only set De La Salle apart but to make national sporting history. How many high school football players get to do that?

"We were talking about something we had been given and carrying it on," Matt Costello recalls. "It wasn't about us. It was about all the people who came before us. We were just a small part of it."

The second half turned into a reunion. Former players and coaches reminisced on the crowded De La Salle sideline. The media turned its collective back on the massacre on the field and took notice of the three men in black jackets and hats standing on the sideline.

Bill Mullaly, Greg Gutierrez, and Chris Monahan hadn't planned on attending the game. When an independent filmmaker shooting a documentary about Hudson High's streak suggested that the former Hudson players make the trip to California, they realized they had no choice.

They remembered what it was like when television sportscaster Brent Musburger came to their tiny farming community when they broke the national record in 1975. Mullaly was the starting free safety on Hudson's 1975 team. His picture appeared on the front page of The *New York Times* the next day.

Now they wanted to share that experience with De La Salle coaches and players and relive it themselves. They left Michigan early Friday morning and were being treated like visiting royalty on the De La Salle campus by Friday afternoon.

"I'll be honest," Mullaly said. "Up until they set the record, we were hoping they would lose. We really were. I guess we can still say we hold the public school record."

Hudson has a population of 2,000 and is located a few miles north of the Ohio border. The town's football team was 1–6–2 in 1965 before hiring the twenty-four-year-old Tom Saylor as head coach. The Tigers were 7–2 and 8–1 during his first two seasons before beginning a streak of six undefeated seasons that spanned the Nixon presidency. The pressure became so intense as the national record approached that Saylor's hands trembled uncontrollably.

"The Hudson teams were just like De La Salle," Mullaly said. "They were well-coached and there was a feeling of family and not letting your uncles and brothers down. We thought we worked harder than any team in the state and were better prepared than anybody."

Ladouceur laughed with former players on the sideline in the final two minutes of the Spartans' 56–0 victory over College Park. He hugged Eidson with a minute left, and his players drenched him with a bucket of ice water as the final seconds ticked down.

His wet hair was slicked flat from the water and he was picking ice cubes out of his collar when he was swarmed by reporters and photographers. After he answered their questions, the Hudson trio presented him with a game ball signed by members of the 1975 team that had held the record for the past twenty-two years.

"I couldn't believe Ladouceur didn't wear a headset," Mullaly said. "I thought all football coaches wore headsets."

Ladouceur had never made The Streak his mission. He understood that it was a big event, a historic milestone. He knew how much it meant to the De La Salle community when he walked out of the locker room before the game and saw a standing-room-only crowd filled with familiar faces.

But it wasn't pride or validation he felt. It wasn't joy in being the coach of a team that held such a distinction. As he tried to make his way to the locker room through the throngs of reporters and well-wishers, Ladouceur was overwhelmed by relief. He was just glad it was over.

THE PLAYOFFS

A Weakness Becomes a Strength

d anny Ladouceur and Zac McNally put on their equipment as quickly and inconspicuously as possible. They have never been this nervous before a football game, and this is only a practice.

They are among the four junior varsity players added to De La Salle's varsity roster for the 2002 playoffs. It's an annual tradition for the best JV players to participate at the varsity level to gain experience at the end of the season. Danny and Zac have been consumed by the thrilling possibilities for weeks, handicapping their chances in hushed whispers.

"You four guys go hard," junior varsity coach Al Bonanno told them in front of their teammates as they huddled in the end zone after the final JV game of the year. "Show those varsity coaches what you can do. Show them what you have in your heart."

Danny knows the responsibility that comes with wearing the De La Salle jersey. More than that, he knows the legacy and power of his uniform number—No. 23.

Danny's physical development hints at what his father once looked like. He is naturally thin but filling out, ropey muscles running down his arms and back. His face is thinner, sharper, his cheeks more hollow than his father's ever were.

He's built more like a track athlete than a gridiron standout, but he's determined to play football, just as his dad was. Like his dad, he is the fastest player on his team.

Bob never pushed his son to play football, even though the boy grew up around the game. Danny took it up in sixth grade at the suggestion of a friend. After that, he began to understand the game and appreciate how good his father's teams were.

One player in particular caught his eye. Anthony Vontoure was the best athlete on the team during the 1996 season and had Division-I recruiters flocking to his games. Anthony played cornerback, just like Danny did for the San Ramon Bears youth team. Not only that, but the Vontoures lived right around the corner from the Ladouceurs' home in San Ramon. Danny would ride his skateboard over to Anthony's house. The all-state football player was always glad to see him, and even let him ride the BMX bike Danny admired.

"He was a real genuine person," Danny says. "He was always nice to me, and not because of my dad. That's the kind of person he was."

Danny got an idea on the way to the cemetery after his father delivered the eulogy at Anthony Vontoure's funeral. He wanted to wear Anthony's No. 23 during his sophomore season. Anthony wore No. 23 because it was his brother's number, even though the school had retired it after Chris' death.

Ladouceur thought Danny's request would be a fitting tribute, but told his son he would have to get Emma Vontoure's blessing first. The woman who buried two of her three sons was touched by the gesture. She thought it was a way to keep her sons' legacies alive.

"Every touchdown was better than touchdowns from previous seasons because it was for Anthony," Danny said about wearing the No. 23 jersey. "I really felt his presence; felt like he was watching me. It's making my season so much more meaningful for me."

Monday's practice is held at Diablo Valley College, where De La Salle will host a first-round playoff game. Players carry their helmets and shoulder pads across the field and sit on the track that frames the electric green synthetic surface of Viking Field.

"I remember getting hit so hard when I was a sophomore playing varsity at Deer Valley that I wanted to cry," Chris Mulvanny says just loud enough for Danny and Zac to hear, a broad smile spreading across the senior's face. "It wasn't fun, but it was."

Cole Smith retells the tale of Andy Briner blocking him onto the track when he was first called up to the varsity as a sophomore. Zac and Danny swallow hard, focusing intently on pulling their jerseys over their shoulder pads and tying their shoelaces, pretending not to hear.

"Little Lad will take some shots just because of his last name," whispers freshman assistant Paul Guaragna, another former player.

Bob Ladouceur already warned his players against abusing the junior varsity call-ups unnecessarily. They are here to learn, he explained, not to be tackling dummies for more physically mature and experienced players. This isn't a father fearing for his son's safety. Ladouceur makes the same speech every year, and every year varsity players listen respectfully and then exchange knowing smiles.

De La Salle's upperclassmen spend a lot of time mentoring underclassmen during the offseason when they train together. Tradition calls for varsity players to make sure their eventual replacements know what is required from a varsity player, and what the coaches will expect from them.

"I think the world of John Chan and Erich Faustman," says Zac's dad, Frank McNally, a junior varsity assistant coach. "During the summer they took my son under their wing. That meant a lot to me as a parent. These guys are seniors and there's an age difference, but they taught him what it's like to be a varsity player here. They do that for a lot of kids. The kids are so mature here."

That doesn't mean they won't try to knock the screws out of the sophomore players' helmets once practice begins, however. That's as much a part of the tradition as the head coach's annual plea for restraint. When the sophomores are seniors, they'll do the same.

High gray clouds cover the sky. Orange and yellow leaves hang loosely from trees on the south end of the field. The Diablo Valley College cross-country team, preparing for the state meet later in the week, stretches in the opposite end zone while De La Salle players get slowly to their feet and make their way onto the field to stretch.

Bob Ladouceur trudges across the field cradling a split cardboard box overflowing with scouting reports.

Ladouceur watched film for eleven hours Sunday to prepare the scouting report, which is even thicker than normal. Antioch is De La Salle's first-round playoff opponent. Film from Saturday's Pittsburg-Antioch game was shot from the third row of the bleachers, making it difficult to watch specific players on the far side of the field. Ladouceur had to watch every play four or five times before he was satisfied.

"This is one of the reasons why we're so good," secondary coach Terrell Ward says, leafing through the thirty-page stapled document. The second page lists Antioch's tendencies. When the Panthers line up in an unbalanced formation, they run a sweep 95 percent of the time. When a receiver goes in deep motion, the defense can expect a misdirection play. When one of four receivers goes in motion, it's always a run with one exception—the halfback pass.

"These guys have so many tendencies, if I was playing against them I'd have twenty-five tackles," Ladouceur tells Eidson.

"You'd pull a hamstring," Eidson says.

"Then I'd just stand where they're going to run and misdirect them," Ladouceur says, sitting down on an aluminum bench.

De La Salle is a top seed in the North Coast Section playoffs for the nineteenth straight year, but Sunday's seeding meeting was like no other.

Usually coaches talk up their teams, hoping to get the highest seed possible. James Logan High School coach Neil Fromson took the opposite tack, purposely pointing out his team's flaws to the seeding committee with hopes of receiving a lower seed and therefore avoiding the possibility of meeting De La Salle in a semifinal game for the third straight year.

Despite having won the Mission Valley Athletic League title and owning an 8–2 record, Fromson was granted his wish. His team could've been seeded as high as fourth, but his reverse lobbying resulted in the sixth seed. The only way the Colts can meet De La Salle is in the finals.

"I guess he got sick of hitting us in the second round," Ladouceur says. "He may have trouble getting through the first round after drawing Foothill. I guess he likes his chances better that way."

The Spartans will open the playoffs against Antioch, whose win-loss record fell to 6–4 after a 31–21 season-ending defeat by archrival Pittsburg in the Big Little Game. First-year Pitt coach Vic Galli led his team to the program's first outright league title since 1980, and the team is rewarded with the seventh seed in the NCS 4A playoff bracket.

Ladouceur says he doesn't care who the Spartans play, even though he and Aliotti have been doping playoff scenarios for the past week.

"What else do we have to do?" he explains innocently. "It's not like we have an outside life this time of year. It's hard to talk about the world's problems when you don't even know what they are."

Eidson is tossing passes to receivers during a pass-catching drill early in practice when a ball bounces off Danny Ladouceur's hands.

"OH NO!" he screams in mock surprise, bending over and slapping his thighs for emphasis. "YOU CAN'T DROP THE BALL IN THIS LINE, DANNY!" Danny is relieved when Cameron Colvin drops a pass moments later.

Low-flying planes constantly buzz overhead, en route to the runways at nearby Buchanan Fields airport.

"Against Pittsburg these guys came upfield hard," Ladouceur tells his linemen. "They're not hitting and reading, they just get off and come upfield. They make a lot of tackles for losses against teams that miss blocks. You should all watch last year's film to see how we blocked them. Watch their film from this year, too."

Zac McNally is a powerfully built linebacker whose frame is only beginning to fill out. The Oakley resident would have started for Freedom High School as a sophomore if he hadn't decided to come to De La Salle.

Zac lines up as the scout team's middle linebacker and hits Cole Smith with such force on the first play of team work that the brawny senior center is knocked to the ground. The collision snaps the laces of Zac's shoulder pads. He hustles off the field to replace them.

Later, Zac drops quarterback Britt Cecil for no gain. Willie Glasper blindsides Zac on the next play, knocking him off his feet.

"HEY, DANNY, GET OVER HERE AND GET BURNED AT CORNER FOR A WHILE!" Eidson shouts later in practice.

Danny hustles over to where the defensive players are standing.

"Why are you playing offense?" Eidson wonders aloud. "It's not like you're going to get any plays over there."

"I told him to go over there, Coach," senior cornerback Damon Jenkins confesses. "I thought he played offense."

"He can play over there so we can drill him for a while, and then he can come over and play defense," Eidson says, enjoying this.

Danny lines up opposite Cameron Colvin, and when Cecil's pass is underthrown he makes the easy interception. He's not sure how to react. He takes a couple half-hearted steps toward the opposite end zone before stopping and tossing the ball back to the offense.

"Hey, JV, we don't walk when we get interceptions up here!" Jenkins scolds before his attention is diverted to the middle of the field, where Zac and Erik Sandie are shoving each other.

∾

The package was on Ladouceur's desk on Thanksgiving morning. Players and coaches regarded the brown shirt box wrapped in brown packaging paper curiously. "To the De La Salle coaches" was written on one side; below it, the words "Happy Thanksgiving."

Inside was a framed letter from former De La Salle player Jonathan Kirkham along with the Navy and Marine Corps Achievement Medal he had recently been awarded.

"OH MY GOD," Eidson says. "He gave us his medal. He didn't tell us he got a medal, the little shit."

"Throughout my playing days in college and most recently my advancement in the Marine Corps, the life lessons you taught me have continued to lead me in doing what is right, just and selfless," Kirkham wrote. "Being placed in a position of leadership, I fall back more and more to the model you presented me as coaches than any military lessons I have been taught. If I maintain half the integrity, discipline and tenacity that you men represent I'll consider myself a success.

"So on this day of giving thanks I thank you with a by-product of your guiding hand in my life and the success it has brought me. I present this to you for your role in my life and the effect of your guidance beyond the field of play."

Eidson, Blasquez, and Ladouceur examine the green and orange ribbon and the shiny gold medal with Navy anchor in stunned silence.

"That makes it all worthwhile," Blasquez finally comments.

"Everybody talks about our victories," Ladouceur says. "Well, we got a victory today."

∾

Parents laugh and talk while they clean up after the team dinner, all the while wondering what goes on behind that closed door.

They know very little about what takes place in the garages after they have organized and prepared the meal. The door that leads from the house to the garage is locked during team meetings.

If a player or coach has to excuse himself to go to the bathroom, the meeting stops until the door is closed and locked once again.

Some parents have peered in windows and tried to listen through the cracks in the door, but even that provides precious few clues.

"We don't understand," says Brian Garrett, a bank president who has had two sons play for Ladouceur. "We don't know what goes on in there. We don't know. We almost don't want to know."

Parents held their own prayer service in the school chapel the week before. They took turns standing and talking about how the program has impacted their sons. Men who haven't cried in years were too emotional to speak. Garrett said it was one of the most moving experiences of his life.

The players bond, and so do their parents.

"I've been though it four times now," says Sue Ottoboni, who also has had two sons play for De La Salle. "Every parent talks and it gets very emotional. By the end of the night it seems like everybody is crying."

Ladouceur is even more of an enigma to them than he is to their sons. He deftly navigates the crowd at these dinners, always polite and friendly but never engaging in anything other than small talk.

There's a trust factor there. There has to be because parents are entrusting their sons to a man they hardly know.

"I don't have any relationship with Lad," says Jess Pittore, whose son Mike has developed into a standout defensive lineman.

"There's not a lot of fluff to him," says Mike Chan, a retired police officer whose son John has played for Ladouceur for three years. "When I talk to him we never talk about John's playing ability."

"Ninety percent of the conversations I've had with him during the past eight years have been non-football-related," says Garrett, whose son Brad is a backup center on the 2002 team.

Ladouceur wants it that way. He tells players that he doesn't want their parents around when he's talking to them. It's not because he might swear or chew them out, but because he's evaluating their performance and he considers that information confidential.

The parents aren't there for all the offseason workouts, the practices, the chapel services, and the team meetings. If they only hear bits and pieces they might misunderstand. As he told players after a summer-league passing tournament: This is your experience, not theirs.

"I'm pretty aloof around the parents," Ladouceur says. "A lot of them want information about their kids, and I don't want to share any of that. I don't want to constantly tell them that his feet are slow, he needs to get stronger in the upper body, he drops his shoulder, his steps are all wrong. They don't understand that. They'll think I'm down on their kids. They don't always understand that it's a process."

Parents often feel like outsiders. Their friends and colleagues ask them how Ladouceur does it, how his teams win season after season. They're often struggling to understand it themselves. They watch their sons compete against larger players from St. Louis and Long Beach and they have no explanation for what they see.

"I'm not a religious person, but maybe this is Bob's destiny," Garrett says. "Maybe he has some sort of spiritual power to enable kids to play beyond themselves, because there's no way our kids should be doing this. There's no way this team should be doing this."

Ladouceur organizes a parent meeting at the beginning of each season. He outlines team rules and how the use of alcohol and drugs is prohibited year-round. He explains how it teaches the kids that they can have fun and do something worthwhile without bowing to peer pressure. He tells them that even if their son never plays a down in a football game that's reason enough for him to participate.

Coaches often complain about meddlesome parents, and Ladouceur has endured a few, but his record eliminates most of the second-guessing that other coaches are often subjected to.

"I'm dealing with your son, not you," Ladouceur tells parents at the meeting. "If your son comes home and complains, don't call me and fight his battles for him. Make him stand up and be heard. That's part of growing up. If he does that and there are still things I need to know, then by all means call me."

It's their sons who ultimately sell them on the program. Mike Chan was boasting to coworkers about De La Salle's success when his son pulled him aside and admonished him for it.

"It sounds like you're bragging and that's not what we're about," John told his dad, who later realized that his son was right.

Jess Pittore asked his son Mike why he was playing defensive tackle instead of his more natural position, defensive end. Mike told him that he played in the middle because he was needed in the middle. It wasn't about playing a position. It was about playing for your friends.

"That blew me away," Jess says. "It sure shut me up."

Parents are grateful. Their kids don't tell them much about the program, but they see the end result. When the boys do have free time, which isn't often considering the time and effort they pour into the program, they choose to spend it together.

They gather at each other's houses before games, after games. They organize camping trips and caravan to Southern California to watch teammates participate in all-star games.

"These kids go on their overnight trips and oftentimes they get in trouble with authorities who can't believe forty unchaperoned high school kids aren't going to get in some sort of trouble," says Jack Weir, whose son Drew is a backup linebacker. "The seniors handle it calmly, confidently, and the juniors see that."

Then the parents see their sons on the football field, doing things they can't believe are possible, and what goes on the behind the closed door on Thursday nights becomes even more mysterious.

"The parents can't explain it and the kids won't tell us," Brian Garrett says. "It's almost like they become supernatural. They get calmer as the game gets closer. We don't understand how it happens."

Ladouceur spends the day of the first playoff game dealing with an incident that occurred in the school parking lot after the team meeting the night before. Players returned to pick up their cars and began wrestling and mock fighting in the glow of the headlights.

De'Montae Fitzgerald grabbed backup offensive lineman Brad Garrett's sweatshirt. "Hey, you're going to stretch it out," Garrett protested, pushing Fitzgerald in the chest. They were both off balance when Fitzgerald's playful roundhouse accidentally caught Garrett above the right eye, opening a gash that would require ten stitches at the emergency room later that night.

Much of the following morning is spent determining just what happened the night before. Players file in and out of Aliotti's office after being questioned by Ladouceur, Eidson, and the dean of students.

"That's one thing Terry is excellent at," Mike Blasquez says. "Kids always get together to get their stories straight, but Terry has an innate way of getting to the bottom of things. He grills them from every angle. Lad and Joey are real good at it, too. There aren't many kids who have pulled the wool over our eyes over the years."

They are comforted to learn it wasn't malicious. Fitzgerald and Garrett weren't fighting. They were merely horsing around.

What bothers Ladouceur is the immaturity of the act. They learn that players have been leaping out of rolling cars to participate in playful rumbles after team meetings all season. But to have such an incident occur the night before the first playoff game is another example of the adolescent behavior that has been typical of this team all season.

Ladouceur feels as if he's talking to his eleven-year-old son Michael when he tells players to keep their hands to themselves from now on.

"These guys disappoint me sometimes," Blasquez says. "They have such a high level of maturity that you're honored to be around them, and then sometimes they revert back to being ten years old."

It's so quiet players can hear the lights buzzing when they take the field at Diablo Valley College for early warm-ups before their first-round playoff game. There are only twenty-five fans in the stands when they begin to stretch.

Paul Guaragna, the assistant freshman coach and former De La Salle player, stands on the sideline talking to a friend about a mutual friend who was supposed to attend the game but may stay home instead.

"I don't know if he's going to come, because there's an Ultimate Fighting Championship on TV," his friend explains.

"De La Salle football or the Ultimate Fighting Championship," Guaragna says, moving his hands up and down like mock scales weighing the entertainment value of the two sporting events. "He's going to see an ass-kicking either way."

Antioch head coach Ferris Anthony is a former professional wrestler who was dubbed "Earthquake Anthony" by promoters. His signature move for the five years he toured the nation and Europe was "The Ferris Wheel," a variation of the airplane spin, where he put an opponent on his shoulders and spun in circles before landing on top of him.

He quit the circuit when he got his first coaching job, which led to the job he currently holds at the school where he once played.

Anthony is a huge, jowly man with small eyes, unruly brown curls, and an avalanche of a stomach that demands an elastic waistband. He wears a black-and-yellow Antioch football jacket and black sweatpants as his offense takes the field for the first possession of the game.

His two star players are running back Brent Casteel, who enters the game with six touchdown runs of 55 yards or more, and quarterback Joey Luoma, who led the area in passer efficiency rating.

Luoma threw only two interceptions during the regular season. Spartan Willie Glasper doubles that total after intercepting Luoma's first two passes of the game. The interceptions are the fifth and sixth of the season for Glasper, who was starting cornerback as a sophomore in 2001.

Glasper was responsible for letting Derrick Jones get deep on the first play of the Long Beach Poly game the year before. He had never played in front of so many people. He didn't expect the opponents to throw deep so soon. Then Jones was sprinting past him, the ball was in the air, and Glasper was trailing hopelessly behind.

A wave of relief washed over him when Jones dropped the pass. Glasper played better after that. Teammate Damon Jenkins was an all-state cornerback, so opposing quarterbacks picked on Glasper all season. He held his own, even being named an all-state underclassman by one magazine.

This year—2002—has been his breakout season. Glasper helped contain the potent offenses run by St. Louis and Long Beach Poly. Now he is leading the team in interceptions. No one else is even close.

Maurice Drew scores on a 9-yard run to put De La Salle up 7–0 after Glasper's first interception. The second touchdown is bizarre.

Britt Cecil rolls to his right and completes a 14-yard pass to De'Montae Fitzgerald at the Antioch 7. Fitzgerald is heading toward the right pylon when he is hit from behind and fumbles. The ball bounces off the turf and into the hands of Cameron Colvin, who tip-toes across the goal line like a ballerina.

Anthony is as demonstrative on the field as he once was in the wrestling ring. After he throws his hat to the ground for the third time while protesting an official's call, it's obvious it is just a prop.

The Antioch punter shanks one off the side of his foot after Antioch fails to pick up a first down on its third possession.

"Are you going to give us anything tonight?" Anthony screams at the officials after a Jackie Bates fumble is negated because the officials ruled he was down. "Do you think it's going to hurt them?"

The De La Salle offensive line is mowing down defenders, opening huge holes on every play. Drew scores on a 2-yard run two plays later to make it 21–0 with 3:43 left in the first quarter.

Anthony is livid. In his six years at Antioch, he thinks that only one of his team's games against De La Salle has been officiated fairly.

"Maybe the officials don't know they're doing it or they're not doing it on purpose, but it's definitely one-sided," he says.

He's not alone. Many area coaches sense that the Spartans get the benefit of the doubt more often than not. Their complaints range from De La Salle's overaggressive play, including late hits, to offensive linemen not being set for the required one second before the snap.

Anthony speculates that officials hear so much about the Spartans' discipline they assume Ladouceur's teams don't make mistakes.

"That's a bunch of B.S.," says Dave Cutaia, who has been assigning officials to games in Contra Costa County since 1978. "They're reacting to what they see. They're not thinking about whether it's De La Salle or the Green Bay Packers. There's no merit to that statement just like there's no merit to those who say the officials watch De La Salle more closely because they've won all those games."

Luoma is being pressured on every pass attempt. Mulvanny sacks him on the first drive of the game. At other times Luoma is forced to scramble or throw an off-balance pass.

"Where's the pressure coming from?" a teammate asks him on the sideline after the Panthers fail to pick up the first down for their fourth straight series. "Everywhere, dude," the quarterback says.

At that moment Cameron Colvin is streaking down the middle of the field, three yards ahead of the nearest defender. Cecil's pass is perfectly thrown but the ball slips right through Colvin's fingers. He can't believe it. He's made that catch a hundred times. He caught more difficult passes in the two biggest games of the year against St. Louis and Long Beach Poly. He stands in the end zone, disgusted.

Antioch's defensive linemen come charging upfield on the next play, just as Ladouceur said they would. Drew collects the ball on a draw play they put in for that very reason and runs 45 yards untouched for his third touchdown of the game.

John Chan, who played one of the worst games of his career the week before, wipes out the safety on the play and is the first player downfield to congratulate Drew when he crosses the goal line.

"We're better than this!" an Antioch player yells to his teammates on the sideline. "What happened to us on the bus ride here?"

Cecil is buried by four Antioch defenders for an 11-yard sack on the first play of the second quarter. An official calls the Panthers for a face-mask penalty on the play. Anthony goes ballistic.

He runs out almost to the middle of the field, throws his hat down once again, and bumps the official while protesting. The back judge standing right on top of the play didn't made the call. Anthony is upset because it was an official 25 yards away who threw the flag.

Antioch is called for defensive holding on the next play.

"I don't know why you're even out here if you're going to call a game like this," Anthony shouts while assistant coaches attempt to restrain him. He still hasn't cooled down when Cecil scores on a 12-yard keeper to make it 35–0 with 10:20 left in the second quarter.

A member of De La Salle's kickoff team nearly gets decapitated on the ensuing kickoff, and although the return nets only a few yards, the Antioch sideline and cheering section roars to life.

The Antioch offense picks up its second first down of the game on the next drive, and a 39-yard run by running back Charles Brown gives the Panthers a first-and-goal from inside the 1-yard line.

Three plays for no gain and two Antioch timeouts later, Casteel takes a pitch on a sweep, slips through the arms of Matt Kavanaugh, who misses a shoestring tackle at the 7, and scores to make it 35–6 with 5:21 left before halftime.

"He played at Deer Valley for two years," an Antioch player tells a teammate on the next drive after Mulvanny makes a tackle.

"They take all our players, man," his teammate says. "I hear they've got a house in Concord where all the Antioch players live during the season. They're beating us with our own players."

"It's bullshit, man," says yet another Antioch Panther.

Drew bolts up the middle and a helmet-to-helmet collision with the Antioch safety creates a sickening thud. Drew spins away, runs five more yards, and there's another sickening helmet-to-helmet thud before he crosses the goal line after scoring a 24-yard touchdown to make it 42–6 with under four minutes left.

This is as well as the offensive line has played all season. Erik Sandie is dominating his man. Chan is following up his worst game with one of his best. The entire line is firing off the ball, moving people back and getting downfield to wipe out linebackers and safeties.

Fitzgerald wrestles the ball away from Luoma on Antioch's next possession. Backup quarterback Kevin Lopina, subbing for a shaken Cecil, throws a 35-yard pass to Colvin, who makes a leaping, twisting catch at the 4-yard line.

Lopina takes a knee on the next play in order to allow the clock to run out. De La Salle goes into the locker room with a 42–6 lead.

Ladouceur tells his team that everyone will play in the second half. That means Danny, Zac, and the two other sophomore call-ups will see their first varsity action.

Drew scores on a 59-yard run on the third play of the second half before Ladouceur empties the bench. Drew finishes with 195 yards on 11 carries and four touchdowns. The starters are huddled around a gas heater on the home sideline during the fourth quarter.

"It ain't over yet," an Antioch player screams emphatically after De La Salle scores to make it 62–6 with 9:23 left in the fourth quarter. "We've still got time. We can still do it!"

The final score is 62–13.

~

A dozen Hayward Farmers fans wait in the parking lot outside Viking Field in the early evening twilight. The ticket booths are boarded up, the gates locked, the stadium empty. The fans hold blankets and thermoses and talk excitedly in the growing darkness.

They're waiting for the gates to open for the NCS semifinal game. Hayward assistant coach Jamond Williams is waiting for the team bus to arrive.

"Good things are going to happen," Williams predicts confidently. "I've got a real good feeling about this."

The Farmers have been working toward this opportunity all season. They made winning the league title and meeting De La Salle in the playoffs their two primary goals.

Their only loss of the season was to league rival San Leandro, a school De La Salle has defeated in the NCS championship game in each of the past three years. That defeat kept the Farmers from winning the league championship, but they did earn the program's first playoff berth since 1992 and the long-awaited showdown with the top-ranked Spartans.

Hayward head coach Casey Moreno has first-hand experience against De La Salle, even if this is the first-ever meeting between the two programs. He was the starting strong safety for Moreau when De La Salle defeated his team 42–16 to win the Catholic Athletic League title in 1984. Moreno got tossed out of that game for spearing a De La Salle player after an onside kick late in the game. That player was Mark Panella.

Moreno steps off the bus looking so young and fresh-faced that it's hard to believe it has been eighteen years since his playing days ended. Several Hayward fans pass through the gate and down the stairs and greet the bus when it screeches to a halt behind the gymnasium.

"It's like these guys are playing a scrimmage or something," Moreno announces proudly. "They're not tripping at all."

NCS event coordinator Bob Johnson watches Hayward players file past on their way to the locker room before he spots Moreno.

"OK, Coach," he says. "The anthem is at 7:25, captains at 7:28, and kickoff at 7:30."

"So, we're really going to do this thing, huh?" Moreno answers, smiling.

This is as big a game as Hayward has been a part of in years. It's easily the biggest game of Moreno's three-year career. He left his old high school coach a message earlier in the week. Tim Walsh, who coached Moreno at Moreau, is now the head coach at Portland State. Moreno's message was a short one: "What do I do?"

Before Moreno could put the receiver to his ear on Walsh's return call he could hear his old coach's advice: "PUNT!"

"It's an absolute honor," Moreno gushes on game day. "We have absolutely nothing to lose and everything to gain. We're not scared at all. We're going to throw caution into the wind."

He notices few differences between Ladouceur's 2002 Spartans and the team he played against in 1984. What impressed him the most then—the offensive line's get-off and special teams—impresses him most now.

He has had his kickoff team practicing high, short, directional kickoffs that he hopes will prevent Drew from breaking long returns. He has even devised a strategy to negate De La Salle's line surge.

"We're going to jump the count," Moreno whispers, as if revealing a military secret. "We'll probably be offsides a few times. If that doesn't work we'll try something else next year because we plan on playing them next year, too."

Hayward fans fill the visitors' bleachers to capacity as the teams go through their pregame routines. It's a loud, boisterous group that blows air horns and begins lustily heckling De La Salle players and coaches as soon as they take the field for warm-ups.

"Hey, Ladouceur!" one man yells as the Spartans coach puts his linemen through their pregame paces. "Don't get blown out. You guys are going to be on skates all night."

Ladouceur and his players refuse to acknowledge the agitators, going about their business as if they are unable to hear.

"What's up, De La Salle?" someone else shouts.

"The streak ends tonight!" comes another shout.

"I don't know why they would heckle us," Eidson mutters, irritated. "High school kids take that kind of stuff seriously. All it's going to do is piss them off."

The De La Salle offense is warming up at the 30-yard line a few minutes later. Those not on the first-team offense stand in a line near midfield as Hayward players bounce up and down in a large scrum, just a few yards away from where the Spartans are calmly standing.

"These guys ain't nothin'!" shouts one Hayward player.

"These guys aren't shit!" yells another.

"Let's end their season!" comes a voice from the center of the scrum. "Let's end it tonight!"

"I see it as a sign of disrespect," Panella says, peering over his shoulder as Hayward players get themselves fired up. "Maybe if they keep saying it they'll start believing it."

Steam rises off Maurice Drew's scalp and into the chilly, damp night air when he takes off his helmet to adjust his chinstrap. "They talk a lot," he says to himself, watching them. "We'll see. We'll see."

The junior college is hosting a basketball tournament in the gymnasium. One of the visiting teams is leaving the locker room as De La Salle players enter for final instructions before kickoff.

"That's the best team in the nation right there," one basketball player tells a teammate as they watch De La Salle players walk past. "They play all their games on TV."

"Hey, how many games have you guys won?" the coach asks.

"One hundred thirty-four," Tony Binswanger answers proudly.

"Actually, it's one-thirty-six," backup quarterback Kevin Lopina correctly points out.

"Really?" Binswanger asks, surprised.

Fans are still standing in lines at the ticket booth as Hayward huddles on the field before the opening kickoff. Hayward players bounce up and down on their toes in their white jerseys and blue helmets, waiting for the referee to signal the start of the game.

Casey Moreno's brother Mark approached him on the sideline earlier, overcome with emotion. The Farmers finished 4–6 the past three years but here they are, meeting De La Salle in the playoffs.

"My heart was in my throat," Casey Moreno would later say. "I could only imagine how nervous the kids were. I just wanted to get the kickoff over with and maybe get an intimidating hit."

Moreno knew how dominant the Spartans' special teams could be and had his kickoff team practicing a special play for two weeks. The kicker would punch a high, short kick toward the right sideline while members of the coverage team thundered down the field, quickly converging on the ball and forcing a fair catch.

The kick is deeper than it should've been. Drew fields the ball at the 22-yard line and begins angling back across the field. By this time, the Hayward player responsible for outside containment is streaking down the middle of the field, allowing Drew to dip outside.

Drew picks up several key blocks while running the width of the field before cutting up the right sideline. A Hayward defender makes a desperate attempt to collar him from behind at midfield, but Drew is too strong and barely slows. Another defender dives at his feet from behind, but it's a futile gesture.

Moreno worked all week to prevent what is happening now before his very eyes. Drew is in the clear now, the near-capacity crowd rising to its feet, the hash marks a green-and-white blur under his feet.

On the Hayward sideline, Moreno stands on his tiptoes with his hands at his sides, his lower jaw jutting out like a petulant child. When Drew crosses into the end zone, no Farmer within 10 yards, the young coach momentarily looks as if he might burst into tears.

"Our kids came into that game so hyped," he said. "I didn't see anybody with fear in their eyes. As soon as that happened their whole demeanor changed. It was like, 'Oh, so this is how it happens.'"

Moreno's offense is led by running back Stevelan Harper, who set a Hayward Area Athletic League record with 26 touchdowns during the regular season. Six-feet-four-inch, 210-pound quarterback John Russell is drawing interest from smaller Division-I programs.

Spartan Terrance Kelly seems to know exactly where Russell plans to throw the ball and almost intercepts his first pass. Fullback Tony Sapiga gains three yards on second down before Erik Sandie and Mike Pittore converge on Russell, sacking him for a 7-yard loss.

The defense has been the strength of Hayward's team all season. It held previously unbeaten Berkeley High to minus-2 yards of offense during a 24–0 win in a first-round playoff game the week before. Yet Jackie Bates runs through a gaping hole in the line for a 20-yard gain on De La Salle's first play. After a penalty and two incomplete passes, Binswanger is called on to attempt a 45-yard field goal.

"A 45-yard field goal is nothing for this kid," Moreno explains to one of his assistants on the sideline.

The Farmers jump the snap as promised, prompting a De La Salle player to jump and get flagged for illegal procedure. Binswanger's 45-yard attempt is short but Eidson lets him try the 50-yarder.

Binswanger's second attempt lands in the middle of the end zone, seven yards short of the crossbar.

"They're making mistakes! They're making mistakes!" Moreno shouts encouragingly as his relieved players run off the field.

Sandie sacks Russell again on Hayward's next possession, setting up third-and-long. The senior quarterback finds a wide-open receiver on the next play, but the ball sails behind the receiver. It's as if Russell was expecting his target to turn one way, and the guy turned the opposite way instead.

Moreno holds a clipboard in his left hand. A pencil is wedged behind his right ear. The keychain dangling from the pocket of his khaki pants reads "I love Jesus."

"What happened?" he yells, exasperated, as Russell comes off the field. "He was wide open."

Russell stands on the sideline a few seconds later, his helmet pushed back on his head, his chinstrap dangling.

"Wow," he says, blinking.

Britt Cecil feels the pressure and scrambles to his left, making four defenders miss and gaining 15 yards. On that one play he displays the quickness that made Ladouceur believe he would be an effective option quarterback at the beginning of the year.

It hasn't turned out that way. Midway through the season, Cecil's longest run from scrimmage was only eight yards. It's hard to categorize Cecil. He wasn't considered an accomplished thrower, but he helped beat St. Louis and Long Beach with his right arm.

He wasn't the running quarterback that Ladouceur and Panella thought he would be, but he has used his feet to pick up key first downs in critical situations, especially in the win over Poly.

Bates takes a pitch from Cecil one play later and cuts back to his left before dipping outside again, his long strides propelling him over the turf. The 49-yard run makes the score 14–0.

"I've never seen a high school team so good at converting the pitch," Moreno says. "It's a great pitch, a great catch, a great block by the wide-out on the cornerback and then he's gone."

It has been obvious since the first play of the Antioch game the week before. The offensive line, De La Salle's greatest weakness during the regular season, has turned into perhaps its greatest strength.

People call De La Salle "The Green Machine," and the Spartans resemble a machine when offensive linemen are blowing off the ball, knocking defensive linemen into the linebackers, and linebackers into the secondary. The whole left side of Hayward's defensive line is collapsed on Bates' touchdown run.

Sandie is dominating on both sides of the ball, similar to the way Derek Landri dominated the year before. He is impossible to ignore, even in the obscurity of the middle of the line. He knocks defenders 10 yards off the ball on some plays. John Chan is ranging far downfield to pick off unsuspecting linebackers and safeties. Steve Fujimoto, the 5'10", 195-pound offensive guard who looked overmatched at times against St. Louis and Long Beach, is firing off low and hard, using his leverage to make much larger defenders slowly give ground.

Chris Biller is back. He subbed for Kyle Balough after the first offensive series. The junior tackle hasn't played since he sustained a hairline fracture of his left fibula against Poly. Now he has recovered and is making the Farmers pay for his time away. On Bates' run, he knocks a linebacker on his rear before peeling back and blindsiding a defender who was turning to pursue Bates from behind.

"Good surge," Ladouceur tells his linemen as they come off the field. "You guys are kicking their asses up front."

Russell drops straight back on third-and-4 on Hayward's next drive and immediately feels Balough pursuing from behind. His hurried pass hits Drew right in the chest. The thump of ball on shoulder pad can be heard on both sides of the field.

Drew's interception sets up yet another touchdown by Bates. Chan and Fujimoto double-team the defensive tackle, taking him completely out of the play. The defensive end hits Cecil after he hands off to Bates on the option dive. Terrance Kelly, the tight end, seals off the linebacker on a play that is executed to near perfection.

Bates breaks two tackles en route to a 19-yard touchdown when Hayward defenders hit him hard but fail to wrap him up.

"This game ain't over until we say it's over," barks an assistant coach on the Hayward sideline. "You've got to take this shit personal."

Jackie Bates is finally developing into the kind of talent Ladouceur expected him to be at the beginning of the season. He expressed his disappointment in Drew's eventual replacement after Drew was forced to bail his teammates out once again in the win over Freedom.

Bates worked hard but was undisciplined, at least in Ladouceur's view, his routes on the veer either too deep or too shallow. He has tremendous speed but always seems to be flat-footed, stutter-stepping, trying to fake out a defender instead of slashing upfield, the way De La Salle backs are taught as freshmen.

No one was more aware of Bates' lack of production than he was. The turning point came during a conversation with Maurice Drew the night before the Pittsburg game. Drew sensed Bates' disappointment over his limited role in the offense and his unspectacular results when he did get the ball.

Drew told Bates that he felt the same way before his breakout game against Poly the year before. Bates admired Drew more than anyone else on the team. He listened when Drew told him it wasn't about touches, but what you did with the ball once it was tucked under your arm.

"Everybody knows how good you are," Drew told him. "Everybody knows you're way better than this. Do you know it?"

Bates quit thinking about making defenders miss and started reacting, letting his instincts and athleticism take over. He had his best game against Pittsburg, rushing for 166 yards on five carries.

Now he is having another great night, and it is all thanks to Drew, at least as far as he is concerned.

"He just talked about my game, and coming from him—the best athlete I've ever seen—it meant a lot," Bates says. "He was real supportive. He has really helped me mature."

Drew's 41-yard run sets up a 15-yard touchdown scamper that makes the score 26–0 with 20 seconds left in the first quarter. A bad snap foiled Binswanger's extra-point attempt after Bates' second touchdown, which now gives Eidson the opportunity to prove Ladouceur wrong once again.

Eidson had his field goal unit working on two different trick plays all week. The first one calls for Drew, who lines up on the far left end of the line with his hands on his knees, to turn around and take a shovel pass from holder Matt Kavanaugh before cutting upfield.

The second is a variation of the same play, only this time Drew throws back to Kavanaugh, who runs into the left corner of the end zone.

"That will never work," Ladouceur said predictably when he saw the first play in practice. "That won't work either. It's too slow-developing," he moaned after watching the throwback unfold.

The shovel pass works to perfection, making it 28–0.

The defense continues to dominate. Eidson knew his secondary would be the strength of his defense, but he didn't expect the defensive line and linebackers to be so strong. Earlier in the week, he and Geldermann agreed that this unit was as balanced as any they could remember.

Defensive linemen aren't giving an inch and are consistently penetrating deep into the Hayward backfield. Linebackers are flying to the ball, and the secondary knows where Russell will throw before he does.

The first quarter ends with Moreno heeding the advice of his former coach. He yells for his punt team to get ready.

A 48-yard pass from Cecil to De'Montae Fitzgerald sets up another touchdown, this one coming on a 1-yard sneak that stretches De La Salle's lead to 34–0 with 6:26 left in the second quarter.

"Hey, you've got to pick up the blitz!" Moreno screams to his running back after Parker Hanks forces Russell out of the pocket.

"I got him. I picked him up," his player yells back defensively.

Moreno stomps his foot in frustration. "Then what's he running around back there for?" he asks, referring to his quarterback.

The running back looks toward the huddle for a moment before placing his curled hands on either side of his mouth, making a megaphone that will help carry his words to his coach on the sideline.

"Because he's scared, Coach," comes the answer.

The ball squirts out of Russell's hand when he tries a fake pump on the next play. Reluctantly, Moreno calls for the punt team again.

The left side of the offensive line clears a wide path on the next offensive play. Biller lines up at right tackle and circles behind the linebackers before blindsiding a Hayward defender near the line of scrimmage who is turning to pursue Drew as he collects a pitch.

The senior running back motors 44 yards untouched to give De La Salle a 41-point lead with 5:20 left in the first half.

"I think we match up against them talent-wise," Moreno says. "Technically, they are so skilled. Most of those kids are average athletes but they play with a passion that is unmatched. That's the way the game is supposed to be played. It's impressive as hell."

Hayward wanted De La Salle, and the Farmers are getting the Spartans at their best. There's no way to know how accurate *USA Today*'s national rankings are. Earlier in the season, when the Spartans were struggling against Archbishop Mitty and St. Francis, their No. 1 ranking seemed suspect. The way they have performed against two playoff opponents, it's difficult to imagine a team in America that could beat them.

Gino Ottoboni makes his first appearance in a game since spraining his knee against Poly, ripping off a pair of 20-yard runs early in the fourth before he's stripped from behind and fumbles.

On the next offensive series, Ottoboni fumbles a handoff on a draw play only to have the ball bounce off the turf and right back into his thick arms. He doesn't even break stride, running 58 yards for a touchdown to make it 47–0. Russell throws a 5-yard touchdown pass with less than a minute left to make the final score 47–7.

"That's an awesome program," Russell says while his parents wait to offer him words of encouragement after the game. "I don't see them losing for another ten years. I bet they win another 137 in a row."

1998

MATER DEI THREATENS THE STREAK

I t was thirty minutes before kickoff in what *USA Today* had billed "the biggest high school football game in history." De La Salle players sat on plastic chairs inside the locker room at Anaheim's Edison Field, showing no outward signs of anxiety. The only sounds that broke the unrelenting silence were occasional coughs and the noise of flushing toilets.

An official knocked on the door less than fifteen minutes before kickoff. The walkup crowd was much larger than anticipated. Fans were standing thirty deep at the ticket windows. Kickoff would be delayed in order for them to purchase tickets and find a seat.

"That's OK," head coach Bob Ladouceur said, shrugging off the delay. "We've waited a year to play this game. We can wait another twenty minutes."

De La Salle players were still celebrating their record-breaking victory over College Park on November 6, 1997, when reporters asked them to respond to criticism that The Streak was a product of inferior competition. The Spartans had established a new national high school record with their seventy-third consecutive win, but it wasn't until a year later that they got the chance to legitimize it.

There are more than nine hundred prep football programs in California, making it virtually impossible to implement a state-wide playoff system. Thus, some were calling the long-awaited 1998 matchup between tradition-rich De La Salle and Southern California private-school powerhouse Mater Dei of Santa Ana the most anticipated high school football game in state history.

The hype had been building for more than a year, and the buzz extended beyond the two campuses. Mater Dei had won three South-ern Section titles in the 1990s, more than any other school. The Mon-archs won mythical national championships in 1994 and 1996 but finished behind De La Salle in *Cal-Hi Sports* state polls in each of those years.

De La Salle had won 78 straight games and was ranked No. 1 in the country, but they had never played such a high-powered opponent before. Mater Dei plays better competition week in and week out in Southern California, which has a denser population, more schools, and therefore more quality athletes and quality teams. The 1998 Monarchs had big-game experience too, playing in front of some of the largest crowds in Southern Section history. The game was close to its private-school campus, while De La Salle had to travel to Southern California.

De La Salle was the most highly decorated program in the nation, but many considered it a decided underdog against another Catholic School that has been accused of recruiting.

"Mater Dei set the standard for high school football in California during the 1990s," Ladouceur says. "They were nationally known and they had a wonderful reputation. There was a battle cry for us to play them. People kept saying we needed to play those guys."

The Southern Section was so competitive and so insular that Mater Dei coach Bruce Rollinson had only a vague awareness of De La Salle until the game was scheduled. The more he learned in the months lead-ing up to the much-anticipated showdown, the more concerned he became.

"You could've hit me on the head with a two-by-four twenty times and I couldn't have told you who Bob Ladouceur was," Rollinson says. "Then I started reading articles as the game approached and seeing the similarities between our two programs. We both pride ourselves on dis-cipline, execution, and conditioning. People talked about how well-coached they were and how technically sound they were. Those were things we took a great amount of pride in, too."

He didn't talk to his players about The Streak. Instead, he told them they would be playing the finest opponent in Mater Dei history. He told them they were going to play the mirror image of themselves.

There were similarities, but when De La Salle players walked hand-in-hand onto the field before kickoff they quickly noticed striking dif-ferences. Mater Dei seemed to have more assistant coaches than De La

Salle had players. Rollinson had an 85-man roster, and his players took up almost the entire field during pregame stretching.

Then, dressed in red helmets with three white stripes, red jerseys with white piping and red pants, they bunched together near their sideline, running in place, their feet chopping furiously. Rollinson, wearing khaki pants, a blue Oxford shirt, and a red print tie, then led them down the field as their fans erupted with applause.

Many of De La Salle's players that year refused to wear elbow pads because they didn't want to differentiate themselves from their teammates. They stood silently on the sideline, blinking.

"De La Salle is more like special ops than the Army," said former player Patrick Walsh, who was a De La Salle assistant coach in 1998. "We truly live a Spartan existence in football. Our coaches don't wear headsets. We only dress forty-five guys. We have guys play both ways. Then we came out and saw this team that looked more like a college or professional program. They had banners and balloons and cheerleaders building pyramids and Coach Rollinson leading them across the field, and we had none of that stuff. In some ways it became an ideological battle."

Rollinson knew he was in a game from the first snap. Few teams in the Southern Section run an option attack. He had spent much of the offseason prepping for De La Salle's veer, but the focus and intensity of his opponent hadn't shown up on film.

"We've got our hands full," one of his assistants said early in the game. "Those guys can get off the ball."

"What the hell did you expect?" Rollinson growled.

It was chaos in the De La Salle locker room at halftime. The Spartans' 21–7 lead felt anything but secure. Offensive players crowded around a blackboard in one corner of the room. Everyone was talking at once, trying to describe Mater Dei's defensive alignment to assistant coaches. Ladouceur stood in the back of the room, strangely detached as coaches and players suggested various blocking techniques that might prove effective in the second half.

"How do you guys feel about the quick trap?" he asked finally. Silence fell over the room as he walked slowly to the board and changed the blocking assignments on the play.

Assistant coach Patrick Walsh walked out of the locker room wondering if Ladouceur had lost his mind. De La Salle basketball coach and former Notre Dame quarterback Frank Allocco entertained similar doubts. "I've seen a lot of halftimes, but I've never seen somebody waste an entire halftime changing the blocking on one play," Allocco commented.

Mater Dei roared back to tie the score in the second half. The game was slipping away when the third-quarter clock expired. De La Salle quarterback Vince Padilla was thrown violently to the ground for a 25-yard loss, setting up a third-and-32 at the Spartans' 19-yard line.

The Monarchs had momentum on their side. Red-clad Mater Dei fans, who made up the vast majority of the crowd of 20,781, were on their feet. Not since the last-second win over Pittsburg in 1993 had The Streak been in such jeopardy.

Ladouceur sent in the play. Running back Atari Callen took the handoff, picked up a key block from Jesse Rodriguez, and flashed into the secondary. He ran diagonally across the field, eight Monarchs in full pursuit. He finally was dragged down after a 58-yard gain.

Ladouceur had called the quick trap out of a passing formation. It was the first time he had called the play during the second half. Allocco immediately recognized it and stared at the field in disbelief.

"That's when I started to wonder if he was magic," he said.

De La Salle hung on for the 28–21 victory. Afterwards, Ladouceur stood before his exhausted players, telling them to be proud of their accomplishment. Because they refused to fold and had pushed their bodies to the extreme, their true character had been revealed. It was by far the biggest victory in school history at the time, but Ladouceur noticed that several of his players wore masks of disappointment.

"It's OK to feel disappointed if you didn't play your absolute best," he told them. "That's what we're all about."

～

Bruce Rollinson of Mater Dei looks like a football coach should. He is a tall, broad-shouldered man with a graying mustache and a voice so gruff it sounds as if he's talking through a mouthful of gravel.

He was an all-Orange County running back at Mater Dei in the mid-

1960s before going to USC and playing on two Rose Bowl teams. He returned to Mater Dei as an assistant in 1976 and led his alma mater to unprecedented success after being named head coach in 1988.

Under his guidance, by 1999 the Monarchs had won five Southern Section titles, nine league championships, and two mythical national championships. Rollinson was named national coach of the year by *USA Today* after the 1994 season.

Rollinson had prepared his team for De La Salle's option attack the year before and now, with the 1999 rematch approaching, he was more convinced than ever that stopping the veer was the key to snapping The Streak. His players had experienced the Spartans now. They had felt the line surge and precision. They would be better prepared this year.

"They get off the ball so fast and hit it so quick it's mind-boggling," Rollinson said. "You've got to get whacked by it a couple times before you even know what you're up against."

Mater Dei's 1999 season-opening loss to Clovis West dropped the Monarchs out of the national polls and stole some of the thunder from the rematch at University of the Pacific's Amos Alonzo Stagg Stadium in 1999.

De La Salle's backfield featured 2003 preseason all-American D.J. Williams and a sophomore quarterback named Matt Gutierrez, who had completed only seven passes in his high school career. Rollinson's game plan was as simple as it was logical. He would crowd the line with defenders to stop the run. He wasn't going to let Williams beat him.

He had a player in safety, Matt Grootegoed, who was talented enough to tackle Williams one on one and make the strategy work.

Grootegoed was also a preseason all-American who had turned in one of the most spectacular performances in state history in the Southern Section championship game the year before. He was named the offensive and defensive player of the game after rushing for 224 yards and two touchdowns and registering seven tackles and a forced fumble in Mater Dei's win over Long Beach Poly.

Grootegoed has icy blue eyes and old-school attitude. He later received a full-ride scholarship to USC. He was such a fearsome hitter that Rollinson referred to him as a "heat-seeking missile."

"He's one of the best natural football players I've ever seen," Ladouceur said. "He knew his way around the football field. His instinct for the ball, his tackling ability, and his athleticism made him so dangerous. He would come up and hurt people. He was that tough."

De La Salle came out in three- and four-receiver sets, but it was only a deception. Ladouceur was not about to throw his sophomore quarterback into the fire, even if he did believe that he had the potential to be the best quarterback in school history.

"I wasn't going to throw over those guys," he said. "I was going to run over them."

It was obvious from the start that Grootegoed was fixated on D.J. Williams. He was flying up from his safety position and punishing De La Salle running backs and receivers. He found his physical match in Williams, who'd had his breakout game against Mater Dei the year before and was now being described as the best prospect in the nation.

The two collided several times in the first quarter, both players refusing to give ground. The game was scoreless when Gutierrez ran what first appeared to be a typical veer option. He backpedaled at the last moment, however, and tossed a touch pass to receiver Demetrius Williams (no relation to D.J.), streaking down the left sideline for a 24-yard touchdown to make it 7–0.

Rollinson felt he had been too conservative offensively in the first game and was determined this time to throw his entire playbook at Terry Eidson's defense. Grootegoed and Matt Leinart would share time at quarterback. Leinart, a junior, was the more accomplished passer. When Leinart entered the game, Grootegoed—a dominant runner—would shift to tailback.

"Their offense had a lot of volume but they only run a few plays out of every offensive set," Eidson said. "To give our kids a chance, I had to make them understand what plays [Mater Dei] ran out of each formation."

Gutierrez completed more passes in the first half than he had all season. His three touchdown passes staked De La Salle to a 21–0 lead. He was only a sophomore, but the skinny 6'4", 196-pounder was doing exactly what Rollinson and his defensive staff had dared him to do by focusing their defense on Williams.

Gutierrez threw every type of pass imaginable in the first half, from long touch passes to quick outs to precise timing patterns. As a boy he had grown up idolizing his Godfather's nephew, Damian Vallis, a running back on the 1991 De La Salle team. Gutierrez wanted nothing more than to play for the Spartans. Now he was dominating as a sixteen-year-old.

"I worried about that game every single night during the summer," Gutierrez recalls. "I had dreams about playing Mater Dei."

Grootegoed continued to dominate defensively. Ladouceur called a screen pass with hopes of exploiting Mater Dei's run-oriented defense. Every time he ran it, Grootegoed sniffed it out.

The play called for four receivers, two split on either side of the field. The screen pass would be run to the widest receiver on the right side. On the snap of the ball the inside receiver would take out the cornerback covering the outside receiver, who would slip down the line, catch the pass, and run upfield behind a convoy of blockers.

Grootegoed was lined up on the inside receiver. When he saw his man go for the cornerback he burst upfield and blew up the play. Ladouceur made the adjustment at halftime. He told receiver Demetrius Williams to take three steps toward the cornerback the next time he called the screen pass and then cut hard up the field.

It worked to perfection. Grootegoed saw the play unfolding and stepped up to make the tackle, but there was no tackle to make. Demetrius Williams was streaking downfield, no one within 20 yards of him. The pass didn't need to be as accurate as it was. Just like that, the Spartans' lead ballooned to 28–0.

"A lot of the stuff we do at halftime isn't planned," Ladouceur says. "I'll pull stuff out of the playbook. It's like I'm fishing."

The final score of De La Salle's 91st consecutive victory was 42–0.

"I don't know how you beat them," Rollinson admitted afterwards. "Hope their bus crashes, I guess."

Rollinson accomplished his goal of stopping D.J. Williams, but in his third varsity start Gutierrez turned in one of the most dominant single-game performances in school history, scorching the unsuspecting Mater Dei secondary for 300 yards and six touchdowns.

"I was shocked at the outcome of that game and how he threw the ball and his poise and composure," Ladouceur recalls. "Not in my wildest dreams did I think he was going to do that that night. I remember walking behind him to the locker room after the game and it was the first time I noticed how big he was. A lot of it had to do with the kind of game he had. He looked like he was six-foot-nine. He looked like a college quarterback. I was absolutely astounded."

A demoralized Rollinson took the team back to its Stockton hotel and made sure players were in their rooms before he gathered his assistants for a staff meeting as night turned into early morning.

"We just ran into a hell of a football staff," Rollinson told his coaches. "I hope everybody realizes that we got outcoached tonight."

Later, Rollinson would say, "We didn't think they had that ability. We thought they were married to that veer and would run it come hell or high water. But they threw three and four receivers at us and no-back formations. Our coaches were scrambling. Our respect for that coach and his staff blew right through the top of that hotel that night."

Mater Dei kicker Brian New grudgingly accepts his role in Streak lore, even if he didn't ask for it, even if he doesn't deserve it. The worst part wasn't even what happened on Saturday night. The worst was waiting for him on Monday morning.

"It was horrible," New remembers. "It made it hard going back to school. I kept waiting for someone to pop off to me. I felt like everybody was talking about me even though they probably weren't."

Mater Dei wasn't a team that was used to losing, especially two games in two years to the same opponent, especially 42–0. The Monarchs won 10 straight after the embarrassing six-touchdown defeat to De La Salle in 1999; they then tied Long Beach Poly 21–21 in the 1999 Southern Section title game.

Mater Dei opened the 2000 season with an impressive victory over the No. 1 team in the San Diego Section, Fallbrook. The Monarchs were ranked eighth in the country by *USA Today* and were led by 6'5", 220-pound quarterback Matt Leinart, who had committed to USC.

De La Salle coaches noticed the difference while watching film of

Mater Dei. This team was not only talented, but hungry. De La Salle assistant coach Patrick Walsh predicted that the 2000 game would be even closer than De La Salle's 28–21 win two years earlier.

By this time the two schools had agreed to extend their home-and-home contract for two more years, which meant that Rollinson had two more chances to avenge the 42–0 loss and end The Streak.

That's what made the first quarter so unbearable. His frustration peaked when De La Salle jumped out to a 21–0 first-quarter lead in front of 17,000 screaming fans at Edison Field.

"I was festering on the sideline," he says. "I thought we were good coaches, and we were flopping around, giving up long passes. I was in everybody's face. I was screaming at my defensive coordinator. I was questioning everything about coaching, everything about myself."

After Mater Dei cut the lead to 21–14 at halftime, Rollinson made a critical decision. His team was having trouble running the ball against Eidson's defense. But he had a difference-maker in Leinart.

"We couldn't run on them," Leinart said. "I remember Coach Rollinson saying we were going to air it out in the second half."

The De La Salle lead was 24–14 late in the third quarter when Ladouceur went for it on fourth-and-12 at the Mater Dei 34-yard line.

"That was the last play I called," Eidson said. "I knew they were going to bring the heat. I said, 'Why don't we just throw a quick screen to Demetrius Williams and let him run with it?'"

The 34-yard touchdown extended the lead to 31–14 and would turn out to be crucial because of something hardly anyone knew at the time.

Gutierrez had gone from a virtual unknown to an up-and-coming star after his six-touchdown performance against Mater Dei the year before. When his first-ever recruiting letter arrived in the mail, it was addressed to Matt Gutierrez, Monarch Killer.

Now he was hurt. He had injured his wrist in the weight room during the offseason. It didn't swell so he didn't worry. But it never healed.

"That was the worst experience of my life," Gutierrez said. "I had a broken wrist and I didn't even know it. All I knew was it hurt and the ball wasn't coming off my hand the way I wanted it to."

De La Salle led 31–28 and had the ball near midfield with less than three minutes left when Ladouceur made one of the few play calls that have ever been second-guessed. Instead of running the ball and milking the clock on third-and-8, he had Gutierrez throw deep for Williams streaking down the middle of the field.

The receiver was wide open, just as Ladouceur predicted he would be, but Gutierrez's broken wrist prevented him from throwing the ball that far. Williams tried to come back to catch the underthrown pass but a Monarch defensive back made the interception at the Mater Dei 10.

"It was a great play call," Walsh said. "It was one of the few times his players didn't execute something that was exploitable. It was a ballsy call but it wasn't like the kid wasn't open."

Mater Dei's offensive line had been giving Leinart time, and he was shredding the Spartans' secondary like no quarterback had ever done. He would finish the game with 26 completions in 42 attempts for 356 yards and four touchdowns.

He engineered a 15-play, 74-yard drive that included two fourth-down completions before it stalled at the Spartans' 16.

Brian New had been an all-state kicker for three straight years and was considered one of the top ten kicking prospects in the nation. Ladouceur was preparing for overtime when New lined up for a 34-yard field goal.

"I should've called a timeout," Rollinson said. "I wish I would've called him over to let him know that it wouldn't be the end of the world if he missed it. I regret that I didn't do that."

New thought he struck the ball well but his foot hit the ball off-center. It curled left with 33 seconds left.

De La Salle hung on for consecutive win No. 103. Ladouceur told his players afterward that he would've been just as proud if the score were transposed. Rollinson even found peace. His players had competed so fiercely that he could find little fault in their performance.

"A lot of people put a lot of blame on him, but that stuff happens," Leinart said of New. "It's hard not to point fingers because it was the game-tying field goal, but [the loss] was by no means his fault."

~

The final game of the four-game series against Mater Dei was an anti-climax. Rollinson didn't have the personnel to match up with De La

Salle, and the game ended predictably with a 34–6 Spartans victory.

He would never have imagined that he wouldn't be able to defeat De La Salle once in a four-game series.

Rollinson remains more fascinated than ever by The Streak. His teams have lost games that he's convinced they would have won nine out of ten times. They lost because they weren't ready. De La Salle is always ready.

"I think Coach Rollinson is the best coach in the country, but to this day he still wonders how to beat them," former Mater Dei quarterback Leinart says.

Rollinson wanted to see the rivalry continue in 2002, but Eidson already had scheduled Long Beach Poly and was close to finalizing the trip to Hawaii. He didn't want his team traveling twice in one season.

Besides, the interest in the games had slowly declined. The final game drew 8,525 fans, which made it difficult to cover expenses. By that time the game between Long Beach Poly and De La Salle was the focus of the high school football community.

One of the residual up sides to the Mater Dei series would benefit De La Salle greatly within the Bay Area high school football community. The series gave the program visibility. It called attention to the Spartans' work ethic and Ladouceur's unique spirituality and perspective.

The more people understood about the program, the less mysterious De La Salle seemed. It didn't hurt that Mater Dei was a Southern California team. Northern California teams that had been bullied by De La Salle for years suddenly found themselves rooting for the Spartans and celebrating their success.

The Mater Dei series—combined with the public school-private school hearings held by the North Coast Section in 1997 and De La Salle's subsequent offer to secede from the Bay Valley Athletic League—reduced the level of animosity many felt toward Ladouceur and the program locally. De La Salle became more a regional symbol than a local whipping post. Respect for the program soared.

If the makeover is less than complete, at least De La Salle is regarded these days as considerably less evil than the dark empire it was considered to be ten years ago. As for the Southern Section, the impact of the Spartans' four victories over Mater Dei seemed limited to Mater Dei.

Before De La Salle's first game against Long Beach Poly, the Long Beach Poly staff requested a meeting with Rollinson and his assistants. The two Southern California schools were fierce rivals. But they found a common ground when it came to trying to beat De La Salle. Rollinson told the Poly coaches everything he had learned.

"I could tell when we were done with the meeting that they didn't understand what they were getting into," Rollinson says. "I told them they better humble their team because De La Salle doesn't give a flying fig about size and speed. They punch the clock, go to work, kick your ass, and get on a plane and go home. They don't get caught up in the hoopla. That's the one thing I couldn't convince the Poly guys of."

THE 2002 TITLE GAME
A Headfirst Slide into History

I I I I I I I I I

an ornate green-and-white quilt hangs in the hallway, the name and number of each De La Salle 2002 varsity player stitched into its design. Candles flicker in the living room where coaches sit with their wives, away from the kids and the parents and the mayhem. Christmas lights twinkle outside the window.

It feels more like a Christmas party than the last team meeting of the season. Beverly Ladouceur and Wendy Aliotti are in the kitchen. Mary Blasquez sits next to her husband, her blond hair pulled back in a bun. Baby Bianca sits at their feet, drooling happily. Mark and Sue Panella's laughter fills the room. Nicole Geldermann is in the final uncomfortable stages of pregnancy.

The feeling of finality that began to settle in before the Ygnacio Valley game was palpable during practice earlier in the week. "I can't coach you anymore," Ladouceur tells his players. "I can't make you better in two or three days. It's all on you now."

He has fantasized about sitting with his assistants in the top row of the bleachers and watching his kids play. He considers it the ultimate test for a high school football team. He might just do it yet. He wonders how parents would react.

They condition after Monday's practice leading up to the North Coast Section 4A championship game against San Leandro just as they always do, Blasquez lording over the workout with a stopwatch.

"Remember this day," he tells them as they try to catch their breath, their sweat-drenched shirts sticking to their backs. "I don't care what you do or where you play, you'll never be in this good a shape again in your lives—never."

The offensive linemen hit the sled forty times after Wednesday's practice the way they always do, firing out low, striking and raising the sled high before dropping it with a crash. Ladouceur rides on the back of the sled barking out the cadence—"Down . . . Set . . . Hut"—again and again, the sled gliding over the grass, rising and crashing to the ground. This workout is different, however. This is the seniors' last long, slow dance with the sled they have pushed around the cramped practice field for the past four years. They keep going, pulling left and hitting the sled, pulling right, every step in unison, as the sun fades behind the distant horizon.

If there's one snapshot that best captures the De La Salle program, this is it: the work ethic, the repetition, the precision. Ladouceur, the sled, the crouching linemen, large beads of sweat dripping from their faces, all cast in black silhouette against the vibrant orange backdrop of autumn twilight.

Ladouceur hasn't been satisfied with the play of his offensive linemen in games against San Leandro for the past three years. He told them as much after the sled was pushed to its winter resting place. They have a chance to rectify that, he tells them. It's all up to them.

He walks off the field in the gloaming, wondering if the excellence shown by his offensive line over the past two weeks—in fact, how his entire team has performed—answers the question he has been asking himself all season:

"If our kids are looking bad in one area, we're never going to throw up our hands," Ladouceur said. "If they can't do something that's fundamental to our program, they're going to get hammered with it all year until the end of the year when we'll finally realize they couldn't do it. We're not going to give up on it. This group is a perfect example. We had to hammer on them a lot at the beginning of the year, but look at them now. We're tough on kids because we believe they can do things they don't believe they can. But when do you keep pushing them and when do you back off and let them settle at their own level? That's a tough question, and it's different for each individual kid."

Justin Alumbaugh returned from Europe on Thursday. Players hold their helmets in the air and chant, "Coach Baugh! Coach Baugh!" when he walks out to the practice field. They circle around him as he entertains with tales of his adventures in Budapest and Prague.

"I can't tell you all the stories until football is over," he says, grinning.

There is another visitor to practice, a stranger who wandered through the gates, unsure. He wants to know if this is the school that has won 137 straight football games. He is told that it is. He looks around, bewildered.

He is in the Navy, he explains, and has followed The Streak in the newspapers while stationed in Virginia. He is on his way to a family wedding in San Diego but wanted to stop here first.

"How do they do it?" he asks, desperate for an answer. "How can they keep winning like this?" He searches the campus for something that isn't there. "I can't believe this is where they play their home games. You think De La Salle and you expect something more."

That evening, pasta is served and duly consumed on long tables in the garage. Players fold up the tables and carry away the trash to make room for the team meeting.

Individual letters spelling out "I LOVE YOU SPARTANS" are taped to the cabinets above the workbench. They are the same homemade placards parents held up during senior night three weeks earlier.

Christmas lights illuminate the eaves outside the open garage door. Ladouceur wears jeans and a black leather jacket. Players wear sweatshirts and rub their hands together to stave off the damp cold.

This is the final team meeting of the season, the last-ever team meeting for the twenty-five seniors. Eidson stands before them, head bowed, as if he is still trying to formulate his words as players quietly clear their throats. This is Eidson's twenty-second year in the program. He could've become a head coach, could've become a college assistant years ago had he not made it known that he would never leave De La Salle.

Never before have his contributions loomed so large. His defense came into the season greener and riddled with even more question marks than the offense. But it was consistent all season, while the offense struggled to find its way, making the staff question the team's ability to defeat St. Louis and Long Beach Poly. The success of his defense and special teams was crucial to this team's success. Eidson begins:

"You have to remember you guys have been in games for six and seven weeks when things have gone your way and the game has been basically over by halftime. It's been somewhat easy. You're playing an undefeated team, 12–0, and they're not going to roll over and die, and if they do, great, but there's no guarantee of that. You may not have the lead tomorrow night. You may fumble the ball on the first possession. They may hit a guy on a bomb on the second play of the game. A lot of things can happen. I anticipate this being a four-quarter game. This is a championship game. This team, outside of us, is one of the best teams in Northern California and could compete with Southern California schools, too. This is a good team. A lot of things can go wrong. Keep your heads about you. Don't panic. Remember what got you here—passion, emotion, hard work, technique—and put it together.

"Go out and enjoy it and make a nice memory for yourself."

Ladouceur is almost always asked to compare teams after each season. He prefers not to. This wasn't his most talented group—not even close. But it maximized its potential, its crowning achievement—his crowning achievement—being the 28–7 win over Long Beach Poly on a day when many believed that a vulnerable team would finally surrender The Streak. For all these reasons the 2002 Spartans will forever hold a special place in his heart.

Still, the last game of the season weighs heavily on his mind. San Leandro is undefeated, tough, well-coached, and possesses the one thing that has always worried him most—speed.

This group played as well as any De La Salle team he could remember in winning playoff games against Antioch and Hayward. The offensive line improved more than he thought possible. The defense has been superb all year, but this team has shown signs of immaturity all season. It would be just like this team to stumble now, after all it has invested and accomplished, regardless of how well it has been playing. Ladouceur not only has had to coach this team, he has had to lead it.

He can't afford to quit leading it now.

"I promised Maurice and Jackie and Gino, all you guys that are going to run the ball tomorrow, we're going to block for you, and goddamn it, you offensive linemen better do that. I'll be very, very disappointed if you don't. Regardless of how I feel about it, you should be disappointed if you don't block for those guys. I have a feeling they're going to come out and give it everything they've got as runners. You have to put the two together. I'm so sick of watching San Leandro lay hit after hit on our running backs and watching our linemen stand around and watch it all happen. When I see that as a coach I get real discouraged because it shows them that they are more aggressive than us, and that's the way it has been offensively.

"This team that we're playing has a lot of grit. They're not in any way, shape, or form afraid of you. They want to lay hits on you. That's been my experience with them. They want to lay hits on you guys, and if you don't fight, scratch, and claw as linemen you're going to betray everything we've worked for. That's what your job is as linemen, scrappers, fighters, grit, right down in the pit. That's what you signed up for. That's what it is. Follow through on that tomorrow.

"Think of where we started back at Mitty. Even in St. Louis, although we gave a great effort, we were still pretty raw and green. Look at our beginnings. After looking at our St. Francis film, we were looking around as coaches and looking at you guys and saying, 'I don't know. I don't know if these guys can pull it together.' It didn't seem like you were going to, but I'll be damned if you didn't.

"I think you had an outstanding year considering where you've been and where you are. There's nothing more gratifying to me, I couldn't have been more proud of you guys after watching your last two games, after watching you play with that kind of heart, that kind of determination, that kind of spirit. It was everything I could ever want as a coach, or even as a fan of the game. I'd love to see it one more time. We're not going to see football like that here at De La Salle all the time. You guys have been playing great, and that's a rare phenomenon to get the eleven guys moving as one like that and playing with that kind of heart. I don't know when we're ever going to see that again. Who knows? Nothing is guaranteed anybody. I'd love to see it one more time.

"I know San Leandro is dangerous. I know they're good, I know they're physical, but I believe in you guys. I believe you can mash those guys. But you've got to bring it. You have to bring what you have been bringing. If you do, you'll ride back on that bus tomorrow and there won't be any greater feeling. That I guarantee. You'll ride back on that bus and you'll say we just did something that was really good, and not just the championship game, the whole thing. You'll have done something that not many guys can do ... I can't envision you guys falling apart as a team. No way. It's not us. It's what I wrote to you seniors in your letter. Be you tomorrow. Be Spartans. Give everybody—teammates, coaches, parents, everybody who comes to watch—give them something; give them a thrill. Let us all walk away and just say, 'Wow.' That's what I've been thinking for the past two weeks. You can do it one more time. You're in perfect position for it."

Responsibility had weighed heavily on the seniors, who were sad to see the regular season end. Deep down they also were relieved.

People always talk about the inherent pressure in being caretakers of The Streak. The seniors didn't think about it that way. They, like the coaches, were too immersed in the details—taking the right first step on 13 veer, memorizing the scouting report, living up to their commitment cards. The Streak is merely a byproduct of those things.

But there's no denying its omnipresence. The Streak is always there, in the back of their minds, if not the front. How could it not be when outsiders are constantly reminding them of it?

They inherited The Streak, put their own personal stamp on it, and prolonged it. One more win and their mission is complete. They can pass the responsibility on to the next class.

"I want to thank Erik Sandie for being the type of player that he is," says senior captain Cole Smith, the first player to stand during the final team meeting of the 2002 season. "Erik, you're so big and strong and gritty. You're everything I always wanted to be as a lineman. I like the amount of heart and hustle you play with. It inspires me. I would just like to thank you for that."

Cameron Colvin rises from his chair, so much more confident and self-assured than he was at the beginning of the season. He carved a niche for himself this season. He set himself up to have the kind of senior season that could take him far, far away from the people who passed him on the streets of his hometown, people who thought they knew everything about his mother, his father, and his uncle after reading about them in the newspaper. People who even thought they knew him.

"When the season started I didn't think I would make it," he says, pausing to make eye contact with players around the room. "It was indescribable. Being out there with you guys made it bearable. I just want to thank everybody here for making the worst time of my life the best time of my life. Everybody should know I love them."

"You made a name for yourself," Damon Jenkins tells quarterback Britt Cecil. "Everyone talked about how you would replace Matt Gutierrez, and you would say how you weren't going to try to replace Matt Gutierrez. You were just going to try to be Britt Cecil. You did that. Even though Maurice did all the scoring, you were the one in charge of the offense. I just want you to know that I respect the hell out of you for that."

Cecil has spoken only rarely in team meetings. He will never forget the feeling of having to be prodded into speaking the night before the season opener against Mitty. Finally, Panella had insisted he say something, even if Cecil felt he had to prove himself on the field before he would have any credibility in the meetings.

He had overcome so much. People said he was inexperienced, had a weird hitch in his delivery, and wasn't a strong leader. Maybe it was true. He hadn't developed into the accomplished running quarterback many had predicted he would become over the course of the season.

But he had come to personify this team. He was raw and untested when the season began. But he played his two best games in the two biggest games on the schedule. He wasn't the player anybody expected him to be, but he got the job done—at times spectacularly.

He proved himself in some of the biggest games in De La Salle history. He feels as if he finally has earned the right to speak.

"I want to thank Coach Lad," he says, looking the head coach right in the eye. "I want to thank you for all the patience you showed me. You were there through all the bad times and I could always see a little twinkle of confidence in your eyes and it kept me going. You made me dig deeper. I thank you for that."

Chris Biller had taken his second injury in stride. He hated watching his teammates play without him but felt fortunate to have played at all considering that his varsity career nearly ended before it began.

He proved himself in the biggest game of the season, earned the respect of everybody in this room, and reserved a starting position for himself on the offensive line during his senior season.

"Coach Blasquez went to bat for me at the beginning of the year," he says. "I don't know what he went through to get me all those appointments. I just want him to know how much I respect him for that."

John Chan played so well against Antioch and Hayward that the memory of his disappointing performance against Ygnacio Valley had quickly faded. Few had ever taken their De La Salle careers as seriously as he did. It frightened him, wondering how he would fill the void.

He and Cole Smith are trying to secure appointments to the Naval Academy. The more he thinks about it, the more it seems like the perfect fit. The discipline, the academics, the demands of being a plebe—it's exactly the type of challenge that would help replace De La Salle football.

"I want to say something about Sam Cheatham," Chan says, referring to San Leandro's standout wide receiver and defensive back. He relates a story.

Brendan Ottoboni, Gino's older brother, was running a pass route across the middle in the previous year's championship game against San Leandro. He leaped high in the air to make the catch. Cheatham timed his hit perfectly, putting his shoulder right on Brendan's exposed midsection. It was a clean hit, but brutal.

Brendan spent four days in the hospital after suffering damage to his internal organs and experiencing internal bleeding.

"When Brendan rolled over and threw up after the hit, I heard a cheer. Not a huge roar but a cheer, and that pissed me off," Chan says. "I remember that. What brought it up is I was talking to Nick Holtz, and Nick and Brendan go to Colorado together, and Colorado has been recruiting Sam Cheatham. Cheatham was on a recruiting trip there earlier this year and had a highlight film. They were showing it in the training room and they saw Brendan's hit. Of course he had that on his highlight film. But he also had Brendan throwing up. Not that he's a horrible person for that, but it pisses me off because I'm Brendan's friend. If I was a DB tomorrow I'd shut that guy down because he's gotten on us the past two years. I've got my own problems to worry about. I didn't play great last year. It's not my place, but I'm asking you DBs to shut that guy down. Do it for Brendan, too."

"I've got something to add to that," Ladouceur says, sitting up in his chair. "In all the films I've watched that guy on, he comes up like a shot, head down, full-speed into runners. You offensive linemen can take care of that yourself. I don't want you head-hunting the guy but he's a touch-down alley guy. A good touchdown alley target is that guy. I'm not telling you to get revenge. I'd never tell you to do that. But he's a good target. He comes in to hurt people. He plays the game hard. No doubt about it. I'm not saying he's cheap or dirty or anything, but that's one guy you want to keep off your runners. I was going to say that before you men-tioned it. Not about Brendan, but I don't like to see guys flying in and putting hats on our runners. That's part of your assignment tomorrow. Touchdown alley blocks mean taking out those secondary guys, too, because they come up and hit."

Chris Wilhelmy's season hasn't turned out the way he imagined it would. Dr. Wilhelmy's son expected to be a key contributor. Instead he has been sidelined for much of the season with various injuries. He worked hard to make it back before the end of the season. Now the sea-son is ending when his was just beginning.

Ladouceur gave seniors a personal letter during chapel service ear-lier that afternoon. Wilhelmy couldn't stop thinking about it.

"When Coach handed out his letter today, it really affected me," he says, wiping the tears from his cheeks with the sleeve of his sweatshirt. "I was touched by it. I was looking at all those names on the top and I knew I would remember them for the rest of my life. I'll always keep it so I can look at it because I know those people care about me. Tomor-row night we're going to be playing for the person next to us, but I'm going to give it my all for every senior and every junior, too, because I want to end my season like Coach said. I want to walk off that field knowing I can look the other seniors in the eye for the rest of my life and we can say, 'We did that together. We were together that night. We were together for that whole season.'"

"I appreciate that," Ladouceur says. "That's heartfelt. I hope everybody feels this way because this team is over in twenty-four hours. This team disbands in one more day. It's sad and it made me sad today. I was going around hugging you seniors today in Chapel and it was difficult for me, but in a good way. Life goes on and we have to push forward, but when I come back tomorrow I want to have the job done, completed. I just don't want to have any blot on what you guys have done. I have a feeling you're going to go out there and fight for each other because that's what you have become. Like I said, in twenty-four hours this team will cease to exist. The only thing that will live is our memories. Our bonds will always be there, but we will not function as a team anymore. That's why you should be really jacked for tomorrow."

The coaches have spoken. The players have spoken. A meal has been consumed and they have methodically gone over the offensive and defensive checklists, just like they have before every game.

But something has been left unsaid. The coaches and players are hesitant to fold up their chairs and disappear into the night.

"You know my personality," Eidson says softly. "I'm not a quiet person. But I really believe this has been my quietest year...."

"Yeah, right," Geldermann snorts.

"Well, I guess I am who I am," Eidson says. "Every day I put my four-year-old daughter in the car and I say, 'Hanna, you don't have to yell.' Then I realize it's God getting back at me."

The room fills with laughter.

Eidson has found himself pondering another question. He never imagined it would come to this when the season started, but twelve weeks of conclusive evidence have convinced him otherwise.

This is by far the best secondary in school history. Not even St. Louis and Long Beach Poly were able to throw against Damon Jenkins, Matt Kavanaugh, Jackie Bates, and Willie Glasper this season.

There was no D.J. Williams, no Kevin Simon or Derek Landri, no so-called superstars among the front seven, yet this has been one of the most balanced defenses he ever has put on the field. Considering the caliber of competition the Spartans faced, it also has been one of the best.

"You guys who played defense this year," Eidson says after the room quiets down. "You caught the attention of Spartan faithful as a very special group. If you finish this season the way you can, I'll be able to say this is one of the best defensive groups I've had. It's up to you. It won't do anything for me. I don't care if people consider me a genius. I'm not looking to move up the ladder. It's all for you."

Ladouceur tells his assistants not to ramble when they talk to the team. Eidson is rambling now, but nobody minds.

"We always talk about retiring," he says. "We've been talking about that for ten years, but teams like this keep bringing us back. Lighting that victory cigar on the beach in Hawaii and watching you guys hit the waves at midnight, what a great memory. That's something I'll never forget. I want to thank you guys for that."

Eidson sits down.

"If you go through life and get to work side by side with your best friends, consider yourself lucky," Ladouceur says. "Not many people get to do that. I've been coaching for twenty-four years but I've never said I'm going to work. I say I'm going to school because I don't consider what I do here work. I don't know why. I haven't thought that out yet. Maybe it's because I'm still learning about myself too."

Players are handed a small bag of candy after they thank the Fujimotos and walk out the door. They start throwing the candy at each other in the front yard and soon there are sweets scattered in the grass.

A streetlight is out and it's very dark. Erik Sandie talks to a teammate as he walks down the sidewalk toward his truck.

"Oh, dude, I thought I lost my letter," he said.

"What letter?" a voice in the dark asks.

"My letter from Coach Lad," Sandie says as he opens the door to his truck, the dome light illuminating his features. "I would've never forgiven myself if I had lost the letter from Coach Lad."

～

Ladouceur gave his seniors the following letter during the final Chapel service earlier that afternoon. He also chose the music, selecting "Forever Young" by Rod Stewart.

12-06-02

To: Chris W., Britt, Chris B., D. Fuji, Matt K., Gino, Maurice, De'Montae, Damon, Aaron, Ian, Carlo, Chris M., Cole, Erich, John C., Eric L., Brad, Ryan, Sean, Joe, Erik S., Garth, Matteo, Tony.

I want to thank you for the opportunity to coach you through your varsity football days at De La Salle. My association with you has been a positive experience for me that will stay with me for the rest of my life. You have provided me with some wonderful memories that I know I will look back on with pride—and smile.

I know you have all improved as football players because I have witnessed the growth. However, this is not what is most important to me. What is my hope and dream is that you have all improved and grown as human beings through your experiences at De La Salle. I believe that you have, but only "the man in the glass" knows for sure.

You all know and lived the "secrets" to De La Salle's success— love, brotherhood, sacrifice, discipline, heart, courage, passion, honesty. These are not just "catch words" we throw around to impress others or justify our existence. We know what these mean because we created it and lived it. Understand that with that knowledge there is no turning back for us—ignorance is not an option. It is your future duty, no matter where you end up, to create the environment you have created here by bringing your best selves to the table.

It is my hope and prayer that your future significant others (friends, wives, children, co-workers) will have the good fortune to experience you as I have. Remember to always take the difficult look at yourselves and have the courage to change, evolve and grow.

Go out tomorrow and play like you are—dare to be you— Spartans. And as for me, you will remain "Forever Young."

With respect,
Coach Lad

≈

De La Salle players gasp as they are led into the Raiders' locker room at the Oakland Coliseum. Plush silver and black-checkered carpeting covers the floor. "Commitment to Excellence" is spelled out in black across the back wall next to the Raiders shield.

Ladouceur is looking for a place for his team to stretch. NCS officials won't allow players participating in the second game onto the field until the 3A game has concluded, but they have not allotted enough time for the Spartans to complete their normal pregame routine. The dilemma is solved as Ladouceur looks around the room. The locker room is so large that his entire team can stretch on the soft carpeting with square footage to spare. They can even do their pregame speed work in here.

"Why can't we just play the game in here?" quarterback Britt Cecil asks before firing a crisp pass to a teammate standing across the room. It's almost as if he is reading Ladouceur's mind.

This is the first time in five years the North Coast Section championship games are being held at the Coliseum. Ending the season in the home of the Raiders and A's has long been the goal for football players competing for North Coast Section schools. But scheduling conflicts with the Raiders have interrupted the tradition.

The majority of the 16,139 fans that fill the lower bowl on the south side of the stadium have not come to watch De La Salle play San Leandro for the fourth straight year. The 3A championship game between Monte Vista and San Ramon is the main attraction.

The two Danville schools are cross-town rivals, and they boast two of the best quarterbacks in the nation. San Ramon Valley's Sam Keller has agreed to attend the University of Michigan on a scholarship, while Monte Vista's Kyle Wright has committed to the University of Miami.

The two teams met earlier in the season in one of the greatest shootouts in the history of Bay Area high school football. Keller completed 22 of 37 passes for 346 yards and four touchdowns in that game. Wright threw for 372 yards, tossing the game-winning touchdown pass with four seconds left to give Monte Vista a 46–44 win. The game featured five lead changes.

It seems as if the entire population of Danville is at the Coliseum to watch the rematch, which proves less compelling than the original. Monte Vista has a comfortable 35–0 lead over Ladouceur's alma mater when De La Salle coaches stroll onto the field.

"It's a big crowd," Eidson says, scanning the stands.

"Do you think they'll stay?" he is asked. Some wonder if many fans will leave before the De La Salle-San Leandro game begins.

"They'll stay for a while," Eidson says matter-of-factly. "But they'll root for San Leandro."

San Leandro has established itself as the best public school program in the Bay Area during the past three seasons, each of which ended with a lopsided loss to De La Salle in the championship game. Those are the only three games the Pirates have lost during that three-year stretch; they came by a combined score of 135–40.

If not for the Spartans, San Leandro would have a 46-game win streak of its own.

Danny Calcagno is one of the top young coaches in Northern California. His Pirates are ranked 22nd in the nation by Rivals.com, making them the third nationally ranked team that De La Salle has played this season. Nobody gives them much of a chance against the Spartans, the team that still stands at No. 1.

The day marks the eleventh anniversary of De La Salle's last defeat, a 35–27 loss to Pittsburg on this same field. In many ways San Leandro resembles the 1991 Pittsburg team, especially at the skill positions.

Three-year starting quarterback Dennis Dixon resembles a young Randall Cunningham. He is the best quarterback prospect in the Bay Area behind Wright and Keller. Sam Cheatham set league records for touchdown catches (13), career touchdown catches (22), and single-season receiving yards (813). The Pirates' other wide receiver, Reggie McPherson, caught five passes for 99 yards in an NCS semifinal win the week before.

San Leandro players wear white jerseys with blue numbers trimmed in red as they unfurl large pirate flags on the field, waving them wildly as the school's cheering section erupts with applause.

De La Salle players walk toward the field with the quiet serenity of parishioners on their way to Mass. They hold hands and walk in parallel lines, emitting a calm confidence.

"I can't believe the growth," says Pat Hayes, who wears an army-green poncho as he watches them take the field. "After St. Francis we thought it was over. The kids were the only ones who believed."

The announcement that Mater Dei has upset Long Beach Poly 21–20 in a Southern Section semifinal game prompts gasps from the crowd. The night before, the St. Louis Crusaders defeated Castle High to capture the program's fifteenth Hawaii state championship in seventeen years.

Starters from both De La Salle and San Leandro are announced over the Coliseum speakers. Ladouceur sits on the bench, looking like someone who might absent-mindedly toss crumbs to pigeons, when his image appears on the scoreboard video screen. The camera also captures Hayes, with his wild white hair, sitting next to him. Ladouceur looks up and laughs at the two of them. Hayes is mildly offended.

Senior captains De'Montae Fitzgerald, John Chan, and Cole Smith join hands and walk deliberately out to the middle of the field for the final coin toss of their high school careers.

"Let it come to you," secondary coach Terrell Ward tells Maurice Drew on the sideline. "Let it come to you and it will come in a big way tonight."

Drew lets it come to him. Dixon reads blitz and rushes his second pass attempt of the night. It hits Drew right in the chest. It's bad enough to throw an interception on the first drive of the game, but now Drew, the best running back in the state, is running in the open field.

The De La Salle crowd cheers wildly while others look on in disbelief as Dixon pushes Drew out of bounds at the 1-yard line. Britt Cecil scores on a quarterback sneak on the next play.

Less than two minutes into the game the Spartans have a 7–0 lead against the best public school team in Northern California.

Calcagno looks young enough to still be playing quarterback for San Leandro, which he did in the mid-1980s. His team lost to the Spartans 54–13 in an NCS playoff game in 1984.

He has tried various strategies against De La Salle through the years, all with limited success. The closest he ever came to being in a game against the Spartans came in 2001, when his team trailed 20–13 with 6:49 left in the third quarter. Ladouceur's team then scored 28 unanswered points to win going away.

Calcagno's game plan calls for the same kind of quick, precise passes that allowed Pittsburg to control the ball for much of the third quarter of their upset victory over De La Salle in 1991. He has the personnel for it. Dixon is being recruited by Oregon. His receivers Cheatham and McPherson have drawn heavy interest from Big 10 schools.

Dixon rolls right and throws a strike to a well-covered McPherson for a 10-yard gain on the first play of San Leandro's second possession. Running back Michael Ignont gains four yards off right tackle on second down before Dixon completes a 16-yard pass over the middle, prompting the San Leandro fans to wave their Pirate flags. The drive stalls after an incompletion on third down near midfield.

"They're going for it, Terry!" Ladouceur yells.

"NO, they're not! This is how they punt," Eidson shouts impatiently. Sure enough, at the last possible moment, Calcagno rushes his offense off the field while his punt team comes running on.

Drew bursts off right tackle for 30 yards on third-and-short on De La Salle's ensuing drive, but the play is called back when Sandie jumps before the snap. Players are in the huddle, waiting for the penalty to be marked off, when they notice that Smith can barely stand.

Cole Smith suffered his first concussion against St. Louis. His second was the result of an accidental head-to-head collision with Fitzgerald on the first drive of the game. It's only midway through the first quarter, the outcome still very much in doubt, but Cole Smith's high school football career is over. He's the only one who doesn't know it.

He has no memory of the hit or why he insisted on staying in the game when he was obviously woozy. He won't even remember sitting on the bench, trembling and sobbing, as his teammates approach one by one to hug and comfort him throughout the first half.

Drew runs off left tackle for 37 yards and a touchdown on the next play, rendering the penalty moot and giving De La Salle a 14–0 advantage as the first quarter comes to a close.

That's when it becomes official, even though De La Salle's defensive players are unaware of it. The defense has not allowed an opponent to score a first-quarter touchdown all season—quite an accomplishment considering that St. Louis, Long Beach Poly, and San Leandro all feature high-powered offenses.

Cheatham's hit on Brendan Ottoboni wasn't his only memorable play from the 2001 championship game. He also beat Damon Jenkins for a 69-yard touchdown. Dixon throws a pass intended for Cheatham in the opening minutes of the second quarter. Jenkins intercepts in midstride and returns it 19 yards to the San Leandro 10.

Jenkins is considered one of the best college cornerback prospects in the state, but his college plans are very much in doubt. He could've had his choice of schools if his grades had been better. He was told during his sophomore year that he had a learning disability that made it difficult for him to retain information. That helped explain why he walked a thin line between eligibility and ineligibility throughout his four-year high school career.

USC, UCLA, Ohio State, Washington, and Washington State are among the schools courting him, but the interest is contingent upon him receiving the minimum score required for freshman eligibility on the SAT. He is scheduled to take the test next month.

Drew runs to the San Leandro 4-yard line before Jackie Bates walks into the end zone behind a wall of green. Binswanger's extra point attempt is blocked, making it 20–0 with 10:27 left before halftime.

Eidson yanks Matt Kavanaugh out of the game after Cheatham catches an 11-yard slant pattern in front of him. Kavanaugh hadn't expected to be the starting safety when the season began, but Chris Wilhelmy was injured and he found himself playing with the first team in practice more and more often.

Kavanaugh knew he wasn't gifted with the athleticism of Jenkins or Willie Glasper, but he did whatever he could to keep his starting position, memorizing the scouting report every week and hitting anything that moved, before and occasionally after the whistle.

He knew he would never catch touchdown passes or return an interception 90 yards for a touchdown. He considered himself a hard-nosed player, even if it did get him in trouble at times.

He was guilty of a cheap shot against Archbishop Mitty in the season opener and was kicked off the special teams unit for the year after another overaggressive play against St. Francis.

He thought the punishment excessive, even though he was still allowed to hold for field goals and extra points. He spent the rest of the season in Eidson's ear, day after day, trying to persuade the special teams coach to give him another chance.

He goes straight for Eidson as soon as he reaches the sideline. Eidson hitches up his pants and signals in the next defensive play, ignoring his antagonist until Kavanaugh, frustrated, stomps away.

"KEEP GIVING ME THAT ATTITUDE, AND YOU WON'T PLAY THE WHOLE GAME!" Eidson shouts at Kavanaugh.

Dixon rolls right on fourth-and-12 near midfield and finds McPherson for a 21-yard gain to keep the drive alive.

"GOD DANG IT!" Eidson shouts on the sideline. "WHAT'S WRONG WITH YOU GUYS?"

He turns and searches for Kavanaugh, who has removed himself from his teammates, his hands on his hips, steaming.

"KAVANAUGH, GET IN THERE!" he shouts.

Kavanaugh races toward the huddle. It's third-and-4 on the Spartans' 20 when Dixon rolls right, feeling the pressure, and throws an incompletion. He attempts a shovel pass on fourth down but Kavanaugh and Hanks read it perfectly, dropping the running back for no gain. Kavanaugh pumps his fist and searches the sideline for Eidson while Ladouceur sends his offense onto the field.

The scholarship offers are pouring in for Drew: USC, UCLA, Cal, Colorado, and Wisconsin are among the schools bidding for his services. He will finish the season with 1,459 yards and 26 touchdowns—including six kickoffs or punts returned for scores. He's a good enough defender that USC is interested in him as a safety.

He sweeps the left side on third-and-3 from the De La Salle 27, patiently waiting for five eager blockers to form a wall in front of him. He gains 40 yards to set up a 24-yard run by Bates that makes the score 28–0 with exactly three minutes left before halftime.

Eidson calls for the shovel pass throwback to Kavanaugh on the ensuing 2-point conversion, but an offsides penalty negates the play.

"It's kind of dumb to go for it from way back there," says a sideline observer when Ladouceur keeps his offense on the field to attempt the 2-point conversion from eight yards away.

"Like I said, good call," the observer says after a wide-open Colvin catches Cecil's pass in the end zone.

San Leandro needs to put together a drive in the final 2:53 if it hopes to carry any momentum into the locker room at halftime. Dixon is trying to set up a screen pass when he sees Sandie burst through the line and come after him.

Kyle Balough sheds his man and sprints toward Dixon. When he recognizes the screen, he stops, just as he has been taught to do.

Dixon tries to flip the ball over Sandie. Balough reaches up and makes the interception. The De La Salle crowd comes alive as Balough rambles 27 yards for a touchdown and a commanding 35–0 lead.

"Now that's how you play the screen!" a delighted Geldermann shouts as he hurries down the sideline to congratulate Balough, who is being mobbed by his teammates in the end zone.

Cole Smith doesn't understand why everyone is so excited. Backup defensive tackle Sean Matlock tries to explain at halftime.

"Balough scored a touchdown on an interception," he tells Smith again.

There's a flicker of recognition in Smith's bloodshot eyes. Then he wrinkles his brow and it's gone, replaced by a look of complete and utter bafflement.

"Who scored a touchdown?" Smith asks dreamily.

"Balough," Matlock replies patiently.

"How did he do it?" Smith wants to know.

Offensive and defensive players are on opposite sides of the locker room, taking instruction from Eidson and Ladouceur.

"This is a good lesson for you juniors," Eidson says. "If we check out of this defense...."

"Parker, what do you see on the load?" Ladouceur asks. "Is that guy in a six?"

"We're pretty much shutting down their running game," Eidson says. "They've gotten some yards. They're not 12–0 for nothing."

The strategy sessions have ended when Fitzgerald approaches Smith: "We went head to head and I cracked your ass for the first time in four years," he tells him.

"I don't remember," Smith says earnestly.

Geldermann walks up to Smith then, flipping him the bird.

"Hey, Cole, how many fingers?" he asks, grinning. Cole laughs.

"Just so you know, in all the years we've played in the championship games, we've never had a shutout," Eidson tells players as they prepare to take the field for the second half.

"What about my senior year?" Geldermann asks. The Spartans defeated James Logan 35–0 for the 1994 NCS 4A championship.

"This would be the second time then," Eidson says, correcting himself. "SORRY. MY BAD."

Smith is as wobbly as he was when he first came off the field. Steve Fujimoto tries to help him up from his chair.

"Where's my helmet?" Smith asks, searching the room.

"Don't worry," Fujimoto says, holding his arm and leading him toward the door. "You don't need it."

Dr. Wilhelmy is concerned after examining Smith at halftime. Players who suffer concussions usually improve. Smith is as confused and unsteady on his feet as he was when he came out of the game.

"Man, am I going to party after this game is over," Smith tells Matlock.

"No, you're not," Matlock says.

Dr. Wilhelmy sends Smith to the hospital for tests midway through the third quarter, as San Leandro is marching down the field on a long, time-consuming scoring drive that ends Eidson's hopes of a shutout.

De La Salle fans sitting above the tunnel leading to the locker room chant Smith's name as he is guided off the field, tears streaming down his face. Ladouceur believes that Smith epitomizes the program. Smith has made himself into a great high school football player, yet football doesn't define him. He raises his hand to acknowledge the chants before disappearing under the stands.

Players try to dump a cooler full of ice water on Ladouceur when the fourth-quarter clock expires on De La Salle's 42–14 victory.

He avoids the soaking. Calcagno isn't as fortunate on the opposite sideline. Ice water drips off the losing coach's visor as he and Ladouceur shake hands in the middle of the field.

"After the fourth time it gets a little frustrating," Calcagno will say later. "We don't play under the same set of rules. It's nothing against De La Salle. But for a public school to compete against a private school every year isn't fair. I just feel sorry for the kids who never had a chance to win an NCS title."

De La Salle players are joyous, their long, arduous journey having finally come to an end with The Streak intact, their legacies secure.

"You can smile, Chan. We won!" Kavanaugh shouts sarcastically. Chan actually smiles.

San Leandro players act as if the game ended under radically different circumstances. There are no long faces or dejected expressions. They congratulate each other, climb into the stands to hug their parents and girlfriends, and pose for pictures on the field where they have watched the Raiders play.

"I'm going to have to put it aside," says Dixon, who threw four interceptions in the game and eleven against the Spartans in three title games. "If it weren't for De La Salle we would've won four straight, but you can't take anything away from them. That's a great football team."

Ladouceur watches his players take turns holding up the championship plaque, but he's worried about Cole Smith and Parker Hanks, who ruptured a bursa sack in his right knee just before halftime. They are unable to savor this moment. The older Ladouceur gets, the more his players' injuries trouble him. Sometimes he has difficulty clearing his head enough to call plays when one of his players goes down.

"These guys showed the most improvement of any team I've had," Ladouceur tells reporters. "And the defense was stellar all year long. Terry did a great job."

Each player puts his NCS championship medal around his neck before posing for a team picture on risers erected on the far side of the field. A local television station does a live interview, the reporter asking Ladouceur another inane question about The Streak.

When they are through with their postgame commitments, De La Salle players do what they have been talking about doing all season. They drop their helmets and sprint to the corner of the end zone where home plate can be found during the baseball season. It's a long-standing tradition. They run as fast as they can, then slide belly first, as if they were Pete Rose or Rickey Henderson stealing home.

Ladouceur watches them go before stooping to pick up the cardboard box filled with pennants and the championship trophy. He dreamed of this season-ending moment on the first day of practice, when he almost dreaded the thought of another three months spent prodding, pulling, cajoling, and exhorting four dozen teenage boys to fulfill potential they didn't know they had.

The experience is both fulfilling and exhausting. The Streak is still alive. More importantly, because winning is a mere byproduct of Ladouceur's true life mission, his methods and core beliefs remain valid.

The season has ended as it usually does—with De La Salle players sliding headfirst in unrestrained adolescent glee into an infinite future, and their coach fatigued and satisfied, having temporarily quieted his conflicted soul and temporarily resolved his ongoing dilemma about how hard he should push his players.

He is not the man you expect him to be, and this is not the reaction to a championship moment you might anticipate. He plods across the field, the architect of a 138-game winning streak, his record now 274–14–1, with the emotionless stride of a worker passing through a factory's gates. It's not the numbing repetition of the moment. It's as if Ladouceur has given so much to his players that he has nothing left for himself, nothing beyond his intuitive gift for approaching football as a portal to life.

All he can think about at this moment is that he doesn't have to watch film tomorrow. He doesn't have to work. He can sleep in.

The stadium lights go dark before he reaches the home sideline, the celebration still raging all around him. He seeks out and finds his wife Beverly in the stands. His eyes lock in on her sweet, shining face and he moves toward her, a man perfectly in step with his time and place.

AFTERWORD

How do they do it? That's what everybody wants to know. How have the De La Salle Spartans won 138 consecutive football games?

There is no easy answer. It's a hundred different things—elite coaching, personal accountability, tradition, a dedication to hard work, and a bond that is created between players on Bob Ladouceur's teams that makes them stronger than the sum of their parts.

But when you add it all up it still doesn't explain 138–0, making their dominance difficult for even the Spartans to comprehend.

"Our teams aren't meant to be defined, for once you define something it loses its mystery and some of its power," Ladouceur told players and their parents at the postseason banquet.

It was an emotional and festive night. Maurice Drew was named Most Valuable Player. Chris Biller was Most Inspirational. De'Montae Fitzgerald and Tony Binswanger were named the Special Teams Players of the Year. Erik Sandie received the award for the Most Valuable Lineman, and Britt Cecil was named the Most Valuable Back.

Tears flowed when Mark Panella read Rick Cecil's tribute to his son. He found the message posted in a high school sports chat room on the Internet that is frequented by parents, boosters, and fans.

"I want to congratulate my son and his teammates on a remarkable season and a wonderful high school experience," the message read. "I have seen the pressure heaped upon you all and marveled at your steady, calm reaction to it. I have learned wonderful lessons from you about patience, poise, dedication and love. Throughout these last four years I have watched you struggle and felt your pain. I have watched you triumph and felt your joy. Thank you for becoming ten times the young man that a father could ever expect. This chapter is coming to a close and a new one will open. I have a warm comfortable confidence about your future because of who you have become, and it gives me great pride to see you blossom. Savor every drop of success because every drop was earned."

The Spartans were crowned mythical national champions by *USA Today* for the third straight year in 2002, and for the fourth time in five seasons. Ladouceur was named Coach of the Year for the fourth time.

Drew was named to the Parade All-America team and accepted a full-ride scholarship to UCLA. Sandie continued his career at Colorado State, and Fitzgerald attended Montana State on a football scholarship. Cole Smith recovered from his second concussion, and along with John Chan received an appointment to the U.S. Naval Academy. Damon Jenkins was offered a scholarship by Fresno State.

Chris Mulvanny, the defensive end, headed to Sacramento State, where he is expected to play safety. Britt Cecil joined the Navy.

Mike Blasquez left the De La Salle program when he was offered the job as head of strength and conditioning at the University of California-Berkeley. He called it one of the most difficult decisions of his life. Ladouceur put Justin Alumbaugh in charge of the offseason conditioning program.

"There's only one word to describe the reason for our success—mystery," Ladouceur said. "The spirit that exists at De La Salle High is mysterious. You can't define, box it, buy or sell it. You just allow it in, with all respect and humility. Our job is to allow the spirit to work within us to change our small corner of the world—one play at a time, one relationship at a time, one love at a time, one child at a time—and when it's all said and done you'll understand that it begins with you."

ACKNOWLEDGMENTS

Writing a book is like playing football for De La Salle. It's all about team.

This book would not have been possible if Bob Ladouceur hadn't felt he had nothing to hide. Without his sincerity and cooperation this project would not have made it past the planning stages. Terry Eidson put up with me all season and endured my tedious follow-up questions. Thanks to Mark Panella for diagramming plays over the phone.

I can never express my gratitude to all the coaches and players, past and present, for sharing their experiences. My heart-felt thanks to Cameron Colvin, Britt Cecil, Marlon Blanton, Mike Blasquez, and Mike Bastianelli for their honesty and deeply personal stories.

I'd like to thank Marlys Gee and Jeffri Chadiha for their feedback, and Kathy Glass and Gary Peterson for their thoughtful editing. They improved this manuscript immeasurably and for that I am very appreciative.

Bob Larson's photographs brought this story to life.

John Armstrong and Jerry Micco, my bosses at the *Contra Costa Times,* gave me the opportunity to pursue this project. I'd like to thank Jerry Southwick for his technical and emotional support and for the use of his dining room table.

Andrea Miller at the Christian Brothers San Francisco District Archives provided key documentation. Dr. David Flakoll's videotapes were invaluable. Thanks to Brother Christopher Brady for access to school records, Erin Jones for providing alumni phone numbers, and Steve Dulas, Mitch Stephens and Joe Stiglich for their careful research.

My professional respect goes out to anybody who has spent a rainy Friday night covering a high school football game. I poured over the work of countless prep writers and was impressed by their accuracy, detail, and insight.

I will forever be grateful to my wife Charlee, who believed in this project and put her own career on hold while I pursued it. Finally, thanks to Nicky and Riley for never complaining when I wasn't around.

Appendix

LADOUCEUR'S RECORD AT DE LA SALLE

YEAR / W-L-T / TITLES WON

Year	W-L-T	Titles Won
1979	6–3–0	
1980	8–2–0	
1981	7–2–0	
1982	12–0–0	NCS 2A champs
1983	8–2–1	
1984	11–1–0	NCS 2A champs
1985	12–0–0	NCS 2A champs
1986	12–0–0	NCS 3A champs
1987	11–1–0	
1988	13–0–0	NCS 3A champs
1989	11–2–0	NCS 3A champs
1990	13–0–0	NCS 3A champs
1991	12–1–0	
1992	13–0–0	NCS 3A champs
1993	13–0–0	NCS 3A champs
1994	13–0–0	NCS 3A champs
1995	13–0–0	NCS 3A champs
1996	12–0–0	NCS 4A champs
1997	12–0–0	NCS 4A champs
1998	12–0–0	NCS 4A champs
1999	12–0–0	NCS 4A champs
2000	13–0–0	NCS 4A champs
2001	12–0–0	NCS 4A champs
2002	13–0–0	NCS 4A champs

PLAYOFFS

53–3 (through 2002 playoffs)

Totals 274–14–1 (.948 winning percentage)

* Hudson High School (Michigan) held the national record for most consecutive wins with 72 (from 1968 to 1975).

LADOUCEUR'S CAREER GAME BY GAME

1979 (6–3)

De La Salle 26, Sacred Heart-San
  Francisco 13
De La Salle 14, Benicia 0
De La Salle 35, Half Moon Bay 7
California 3, De La Salle 0
De La Salle 14, Bishop O'Dowd 13
De La Salle 20, St. Mary's 6
Salesian 32, De La Salle 0
Moreau Catholic 26, De La Salle 24
De La Salle 42, St. Patrick-Vallejo 7
  NOTE: The 32–0 loss to Salesian is
  the worst loss of Ladouceur's career
  and the second and last time he has
  been shut out.

1980 (8–2)

De La Salle 52, Pacific 6
De La Salle 49, Sacred Heart-San
  Francisco 7
Riordan-San Francisco 24, De La Salle 14
De La Salle 43, Ceres 16
De La Salle 34, San Leandro 15
De La Salle 16, St. Mary's 8
De La Salle 16, Salesian 8
De La Salle 26, Moreau Catholic 14
De La Salle 28, Bishop O'Dowd 7
St. Patrick-Vallejo 24, De La Salle 21

1981 (7–2)

De La Salle 35, Pacific 7
College Park 19, De La Salle 17
De La Salle 36, Riordan-San Francisco 13
De La Salle 54, San Leandro 6
Salesian 21, De La Salle 17

De La Salle 14, Moreau Catholic 12
De La Salle 34, Bishop O'Dowd 14
De La Salle 20, St. Mary's 12
De La Salle 27, St. Patrick-Vallejo 0

1982 (12–0)

De La Salle 54, Dublin 0
De La Salle 21, College Park 18
De La Salle 21, Concord 0
De La Salle 21, Miramonte 6
De La Salle 9, Benicia 6
De La Salle 34, St. Patrick-Vallejo 7
De La Salle 55, Moreau-Catholic 0
De La Salle 63, Bishop O'Dowd 13
De La Salle 33, St. Mary's-Berkeley 20
De La Salle 48, Salesian 0

NCS 2A playoffs
De La Salle 17, Campolindo 6
De La Salle 49, Arroyo 0
(10–0 regular season, 2–0 playoffs)
No. 2 in final *Cal-Hi Sports* 2A poll

1983 (8–2–1)

De La Salle 7, San Ramon Valley 7
De La Salle 21, Oakland 12
De La Salle 41, Concord 0
De La Salle 13, Miramonte 3
De La Salle 45, Piedmont 14
Salesian 24, De La Salle 13
De La Salle 40, Moreau 16
De La Salle 7, Bishop O'Dowd 6
De La Salle 26, St. Patrick-Vallejo 7
De La Salle 21, St. Mary's-Berkeley 0

NCS 2A playoffs
Miramonte 13, De La Salle 7
(8–1–1 regular season, 0–1 playoffs)

1984 (11–1)
De La Salle 22, Piner 0
(game called at halftime because of
official treated for dehydration)
De La Salle 31, Oakland 14
Skyline 22, De La Salle 21
De La Salle 31, Serra-San Mateo 0
De La Salle 49, Piedmont 7
De La Salle 21, St. Mary's 0
De La Salle 42, Salesian 7
De La Salle 45, Moreau 14
De La Salle 44, Bishop O'Dowd 0

NCS 2A playoffs
De La Salle 42, Miramonte 6
De La Salle 54, San Leandro 13
De La Salle 39, Cardinal Newman 20
(8–1 regular season, 3–0 playoffs)
No. 8 in final *Cal-Hi Sports* 3A poll

1985 (12–0)
De La Salle 37, Bellarmine-San Jose 14
De La Salle 53, Campolindo 7
De La Salle 42, Skyline 18
De La Salle 49, Pinole Valley 6
De La Salle 35, El Cerrito 0
De La Salle 47, Salesian 24
De La Salle 50, St. Mary's 13
De La Salle 60, Moreau 22
De La Salle 54, Bishop O'Dowd 6

NCS 2A playoffs
De La Salle 41, Encinal 0
De La Salle 54, Miramonte 14

De La Salle 45, Marin Catholic 14
(9–0 regular season, 3–0 playoffs)
No. 1 in final *Cal-Hi Sports* 3A poll
No. 23 in final *USA Today* Super 25 Poll

1986 (12–0)
De La Salle 32, Bellarmine-San Jose 28
De La Salle 24, Campolindo 7
De La Salle 27, Antioch 20
De La Salle 54, South San Francisco 3
De La Salle 62, El Cerrito 16
De La Salle 61, Berkeley 16
De La Salle 41, Alameda 6
De La Salle 56, Kennedy-Richmond 21
De La Salle 49, Pinole Valley 25

NCS 3A playoffs
De La Salle 56, Eureka 7
De La Salle 24, Clayton Valley 6
De La Salle 24, Monte Vista 7
(9–0 regular season, 3–0 playoffs)
No. 2 in final *Cal-Hi Sports* 4A poll

1987 (11–1)
De La Salle 32, Bellarmine 7
De La Salle 29, St. Francis-Mountain
View 23
De La Salle 40, Antioch 6
De La Salle 39, El Camino 14
De La Salle 37, El Cerrito 9
De La Salle 54, Berkeley 7
De La Salle 53, Alameda 7
De La Salle 24, Kennedy-Richmond 21
De La Salle 49, Pinole Valley 33

NCS 3A playoffs
De La Salle 32, Rancho Cotate 6
De La Salle 34, Ygnacio Valley 7

Monte Vista 14, De La Salle 13
(9–0 regular season, 2–1 playoffs)
No. 3 in final *Cal-Hi Sports* 4A poll

1988 (13–0)
De La Salle 35, Bellarmine 14
De La Salle 28, St. Francis-Mountain
    View 7
De La Salle 35, Berkeley 6
De La Salle 24, Valley 7
De La Salle 44, Antioch 0
De La Salle 28, Pittsburg 21
De La Salle 33, Ygnacio Valley 21
De La Salle 28, Pinole Valley 25
De La Salle 29, El Cerrito 13
De La Salle 31, Clayton Valley 0

NCS 3A playoffs
De La Salle 41, Eureka 6
De La Salle 35, Montgomery 13
De La Salle 42, Granada 0
(10–0 regular season, 3–0 playoffs)
No. 2 in final *Cal-Hi Sports* 4A poll
No.10 in final *USA Today* Super 25 Poll

1989 (11–2)
De La Salle 35, San Ramon Valley 14
St. Francis-Mountain View 18, De La
    Salle 16
De La Salle 41, Napa 28
El Cerrito 14, De La Salle 13
De La Salle 28, Berkeley 12
De La Salle 31, Antioch 7
De La Salle 43, Pittsburg 18
De La Salle 27, Ygnacio Valley 7
De La Salle 28, Pinole Valley 22
De La Salle 21, Clayton Valley 7

NCS 3A playoffs
De La Salle 49, Eureka 7
De La Salle 28, San Ramon 3
De La Salle 41, James Logan 6
(8–2 regular season, 3–0 playoffs)
No. 8 in final *Cal-Hi Sports* 4A poll

1990 (13–0)
De La Salle 35, San Ramon Valley 18
De La Salle 35, St. Francis-Mountain
    View 12
De La Salle 20, Napa 3
De La Salle 42, Berkeley 0
De La Salle 35, El Cerrito 12
De La Salle 33, Clayton Valley 6
De La Salle 31, Antioch 28
De La Salle 28, Ygnacio Valley 14
De La Salle 49, Pittsburg 14
De La Salle 35, Pinole Valley 14

NCS 3A playoffs
De La Salle 42, Cardinal Newman 14
De La Salle 31, Foothill 6
De La Salle 49, Piner 24
(10–0 regular season, 3–0 playoffs)
No. 4 in final *Cal-Hi Sports* 4A poll

1991 (12–1)
De La Salle 54, San Ramon Valley 0
De La Salle 35, Merced 21
De La Salle 29, St. Francis-Mountain
    View 14
De La Salle 28, Pittsburg 16
De La Salle 49, Berkeley 19
De La Salle 40, El Cerrito 0
De La Salle 52, Clayton Valley 7
De La Salle 21, Antioch 3

De La Salle 13, Ygnacio Valley 9

De La Salle 51, Pinole Valley 18

NCS 3A playoffs

De La Salle 61, Montgomery 14

De La Salle 33, Washington 7

Pittsburg 35, De La Salle 27

(10–0 regular season, 2–1 playoffs)

No. 6 in final *Cal-Hi Sports* 4A poll

1992 (13–0)

De La Salle 34, Merced 14

De La Salle 54, Riordan-San Francisco 0

De La Salle 41, Fairfield 20

De La Salle 48, Ygnacio Valley 0

De La Salle 44, Pittsburg 7

De La Salle 64, Berkeley 6

De La Salle 43, El Cerrito 0

De La Salle 59, Clayton Valley 6

De La Salle 49, Antioch 14

De La Salle 62, Pinole Valley 12

NCS 3A playoffs

De La Salle 35, Montgomery 7

De La Salle 55, James Logan 20

De La Salle 41, Pittsburg 6

(10–0 regular season, 3–0 playoffs)

Outscored opponents 629–112

No. 1 in final *Cal-Hi Sports* 4A poll

No. 3 in final *USA Today* Super 25 Poll

1993 (13–0)

De La Salle 58, Alhambra 13

De La Salle 46, Riordan-San Francisco 6

De La Salle 53, Fairfield 13

De La Salle 63, Antioch 14

De La Salle 69, Berkeley 0

De La Salle 26, Pittsburg 21

De La Salle 55, Mission San Jose-
Fremont 13

De La Salle 56, Monte Vista 7

De La Salle 41, Liberty 0

De La Salle 47, Pinole Valley 6

NCS 3A playoffs

De La Salle 55, American 6

De La Salle 50, Washington 7

De La Salle 46, Pinole Valley 14

(10–0 regular season, 3–0 playoffs)

Outscored opponents 665–120

No. 2 in final *Cal-Hi Sports* 4A poll

No. 7 in final *USA Today* Super 25 Poll

1994 (13–0)

De La Salle 45, Alhambra 6

De La Salle 55, Tracy 19

De La Salle 42, St. Mary's-Stockton 0

De La Salle 35, Antioch 21

De La Salle 35, Berkeley 0

De La Salle 55, Pittsburg 26

De La Salle 60, Mission San Jose-
Fremont 0

De La Salle 55, Monte Vista 15

De La Salle 45, Liberty 14

De La Salle 47, Pinole Valley 0

NCS 3A playoffs

De La Salle 35, Eureka 6

De La Salle 45, Antioch 8

De La Salle 35, James Logan 0

(10–0 regular season, 3–0 playoffs)

Outscored opponents 589–115

No. 1 in final *Cal-Hi Sports* 4A poll

No. 2 in final *USA Today* Super 25 Poll

1995 (13–0)

De La Salle 35, Rancho Buena Vista-
    Vista 14
De La Salle 68, Tracy 14
De La Salle 35, St. Mary's-Stockton 25
De La Salle 27, Berkeley 0
De La Salle 28, Pittsburg 7
De La Salle 49, Antioch 20
De La Salle 67, Pinole Valley 13
De La Salle 55, Liberty 0
De La Salle 41, James Logan 8
De La Salle 56, Monte Vista 0

NCS 3A playoffs
De La Salle 54, Montgomery 6
De La Salle 56, Berkeley 31
De La Salle 35, Pittsburg 14
(10–0 regular season, 3–0 playoffs)
Outscored opponents 606–152
No. 1 in final *Cal-Hi Sports* 4A poll
No. 3 in final *USA Today* Super 25 Poll

1996 (12–0)

De La Salle 36, Rancho Buena Vista-
    Vista 19
De La Salle 55, Ygnacio Valley 0
De La Salle 64, College Park 0
De La Salle 28, Skyline 0
De La Salle 55, Liberty 14
De La Salle 42, Antioch 0
De La Salle 75, Clayton Valley 0
De La Salle 36, Pittsburg 7
De La Salle 58, Pinole Valley 6
De La Salle 60, Northgate 0

NCS 4A playoffs
De La Salle 50, Berkeley 0
De La Salle 35, Pittsburg 7

(10–0 regular season, 2–0 playoffs)
Outscored opponents 594–53
No. 1 in final *Cal-Hi Sports* 4A poll
No. 3 in final *USA Today* Super 25 Poll
The seven shutouts this year set the
    school record (old 5; set in '82
    and matched in '94)

1997 (12–0)

De La Salle 48, Nevada Union-Grass
    Valley 14
De La Salle 62, Ygnacio Valley 7
De La Salle 66, Clayton Valley 10
De La Salle 62, Deer Valley 13
De La Salle 53, Northgate 8
De La Salle 44, Antioch 17
De La Salle 53, Liberty 7
De La Salle 55, Pittsburg 7
De La Salle 56, College Park 0
De La Salle 28, Pinole Valley 6

NCS 4A playoffs
De La Salle 56, Pittsburg 0
De La Salle 35, James Logan 15
(10–0 regular season, 2–0 playoffs)
Outscored opponents 618–104
No. 1 in final *Cal-Hi Sports* 4A poll
No. 6 in final *USA Today* Super 25 Poll

1998 (12–0)

De La Salle 48, Nevada Union-Grass
    Valley 13
De La Salle 48, Bakersfield 20
De La Salle 28, Mater Dei-Santa Ana 21
De La Salle 21, St. Francis-Mountain
    View 0
De La Salle 41, Skyline 7
De La Salle 60, Pittsburg 12

De La Salle 70, Northgate 0
De La Salle 61, Liberty 23
De La Salle 45, Clayton Valley 7
De La Salle 42, Pinole Valley 0

NCS 4A playoffs
De La Salle 48, Pittsburg 14
De La Salle 55, Castro Valley 13
(10–0 regular season, 2–0 playoffs)
Outscored opponents 567–130
No. 1 in final *Cal-Hi Sports* 4A poll
No. 1 in final *USA Today* Super 25 Poll

1999 (12–0)
De La Salle 57, Richmond 6
De La Salle 35, Bakersfield 8
De La Salle 42, Mater Dei-Santa Ana 0
De La Salle 35, St. Francis-Mountain
    View 7
De La Salle 37, Skyline 0
De La Salle 71, Ygnacio Valley 32
De La Salle 48, Antioch 9
De La Salle 55, Clayton Valley 7
De La Salle 61, Pittsburg 14
De La Salle 60, College Park 12

NCS 4A playoffs
De La Salle 55, Castro Valley 21
De La Salle 38, San Leandro 14
(10–0 regular season, 2–0 playoffs)
Outscored opponents 594–130
No. 1 in final *Cal-Hi Sports* 4A poll
No. 3 in final *USA Today* Super 25 Poll

2000 (13–0)
De La Salle 30, Buchanan-Clovis 24
De La Salle 49, Marin Catholic 7
De La Salle 31, Mater Dei-Santa Ana 28

De La Salle 42, St. Francis-Mountain
    View 7
De La Salle 56, Bishop Amat-La Puente 6
De La Salle 55, Freedom 7
De La Salle 64, Clayton Valley 21
De La Salle 35, Ygnacio Valley 7
De La Salle 37, Pittsburg 14
De La Salle 41, Deer Valley 10

NCS 4A Playoffs
De La Salle 68, San Ramon Valley 0
De La Salle 34, James Logan 10
De La Salle 49, San Leandro 13
(10–0 regular season, 3–0 playoffs)
Outscored opponents 592–144
No. 1 in final *Cal-Hi Sports* 4A poll
No. 1 in final *USA Today* Super 25 Poll

2001 (12–0)
De La Salle 56, Buchanan 14
De La Salle 34, Mater Dei 6
De La Salle 42, St. Francis 0
De La Salle 29, Long Beach Poly 15
De La Salle 42, Pittsburg 14
De La Salle 64, Antioch 0
De La Salle 65, Liberty 0
De La Salle 31, Ygnacio Valley 13
De La Salle 57, Deer Valley 6

NCS 4A Playoffs
De La Salle 54, Washington-Fremont 15
De La Salle 45, James Logan 0
De La Salle 48, San Leandro 13
(9–0 regular season, 3–0 playoffs)
Outscored opponents 567–96
No. 1 in final *Cal-Hi Sports* 4A poll
No. 1 in final *USA Today* Super 25 Poll

2002 (13–0)

De La Salle 24, Archbishop Mitty 0

De La Salle 31, St. Louis-Honolulu 21

De La Salle 14, St. Francis-Mountain
View 0

De La Salle 56, La Costa Canyon-
Carlsbad 27

De La Salle 28, Long Beach Poly 7

De La Salle 48, Liberty 0

De La Salle 46, Freedom 7

De La Salle 65, Pittsburg 6

De La Salle 42, Clayton Valley 0

De La Salle 35, Ygnacio Valley 0

NCS 4A Playoffs

De La Salle 62, Antioch 13

De La Salle 47, Hayward 7

De La Salle 42, San Leandro 14

No. 1 in final *Cal-Hi Sports* poll

No. 1 in final *USA Today* Super 25 Poll

INDEX

Wisconsin, 375
Wooden, John, 6
Wright, Kyle, 370–371
Wright, Louis, 63
Wright, Manuel, 159, 160, 162
Wurzel, Linda, 217
Wurzel, Luke, 217, 219, 245

Y
Yeoman, Bill, 90, 109
Ygnacio Valley High, 30, 33, 217, 221,
    234, 245, 278, 290–307, 358, 365
Ygnacio Valley Warriors, 59
Yolo County, 315
Young, Chuck, 113, 116
Young, Eugene "Choo Choo", 178